SOURCES IN BRITISH POLITICAL HISTORY 1900–1951

Volume 5

Also by Chris Cook

The Age of Alignment: Electoral Politics in Britain, 1922–29
A Short History of the Liberal Party, 1900–76
By-Elections in British Politics (*ed. with John Ramsden*)
European Political Facts, 1918–73 (*with John Paxton*)
The Politics of Reappraisal, 1918–39 (*ed. with Gillian Peele*)
The Decade of Disillusion (*ed. with David McKie*)
British Historical Facts, 1830–1900 (*with Brendan Keith*)
Atlas of Modern British History, 1700–1960 (*with John Stevenson*)
European Political Facts, 1848–1918 (*with John Paxton*)
The Slump: Society and Politics during the Depression (*with John Stevenson*)
Sources in British Political History, 1900–1951, Volumes 1–4

Also by Jeffrey Weeks

Socialism and the New Life (*with Sheila Rowbotham*)
Coming Out

Sources in British Political History 1900–1951

compiled for the British Library of
Political and Economic Science by
CHRIS COOK AND JEFFREY WEEKS

Volume 5

A Guide to the Private
Papers of Selected Writers
Intellectuals and Publicists

First published 1978 by
THE MACMILLAN PRESS LTD
London and Basingstoke
Associated companies in Delhi
Dublin Hong Kong Johannesburg Lagos
Melbourne New York Singapore Tokyo

Printed in Hong Kong by
Shanghai Printing Press Ltd

British Library Cataloguing in Publication Data

Cook, Chris
Sources in British political history 1900–1951
Vol. 5: A guide to the private papers of
selected writers, intellectuals and publicists
1. Archives – Great Britain 2. Great Britain –
History – 20th century – Sources 3. Great Britain –
Politics and government – 20th century – Sources
I. Title II. British Library of Political and
Economic Science III. Weeks, Jeffrey
941.082 DA566.7

ISBN 0-333-22124-9

Contents

Foreword

This is the fifth and last in the series of volumes reporting the results of a major survey of twentieth-century British political archives, which has been undertaken over the past six years by the British Library of Political and Economic Science with the generous support of the Social Science Research Council.

The project originated from a meeting of archivists, historians and librarians, held in October 1967 on the initiative of Nuffield College, Oxford. As a result of this meeting a Political Archives Investigation Committee was established (its membership is listed on p. x) to explore the possibility of making a major effort to locate and list modern British political manuscripts and encourage their preservation.

With the assistance of a grant from the Social Science Research Council a two-year pilot project, directed by Dr Cameron Hazlehurst, was begun at Nuffield College in 1968, with the object of locating the papers of Cabinet Ministers who held office between 1900 and 1951. The Political Archives Investigation Committee acted as an advisory body to the project. The survey of Cabinet Ministers' papers was an undoubted success and a guide to the papers was published in 1974.[1]

In view of the favourable outcome of the pilot project, the Committee had no hesitation in recommending that a more comprehensive survey should be undertaken; and particularly bearing in mind the bibliographical facilities and geographical convenience of London, as well as the number of scholars active in relevant fields working in the London School of Economics, it was proposed that this phase of the investigation should be carried out under the auspices of the British Library of Political and Economic Science.

A generous grant was accordingly made to the BLPES by the Social Science Research Council and on 1 October 1970 a research team directed by Dr C. P. Cook began work on a six-year project intended to locate the papers of all persons and organisations influential in British politics between 1900 and 1951, encourage their preservation, and publish guides.

The records of political parties, societies, institutions and pressure groups were described in the first volume in this series. The second volume was concerned with the private papers of senior public servants, colonial administrators, diplomats and senior officers of the armed forces. The third and fourth volumes were devoted to reporting the findings of a comprehensive search that was made for the papers of all Members of the House of Commons between the General Elections of 1900 and 1951.[2]

---

[1] Cameron Hazlehurst and Christine Woodland, *A Guide to the Papers of British Cabinet Ministers, 1900–1951* (London: Royal Historical Society, 1974).

[2] Chris Cook with Philip Jones, Josephine Sinclair and Jeffrey Weeks, *Sources in British Political History, 1900–1951*
Vol. 1: *A Guide to the Archives of Selected Organisations and Societies* (London: Macmillan, 1975).
Vol. 2: *A Guide to the Private Papers of Selected Public Servants* (London: Macmillan, 1975).
Vols 3 and 4: *A Guide to the Private Papers of Members of Parliament* (London: Macmillan, 1977: A–K and L–Z).

The final volume deals with the papers of selected writers, intellectuals and publicists, religious leaders, leading trade unionists, businessmen and others. It completes the initial programme set out in 1970, and the five volumes now constitute a comprehensive guide to the whereabouts of twentieth-century political records.

Inevitably some of the information contained in these volumes will become outdated, through the changes of address of owners, through deposits, or through the reorganisation of library or record services. I would hope, therefore, that those who have so generously provided information over the years will continue to do so in the coming years by writing to the Librarian, British Library of Political and Economic Science, 10 Portugal Street, London WC2A 2HD. The resulting file of up-to-date information will be made available to enquirers.

It remains for me, on behalf of the British Library of Political and Economic Science, to thank my colleagues on the Political Archives Committee and the staff of the project for their work in ensuring the success of this survey.

D. A. Clarke
Librarian
British Library of Political and Economic Science

March 1977

Acknowledgements

This book is the fifth in the series, and like its predecessor volumes could not have been compiled without a large grant from the Social Science Research Council, and the help and guidance of Derek Clarke, Librarian of the British Library of Political and Economic Science. The facilities of that Library have been essential to the success of this project, and we owe its staff a major debt. We must also thank the members of the Political Archives Investigation Committee for their advice over the whole period of this project.

This volume has been completed only with the unstinting help of many individuals, and it would be impossible to thank them all by name. We are, however, especially indebted to the following: Maurice Bond at the House of Lords Record Office; D. S. Porter of the Bodleian Library, Oxford; A. E. B. Owen of Cambridge University Library; Daniel Waley, Keeper of Manuscripts at the British Library; J. K. Bates, Secretary of the National Register of Archives (Scotland); J. S. Ritchie at the National Library of Scotland; Sir John Ainsworth, Bt., at the National Library of Ireland; G. M. Griffiths at the National Library of Wales; the Keeper and the staff at the Public Record Office, London, and their colleagues at the Public Record Office of Northern Ireland.

A variety of related research projects have supplied helpful information, and we must especially thank Joyce Bellamy and Professor John Saville, of Hull University, editors of the invaluable *Dictionary of Labour Biography*; Martin Sieff and Philip Jones of the British Academy's Anglo-Palestinian Archives Project; Richard Storey and Janet Druker of the Modern Records Centre, University of Warwick Library.

It goes without saying that we owe a major debt to the archivists and staff of various record offices and libraries. Particular thanks are due to the staff of the British Library, the Bodleian Library, Cambridge University Library, the House of Lords Record Office, the Imperial War Museum, the Liddell Hart Centre for Military Archives, Churchill College, Cambridge, the India Office Library, the Middle East Centre at St Antony's College, Oxford, King's College, Cambridge, the University of Warwick Library, Sussex University Library, the National Library of Scotland, Edinburgh University Library, John Rylands University Library of Manchester, Manchester Central Library, Liverpool University Archives and many others.

We have also relied greatly on suggestions, advice and information supplied by colleagues and friends, especially David Bovey, Stephen Koss, Jean L'Esperance, Ian Nish, Roderick Suddaby, John Ramsden, Angela Raspin, Anthony Reid, Arthur Searle, Julia Sheppard, Martin Sieff, Paul Sturges, Philip Woods. We owe a major debt to Dr Godfrey Davis and the staff of the Historical Manuscripts Commission who have given continuous and vital assistance.

Finally, we must warmly thank Philip Jones and Josephine Sinclair, who worked with us on the compilation of the earlier volumes of this series, and did much preparatory work for this; and Eileen Pattison and Janet Scott, without whose patience and skill this book could not have been completed.

CHRIS COOK
JEFFREY WEEKS

Members of the Political Archives Investigation Committee

Mr John Brooke, formerly Historical Manuscripts Commission (1967–77)
  (Chairman, 1972–7)
Mr D. A. Clarke, British Library of Political and Economic Science (1967–77)
Dr C. P. Cook, Historical Manuscripts Commission (1970–7)
Mr Martin Gilbert, Merton College, Oxford (1967–70)
Dr R. M. Hartwell, Nuffield College, Oxford (Chairman, 1967–72)
Dr Cameron Hazlehurst, Nuffield College, Oxford (1967–70)
Professor A. Marwick, The Open University (1972–7)
Dr H. M. Pelling, St John's College, Cambridge (1967–77)
Dr John Roberts, Merton College, Oxford (1973–7)
Mrs Felicity Strong, formerly Historical Manuscripts Commission (1967–77)
Mr A. J. P. Taylor, Magdalen College, Oxford (1972–7)
Professor D. C. Watt, London School of Economics and Political Science (1967–77)
Mr Jeffrey Weeks, British Library of Political and Economic Science (1975–7)
Dr Edwin Welch, Churchill College, Cambridge (1967–71)

Introduction

1. Scope of the Survey

This volume is concerned with the private papers of writers, intellectuals and publicists who played a prominent role in British public life during the first half of the twentieth century. Broadly, it lists the papers of those whose political influence was personal rather than *ex officio*. Inevitably, these categories are less clear cut than those of Public Servants (Vol. 2) or Members of Parliament (Vols 3–4). Nevertheless, an attempt has been made to discover papers in the following categories: newspaper proprietors; editors of major daily newspapers (especially *The Times* and *Manchester Guardian*); the editors of influential weeklies (e.g. *The Spectator, New Statesman*); other selected journalists and foreign correspondents; political theorists; religious leaders (Anglican, Roman Catholic, Nonconformist, Jewish); leading economists; socialist theorists and publicists of the Labour Movement; some leading Trade Union officials; publicists of the Co-operative Movement; some leading businessmen; publicists and theorists of the Conservative and Liberal parties; writers whose work brought them into political controversy; leading educationalists and academics; publicists and leaders of the feminist movement; tariff reformers; pacifists; proponents of Empire; anti-imperialists; military writers and international strategists; leading social psychologists, sociologists and anthropologists; criminologists; and town planners and environmentalists.

For obvious reasons, no attempt to be comprehensive could be made in any of these areas. Nor will all the obvious names appear in this volume. This is because many of the individuals who were primarily publicists or writers also entered the public service or became Members of Parliament at various times of their lives, and descriptions of their papers have appeared in previous volumes (William Beveridge is an obvious example). Contrariwise, several individuals who did sit in Parliament for short periods could not be excluded from this volume (e.g. C. P. Scott). The result is a volume of over 700 entries which attempts to provide a conspectus of British intellectual life during the first half of the century.

2. The Reports

As in the previous volumes the reports are in two parts: a biographical description of the main outline of an individual's career; and a description of the papers. The biographical note is necessarily brief, and readers are urged to use entries in conjunction with the *Dictionary of National Biography, Who Was Who* and the more specialist biographical works, such as the *Dictionary of Labour Biography* (ed. Joyce Bellamy and John Saville, published by Macmillan: London, 1972–).

The note on the papers attempts to describe the extent and nature of those private papers which have survived, both in private hands and in public repositories. Where it has been found that no private papers are extant, this information has been included. No systematic attempt has been made to locate the papers of those who are still alive, but when their papers have been deposited, and are available for research purposes, this information has been included. Where appropriate, reference has been made to published biographies, memoirs or other works, especially where these make use of manuscript sources. The reports vary a great deal in length. Some collections, especially those in libraries, are fully catalogued, and use has been made of the information in the published guides. In other cases, especially for those papers still in private hands, where access is often restricted, it has only been possible to provide a summary description. The brevity of a description should not, therefore, be taken as an indication of the lack of importance of a collection. Where appropriate, reference has also been made to relevant papers or correspondence of an individual to be found in another collection. For frequently updated information in this context, readers are urged to consult the Personal Index at the Historical Manuscripts Commission. Cross-references will also be found in the text to previous volumes of this series (referred to as *Sources*), especially Vol. 1, *A Guide to the Archives of Selected Organisations and Societies*, where efforts have been made to relate personal collections to relevant institutional records described there. There are also cross-references where relevant to other guides to sources, especially Paul Sturges' *Economists' Papers 1750–1950* (London: Macmillan, 1975).

3. Research Procedure

This volume is the result of a search for the papers of over 700 individuals. In the first place this involved the collation of existing information. Much information on collections of papers had been gathered by a survey of major libraries in Britain, the USA and Commonwealth countries undertaken by this project. This was supplemented by the information available in the lists and reports of the Historical Manuscripts Commission, published sources such as the *National Union Catalog of Manuscript Collections* (Washington: Library of Congress, 1962–), and by close cooperation with the major libraries in this country and with related archives research projects. The editors owe a great debt to the work of the British Academy's Anglo-Palestinian Archives Project, the Contemporary Scientific Archives Centre, Oxford, the University of Sussex 'Survey of Men of Science', the Modern Records Centre at the University of Warwick, and various other projects.

In a number of cases, however, no information on papers was publicly available. Efforts were then made to trace the owners of papers presumed still to be in private hands. When the name of a descendant or heir was not accessible in a standard reference work such as *Who's Who*, *Kelly's Handbook* or *Burke's Peerage*, a search was made of the Wills and Probate Acts available at the Principal Probate Registry at Somerset House, London. In many cases this enabled contact to be made with the surviving family, executor or solicitors, and a number of collections of papers were discovered in this way. The results are described in the text of this volume. Unsuccessful approaches have also been recorded. Nevertheless, despite our efforts it is unavoidable that there will still remain considerable omissions in this volume. For any number of reasons it may not be possible to include details of papers of certain figures who should be included. It may be impossible to trace a family; an address may change; illness or incapacity may prevent a reply to an enquiry; papers may be in store and details thus not available. In such circumstances, omissions are inevitable. Equally, the information presented here may change. For this reason, where the address of a person mentioned in the text can be obtained from the current *Who's Who*, or similar sources which are constantly updated, it is not cited in the text.

For all these reasons the editors of this book would request that, if scholars obtain information additional to that included here, they would inform the BLPES and the Historical Manuscripts Commission so that this information may be added to the project's findings.

4. Arrangement

The entries in this guide are arranged alphabetically under the last known name of the person concerned. Peers are listed under their senior title, not under the family name. Hyphenated surnames are generally under the last part of the name. Where names have changed, either through elevation in or to the peerage, or otherwise, cross-references will be found in the appropriate alphabetical place.

An appendix provides a list of addresses of the major libraries mentioned in the text, together with a list of the collections of papers to be found in each library.

5. *Availability of Papers*

The mention of the existence of private papers in this volume in no way implies that these collections are necessarily available for research. Where papers are *known* to be closed to scholars, an attempt has been made to incorporate this information. For all collections in libraries and record offices, a preliminary letter to the appropriate archivist is very strongly advised. For collections in private hands, a letter is absolutely essential. No research worker should expect private collections necessarily to be opened up for his work. A subsequent letter of thanks to custodians of private papers is also a matter of common courtesy. Scholars are reminded of the law of copyright – and, in particular, that copyright lies with the writer of a letter, not the recipient or owner of a collection.

6. *Abbreviations*

To save needless repetition, standard abbreviations have been used for ranks and appointments. A Life Peer has been styled Baron. Otherwise, titles have been abbreviated as follows: D (Duke); M (Marquess); E (Earl); Vt (Viscount); B (hereditary Baron); Bt (Baronet). The British Library of Political and Economic Science is referred to throughout as BLPES.

7. *Further Information*

Deposits of papers too recent to be included in this volume are recorded in the annual list of Accessions to Repositories published by H.M. Stationery Office for the Historical Manuscripts Commission. More detailed unpublished lists of archives both in repositories and libraries and in the custody of their originators may often be found in the National Register of Archives maintained by the Historical Manuscripts Commission, Quality House, Quality Court, Chancery Lane, London WC2A 1HP, where known alterations and additions to the information given in this volume will be recorded.

It is hoped that the information in this volume is correct at the time of going to press, but apart from the possible changes mentioned earlier, it must be remembered that many details of papers were often supplied by persons whose knowledge of the records was imperfect, by archivists who had not yet been able to catalogue records fully, or by scholars whose interests might be limited to certain aspects of their work. Both the British Library of Political and Economic Science and the Historical Manuscripts Commission will be grateful to be informed of alterations, additions and amendments.

CHRIS COOK
JEFFREY WEEKS

Private Papers

ABERCROMBIE, Sir (Leslie) Patrick (1879–1957)

Architect and Town Planner. Professor of Civic Design, Liverpool University, 1915–35. Professor of Town Planning, University College London, 1935–46. President of the Town Planning Institute. Member of the Royal Commission on the Location of Industry.

The papers of Sir Patrick Abercrombie are currently in the care of Professor G. B. Dix of Liverpool University, Department of Civic Design, who is using them for a biography. They may eventually, it is understood, be deposited with Liverpool University Archives. At present they are not available for research.

Correspondence, 1941–5, in connection with the Greater London Plan, 1944, is in the Public Record Office (HLG 85). Correspondence, 1955, with Sir Sydney Cockerell is in the British Library (Add. MS 52703).

ACLAND, Lady
Alice Sophia Acland (1849–1935)

Founder, Women's League for the Spread of Co-operation (later Women's Co-operative Guild). Secretary, 1883–4, President, 1884–6.

Records of the Women's Co-operative Guild, in BLPES and in Hull University Library, are described in *Sources* Vol. I, pp. 77–8. Certain other relevant material can be found in the Acland family collection at the Devon Record Office. A note on her career appears in *Dictionary of Labour Biography* Vol. I, pp. 5–6.

ACLAND, Sir Arthur Herbert Dyke, 13th Bt (1847–1926)

Politician. M.P. (Lib.) Rotherham, 1885–99. Chairman of the Executive Committee, Imperial College. Supporter of co-operative movement.

It is believed that most of his papers were destroyed, though there is family material in Devon Record Office. Correspondence with his father, Sir T. D. Acland, Bt, can be found in Duke University, North Carolina. Relevant material can also be found in the National Library of Wales (in the T. E. Ellis and Rendel collections) and there are letters to Asquith, 1898–1920, in the Bodleian Library, Oxford.

ACTON, 1st B
Sir John Emerich Edward Dalberg-Acton, 8th Bt (1834–1902)

Historian, politician and Liberal philosopher. M.P. (Lib.) Carlow, 1859–65; Bridgnorth, 1865–6. Lord-in-Waiting, 1892–5. Professor of Modern History, Cambridge University, 1895–1902. Founder of *English Historical Review*. Editor, *Cambridge Modern History*.

Cambridge University Library has a collection of Acton's papers. The collection includes a number of original MSS acquired by Acton; and transcripts made by or for Acton, mainly from Italian and French archives. Acton's working notes, either on slips or in notebooks, also survive. Often there are general boxes or notebooks on a single theme, e.g. History of Liberty, Dollinger, but many of the notebooks are miscellaneous in character, and cover the whole range of Acton's interests. Family papers were also included in the original deposit, some dating back to the sixteenth century. More recently the Library has acquired a substantial collection of Acton's correspondence, including letters from professional and political colleagues as well as members of his family (some 29 boxes in all). In addition the Library has other relevant correspondence, e.g. with Mandell Creighton, R. L. Poole, and letters concerning the *Cambridge Modern History*.

The Mirfield deposit in the Borthwick Institute of Historical Research has some correspondence with Figgis, as well as letters concerning Acton and the *Cambridge Modern History* (in the Figgis papers). Some correspondence with Sir Percy Bunting is available in the University of Chicago Library, while letters to Richard Garnett are in the University of Texas Library, Austin. The Bryce papers at the Bodleian Library have 137 letters from Acton, 1885–1901. Letters to Rendel are in the National Library of Wales, and to Wolseley in Hove Central Library. Relevant material can also be found in the archives of the English Benedictine Congregation, at St Gregory's, Downside.

ADDIS, Sir Charles Stewart (1861–1945)

Banker. Worked in London, and in India, Burma, China and the Straits Settlement, 1880–1904. London manager, Hongkong and Shanghai Bank, 1905–21. Chairman, London Committee, 1922–3. Director, Bank of England 1918–32. President, Institute of Bankers, 1921–3. Vice-Chairman, Bank for International Settlements, 1929–32.

Sir John Addis (son), Woodside, Frant, Tunbridge Wells, Kent TN3 9HW, has a collection of his father's diaries from 1879 to 1945; files of letters received; copies of letters sent; and two volumes of press cuttings of the 1880s. The diaries consist of brief entries, chiefly concerned with personal and family affairs. The Bland papers in the University of Toronto Library contain further relevant papers.

ALDRED, Guy Alfred (1886–1963)

Socialist journalist and propagandist. He worked with various socialist organisations including the Social Democratic Federation, 1905; with the educational Communist Propaganda Groups, 1906–20; the Anti-Parliamentary Communist Federation, 1920–33; and the United Socialist Movement, 1933–63. He founded the Strickland Press, Glasgow, which published numerous pamphlets with socialist and pacifist themes.

The surviving papers of Guy Aldred, depleted by various confiscations, were deposited in the Baillie's Library, Glasgow. The collection includes letters from various public figures, including Boyd-Orr, Fenner Brockway, Sir Patrick Dollan and John McGovern. There are over 70 letters from Arthur Creech Jones, 1941–50, including 63 to Guy Aldred, the majority of which relate to various aspects of foreign policy. The collection also includes the Spanish correspondence of Ethel MacDonald and Jenny Patrick (Mrs Guy Aldred). The Library has Aldred's books of press cuttings, 1912–60. A calalogue of the material has been prepared.

The Strathclyde Regional Archives Office, Glasgow, has the documents relating to the Strickland bequest on which the Strickland Press was founded. Aldred's pamphlet library has been purchased by Strathclyde University Library. Hull University Library has letters from Guy Aldred in the C. W. Brook Collection. These number 81 in all with three copy replies and cover the period 1942–8. They relate to politics, printing, the British People's Party, India, Aldred's parliamentary candidature, etc. Aldred's autobiography, *No Traitors Gait!*, is an important source. The material described here has been used by John T. Caldwell in *Guy A. Aldred*, an unpublished biography. A short typescript version of this work is in the People's Palace Museum, Glasgow Green.

ALLEN OF HURTWOOD, Ist B
Reginald Clifford Allen (1889–1939)

Socialist propagandist. Secretary and General Manager, *Daily Citizen*, 1911–15.Chairman, Cambridge University Socialist Federation, 1912–15. Chairman, No-Conscription Fellowship, papers, including Chairman's letterbooks, directors' report books, minutes of boards, and general correspondence.

VOIGT, Frederick Augustus (1892–1957)

Journalist. On staff of *Manchester Guardian* from 1918, specialising as a foreign correspondent; Diplomatic Correspondent, 1933–9. Author. Editor of *Nineteenth Century and Afterwards*, 1938–46.

Reference should be made to the archives of the *Manchester Guardian* in John Rylands University Library of Manchester.

WADSWORTH, Alfred Powell (1891–1956)

Journalist. On staff of *Manchester Guardian* from 1917; editor, 1944–56.

Miscellaneous papers can be found in the archives of the *Manchester Guardian* in John Rylands University Library of Manchester.

WALKER, Eric Anderson (1886–   )

Historian. Professor of Imperial and Naval History, Cambridge, 1936–51.

The African Studies Centre, University of Cambridge, has 23 box-files of material, containing chiefly manuscript notes on various aspects of Southern Africa which Professor Walker once worked on. There are some press cuttings, the majority relating to his work, though some are of a more personal nature; and there are several letters concerned with his writings.

WALLACE, Alfred Russel (1823–1913)

Naturalist and author. President, Land Nationalisation Society. Author of works on evolution, botany, vaccination, progress, etc.

The British Library has manuscripts and correspondence, 1856–1912 (Add. MSS 46414–442). They include drafts of *Bad Times*; *Darwinism*, *The Wonderful Century*, *My Life*, etc.; his contributions to periodicals, 1890–1908; and correspondence, general, scientific (with Charles Darwin, among others) and concerning spiritualism, land nationalisation, socialism and anti-vaccination. Notebooks are in the Natural History Museum, and there are letters and notebooks with the Linnean Society. There is correspondence with the Hope Department of Entomology, Oxford University. The Zoological Society of London also has material.
There is correspondence in the Darwin papers, Cambridge University Library.

WALLACE, Sir Donald Mackenzie (1841–1919)

Journalist and author. Private Secretary to Viceroys, of India, 1884–9. Director of the Foreign Department, *The Times*, 1891–9. Editor of 10th edition, *Encyclopaedia Britannica*.

Cambridge University Library has papers collected by Wallace. They consist chiefly of notes for his unpublished 'History of Foreign Policy' and notes on the Russian Revolution of 1905. There is also some correspondence with Chirol.
Three boxes of office papers and correspondence are in the archives of *The Times*. The London Library has a small collection of manuscript notes of the 1st and 2nd Dumas, and the Russian revolutionary movements, 1861–1914.

and notes and memoranda relating to Calcutta can be found in the Hardinge papers at Cambridge University Library.

ALTHAM, Edward (1882–1950)

Naval career; journalist. Senior officer, Archangel River Expeditionary Force, 1919. Naval correspondent, *Morning Post*, 1922. Editor, *Journal of the Royal United Service Institution*, 1924; Secretary of the Institution from 1927. Head of the Postal and Telegraph Censorship Section, Naval Staff, World War II.

Papers at the National Maritime Museum include naval manuscripts and loose papers.

ANDERSON, Sir Kenneth Skelton, 1st Bt (1866–1942)

Businessman and shipping magnate. Chairman, General Shipowners Society, 1913. President, Chamber of Shipping of the United Kingdom, 1915. A member of the Committee on Detention of neutral ships, 1916; of Food Investigation Board, 1918; of Shipping Control Committee, and of the Imperial Shipping Committee.

Five files of papers are deposited at BLPES. The first two include a typescript (approximately 1200 pp.), 'Report on Shipping Control' (1914–15). Another includes correspondence and papers, 1940–2, on post-war shipping; the main correspondent is I. C. Geddes. The final two files contain papers and correspondence relating to expected post war problems. Correspondents again include Geddes, and also Sir Alan Anderson. There are also copies of the privately printed pamphlet, 'The War of Ideas', Feb 1941.

ANDREWS, Charles Freer

Missionary and educator. Closely associated with Gandhi, he worked to improve the lot of Indians in East and South Africa and elsewhere. Author of works on India, Christianity, Labour etc.

Professor Hugh Tinker has used available material in his biography of Andrews.

ANDREWS, Sir (William) Linton (1886–1972)

Journalist. Editor of the *Leeds Mercury*, 1923–39; and of the *Yorkshire Post*, 1939–60. Chairman of the Press Council, 1955–9.

A collection of papers was presented to Leeds University Library in 1973. It is divided into five sections. The first contains material relating to the discussion between the Press Council and the medical profession in 1955 and 1966, on the release of medical information to the press. The second section contains material concerning the Press Council's investigation of the conduct of the British press after the Munich air crash in 1958. The other three sections contain miscellaneous papers by Sir Linton and various items referring to the press.

ANGELL, Sir (Ralph) Norman (1874–1967)

Author and lecturer and socialist politician. Editor, *Salignani's Messenger*, 1899–1903. General Manager, Paris *Daily Mail*, 1905–14. Editor, *Foreign Affairs*, 1928–31. M.P. (Lab.) Bradford North, 1929–31. Member of the Council of the Royal Institute of International Affairs, 1928–41. Co-President, Comité Mondial contre la Guerre et le Fascism. Awarded the Nobel Peace Prize for 1933.

The Angell papers are preserved at Ball State University, Muncie, Indiana, and cover a period of approximately 70 years. They are particularly relevant for Angell's period with the Northcliffe organisation, the war years, and the early 1930s, with some material from the

1960s.The material is extensive and includes several thousand letters. Correspondents include Clifford Allen, Lord Astor, the Duchess of Atholl, Gerald Bailey, Hilaire Belloc, Lady Violet Bonham-Carter, H. N. Brailsford, C. R. Buxton, Andrew Caird, George Catlin, Lord Robert Cecil, Sir Winston Churchill, G. D. H. Cole, Hugh Dalton, G. Lowes Dickinson, R. Palme Dutt, A. G. Gardiner, J. L. Garvin, G. P. Gooch, Lord Haldane, Lord Halifax, Basil Liddell Hart, J. A. Hobson, Julian Huxley, J. M. Keynes, George Lansbury, Harold Laski, J. R. MacDonald, Gilbert Murray, H. W. Nevinson, Lord Northcliffe, Violet Paget, J. B. Priestley, Bertrand Russell, Philip Snowden, J. A. Spender, John Strachey, Arnold Toynbee, Henry A. Wallace, Graham Wallas, H. G. Wells and Sir Evelyn Wrench. The collection also includes a large number of typescripts of various articles and broadcasts, and copies of pamphlets and books. There are, in addition, copies of letters to editors, addresses and reviews, together with notes and memoranda, some of which are in shorthand.Press cuttings for the years 1898–1968 are housed in 21 large boxes. The collection also includes many calendars, appointment books, address books, photographs and personalia.

Miscellaneous letters and papers of Angell, including correspondence with Gilbert Murray and W. A. White, and MSS of articles and essays are available in Columbia University Library, New York.

Further correspondence can be found in the Creech Jones papers at Rhodes House Library, Oxford; and in the Edwin and Lucia Mead papers, Swarthmore College Peace Collection.

ARBERRY, Arthur John (1905–69)

Authority on Arab civilisation. Head of Department of Classics, Cairo University, 1932. Professor of Persian, University of London, 1944; of Arabic, 1946, and Head of Near and Middle East Department, School of Oriental and African Studies. Professor of Arabic, Cambridge University, from 1941.

Five boxes of unsorted correspondence and notes are in Cambridge University Library.

ARCH, Joseph (1826–1919)

Trade unionist. Organiser of agricultural workers.

Patricia Horn, *Joseph Arch* (1971), made full use of available sources. Records of the National Union of Agricultural and Allied Workers (described in *Sources* Vol. 1, p. 191) contain much relevant material. The collection is deposited with the Institute of Agricultural History, University of Reading.

ASHBEE, Charles Robert (1863–1942)

Architect, craftsman and town planner. Master of the Art Workers Guild, 1929. Founder and first Director of the Guild of Handicrafts. Founder of London Survey Committee, and editor of its early publications. Founder of the Essex House Press. Civic Adviser to the Palestine Administration, 1918–22.

The Library of King's College, Cambridge, has Ashbee's Journals, in 40 volumes, covering the years 1880–1941. These contain entries by himself and his wife Janet, correspondence between them and to and from many others, members of the family, friends, colleagues, etc. Correspondents include Edward Carpenter, Laurence Housman, Lowes Dickinson, etc. The Journals also include newspaper cuttings, cartoons, photographs and sketches. The Library also has sketchbooks and other material. Ashbee's 'Memoirs', in six volumes of typescript and based on the Journals, are also in King's College. A seventh volume, *A Palestine Notebook*, was published.

Ashbee gave further typescript copies of his 'Memoirs' to the Library of Congress, the London Library and to the Victoria and Albert Museum. The copy at the Museum is interleaved with MS amendments and additions, photographs, letters and printed matter. It also holds various other relevant papers, including letters for the 1880s; letters relating to the Guild of publishing material, including the Memorandum and Articles of Association of the Fisher Unwin firm; papers and correspondence on Ireland; correspondence dating from 1887 from various sources, and scrapbooks on Ireland which include cuttings, pamphlets, notices of lectures, photographs and broadsheets. There are miscellaneous personal records, including the birth, marriage, and cremation certificates of Fisher Unwin, personalia, passports, correspondence about Dr Johnson's house, a list of members of the South African Conciliation Commission, scrapbooks of miscellaneous items, a record of Fisher Unwin's last words. There are also scrapbooks containing various personal and political items, broadsheets, minutes, agenda, press cuttings, photographs, pamphlets, cartoons, memoranda, correspondence on various topics. The family papers generally contain relevant papers, including material on the Cobden Clubs in London and Heyshott.

The National Liberal Club collection includes a box of unsorted correspondence and papers chiefly relating to Mrs Cobden Unwin, and containing material on the Boer War period and radical organisations with which she was involved. There is correspondence with Lord Hardinge, 1912–15, in Cambridge University Library, while the Bernstein collection in the International Institute of Social History, Amsterdam, contains some items of correspondence, 1896–9. The Norman Angell collection, Ball State University, also has some relevant correspondence.

VARLEY, Julia (1888–1953)

Trade unionist and suffragette.

Hull University Library has a collection of papers. There is some correspondence with members of the royal household, plus press cuttings, photographs, poems and some publications.

VEITCH, George Stead (1885–1943)

Historian. Professor of Modern History, Liverpool University from 1923.

Papers in the Liverpool University Archives reflect Professor Veitch's academic and professional interests. There are various notes taken from primary and secondary sources covering a range of historical topics; and there are lectures and notes for lectures and syllabuses on various subjects – Industrial History, Communications, the Teaching of History, etc. The collection also includes the drafts, typescripts and manuscripts of books and articles, together with relevant correspondence concerning publication. The miscellaneous papers include material relating to his period as a student and later a member of the staff of Liverpool University, plus papers on the history of the University; material relating to work as an examiner at the University and for the Civil Service; illustrative material (slides); personal material such as insurance policies and photographs (slides); plus press cuttings, etc. There is also correspondence with Ramsay Muir, 1908–37, concerning professional and political matters.

VERNEY, Hon. Richard Greville, see WILLOUGHBY DE BROKE, 19th B

VICKERS, Albert (1838–1919)

Businessman. Chairman of Vickers Ltd, shipbuilders and maker of armaments.

Vickers Ltd, Vickers House, Millbank Tower, Millbank, London SW1, has many relevant

Other Joyce material deposited by Harriet Shaw Weaver is at Add. MSS 47471–89 (autograph drafts of *Finnegan's Wake*, proof sheets, etc.); and Add. MS 49975, which includes part of an early draft of Joyce's autobiography, and notes for the last seven chapters of *Ulysses*, 1919–21. Some of the correspondence is reproduced in Jane Lidderdale and Mary Nicholson, *Dear Miss Weaver* (1970).

WEBB, (Martha) Beatrice
Beatrice Potter (1858–1943)

Political scientist and socialist author. Contributed to Charles Booth's *Life and Labour of the People*. Member of Royal Commission on the Poor Law and Unemployment, 1905–9, and joint author of the Minority Report. Member of various government committees. With her husband Sidney Webb wrote numerous works of social investigation and labour history.

BLPES has a large collection of the papers of both Beatrice and Sidney Webb (1st Baron Passfield) (ref. Passfield Papers). The collection consists of both public and private papers. The former include 350 volumes of material collected for the Webb's history of English local government, two volumes of papers related to their Board of Trade activities, 1911–18, twenty volumes relating to *New Statesman* special supplements, 1915–17 (the Webbs founded the *New Statesman* in 1913), and six volumes of papers on East African politics, 1929–31. There are also nine boxes of papers from the reconstruction committee of the Ministry of Reconstruction, 1916–18, and five boxes on the relief of distress, 1914–15.

The most important section of the private papers is Beatrice Webb's diaries, 1873–1943. The manuscript version fills 58 notebooks and includes some letters and photographs. A typescript copy exists. Beatrice Webb herself typed out many of her diaries and began editing them for publication. They were published as follows: Beatrice Webb, *My Apprenticeship* (1926), *Our Partnership*, ed. Margaret I. Cole and Barbara Drake (1948), *Beatrice Webb's Diaries 1912–1924* and *1924–32*, ed. Margaret I. Cole (1952–6), *Beatrice Webb's American Diary 1898*, ed. David A. Shannon (Madison, Wisc., 1963), and *The Webbs' Australian Diary 1898*, ed. A. G. Austin (Melbourne, 1965). Margaret Cole has also written a memoir, *Beatrice Webb* (1945). Kitty Muggeridge, Beatrice Webb's niece, has written a biography (co-author Ruth Adam), *Beatrice Webb:A Life* (1967), based on Potter family papers as well as the Webb collection.

In addition to the diaries, the papers include Potter family letters, Sidney Webb's letters to Beatrice, 1890–1940, and letters from the Webbs given to the library after an appeal in 1956 and subsequently. There are personal papers concerning the various honours and certificates granted to the Webbs, their personal finances and their houses, including a catalogue to the sale of contents in 1948. There are papers related to the Webbs' political and public work, including a collection of papers made by Sidney Webb concerning the 1931 crisis. There is material concerning their many publications, lecture notes, articles, broadcasts and speeches, their bibliographies on various subjects such as the poor law and syndicalism, six boxes of Fabian Society papers, particularly concerning resident summer schools, and papers concerning the foundation, history and administration of the London School of Economics. Two volumes of the letters of Beatrice and Sidney Webb are to be published (ed. Professor Norman Mackenzie). A microfilm of Beatrice Webb's diary is also being prepared.

The Fabian Society archive at Nuffield College, Oxford, contains a mass of correspondence of Beatrice and Sidney Webb, 1891–1941. There are also letters in the War Emergency Workers National Committee papers in the Labour Party archive at Transport House.

Correspondence can be found in a number of collections. There are five letters, 1881–1903, in the Herbert Spencer papers (NRA 16255). At the British Library there are letters to George Bernard Shaw, 1913–42 (Add. MS 50553) and John Burns (Add. MS 46287). The Horace Plunkett papers include letters concerning the *New Statesman* supplement on Ireland, and German Industrial Development. The W. A. S. Hewins papers in Sheffield University Library contain further letters. At the Bodleian Library, Oxford, there is correspondence with Asquith,

BAIRD, Sir Robert Hugh Hanley (1855–1934)

Newspaper owner. Published the *Belfast Telegraph*. Founded Irish *Daily Telegraph*, 1904; *Ireland's Saturday Night*, 1894; *Belfast Weekly Telegraph*, 1873. President Irish Newspaper Society, 1913–25.

The Trustees of the Baird Estate, who have the papers, including diaries, can be contacted c/o Belfast Telegraph Offices, Royal Avenue, Belfast. The Public Record Office of Northern Ireland has xerox copies of some parts of the diaries.

BALDWIN, James Mark (1861–1934)

Psychologist. Stuart Professor of Psychology, Princeton University, 1893–1903. Professor of Philosophy and Psychology, Johns Hopkins University, 1903–9. Professor at the Ecole des hautes études sociales, Paris, 1916–18. Editor, *The Psychological Review*, 1894–1909.

Some papers are available at the Bodleian Library, Oxford. They include letters to Baldwin, chiefly on philosophical subjects, from among others, H. Bergson, F. H. Bradley, T. D. A. Cockerell, H. W. Conn, Samuel Langhorn Clemens (Mark Twain), C. B. Davenport, F. H. Giddings, C. L. Herrick, S. H. Hodgson, Henry James, William James, Sir E. R. Lankester, C. L.Morgan, H. F. Osborn, Josiah Royce and C. F. Stout.

BALL, Willet (1873–1962)

Journalist. Member of National Union of Railwaymen and Social Democratic Federation, 1893. Editor, *Railway Review*, 1917–33.

A small collection of material is in the Library of Nuffield College, Oxford. It includes a few letters, chiefly relating to Socialist politics; some election literature dating from 1895; a few items relating to railways; and various miscellaneous papers, including a minute book of the Luton and District Socialist Party, 1909–11, and certain trade union material.

BARKER, Sir Ernest (1874–1960)

Historian and political thinker. Principal of King's College, London, 1920–7. Professor of Political Science and Fellow of Peterhouse, Cambridge, 1928–39. Professor of Political Science, Cologne, 1947–8.

Peterhouse Library, Cambridge has some lecture notes and other manuscripts together with printed material. Correspondence was retained by Mr Nicolas Barker (son) and may be deposited. The Bodleian Library, Oxford, has his letters to Marvin, and there is correspondence, 1941–53, in the Brett Young papers (NRA 13482).

BARNES, Leonard (1895–1977)

Writer, philosopher and poet. Critic of British colonial policy in the 1930s and 1940s. Author of *Caliban in Africa* (1930), *The Duty of Empire* (1935), *Empire or Democracy* (1939), etc. Lecturer in Education, University of Liverpool, 1936–45. Secretary of the Delegacy for Social Training, Oxford University, 1947–62.

Barnes left an unpublished autobiography, 'Let them Scratch', which has been edited by Dr Anthony McAdam, St Antony's College, Oxford. The complete work is on microfilm in the Library of the School of Oriental and African Studies. There are letters in the Creech Jones papers, Rhodes House Library, Oxford. His work is discussed in Anthony McAdam, 'British Liberal and Left-Wing Critics of the Dependent Empire 1918–1939', unpublished Ph.D. thesis, Edinburgh University, 1977.

BARNETT, Dame Henrietta Octavia (1851–1936)

Social reformer. Hon. Secretary, State Children's Aid Association. Founder and President of London Pupil Teachers' Association. Vice-President, National Association for the Welfare of the Feeble-Minded. Founder of Hampstead Garden Trust, 1903, and a prominent supporter of the Garden City ideal. Lecturer on Housing, Poor Law and Social Subjects.

Papers collected by Dame Henrietta with regard to her biography of her husband, Canon S. A. Barnett, can be found at the Greater London Record Office. These contain various references to her own work. The Greater London Record Office also has letters between Henrietta Barnett and Lord Milner, 1913, and 1917, and those between her and E. St John Catchpool, 1925, 1928–49, which were deposited with the records of Toynbee Hall. Some correspondence with Canon Barnett is in the Barnett papers at Lambeth Palace Library. Dame Henrietta's correspondence with Francis and Edith Marvin can be found in the Marvin papers, and some correspondence with Octavia Hill is available in BLPES. The Jane Addams correspondence in the Swarthmore College Peace Collection includes letters from Dame Henrietta in the Settlement House Work correspondence, 1889–96.

BARNETT, Samuel Augustus (1844–1913)

Social Reformer and Churchman. Vicar of St Jude's, Whitechapel. Founded Charity Organisation Society, 1869. A founder and Warden of Toynbee Hall, 1884–1906; President of Toynbee Hall, 1906–13. Canon of Westminster from 1906; Steward, 1911–13.

Various personal papers are in the care of the Greater London Record Office. These were chiefly collected by Dame Henrietta Barnett from various members of the family and were used in the compilation of her biography of her husband, *Canon Barnett, his Life, Work and Friends* (2 vols, 1918). The collection consists of correspondence, sermons and lecture notes, together with miscellaneous items. The correspondence largely consists of weekly letters from Canon Barnett to his brother, F. G. Barnett, and after his death to the widow, daughter and son. These date from c. 1883. There are also letters from Barnett to his mother and family, relating chiefly to his trips to Egypt in 1879–80, and round the world, 1890–1. The collection also includes a series of bound sermon notebooks and various lecture notes. The sermons are essentially for the period at St Jude's, 1875–88. Amongst the miscellaneous papers are formal documents relating to posts, photographs, etc.

The Greater London Record Office also has records of Toynbee Hall. The bulk of the records were destroyed during World War II but the fragmentary material that survives contains references to Barnett's work.

Lambeth Palace Library has papers of Barnett relating to the National Church Reform Union. Amongst these are newspaper cuttings, mainly of articles and letters by the Canon, 1885–96; and letters to Barnett from E. A. Abbot, H. M. Butler, P. L. Gell, Thomas Hughes, the Bishop of Lichfield and Arnold Toynbee, as well as letters from Barnett to his wife. Other papers include notes and memoranda and extracts from letters by Barnett.

Barnett's correspondence with the US National Federation of Settlements and Neighbourhood Centers can be found in the Louis Helberg Towley papers, in the University of Minnesota Library. His correspondence with Herbert Samuel, 1888–1908, is in the House of Lords Record Office. Correspondence with Beveridge regarding Toynbee Hall can be found at BLPES, as can some correspondence with Octavia Hill.

BARRINGTON-WARD, Robert McGowan (1891–1948)

Journalist. Editorial secretary, *The Times*, 1913. Assistant editor, *The Observer*, 1919–27; *The Times*, 1927–41. Editor of *The Times* from 1941.

Mr Mark Barrington-Ward (son), 8 Apsley Road, Oxford, OX2 7QY has a collection of papers. Amongst these is a diary, 1924–48 (with the volume for 1933 missing). Until the later

WARD, Thomas Humphry (1845–1926)

Journalist and author. Fellow of Brasenose College, Oxford, 1869; tutor, 1870–81. Contributor and leader writer, *The Times*.

Papers can be found in collections of Ward family papers at Pusey House, Oxford, and in University College Library, London, as described above. These include correspondence, diaries and appointments books.

Social correspondence, 1910–12, is in the Sladen papers, while his publishing correspondence with Macmillans, 1869–1901, can be found in the British Library (Add. MS 54927). The University of Texas, Austin, has correspondence with Thomas Hardy and Henry James.

WARE, Sir Fabian Arthur Goulstone (1869–1949)

Administrator and author. Acting Director of Education, Transvaal, 1901; Director, 1903–5. Editor of the *Morning Post*, 1905–11. Founder, Imperial War Graves Commission; Vice Chairman, 1917–48. Chairman, Parents' National Educational Union.

No papers are known, but there is correspondence with Richard Jebb, 1907–17, in the Institute of Commonwealth Studies. Papers of PNEU are in London University Library.

WARREN, Sir (Thomas) Herbert (1853–1930)

President of Magdalen College, Oxford, 1885–1928. Vice-Chancellor, University of Oxford, 1906–10.

Magdalen College, Oxford, has Warren's 'official' papers in the College records. They chiefly relate to tutorial and bursarial matters. Family and personal papers are in the care of Mr C. A. Brodie, Squires Farm, Coldharbour, near Dorking, Surrey. They are contained in several deed boxes, but are at present unsorted. There is correspondence with Douglas Sladen, 1908–9, concerning his book on Egypt, and letters, 1915, on recruitment for the army. Letters to Ruskin are in Hull University Library, and there is correspondence in the Edward Arber collection (NRA 10731).

WATSON, Robert Spence (1837–1911)

Political, social and educational reformer. Helped found Armstrong College, Durham, 1871; first President, 1910. Pioneer of University extension teaching in North of England. President of the National Liberal Federation, 1890–1902. President of the Peace Society.

The House of Lords Record Office has photocopies of correspondence and papers, including correspondence with John Morley. It also has some 25 letters from Spence Watson in the Soskice collection.

WEAVER, Harriet Shaw (1876–1961)

Feminist and literary patron. Editor of *The New Freewoman*, later known as *The Egoist*, and of the *Egoist Press*. Patron of James Joyce.

The British Library has a collection of correspondence and papers both literary and business, and including material relating to James Joyce (Add. MSS 57345–65). There is a substantial grouping of letters from' or concerning Joyce, 1914–41, together with letters from Nora and Lucia Joyce and other members of the family. Other correspondents include Archibald Macleish, Ezra Pound, John Quinn, G. B. Shaw, H. G. Wells, Sylvia Beach, T. S. Eliot, Edmund Gosse, Virginia Woolf and Dora Marsden (1912–35). There are also literary and business papers concerning *The New Freewoman*, and *The Egoist*, such as articles of association, press cuttings, articles, minutes, notices to shareholders, accounts, etc.

them, by subject. The topics covered by the collection include gunnery, 1903 to 1905; naval policy and strategy, on which White exchanged letters with Lord Fisher, Lord Charles Beresford, and Sir Percy Scott. On lower-deck conditions the correspondence is largely with Lionel Yexley, and there are general papers on Ireland, emigration and eugenics. A number of original letters were removed by White but it was his practice to leave typed copies in their place; those of Lord Fisher come into this category. Correspondence, 1911–16, can be found in the Blumenfeld papers, House of Lords Record Office.

WICKSTEED, Philip Henry (1844–1927)

Economist. Unitarian minister from 1867. University Extension Lecturer, 1887–1918.

Wicksteed stated that he kept 'next to no documents' (see Sturges, *Economists' Papers*, p. 128). BLPES has one volume of papers, including MSS, typed and printed material connected with his work on economics. It includes a few notes for University Extension lectures, a syllabus for lecture courses, two letters to and one from Wicksteed and some printed pamphlets, and covers the period 1887–1924. Correspondence with F. E. Colenso concerning colonial affairs is in Rhodes House Library, and further correspondence is available in the Cannan and Wallas papers (BLPES) and James Macluckie Connell collection (Dr Williams' Library).

WIDDRINGTON, Percy Elborough Tinling (1873–1959)

Anglo-Catholic priest. Advocate of a Christian Sociology. A founder member of the League of the Kingdom of God, and founder of *Christendom*.

Papers, including correspondence with his first wife Enid Stacy (q.v.) are in the care of his son, Mr Gerard Widdrington of Toronto. Enquiries may be directed to Mrs Angela Tuckett (niece), 5 Liddington Street, Swindon, Wilts. Maurice B. Reckitt, *P. E. T. Widdrington* (1961), quotes from correspondence and papers in the care of family and friends.

WILKINSON, (Henry) Spenser (1853–1937)

Military historian; author and journalist. Fellow of All Souls, Oxford. Chichele Professor of Military History, University of Oxford, 1909–23.

Material with the Army Museums Ogilby Trust includes letters concerning the Niger and Congo Conference, Berlin, 1885; 37 letters from Lord Milner about political questions in South Africa, 1888–1918; letters from General Sir Ian Hamilton, mainly about South Africa, 1898–1931; and letters and papers dealing with the setting up of the Navy League, 1894–1919. There is correspondence from the Duke of Devonshire, Asquith, Haldane, Fisher, Methuen, Sir John Colomb, M.P., Sir William Robertson, Kitchener, General Sir Aylmer Haldane, Admiral Sir Reginald Custance, Colonel J. L. A. Colin and US Admiral William S. Sims. In addition, the Trust holds various draft articles and leaders, letters to newspapers, typescripts and notes, lectures, press reviews, appreciations of his books, press cuttings, etc.

Two boxes of notebooks, containing many of Wilkinson's lectures and research notes were given to the National Army Museum by the Royal United Service Institution, of which he was Secretary.

In addition, correspondence 1891–1909 can be found in the papers of Earl Roberts, also at the National Army Museum.

WILLERT, Sir Arthur (1882–1973)

Journalist. Chief correspondent of *The Times* in the USA, 1910–20. Secretary of the British War Mission, USA, 1917–18. Head of the News Department and Press Officer, Foreign Office, from 1921. Head of the Ministry of Information Office for Southern Region, 1939–45.

Sir Arthur Willert's papers were bequeathed to Yale University Library.

BEARSTED, 1st Vt
Sir Marcus Samuel, 1st Bt (1853–1927)

Businessman; founder of Shell Petroleum Company. Lord Mayor of London, 1902–3.

The present Viscount Bearsted has no papers. A holograph diary kept during the 1st Viscount's period as Lord Mayor is in the Guildhall Library.

The archives of Hill, Samuel and Co. Ltd, merchant bankers, 100 Wood Street, London EC2, contain relevant records. These include a press cuttings book of obituary notices; and correspondence relating to trading in the Far East. His interest in World Jewry is reflected in a memorandum by Neville Laski on the position of Jews in Czechoslovakia, 1938. The records of Hill, Samuel, together with those of Shell, were used by Robert Henriques in his biography.

BEAVER, Sir Hugh Eyre Campbell (1890–1967)

Industrialist. Partner in Sir Alexander Gibb and Partners, consulting engineers, 1932–42. Managing Director, Arthur Guinness Son and Co. Ltd, 1946–60. Director General and Controller General, Ministry of Works, 1940–5. Director, Colonial Development Corporation, 1951–60. Chairman, Advisory Council for Scientific and Industrial Research, etc.

BLPES has a collection of papers. Biographical material includes miscellaneous notes prepared by Sir Hugh for his autobiography; correspondence with his mother, and other letters to him as a boy; honours; letters of congratulations, notebooks and memoranda, a private journal, diary notes and pocket diaries; press cuttings; letters of a personal nature from Indians, fellow officers etc. There is extensive correspondence relating to the firm of Sir Alexander Gibb and Partners; papers concerning the Ministry of Works, including correspondence, committee papers, etc.; papers relating to the Guinness company; material on the Federation of British Industries, 1957–60s, and correspondence relating to educational institutions with which he was involved. There is a grouping of personal correspondence arranged chronologically, 1929–66, including Christmas greetings, family news, social engagements, letters of sympathy, of congratulation, etc. There are also various lectures, speeches and addresses dating from 1937. Another section of the collection contains various reminiscences by Sir Hugh. There are also papers, correspondence, etc., relating to Lord Reith, 1940–66; and material relating to Winston Churchill. Documents and correspondence dealing with Wellington College are in the archives of the College.

BEAZLEY, Sir (Charles) Raymond (1868–1955)

Historian and diplomatist. Professor of History, University of Birmingham, 1909–33.

The Library of Birmingham University holds 25 boxes of papers containing some 170 items. Box 1 contains a collection of personal letters, many from other historians, together with his student notes on historical problems and notes on his own history students. Boxes 2–14 contain lecture notes, notes for publications, manuscript drafts of publications and offprints of articles. Boxes 15–17 hold materials from Foreign Office papers, dating from 1872. Boxes 18–20 have material relating to Germany, Poland and Russia, while Boxes 21–4 have miscellaneous papers, notebooks and press cuttings relating to the same themes and period. The final box, 25, has material relating to Birmingham University and to Beazley's schooldays.

Correspondence with W. H. Dawson, also in Birmingham University Library, relates to the Saar, Disarmament and the defence of Germany.

BEESLY, Edward Spencer (1831–1915)

Positivist thinker and historian. Principal, University Hall, London, 1859. Professor of History, University College London, 1860–93; Professor of Latin, Bedford College London, 1860–89. Editor, *Positivist Review* from 1893.

A collection of correspondence, lecture notes, press cuttings, miscellaneous papers and printed books was given by Beesly's grandchildren to University College London. The correspondence is rather slight in content, and only isolated letters from individual correspondents are preserved. The collection includes groups of Beesly's own letters to Harry Crompton and to Frederic Harrison, and a few letters to Beesly's brother, A. H. Beesly, and E. S. Beesly's son, Alfred. The lecture notes cover Classical, English, and French history. The newspaper cuttings include a notebook containing cuttings of articles, letters and speeches by Beesly, and reviews, 1874–84; another, 1896–1911, containing the same range of matters; cuttings on the suicide of Paul and Laura Lafargue, 1911; and an album of obituaries, 1915. Amongst the family papers are three letters to Mrs Beesly from Irish M.P.s, 1888, and material relating to Alfred Beesley. The printed matter includes reports relating to positivism, offprints of articles by Beesly, copies of his review articles, 1861–95, pamphlets, copies of journals, and articles about Beesly.

Letters from Frederic Harrison to Beesly (1852–70) can be found in the Harrison Papers at BLPES. Records of the London Positivist Society are also available at BLPES. (*Sources*, Vol. 1, p. 157).

BELGION, (Harold) Montgomery (1892–1973)

Journalist and author. On staff of *Daily Mail*, 1919–21, 1922–4; *New York World*, 1921–2; *Westminster Gazette*, 1924–5; *Daily Mirror*, 1935–7; *Daily Sketch*, 1939.

Churchill College, Cambridge, has a collection of papers, contained in some 46 boxes. The collection, at present uncatalogued, contains personal material; papers concerning war crimes and the Nuremburg trials; books, reviews and articles; papers on Art; notes, cuttings and correspondence about his work on 'Megalopolitics'; and drafts of unfinished novels.

BELL, Charles Frederic Moberly (1847–1911)

Journalist. Correspondent of *The Times* in Egypt, 1865–90. Assistant Manager of *The Times*, 1890–1908; Managing Director from 1908.

The archives of *The Times* has three boxes of materials, including letter books, 1865–1909, letters to colleagues on *The Times*, such as Buckle and members of the Walter family, and some family material. Bell had the habit of writing many letters from home, and these have been lost. The manager's letterbooks contain copies of Bell's out-correspondence. The Cromer papers at the Public Record Office include correspondence concerning Egyptian matters, including Bell's work in Egypt and Cromer's *Modern Times*, material on the reorganisation of *The Times*, and tariff reform. Correspondence with Macmillans, the publishers, is in the British Library (Add. MSS 55038). The papers of Ernest Gedge contain some correspondence while correspondence with Earl Roberts is in Duke University, Durham, North Carolina.

BELL, George Kennedy Allen (1883–1958)

Bishop of Chichester, 1929–58. Member of Archbishops' Committee on Social and Industrial Problems, 1917. Member of Royal Institute of International Affairs, 1923. Chairman of Universal Christian Council for Life and Work, 1934–6.

Lambeth Palace Library has various relevant papers. Amongst these are 61 volumes of 'German Papers', 1925–57, which chiefly relate to Bishop Bell's work with peace movements and his contacts with the German resistance. Four volumes, 1919–55, concern peace campaigns and the National Peace Council; while another 20 volumes contain material relating to the German Church struggles and correspondence and papers about refugees, 1933–49. There is correspondence with, and concerning Dietrich Bonhoeffer, and with Martin Niemöller, together with correspondence with a number of German pastors. Other material relates to post-war Germany and denazification, resistance movements, war criminals and evangelical Church meetings. Lambeth Palace Library also has correspondence between Bell and Gerhard Leibholz;

Weldon's papers passed to his literary executor, Karl Pearson, and are now in the Pearson collection in the Library of University College London. They include working papers, correspondence and papers relating to *Biometrika*. A substantial grouping of correspondence can also be found in the Galton papers in University College London.

WELLS, Herbert George (1866–1946)

Novelist and social critic. Author of many works of fiction, science fiction, political pamphlets and articles (with socialist themes), etc.

The University of Illinois Library has a large collection, some 65,000 items in all, covering the years 1880–1946. The correspondence consists of some 60,000 letters received, from a large range of political and literary correspondents, and around 1500 letters from Wells. There are also the typescripts and proofs of 40 novels, 37 sociological books and 11 pamphlets; typescripts and clippings of some 150 unpublished articles, stories, speeches, plays, films and other papers. Personal papers include pocket diaries, personal financial material, family records, contracts and publishers' statements, address books, house inventories, photographs, etc. Correspondence concerning his publications, and a collection of his wife's letters are in the University of Virginia Library (Charlottesville). Correspondence of Wells and his family with William Baxter and notes by Baxter concerning Wells are in Bromley Central Library. Correspondence with the Society of Authors, 1909–39, and with Macmillans the publishers, 1895–1944, can be found in the British Library (Add. MSS 56843–4 and 54943–5 respectively). The British Library also has Wells' correspondence with G. B. Shaw and his wife, 1901–4 (Add. MS 50552) and with Lady Aberconway, 1925–46, (Add. MSS 52551–3). The Wells letters in the PEN archive have been purchased by the University of Texas, Austin.

Wells' correspondence with Frank Swinnerton is in Arkansas University Library; with William Smith Culbertson and with Charles Anderson Dana in the Library of Congress; with H. J. Laski and with Coronet Magazine in Syracuse University Library; with Howard Vincent O'Brien in the Newberry Library, Chicago; with Marie Meloney in Columbia University Libraries; and with Norman Angell in Ball State University. There are also letters to Sir Edmund Gosse, 1897–1912, in Leeds University Library; to R. Murray Gilchrist in Sheffield City Library; personal, social and literary correspondence with Douglas Sladen, 1915–20; letters to Lloyd George, 1927, 1934–9, in the House of Lords Record Office. The Ashbee journals at King's College, Cambridge, also have references.

The Fabian Society archive at Nuffield College, Oxford, contains correspondence and lectures by Wells, and papers relating to the H. G. Wells controversy, 1907, including reports of the Special Committee and the Executive Committee, the report on the reconstruction of the Fabian Society, printed circulars, various letters and notes, letters to Wells, agenda, etc.

The Kingsley Martin collection in Sussex University Library has relevant papers, including general correspondence to Martin, and three files of manuscript, typescript and printed material specifically concerning Wells. These include his letters to the *New Statesman*; drafts, notes by Martin and others on Wells, a bibliography, etc.

Norman and Jeanne Mackenzie, *The Time Traveller: The Life of H. G. Wells* (1973) made full use of the Wells archives in Illinois and elsewhere. Lovat Dickson, *H. G. Wells: His Turbulent Life and Times* (1969), quotes from correspondence. Gordon N. Ray, *H. G. Wells and Rebecca West* (1974) uses the c. 800 letters from Wells to Rebecca West in her care (hers to Wells have been destroyed). Ray is also editing the *Life and Letters*.

WHITE, Arnold Henry (1848–1925)

Author and journalist. Writer on social problems, colonisation, Jewish settlement. Advocate of a strong navy as 'Vanoc' of the *Referee*.

The papers were deposited on permanent loan in the National Maritime Museum by the Bedford Estate Office in 1972. They consist of 202 files arranged alphabetically, as White left

WRENCH, Sir (John) Evelyn Leslie (1882–1966)

Writer and politician. Promoter of Commonwealth unity. Founder of the Overseas Club (later League) and of the English-Speaking Union of the Commonwealth, 1918. Chief Private Secretary, Air Minister, 1917–18. Deputy controller, British Empire and USA Section, Ministry of Information, 1918. American Relations Officer to government of India, 1942–4. Editor of *The Spectator*, 1925–32; its chairman from 1925.

Correspondence and diaries are located in the British Library (Add. MSS 59541–597). The correspondence chiefly consists of letters addressed to Wrench and dates from 1887. One volume, Add. MS 59541, consists chiefly of letters to his father, Rt. Hon. Frederick Wrench. Vol. VIII of the correspondence, Add. MS 59548 consists of six letters from T. E. Lawrence to Francis Yeats-Brown of *The Spectator*, 1926–7. The diaries cover the years 1897–1950, and are mostly records of travel abroad, including some typewritten versions, consisting of copies of, or extracts from, the diaries.

Correspondence can be found in the Edward Carson papers, Public Record Office of Northern Ireland.

YOUNG, Sir Frederick (1817–1913)

Colonial Administrator; advocate of Imperial Federation. Secretary of the Royal Colonial Institute.

The Royal Commonwealth Society Library has a collection of material. It includes both correspondence to him personally and letters addressed to him as Secretary of the Institute (these are filed in the main collection of autograph letters). There are two letterbooks, including letters from Young, dating from 1837, and letters to him. There is also an 85-page manuscript autobiography. In addition, there are two volumes of press cuttings on his activities, covering subjects of interest to him. Three files contain letters and memoranda, and copies of pamphlets by Young.

YOUNG, George Malcolm (1882–1959)

Historian.

Material concerning his biography of Stanley Baldwin is in Cambridge University Library. All Souls College, Oxford, has some typescripts by Young.

ZANGWILL, Israel (1864–1926)

Man of letters. Author of novels, poetry, plays, essays. President of the Jewish Historical Society.

The bulk of his papers are in the Central Zionist Archives, Jerusalem, including diaries and notes from meetings with Foreign Office officials. Relevant items can be found in the Anglo-Jewish Archives, University College London. His unfinished novel 'The Baron of Offenbach' is in the British Library (Add. MS 41485). There is correspondence, 1894–1900, 1915–20, on social, business and literary matters in the Douglas Sladen papers. Correspondence with Annie

Middle East Centre, St. Antony's College, Oxford. This material includes letters to Bentwich in Palestine, 1921–9, written in Arabic and English. Relevant material may also be found in the records of the Central British Fund for Jewish Relief and Rehabilitation, Woburn House, Upper Woburn Place, London WC1H 0EX. His autobiographical work, *Mandate Memories*, is a useful memoir for the period.

BERNAL, John Desmond (1901–71)

Scientist; writer on science and society; Marxist publicist. Fellow of the Royal Society. Professor of Physics, Birkbeck College, University of London, 1937–63; Professor of Crystallography, 1963–8. Foreign member, Academy of Sciences, USSR, 1958. Awarded Lenin Peace Prize, 1953. Author of *The Social Function of Science* (1939), *Marx and Science* (1952), *Science in History* (1954), etc.

There are some 56 boxes of material in Cambridge University Library. These cover a wide range of his interests, from crystallography to his membership of progressive organisations, and include correspondence, diaries, notebooks, material on 'Science and the Labour Party', 'Origins of Life', 'Science in History', etc. Birkbeck College, London, has a further collection of papers, which includes many of his scientific writings (both published and unpublished), writings on the social relations of science (political, philosophical, economic, etc.) and details of broadcasts. A catalogue of these papers is being prepared by Miss A. Rimel, former secretary to Professor Bernal; when this is completed the papers will be made available for consultation.

BLPES has material concerning his international peace activities. Martin Bernal, 15 Manor Mansions, Belsize Grove, London NW3, is collecting material for the authorised biography.

BERNARD, Archbishop John Henry (1860–1927)

Churchman and educationalist. Archbishop of Dublin, 1915–19. Provost, Trinity College Dublin, 1919–27. Closely involved in moves towards Irish independence.

Correspondence and papers are available at the British Library (Add. MSS 52781–4), and include general correspondence (1912–25), and correspondence with Lloyd George and his secretaries (1916–22), with the 1st Earl of Midleton (1917–26), the 5th Earl of Desart (1916–24) and A. V. Dicey (1910–20). In addition, the collection includes literary manuscripts, proofs, speeches, and press cuttings, 1917–25.

Other papers are housed at Trinity College Dublin. The collection consists of some 868 items, relating directly to Bernard, together with one box of printed material; also eight other volumes concerning Bernard's work, and referring especially to George Salmon, the theologian; and two boxes of papers concerning the Irish Convention.

BESANT, Annie (1847–1933)

Socialist pioneer, Theosophist, educationalist and Indian politician. Member of National Secular Society from 1874; co-editor with Charles Bradlaugh of *National Reformer*; with Bradlaugh published Knowlton's tract, *Fruits of Philosophy*, and subsequently prosecuted, 1877. Fabian Essayist, 1889. Helped organise unskilled labourers; organiser of the Match Strike, 1888. Member of Theosophical Society, 1889; President from 1907. A leader of the Indian Liberal Party. Author of various publications on political, religious, philosophical and scientific matters.

The Theosophical Society, International Headquarters, Adyar, Madras 600020, India, has various papers relating to Annie Besant. These do not pre-date her involvement in the Theosophical Movement, and therefore have little on her work with Bradlaugh and the Fabian Society, etc. The political papers in the archive date from c. 1914, and concern the nationalist movement in India. There are some 200 letters from various government officials, some concerning the Boy Scout movement of which she was a commissioner, and there is correspondence with three prominent Indian political personalities, Taj Bahadur Sapru (c. 1926, concerning the Round Table Conference), G. K. Gokale (c. 1914, concerning the Servants of India Society) and V. S. Srinivasa Sastri (1921–3). Diaries start from the year 1892, and continue to 1932, but they are effectively appointment books, with little detail. Scrapbooks, chiefly relating to her theosophical works date from September 1890. Other manuscript material includes her internment diary and minute books of various organisations started by her, such as the Madras Parliament.

Her political activities in Britain can be traced in various collections. The Socialist League archive, at the International Institute of Social History, Amsterdam, contains a few letters, 1887–8. There are letters to G. B. Shaw, 1885–1919, in the British Library (Add. MS 50529); letters to Edward Carpenter in Sheffield City Libraries; and letters to S. L. Bensusan in the University of Essex Library. Archives in India also contain relevant material, e.g. the state archives of West Bengal in Calcutta, and the National Archives in New Delhi.

The archives of the Fabian Society are in Nuffield College, Oxford, and these contain relevant material. A note on archives relating to Indian Affairs can be found in *Sources* Vol. 1, pp. 111–14. Available manuscript sources and interviews with people who knew Annie Besant were used in Arthur H. Nethercot, *The First Five Lives of Annie Besant* (1961), and *The Last Four Lives of Annie Besant* (1963).

BLACKETT, Baron
Patrick Maynard Stuart Blackett (1897–1974)

Scientist, Fellow of the Royal Society, Government adviser. Fellow of King's College, Cambridge, 1923–33. Professor of Physics, Birkbeck College, University of London, 1933–7. Professor of Physics, University of Manchester, 1937–53. Professor of Physics, Imperial College of Science and Technology, 1953–65. Chairman, Research Grants Committee, 1956–60. Scientific Adviser, Ministry of Technology. President, British Society for the Advancement of Science, 1957–8. President of the Royal Society, 1965–70.

The Blackett papers have been listed by the Contemporary Scientific Archives Centre, and are to be deposited with the Royal Society. The collection is wide-ranging, covering both Blackett's scientific and public career. All the major aspects of his scientific work are represented in papers and scientific correspondence.There is also biographical material, papers covering his work on various scientific and non-scientific committees, papers on his involvement with the Labour Party, his role in the foundation of the Ministry of Technology, papers on University expansion, Imperial College, material on disarmament and defence, lectures etc.

BLAIR, Sir Robert (1859–1935)

Educationalist. School inspector in Scotland, 1894–1900. Chief Inspector for Technical Education, Ireland, 1900–1; Assistant Secretary, Technical Instruction, Department of Agriculture and Technical Instruction for Ireland, 1901–4. Education Officer, London County Council, 1904–24.

Private papers are in the care of Heriot-Watt University Library. They include evidence and relevant papers concerning the Royal Commission on London Government, 1922; papers on the Irish and L.C.C. Inspectorate; material concerning the Liberal Party and education; notes on London Public Schools; a paper concerning Lord Haldane's Committee; a folder of lectures on education; papers concerning superannuation, salaries, finance and education, training and education, including notes for speeches; four small personal notebooks; and various pamphlets and reports.

Blair's activities for the London County Council can be traced in its records at the Greater London Record Office.

Press, 1917. Secretary of Labour Party Advisory Committee on International Affairs.

The University of Sussex Library has a collection of Woolf's papers. This includes boxes of miscellaneous letters, from the 1930s to 1969; family correspondence and two boxes of letters from eminent persons; 11 boxes of work and business papers, up to 1968; and papers relating to his autobiographical volumes, *Sowing, Growing, Beginning Again, Downhill All The Way* and *The Journey not the Arrival Matters*. Political papers include documents relating to the Labour Party International Advisory Committee, the Fabian Society Research Group, the League of Nations, reviews of political works, and miscellaneous political letters and papers. Amongst literary material are university essays and translations, volumes of university notes, papers, articles and reviews relating to Ceylon, correspondence and reviews relating to Virginia Woolf and to his own books, unsorted manuscripts and typescripts, offprints of articles, etc. There is in addition, a collection of domestic papers, and 'bills paid'. Other miscellaneous material includes a box-file of papers on Africa, War, League of Nations Mandates, plus reviews, press cuttings, photostats, etc.

Correspondence regarding Labour Party policies towards the colonies can be found in the Creech Jones papers at Rhodes House Library, Oxford. Letters of Virginia and Leonard Woolf can also be found in the J. M. Keynes papers at King's College, Cambridge, and in the Charleston papers there. A considerable amount of material relating to Virginia Woolf, Leonard's wife, can be found in the Berg collection, New York Public Library.

Documents of the Labour Party Advisory Committees on International and Imperial Affairs at Transport House are briefly described in *Sources*, Vol. 1, p. 130. The Greenidge papers contain miscellaneous notes and papers, while correspondence concerning Ceylon is in the Cambridge Centre for South Asian Studies.

WORSFOLD, William Basil (1858–1939)

Barrister, lecturer and author. Confidant of Lord Milner in South Africa. Editor of the *Johannesburg Star*, 1904–5.

A collection of material survives at Rhodes House Library, Oxford. The papers cover the years 1902–33 and are concerned almost entirely with his association with Milner until his death in 1925. Correspondence in the collection reveals the accord between the two men, and the extent to which Milner influenced the *Star*'s editorial policy. There are also letters between them concerning the publication of books by Worsfold on Milner's South African policy. There is a draft of his 1913 book on *The Reconstruction of the New Colonies under Lord Milner 1902–1905*, together with notes and extracts made by Worsfold from Milner's diaries and correspondence with Chamberlain and others.

There are also articles by Worsfold on Imperial questions, which appeared in the *Nineteenth Century* and a file of papers is concerned with the memoir of Milner prepared by Worsfold at the request of *The Times*, and printed after Milner's death in May 1925. Other files contain drafts and other papers connected with a biography of Milner originally intended to form one of a series of biographical sketches entitled 'Empire Builders', edited by Worsfold. It was unfinished at the time of Milner's death, and his widow did not feel able to give permission for Worsfold to complete it in an extended form.

A further file of papers was listed by Worsfold under the heading 'Obituary Packet'; it includes his memoir of Milner, printed in *The Times* of 14 May 1925. There are also articles and papers which Worsfold wrote about the Doullens Conference held on 26 Mar 1918, in which Milner took part and at which was established the single command of the Western Front under Foch. These papers include pencil sketches made by Worsfold in 1925 at Doullens and Beauvais. Twenty bound volumes of photographs, line drawings and watercolour sketches made by him in various parts of the world have been deposited in the Bodleian Library, Oxford. The Milner papers are also in the Bodleian Library and should be referred to.

balance sheets, printing estimates, etc., 1891–5. These records and other material relating to the Clarion Movement, in Manchester and in other libraries are described in *Sources*, Vol. 1, pp. 42–3. Correspondence (1916–17) regarding a review in *The Clarion* can be found in the Sladen papers (NRA List 14252). Two letters from Blatchford giving his views on the working class can be found in the Labour Party archive at Transport House. The Edward Carpenter Collection in Sheffield City Library contains several letters written in the early 1890s. Letters to J. Burns can be found in the British Library (Add. MS 46287). A variety of other Blatchford papers at present remain with the family.

BLUMENFELD, Ralph David (1864–1948)

Journalist. Worked in USA; editor of the New York *Evening Telegraph* until 1894. News editor, *Daily Mail*, 1900–02. Editor, *Daily Express*, 1902–32. President, Institute of Journalists, 1928. Propagandist of Tariff Reform. A founder of the Anti-Socialist Union.

Blumenfeld's papers were given to the Beaverbrook Library by his family, and are now deposited in the House of Lords Record Office. The collection includes some 1600 letters received by Blumenfeld, 1889–1948, though the bulk of these are dated after 1900. Most of the correspondence derives from his work on the *Daily Express*, and can be divided into three main categories. The first, personal correspondence, forms the largest part of the papers, and are miscellaneous in nature. They include letters of congratulations on the publication of his books; letters concerning subscriptions to charities; letters of praise for the *Daily Express*; invitations to functions; acknowledgements from various M.P.s for the paper's electoral support; acknowledgements for reviews; requests for publicity, etc. Correspondents include friends such as Arnold Bennett, T. P. O'Connor, H. A. Gwynne, H. G. Wells, Viscounts Rothermere and Northcliffe. A group of letters from Lady Warwick, 1907–38, relate to her journalism and her political differences with Blumenfeld. Other letters reflect Blumenfeld's involvement with organisations such as the Institute of Journalists.

The second category of papers consists of letters relating to politics, particularly Conservative politics, the campaign for Tariff Reform, and the Anti-Socialist Union. Correspondents include a wide range of leading political figures, including Lord Carson, Lord St Audries, Viscount Long, Lord Croft, the Earl of Birkenhead, Lord Willoughby de Broke, and John Sandars. A number of letters relate to Irish affairs, 1910–22, and particularly to the 1914 Home Rule crisis.

The third category of letters relates to World War I, and to naval and military affairs generally. A number of letters, 1907–15, from Lord Beresford, Admiral Fisher and the Navy League criticise naval policies. Some 50 letters are from the 17th Earl of Derby and relate to wartime recruitment and post-war French policy. There are also ten letters from Sir Samuel Hoare concerning the state of the Royal Air Force, 1924–8.

The Imperial War Museum have several relevant items, including a copy of a press bureau instruction, dated 1 September 1914, annotated by Blumenfeld, and a letter from Lloyd George as Minister of Munitions relating to the labour unrest and the voluntary system, 1915.

Further correspondence can be found in the Elibank papers (NRA 11852). Reference should also be made to the Beaverbrook papers, deposited at the House of Lords Record Office.

BLUNT, Wilfrid Scawen (1840–1922)

Poet, writer, traveller. Travelled in Arabia, Syria, Mesopotamia, Egypt, and India, 1877–84. Stood for Parliament as a Tory Home Ruler, 1885; later stood as a Liberal. Writer on political and imperial matters.

The Fitzwilliam Museum, Cambridge, has a large collection of papers and correspondence, including most of his autograph diaries, a large group of letters to him, and miscellaneous manuscripts, notes and memoranda. In addition, the Lytton family have deposited some 6500 letters to Scawen Blunt together with a smaller batch of other family letters. These papers are closed while being used by Elizabeth Lady Longford for an official biography. The Wentworth Bequest at the British Library (Add. MSS 53817–54155) contains material relating to Blunt and Lady Anne Blunt. The material includes diaries, sketch books, notebooks, and papers of Lady Anne Blunt, 1847–1917; diaries, notes, sketches and papers of W. S. Blunt, including an autobiography of his youth, diaries for 1873, 1878–9, a notebook, 1880, and a collection of material regarding his public career, mostly printed papers and press cuttings. There is a collection of correspondence, chiefly family letters; correspondents include Baron Wentworth, and Mary, Countess of Lovelace. Various papers relate to horse racing, and there is also a selection from Lady Wentworth's personal papers.

The Lytton family papers (to be consulted at West Sussex Record Office) contain some early family material. Correspondence regarding Egyptian affairs, 1883–97, can be found in the Cromer papers at the Public Record Office. Letters to William Morris, concerning literary matters, are in the Victoria and Albert Museum, while letters to R. B. Cunninghame Graham can be found in the Baker Library, Dartmouth College, Conn, USA. Blunt published *My Diaries* in two parts in 1919 and 1920. *The Cousins: The Friendship, opinions and activities of Wilfrid Scawen Blunt and George Wyndham* by Max Egremont (1977) uses manuscript sources.

BODLEY, John Edward Courtenay (1853–1925)

Civil servant and historian. Private secretary to the President of the Local Government Board, 1882–5. Secretary to the Royal Commission on Housing of the Working Classes, 1884–5; author of its three Reports on England, Scotland, and Ireland. Corresponding Member of the French Institute, 1902. Author of works on French history.

The Bodleian Library, Oxford, has various papers and miscellaneous material. Journals date from 1874, and there is a commonplace book, 1921–4, together with newspaper clippings and notes on the Church in France. Correspondence includes two volumes of letters to Bodley, 1877–1925, plus miscellaneous other correspondence: letters relating to the Royal Commission, eight letters to Sir Charles Dilke, 1884–5, and four letters from him, 1906–8; letters from correspondents in South Africa, 1887–8, and from correspondents in Canada and America, 1888–90; letters about articles by him, 1889–92; and letters concerning his book on *The Coronation of Edward VII* (1903). There are also letters from Bodley to his mother and other members of his family, and letters and telegrams on his election to the French Institute.

His journal and a memoir by his wife are in the Library of Balliol College, Oxford.

BONAR, James (1852–1941)

Economist and Civil Servant. Senior Examiner, Civil Service Commission, from 1895. Deputy Master, Canadian Branch of the Royal Mint, 1907–19. President of Section F, British Association, 1898. Vice-President, Royal Statistical Society, 1920, and of the Royal Economic Society, 1930. Fellow of the British Academy, 1930.

Sturges, *Economists' Papers*, pp. 12–13, mentions papers relating to Adam Smith collected by Bonar and four volumes of notes taken from Edward Caird's lectures on moral philosophy, 1870–1, in Glasgow University Library; an unpublished manuscript of a Life of Malthus, in the Library of the University of Illinois; and a manuscript account of the origins of the Royal Statistical Society, in BLPES. Relevant material in other collections is also listed.

BOOTH, Charles (1840–1916)

Shipowner and social researcher. Chairman of Alfred Booth & Co. Ltd, Liverpool. Director of Booth Steam Shipping Co. President of the Royal Statistical Society, 1892–4. Member of Tariff Commission, 1904. Author of *Life and Labour of the People in London*.

A collection of correspondence and papers has been deposited in the University of London

Library (MS 797). There are about 1000 letters from Charles Booth, nearly all to his wife, Mary. Many of these were written from abroad, and describe in detail his travels in North and South America and Europe. Letters addressed to Booth are also numerous, and include correspondence from business colleagues, from collaborators on *Life and Labour*, and from other colleagues in his public activities. Correspondents include Joseph Chamberlain, Octavia Hill, Sir Charles Loch, Alfred Marshall, A. C. Humphreys-Owen, Lancelot Phelps, B. S. Rowntree, J. A. Spender, Beatrice Webb and H. G. Wells. The letters of Mary Booth (some 1400 in number, mostly addressed to Charles) are more domestic in character, but public affairs are discussed, and advice given about Booth's various activities. The collection also includes letters from three of the Booths' children. The Booth correspondence has been used in Mary Catherine Booth, *Charles Booth: A Memoir* (1918), and T. S. Simey and Margaret Simey, *Charles Booth: Social Scientist* (1960). The collection at the University of London also includes deeds; essays (on 'Religious Questions', 'Political Economy', 'Bimetallism', 'Irish Land Question', etc.); papers connected with *Life and Labour* and *Memoir* (proof corrections, tables, notes, reviews, press cuttings, etc.); some pamphlets; obituary notices; travel diaries (dating from 1862) and sketches; and some newspaper cuttings.

Alfred Booth and Co. Ltd holds some 75 volumes of partnership letters written from England to America, and from America to England (1863–1935). There is a further collection at the University of Liverpool Library. This consists of 14 boxes, containing the draft for the printer of *Life and Labour*, with certain other items. BLPES holds the original material (392 notebooks, loose papers, etc.) used in the compilation of *Life and Labour* and other works. Further relevant material can be found in the Passfield papers at BLPES and correspondence with Herbert Samuel, 1888–95, can be found at the House of Lords Record Office.

BOOTH, Eva Gore- (1870–1926)

Writer and Irish politician.

Papers, 1868–1928, are in Pennsylvania State University (University Park). They include letters, exercise books, paintings, sketches, poems and other literary drafts, press cuttings, photographs and magazines.

BOOTH, William (1829–1912)

Founder of the Salvation Army, 1878; General and Commander-in-Chief.

See below.

BOOTH, William Bramwell (1856–1929)

Salvation Army Leader. Chief of Staff, Salvation Army, 1880–1912; General, 1912–1929. Vice-President, British and Foreign Bible Society.

It is believed that personal correspondence survives with Commissioner Catherine Bramwell-Booth, North Court, Finchampstead, Herts. Surviving records of the Salvation Army are described in *Sources* Vol. 1, pp. 231–2. These records contain much relevant material, though a great deal was destroyed by enemy action in World War II. The papers are at present being sorted.

BOOT, Sir Jesse, 1st Bt, see TRENT, 1st B

BOSANQUET, Bernard (1848–1923)

Philosopher. Lecturer, University College, Oxford, 1871–81. University Extension Lecturer and worker for Charity Organisation Society, 1881–97. Professor of Moral Philosophy,

University of St Andrews, 1903–8. Author of *Essentials of Logic, The Philosophical Theory of the State*, etc.

The Bosanquet papers are preserved in the Library of the University of Newcastle upon Tyne. They include material relating to both Bernard Bosanquet and to his wife, Helen (see below). The papers concerning Bernard Bosanquet's work consist of correspondence, manuscripts, notebooks, offprints and miscellaneous material. A box marked 'Letters returned by Professor Muirhead, July 1934' contains letters used by Muirhead for his book *Bernard Bosanquet and his friends* (1935). This contains personal correspondence, some family material, some letters regarding the International Congress of Philosophy, 1915, letters of condolence after his death, and a notebook 'Bernard Bosanquet – Dates roughly gathered for Memoir . . .' by Helen Bosanquet. In addition to material in this box there are several packets of correspondence, including 47 letters from Bosanquet to F. H. Peters; a small group of 'Italian Letters' from L. Vivante, Armando Carlini and C. Pellizzi, and the memorandum *Parodi on Freedom*; Bosanquet's letters to Plater, and Plater's to Helen Bosanquet about him, 1920s; and correspondence between Bosanquet and F. H. Bradley. The collection also includes Helen Bosanquet's notes for her book on Bernard; two notebooks containing undergraduate notes on essays, 1869; several manuscripts by Bosanquet; a collection of offprints of various articles by Bosanquet; and a notebook containing a translation in Bosanquet's hand of parts of Lotze's *Geschichte der Aesthetik in Deutschland* (1868). There are also various personal items, but there appears to be no correspondence between Bernard and Helen Bosanquet. Bosanquet's letters to Norman Kemp Smith are available in Edinburgh University Library.

BOSANQUET, Helen (1860–1925)

Social reformer. District Secretary to the Charity Organisation Society. A University Extension Lecturer. Member of Royal Commission on Poor Laws from 1905. Writer on social subjects (poverty, the Poor Law, the family, etc.)

Much relevant material can be found in the Bosanquet papers at the University of Newcastle upon Tyne (see above). There is a quantity of correspondence, including letters from Helen to her mother; letters from various friends and members of the family; letters on social reform matters, 1908–24; and business correspondence with publishers, 1920s. A literary notebook, notes covering holidays in Greece, Italy and England, engagement diaries, 1920–4, personalia, offprints, and pamphlets also survive. A considerable amount of material relates to the Poor Law Commission. This includes letters from Lord George Hamilton, 1907–9; and letters from John Jeffrey, Secretary of the Commission, R. G. Duff, Assistant Secretary, and other interested parties, 1907–9.

BOSANQUET, Theodora (1880–1961)

Literary editor. Secretary to Henry James, 1907–16. Assistant, 'Who's Who' Section, War Trade Intelligence Department, 1917–18. Assistant to Secretary, Ministry of Food, 1918–20. Executive Secretary, International Federation of University Women, 1920–35. Literary Editor, *Time and Tide*, 1935–43; Director, 1943–58.

A largely literary collection of c. 425 items has been purchased by the Houghton Library, Harvard University. It consists of correspondence, diaries, typescripts of writings by Henry James, writings by Theodora Bosanquet, material relating to James, press cuttings, photographs, etc. Correspondents include Julia De Beausobre, Leon Edel, T. S. Eliot, Rupert Hart-Davis, Henry James, Dan H. Laurence, Nancy Lord, Anne Isabella Ritchie, Edith Sitwell, Howard Sturgess, Renee Haynes, Edith Wharton, Charles Williams and Virginia Woolf.

BOURCHIER, James David (d. 1920)

Journalist. Special correspondent of *The Times* in Romania and Bulgaria, 1888; thereafter correspondent of *The Times* in S.E.Europe. In 1911–12 he played an important role in the foundation of the Balkan League.

A small collection of relevant material can be found in the archives of *The Times*. This includes correspondence from Bourchier to colleagues on *The Times*, dating from the 1880s. The correspondence is addressed to Moberly Bell, Steed, Dawson, among others, and relates to articles, responses to enquiries, telegrams, etc. There are also some letters from Chirol and Dawson, and letters from Bourchier in Russia, 1917–18, and some papers relating to Bourchier after his death.

BOURNE, Cardinal Francis Alphonsus (1861–1935)

Roman Catholic ecclesiastic. Bishop of Southwark from 1897. Archbishop of Westminster from 1903. Cardinal from 1911.

Bourne papers are deposited in the Westminster Diocesan Archives. They include his Pastorals, 1903–34; Instructions to the Clergy, 1904–20s; various circulars, pamphlets, writings and letters; and an Address of the Hierarchy of England and Wales to Cardinal Bourne on the fiftieth anniversary of his ordination.

Further papers, especially concerning his family and early life, are in the Ushaw College Library. There are c. 100 items, including letters from his father, and letters from Francis Bourne to his family, including his mother and aunt.

Correspondence can also be found in the Asquith papers.

BOUTWOOD, Arthur
Hakluyt Egerton* (1864–1924)

Conservative writer on politics and theology. Civil Servant.

A collection of papers is housed in the Library of Corpus Christi, Cambridge. This includes correspondence, 1900–24, particularly with Lords Selborne and Willoughby de Broke, but also with a wide variety of writers, including Asquith (14 letters), Leo Maxse (three) and Lord Salisbury (nine). There are a number of articles, on the efficiency and reform of the Civil Service, on politics, religion, particularly Roman Catholicism, theology, patriotism, British supremacy, National Renewal, the Empire, together with notes and cuttings on theology and politics. Other material includes love poems; political pamphlets; 'The Politicians' Vade Mecum', being classified quotations from his notebooks; a memorandum to the Royal Commission on the Civil Service, 1914; a memo to Lord Selborne, 1913; and copies of *Ignotus*, (which refers to his life) and 'Love Letters'. Copies of these last two items are available at the London Library.

* Pseudonym.

BOWLEY, Sir Arthur Lyon (1869–1957)

Economist. Lecturer at the London School of Economics from 1895. Professor of Mathematics and Economics, Reading, 1907–13. Professor of Statistics, London University, 1919–36. Acting Director of Oxford University Institute of Statistics, 1940–4.

The Royal Statistical Society has a copy of an unpublished lecture on Socialism, c. 1896, with related correspondence between Bowley and R. F. George, 1953; some 15 letters from various correspondents, 1895–1935; and some newspaper cuttings. Sturges, *Economists' Papers*, pp. 13 and 14, mentions this and letters in the Beveridge, Cannan, Keynes, D'Arcy Wentworth, Thompson and Wallas Collections.

BOWRA, Sir (Cecil) Maurice (1898–1971)

Classical · scholar, academic and poet. Warden of Wadham College, Oxford, 1938–70. Professor of Poetry, Oxford University, 1946–51. Vice Chancellor, Oxford University, 1951–4. President, British Academy, 1958–62.

The bulk of the papers which survive in Wadham College are personal and are not available for study.

BRADLEY, Francis Herbert (1846–1924)

Philosopher.

A collection of papers and some three hundred letters, chiefly from Bradley, in copy or draft to and from 55 different correspondents, are in the Library of Merton College, Oxford. Many letters are undated. Copies of the eleven letters to Bertrand Russell are also kept at the Bertrand Russell Archive at McMaster University, Canada. The collection was used extensively for *Etudes Philosophiques* (1960), ed. P. C. Fruchon.

BRAHAM, Dudley Disraeli (1875–1951)

On staff of *The Times* from 1897. Correspondent in Berlin, St Petersburg, Constantinople. Head of the Imperial and Foreign Department of *The Times* from 1912. Editor, *Daily Telegraph* of Sydney, NSW, 1914–22. Founder, and editor, the *Forum* (Australia), 1922. Editor, *West Australian*, 1924–30. Rejoined staff of *The Times* in London in 1930. Served as leader-writer until 1945.

The archives of *The Times* have various items concerning Braham's work for the newspaper.

BRAILSFORD, Henry Noel (1873–1958)

Journalist and historian. Leader-writer successively with the *Manchester Guardian*, *Daily News* and *Nation*. Hon. Secretary to Conciliation Committee for Women's Suffrage, 1910–12. Editor, the *New Leader*, 1922–6. Author of works on socialism, international affairs, literature.

There is no private collection of Brailsford papers, but a considerable number of letters survive. The most important of these can be found in the Gilbert Murray papers, the J. L. Hammond papers, and the Lord Bryce papers at the Bodleian Library; in the R. C. K. Ensor papers at Corpus Christi, Oxford; in the Kingsley Martin papers at the University of Sussex; in the Manchester Guardian archive (letters to C. P. Scott) at the John Rylands University Library of Manchester; in the Millicent Garrett Fawcett collection at the Manchester Central Library; in the Leonard Courtney papers and the George Lansbury papers at the BLPES; in the Clifford Allen (Lord Allen of Hurtwood) papers at the University of South Carolina Library; in the Bertrand Russell papers at McMaster University; in the Catherine Marshall papers at the Cumbria Record Office; in the Viscount Gladstone papers at the British Library; and in the J. Ramsay MacDonald papers at the Public Record Office. There is further material relating to Brailsford's editorship of the *New Leader* in the I.L.P. collection which is to be deposited in the BLPES. There are scattered letters in the Labour Party archive. The manuscript of *The Levellers* is in the International Institute of Social History, Amsterdam.

Professor F. M. Leventhal of Boston University is preparing a biography.

BRAITHWAITE, Catherine Lydia (1864–1957)

Quaker social worker. A founder of the Germany Emergency Relief Committee during World War I.

Papers are available in the Library of Friends' House, London.

BRIFFAULT, Robert Stephen (1876–1948)

Social anthropologist and novelist. Author of works such as *The Mothers* (1927), *The Decline and Fall of the British Empire* (1938).

The British Library has a collection of letters (Add. MSS 58440–3) presented by Briffault's younger daughter. The first volume is devoted to Briffault's letters to his mother, 1886–1902, and to his daughters, 1915–March 1917. These latter letters are the most complete series in the collection. They were written by Briffault during his military service on the Western Front, and provide a vivid picture of the situation there. There is, for instance, a powerful letter written during the Battle of Passchendaele. The second volume consists of letters from Briffault to his daughters, 1917–48, while the third volume consists of letters to him, and personal papers, 1874–1952, together with family papers, 1799–1906. Among the latter are two letters to Briffault's father from Louis Napoleon, 1846 and 1847. The final volume (Add. MS 58443) consists of family photographs.

BRITTAIN, Vera (d. 1970)

Feminist and pacifist; writer and lecturer. Author of some twenty-nine books, 1933–68. President, Society of Women Writers and Journalists; Married Women's Association. Vice-President, Women's International League for Peace and Freedom; National Peace Council.

Large collections of the papers of Vera Brittain and her husband, Sir George Catlin, are preserved in the Library of McMaster University, Hamilton, Ontario. The Brittain collection contains the original manuscripts and typescripts of nearly all Vera Brittain's published writings, with in addition a large collection of unpublished fiction and other material. There are substantial files of background and source material, plus some 100 scrapbooks and files of press cuttings. The personal correspondence files include a very large collection of letters between herself and George Catlin over a period of nearly 50 years. In all there are some 25,000 letters from other writers, politicians, publishers, readers and friends. The majority have carbon copies of her replies. Correspondents include L. S. Amery, Harold Macmillan, Alex Comfort, Nevill Coghill, Hugh Gaitskell, Julian Huxley, C. E. M. Joad, Kingsley Martin, Vanessa Redgrave, Bertrand Russell, Eleanor Roosevelt, Beatrice Webb, Virginia Woolf and Ellen Wilkinson. Additionally, there are letters to her daughter, Mrs Shirley Williams, M.P., with about 450 press cuttings about her career. Vera Brittain's collection of her own and Winifred Holtby's books is also housed in McMaster University.

Vera Brittain's interest in Anglo-Indian relations is reflected in a further deposit at the Bodleian Library, Oxford. This consists of miscellaneous notebooks, 1949–50, which are chiefly concerned with Vera Brittain's participation in the World Pacifist Conference in India.

A book, *Selected Letters of Winifred Holtby and Vera Brittain*, was published in a limited edition in 1960.

BROCK, Arthur Clutton (1868–1924)

Journalist. Art critic of *The Times*. Literary editor of the *Speaker*, 1904–6. On staff of *The Times* from 1908.

The archives of *The Times* have a folder of miscellaneous items.

BRODETSKY, Selig (1889–1954)

Academic and Zionist leader. Professor of Applied Mathematics, Leeds University, 1924–48. President, Hebrew University of Jerusalem, 1949–51. Member of the Executive, World Zionist Organization and the Jewish Agency for Palestine. Hon. President, Zionist Federation of Great Britain. President, Board of Deputies of British Jews, 1940–9.

The Anglo-Jewish Archives collection in the Mocatta Library, University College London, includes many relevant papers (ref. AJ/3). These include papers concerning Brodetsky's early scholastic achievements, 1900–8; academic matters 1910–29; and his involvement with the Board of Deputies and Zionism, 1939–53. There is also a collection of press cuttings (ref AJ/106) covering his career from 1916. The records of the Board of Deputies (*Sources* Vol. 1, pp 20–1) include a series of President's and Secretaries' papers. Material concerning Brodetsky (ref. B5/2) covers his period as President, 1940–9. The collection is divided into 13 sub-sections, e.g. Board affairs; refugees; defence matters; Palestine. Correspondents include A .G. Brotman (Secretary, 1934–66), E. Benes, Sir Anthony Eden, N. J. Laski and S. Salamon. Other material relating to his work is scattered through the Board's files.
    The Central Zionist Archives, Jerusalem have other papers (ref. A82), concerning the Constitutional Council and the legal status of the Hebrew University, 1930–43.
    There is some correspondence in the James Parkes collection, Parkes Library, University of Southampton.

BRODRIBB, Charles William (1878–1945)

Journalist and poet. Assistant editor of *The Times*.

The archives of *The Times* contain certain relevant items.

BROOKE, Stopford Augustus (1832–1915)

Writer and preacher.

A few letters, chiefly of a formal nature, 1906–15, are in Reading University Library. Reference should be made to L. P. Jacks, *The Life and Letters of Stopford Brooke* (2 vols, 1917).

BROOKS, Sydney (1872–1937)

Journalist. Editor, *Saturday Review*, 1921; *Sperling's Journal*, 1917–22. Writer on current politics, particularly Irish matters.

Some 27 letters relating to Irish and personal matters can be found in the Sir Horace Plunkett papers.

BROWN, Alfred Barratt (1887–1947)

Educationalist. Principal of Ruskin College, Oxford, 1926–44. Regional Welfare Officer, Ministry of Labour, 1940–1.

Papers remain with the family. Enquiries should be directed to Mr Michael Barratt Brown, c/o the Department of Extramural Studies, University of Sheffield.

BROWN, Sir Frank Herbert (1868–1959)

Journalist. Leader writer and assistant editor, *Bombay Gazette*; edited *Indian Daily Telegraph*, Lucknow. London correspondent of *The Times of India*. On editorial staff of *The Times* from 1902. Hon. Secretary, East India Association, 1927–54. Author of works on India and the British Empire and Commonwealth.

Papers of Sir F. H. Brown are located in the India Office Library. The collection includes correspondence, notes and accounts. The chief correspondent is Sir Gilbert Laithwaite, and relates to the administration of Lord Linlithgow. There are also letters from leading Indian statesmen, papers on Indian reforms etc.

Some papers can also be found in the archives of *The Times*.

BROWN, Herbert Runham (1879–1949)

Pacifist. Secretary and Chairman of War Resisters International.

Miss Joyce Runham Brown (daughter) has no personal papers, apart from obituary letters and photographs. A short biography of Runham Brown appears in the *Dictionary of Labour Biography* Vol II. Records of War Resisters International are described in *Sources* Vol. 1, p. 276.

BROWN, Ivor John Carnegie (1891–1975)

Author and journalist. London dramatic critic and leader-writer for the *Manchester Guardian*, 1919–35. Dramatic critic, *Saturday Review*, 1923–30; *The Observer*, 1929–54. Director of Drama, Council for Encouragement of Music and the Arts, 1940–2. Editor, *The Observer*, 1942–8.

Surviving papers would be with the family. The contents of his letters were used in his autobiographical works, *The Way of My World* (1954) and *Old and Young* (1971).

BROWNING, Oscar (1837–1923)

Historian, author and teacher. Master at Eton College, 1860–75. Fellow of King's College, Cambridge from 1859. University lecturer in History, and Principal of Cambridge University Day Training College, 1891–1909. Liberal Parliamentary candidate.

A large collection of some 40–50,000 letters, deposited with Hastings Public Library, has now been catalogued by the Historical Manuscripts Commission. The material, which has been arranged by name of the individual correspondent, reveals the wide range of Browning's interests. Browning's concern for boys and young men is indicated by a large number of letters from boys at Eton, Cambridge undergraduates and working-class youths. There is wide evidence of his concern with adult education and the teaching of history. There are letters from teachers, and a considerable group of letters from Lord Acton. Browning's own writing activities are reflected in letters from book and periodical publishers. There is also a considerable corpus of correspondence about India, perhaps reflecting Browning's friendship with the young G .N . Curzon. Browning's general involvement with Liberal politics is widely observable also.

Letters from Browning to various correspondents can be found in collections at King's College, Cambridge, and correspondence with Herbert Samuel is available at the House of Lords Record Office.

BUCHAN, (Hon) Alastair Francis (1918–76)

Journalist and author. Assistant editor of *The Economist*, 1948–51. Washington correspondent, *The Observer*, 1951–5; Diplomatic and Defence correspondent, 1955–8. Director, Institute for Strategic Studies, 1958–69. Commandant, Royal College of Defence Studies, 1970–1. Professor of International Relations, Oxford University, from 1972.

Mrs Hope Buchan (widow), The Old Swan, Brill, Aylesbury, Bucks, retains certain papers, at present unsorted. They include correspondence to and from Buchan; drafts of his various writings, including notes and early chapters of his uncompleted work on American foreign policy.

BUCKLE, George Earle (1854–1935)

Journalist. Editor of *The Times*, 1884–1912. Fellow of All Souls, 1877–85. Author (with W. F. Monypenny) of *The Life of Disraeli*.

According to information supplied by the archivist of *The Times*, Buckle made a habit of destroying his correspondence. Little survives in the archives of *The Times* apart from one box of miscellaneous material. This, however, includes letters to Bell, Walter and Dawson. The Bodleian Library has letters to J. E. C. Bodley, Sir Sidney Lee, 2nd Earl of Selborne, Asquith, Balfour and Sandars. Reference should also be made to the Gladstone papers at the British Library. Correspondence with Lord Randolph Churchill can be found in the Churchill papers (NRA 13273) and social correspondence, 1897–1900, can be found in the Douglas Sladen papers (NRA 14252).

BUNTING, Sir Percy (1840–1911)

Journalist and social reformer. Editor of *Contemporary Review* from 1882; and of *Methodist Times*, 1902–7.

Correspondence, 1882–1911 (2310 items) is housed in the University of Chicago Library. The collection largely consists of letters to Bunting as editor of the *Contemporary Review*. Most of them are simply statements declining, for various reasons, an invitation to write for the *Review*. The letters from each correspondent vary in number, from one by several minor figures to as many as 39 from Herbert Spencer. Many of the letters are, however, from prominent writers and politicians, such as Lord Acton, Matthew Arnold, J. M. Barrie, Rupert Brooke, Robert Browning, Andrew Carnegie, G. K. Chesterton, Winston Churchill, Clemenceau, Wilkie Collins, Austin Dobson, James A. Froude, Gladstone, Benjamin Harrison, Bret Harte, Henry James, James Russell Lowell, Sir John Lubbock (Lord Avebury), Maeterlinck, Cardinal Manning, George Meredith, Cardinal Newman, Florence Nightingale, Walter Pater, Theodore Roosevelt, George Bernard Shaw, Herbert Spencer, Robert Louis Stevenson, John. A. Symonds, and many others whom for one reason or another Sir Percy considered worthy of appearing in the *Contemporary Review*. The letters cover the entire span of Sir Percy's editorial years on the *Review*, from 1882 to 1911.

BURDETT, Sir Henry (1847–1920)

Author, medical statistician and philanthropist. Founder and editor of *The Hospital*. Author of works on medicine, nursing, housing, etc.

Papers are deposited in the Bodleian Library, Oxford.

BURDETT-COUTTS, 1st Baroness
Angela Georgina Burdett-Coutts (1814–1906)

Philanthropist. Partner in Coutts & Co., bankers.

A collection of material made by C. C. Osborne for his biography of Baroness Burdett-Coutts is at the British Library (Add. MSS 46402–08), as is correspondence with Sir James and Sir Charles Brooke, of Sarawak (Add. MSS 45274–82, 83). Extensive correspondence and papers, largely relating to the Church and education, can be found at Lambeth Palace Library, while business correspondence can be found in the Harrowby papers (NRA 1561). Further papers can be found in the Westminster City Library, Archives Department, Victoria.

  A biography by Edna Healey appeared in 1978.

BURLEIGH, Bennet (d. 1914)

Journalist. On staff of *Daily Telegraph* from 1882; war correspondent.

No private papers have been discovered but there is miscellaneous correspondence in the Wolseley papers in Hove Central Library.

BURNAND, Sir Francis Cowley (1836–1917)

Journalist and author. Editor of *Punch*, 1862–1906

Miscellaneous letters of Burnand and his family, 1885–1950s are in the British Theatre Museum collection at the Victoria and Albert Museum. The British Library has his correspondence with F. Anstey. Over 30 letters, 1880–5, mainly on journalistic matters, are in the Escott papers, while there are a few letters, 1881–90, in the Wolseley papers in Hove Central Library.

BURNS, Cecil Delisle (1879–1942)

Ethical reformer, social philosopher and academic. British editor of *Ethics: an International Journal of Social Philosophy*. University Extension lecturer, 1908–15. Worked at Ministry of Reconstruction, 1917–19. Assistant Secretary, International Organising Committee, Labour Office, League of Nations, 1919; at Intelligence Division, Ministry of Labour, 1919–20. Assistant Secretary, Joint Research Department of TUC and Labour Party, 1921–4. Lecturer in Social Philosophy, London School of Economics, 1925–7. Stevenson Lecturer in Citizenship, Glasgow University, 1927–36.

Some correspondence can be found in the Angell Collection at Ball State University. No papers survive in BLPES or in Glasgow University Library.

BURROWS, Christine Mary Elizabeth (1872–1959)

Principal of St Hilda's Hall (later College), Oxford, 1910–19. Principal of the Oxford Society of Home-Students, 1921–9.

Papers are housed at St Hilda's College, Oxford. They are at present unsorted and enquiries should be directed to the College Librarian.

BURROWS, Herbert

Socialist pioneer. Foundation member, Social Democratic Federation.

BLPES has relevant papers, including Burrows' reports on the South Staffs. miners' strike, manuscripts of contributions to *Justice* and a few letters to the SDF, 1884–9.

BURROWS, Winfrid Oldfield (1858–1929)

Churchman and theologian. Bishop of Truro, 1912–19; of Chichester, 1919–29.

His revisions of the Prayer Book, 1925–7, can be found at Lambeth Palace Library.

BURT, Sir Cyril Lodowic (1883–1971)

Psychologist. Advocate of intelligence testing. Psychologist to the London County Council (Education Department), 1913–32. Professor of Education, London University, 1924–31. Professor of Psychology, University College London, 1931–50. Editor, *British Journal of Statistical Psychology*.

Sir Cyril Burt's papers are largely in the care of Emeritus Professor L. S. Hearnshaw at present, while he is preparing a study of Burt's life and work. When this has been completed the papers will be placed in the University of Liverpool Archives.

BURTON, Sir Montague (1885–1952)

Businessman and leading Zionist. Chairman, Montague Burton Ltd. Provincial Vice President, Zionist Federation.

The Burton Group has deposited its records with Leeds City Libraries, Archives Department. The business records are currently available, but special permission is necessary for access to the personal papers containing material concerning Sir Montague. *Globe Girdling* (Vol. 1, 1936; Vol. 2, 1938) are published versions of his travel diary.

BUTLER, Josephine Elizabeth (1828–1906)

Social reformer and moral campaigner. Involved in movements for the higher education of women, for rights for married women, and against the Contagious Diseases Acts. Secretary, Ladies' National Association for the Repeal of the Contagious Diseases Acts, 1869–85. Campaigned against White Slave traffic; advocate of social purity. Author of numerous tracts and pamphlets, and books.

There is no single collection of Josephine Butler papers, though a substantial amount of material is housed in three separate libraries. St Andrews University Library holds a collection of Josephine Butler correspondence. The letters are contained in an autograph album, and comprise 67 complete letters, 25 parts of letters, and ten items where only the autograph remains. Most of the letters are addressed to Josephine, but some are addressed to her husband, Canon George Butler, and to several other individuals. Most of the letters are concerned with the campaign against the state regulation of prostitution, both at home and abroad. Correspondents include a number of prominent public figures.

Liverpool University Library has a further collection of material. Part of this consists of letters used in the preparation of A. S. G. Butler's *Portrait of Josephine Butler* (1954). Amongst these are letters from Josephine Butler to her family and colleagues, 1853–1906. Some 149 letters are addressed to her son, Arthur Stanley and his wife, while another 157 are addressed to Fanny Forsaith, a colleague in the campaign against the Contagious Diseases Acts. A further recent accession to the Liverpool University Library from the Josephine Butler Memorial House in Liverpool consists of 214 items, including letters to and from Josephine Butler (on family and public matters), pamphlets and. cuttings.

Letters and documents owned by the Josephine Butler Society (formerly the Association for Moral and Social Hygiene, the successor of the organisations fighting the Contagious Diseases Acts) have been deposited with the Fawcett Library collection. These papers include a substantial collection of Josephine Butler letters relating both to her campaigns and to personal matters. They were used in connection with a biography of Josephine Butler by Enid Moberly Bell. The formal records of the Association for Moral and Social Hygiene and its predecessors are also relevant and are described in *Sources* Vol. 1, pp. 125–6.

Other letters (28 in number) from Josephine Butler to Hannah and Emily Ford and others on prostitution, 1860–85, can be found in the Brotherton Library, University of Leeds. The papers of H. J. Wilson, particularly those in Sheffield Public Library, are also relevant (see *Sources* Vol. 4, p. 245).

BUTLER, Kathleen Teresa Blake (1883–1950)

Educationalist. Vice-Mistress, Girton College, Cambridge, 1936–8, 1941–2; Mistress, 1942–9.

Girton College, Cambridge, has various papers, being chiefly her collections relating to Italian letter-writers.

CADBURY, George (1839-1922)

Cocoa and chocolate manufacturer. Chairman of Cadbury Brothers Ltd. Founder of Bournville Model Village.

Birmingham Public Libraries has a collection of papers relating to George Cadbury and Dame Elizabeth M. Cadbury. These are at present not fully sorted but include sundry personal letters of George Cadbury, 1893–1922; Holiday Journals, 1893–1902, of George and Elizabeth Cadbury, and a Family Journal and letters, 1904–48; and papers relating to Elizabeth Cadbury, including a miscellaneous collection of addresses and speeches, letters, 1864–75, and personal diaries, 1888–1951.
Further material relating to Cadbury Brothers Ltd and to George Cadbury is in Birmingham University Library. There is correspondence to George and Dame Elizabeth Cadbury, chiefly of a social nature.
The Labour Party archive at Transport House, London, has letters and related papers, 1906.

CAM, Helen Maud (1885-1968)

Historian. Lecturer in History, Cambridge, from 1930. Zemurray Radcliffe Professor in History, Harvard University, 1948–54.

Churchill College, Cambridge, has 11 boxes of material, largely printed material for her study of US affairs, 1960–5. Other papers are in the Library of Girton College, Cambridge.

CAMMAERTS, Emile (1876-1953)

Academic. Professor of Belgian Studies, University of London, 1931–47.

London University Library has a collection of papers, including papers on both World Wars and reflecting his defence of King Leopold III from 1940 to the abdication crisis of 1950.

CAMPBELL, Dame Janet Mary (d. 1954)

Senior Medical Officer for Maternity and Child Welfare, Ministry of Health, and Chief Woman Medical Adviser, Board of Education, 1919–34. Later worked with National Birth Control Association.

Lloyds Bank Ltd Trust Division, who acted in the estate, had no relevant information. Attempts to contact a niece proved unsuccessful. Records of the Family Planning Association (the present name of the National Birth Control Association) are described in *Sources* Vol. I, pp 96–7.

CAMPBELL, John Ross (1894-1969)

Communist journalist. Editor, *Glasgow Worker*, 1921–4; *Worker's Weekly*, 1924–6. Member of the Executive Committee, Communist Party of Great Britain, 1923–64; Communist International, 1925–35. Editor, *Daily Worker*, 1949–59.

The Communist Party of Great Britain has his books and a very small number of office papers. He tended to destroy personal papers.

CANNAN, Edwin (1861-1935)

Economist. Lecturer, London School of Economics, 1897–1926. Professor of Political Economy, University of London, 1907–26. President, Royal Economic Society, 1932–5.

Cannan's library was presented to the BLPES after his death. Consisting largely of published works, it also included a number of manuscript and printed papers, and correspondence. The bulk of the miscellaneous papers (manuscript, printed and typed material) are bound in one chronological sequence from 1876 to 1935. A smaller sequence consists of agreements, accounts and letters with publishers, 1887–1936. The general correspondence is largely concerned with professional matters, Cannan's share being represented almost entirely by duplicates or drafts. The letters cover the period 1889–1938. Reference should also be made to relevant Cannan material in the Sir Theodore Gregory papers at BLPES. Sturges, *Economists' Papers*, p. 18, also mentions material which can be found in other collections.

CANNON, Sir Leslie (1920–70)

Trade union leader. General President of the Electrical Trades Union from 1963. Member of the TUC General Council from 1965; and of the Industrial Reorganisation Corporation from 1966.

A group of papers relating mainly to his campaign against the Communist leadership of the Electrical Trades Union has been placed in the Modern Records Centre, University of Warwick Library.

CAPPER, John Brainerd (1855–1936)

Journalist and man of letters. On staff of *The Times* from 1878. Principal Assistant Editor, 1884–1913.

Various relevant items can be found in the archives of *The Times*.

CARPENTER, Edward (1844–1929)

Socialist author and publicist. Promoter of women's rights and sex reform. Author of *Civilisation: its Cause and Cure, Towards Democracy, Love's Coming of Age, The Intermediate Sex*, etc. Hon. President, British Society for the Study of Sex Psychology.

There is a large collection of correspondence, papers, press cuttings, drafts, proofs, books and pamphlets with Sheffield City Libraries. *A Bibliography of Edward Carpenter* (Sheffield City Libraries 1949) describes the main part of the collection. A supplementary collection of letters and papers was presented to the Library by Gilbert Beith, one of Carpenter's executors, in 1958. The collection includes manuscripts and typescripts of Carpenter's works, published and unpublished, from 1866, and includes manuscripts of all his books. There are diaries (chiefly of engagements), 1915–20; letters from Carpenter to Alfred Mattison, 1889–95; letters and accounts from Carpenter's principal publishers in Britain and America, and correspondence with other foreign publishers and translators; notebooks dating from 1862, and including commonplace books, address books etc. There is a collection of financial accounts from 1878; royalty agreements, family deeds etc; his ordination papers, 1869, the marriage settlement of his sister, etc.; books and articles about Carpenter and extensive press cuttings relating to his books. The correspondence is wide-ranging, including letters from friends, 1880–1931. The later deposit includes family letters and papers dating from 1863, and including letters from Edward to his parents, letters to him from his parents and sisters and other members of his family and close friends and early formative influences. Amongst the varied correspondence are letters to Charles G. Oates, 1869–1901, and Oates' letters to Carpenter; letters from Kate Salt, 1888–1919; letters from Henry Salt, 1890–1921; Havelock Ellis's letters, 1893–1920; letters from Olive Schreiner, 1886–1914; letters to George E. Hukin, 1886–1909, and letters from Hukin, 1886–1913. There are letters from George Merrill, Carpenter's long-time companion, 1896–1912, together with the typescript of Carpenter's paper on Merrill. Other frequent correspondents include Max Flint, Harry Bishop, H. B. Cotterill, Joseph Hobson, E. B. Lloyd, Lily Nadler-Nuelleus, Countess Batthyani, James Brown, and correspondents in Australia, New Zealand, the British West Indies, Malaya, South Africa, France, Germany, the

Netherlands, Italy, India and Ceylon, Japan, Russia, etc. In addition there is general correspondence, 1868–1926, with occasional letters from a long list of people. Other material includes correspondence and press cuttings concerning Carpenter's centenary, 1944, including letters from E. M. Forster (and the typescript of his broadcast), Leonard Green and others, to Gilbert Beith. There is also a minute book of the Edward Carpenter International Memorial Trust, 1931–4, and the Memorial Fellowship, 1934–55.

John Rylands University Library of Manchester has Carpenter's 'autobiographical notes', which are a draft of his autobiography, *My Days and Dreams*. Other relevant material in this Library includes the papers of his friend, Charles Sixsmith, which contain letters from Carpenter. There are also relevant items in the Richard Hawkin collection.

The papers of Alfred Mattison contain further correspondence and papers. At the Brotherton Library, University of Leeds, there is Mattison's diary, with frequent reference to Carpenter, and letters from Carpenter, 1897–1922.

The C. R. Ashbee journals at King's College, Cambridge, contain letters, 1885–95.

Some 12 letters to Granville Bantock are in Birmingham University Library. A few letters, 1885–7, are in the Socialist League archive at the International Institute of Social History, Amsterdam.

The Havelock Ellis collection in the University of Texas, Austin, has further correspondence.

CARPENTER, William Boyd (1841–1918)

Churchman. Canon of Windsor, 1882–4. Bishop of Ripon, 1884–1911. Sub-Dean and Canon of Westminster from 1911.

The British Library has a collection of papers (Add. MSS 46717–65). This includes Royal correspondence, a group of general correspondence, diaries and notebooks. Many of the documents in the collection were used in Boyd Carpenter's *Some Pages of My Life* (1911) and *Further Pages of My Life* (1916) and by Henry Dewsbury Alves Major in *The Life and Letters of William Boyd Carpenter* (1925).

CARRON, ℾ•aron
Sir William John Carron (1902–70)

Trade union leader. President, Amalgamated Engineering Union, 1956–67. Chairman, British Productivity Council, 1959–68. A Director of the Bank of England from 1963.

Some 47 boxes of material are preserved in Churchill College, Cambridge. The material is at present uncatalogued, but consists largely of pocket diaries dating from the 1940s, some fairly late correspondence, plus printed material.

CARTWRIGHT, Albert (1868–1956)

Journalist. Editor, *Diamond Fields Advertiser*, 1896–8; *South African News*, 1899–1905. London editor, *Rand Daily Mail*, 1905–7. Responsible editor, *Transvaal Leader*, 1907–11. Editor, *West Africa*, 1916–47.

Correspondence with Lord Hardinge and a memorandum of his conversation with Baron d'Aehrenthal, 1908–10, can be found in the Hardinge papers, Cambridge University Library. No personal papers have been traced.

CARY, (Arthur) Joyce Lunel (1888–1957)

Novelist and writer on African affairs. Nigerian Political Service, 1913–20. Author of *The Case for African Freedom*, *The Process of Real Freedom* etc.

Papers are available in the Bodleian Library, Oxford. His political writings have been edited by Christopher Fyfe.

CASEMENT, Sir Roger David (1864–1916)*

Consular official and Irish patriot. Entered the British consular service in 1892. Member of the Irish National Volunteers, 1913. Visited Berlin as a propagandist for Irish nationalism, 1914. Executed for treason by the British Government, 1916.

The major archive of papers concerning Casement is in the National Library of Ireland. MSS 13,073–92 represents papers of Casement and some of his cousin, Gertrude Bannister. They comprise some 4000 documents, 1889–1916, including many letters to Casement from correspondents such as J. M. Plunkett, H. W. Nevinson, Hyde and Devoy. There are also letters by him to Miss Bannister; drafts of other letters by him; papers relating to his family and to his nationalist activities; material concerning his journeys to the USA and Germany, his investigations in the Congo and Putumayo; papers to do with his trial in 1916; and some literary papers. MS 8358 in the National Library consists of letters from Casement, 1905–16, chiefly to W. A. Cadbury, dealing with political and humanitarian subjects, with a few letters from Cadbury to Casement. There are also typed copies of a personal statement made by Cadbury after Casement's death, and of a petition to Herbert Samuel, Home Secretary, for a remission of the death sentence. Further groupings of relevant letters were given to the National Library of Ireland by President de Valera, and the Library also has Casement's Putumayo Journal, 1910–11, and his German Diaries, 1914–16. Material concerning Casement can be found in other collections in the National Library: e.g. 81 letters to Alice Stopford Green.

The Public Record Office in London has papers on his colonial investigations and material on his arrest, trial and execution and five volumes of his diaries, 1901–11, to which special conditions of access apply (ref. CO 904 and HO 161). The Public Record Office of Northern Ireland has notes compiled by J. R. Savage-Armstrong in 1956, relating to Casement, his arrest and his diaries (ref. D 760).

The Herbert Samuel papers in the House of Lords Record Office include copies of Cabinet papers and despatches from the British Ambassador in the USA concerning Casement's trial. Letters from Casement (some 283) can be found in the E. D. Morel papers at BLPES, while letters from him concerning the Putumayo Enquiry are in the records of the Anti-Slavery Society at Rhodes House Library, Oxford. Letters to William B. Cockran are in the New York Public Library.

* Casement's knighthood was withdrawn in 1916.

CASEY, William Francis (1884–1957)

Journalist. On staff of *The Times* from 1913. Deputy editor, 1941–8. Editor, 1948–52.

The archives of *The Times* have a few items only, contained in a folder. Amongst the material are a few items of editorial correspondence and remembrance of Casey.

CATLIN, Sir George Edward Gordon (1896–   )

Political scientist. Professor of Politics, Cornell University, 1924–35. Provost, Mar Ivanios College, South India, 1951. Bronman Professor of Political Science, McGill University, 1956–60. Special·foreign correspondent in Germany, Russia, Spain, Italy and India in 1930s. Co-founder with H. G. Wells and others of *The ·Realist*. One-time member of Executive Committee, Fabian Society. Labour Parliamentary candidate, 1931, 1935. Supporter of Atlantic Community policy. Joint founder, America and British Commonwealth Association.

A very large collection of papers concerning Sir George Catlin and his wife, Vera Brittain, is housed in the Library of McMaster University, Hamilton, Ontario. The collection includes a very extensive correspondence between the two, covering some 50 years, as well as Catlin's correspondence with literary, political and governmental figures in Britain and the United States. Also in the collection are lecture notes, the manuscripts of Catlin's books (over 20 in number) as well as material used in compiling his autobiography.

CEANNT,* Eamonn (1882–1916)

Irish nationalist. Member of the Irish Republican Brotherhood Military Council, and active in the Gaelic League and Sinn Fein. Founder member of the Irish volunteers; Director of Communications.

The National Library of Ireland has relevant material (MSS 13069–70) relating to Ceannt and his activities in the Gaelic League, Cumann na bPiobairi and the Irish Volunteers; and to his personal and business affairs, with some literary papers, c. 1900–16.

*Formerly known as Edmund Kent.

CHAMPION, Henry Hyde (1859–1928)

Socialist propagandist. First Secretary, Social Democratic Federation. Parliamentary candidate, Independent Labour Party. Assistant editor, *Nineteenth Century*. Emigrated to Australia, 1893. Leader-writer on *The Age*. Founded Book-Lovers' Library and Australian Authors' Agency.

No substantial collection of papers is known, though correspondence can be found in various collections.

CHAPLIN, Sir (Francis) Drummond Percy (1866–1933)

Journalist, colonial administrator and businessman.

No personal papers have been found but there is extensive relevant material in the P. L. Gell British South Africa Co. papers, while correspondence with Hardinge, 1898–1915, and notes on his discussions with the British India Committee can be found in the Hardinge papers, Cambridge University Library.

CHAPMAN, Guy Patterson (1899–1972)

Historian and author. Served in Army Bureau of Current Affairs from 1943. Professor of Modern History, Leeds University, 1945–53. Member, Institute for Advanced Studies, Princeton, 1957.

The manuscript of his work *A Passionate Prodigality* is in Churchill College, Cambridge, together with a small amount of other material (including campaign maps), some items concerning his wife, Storm Jameson, and letters from Liddell Hart.
     The Liddell Hart papers contain much further correspondence.

CHESSER, Eustace (1902–73)

Lecturer and consultant psychiatrist. Hon. Sec., Society for Sex Education and Guidance, until 1953. Research Director, Research Council into Marriage and Human Relationships. Author of various works on marriage, sexual problems, etc.

Mrs Sheila Chesser (widow) knows of no surviving papers, apart from some typescripts of his books and lectures. These are now housed in the University of Texas Library, Austin.

CHESTERTON, Cecil Edward (1879–1918)

Journalist and polemicist. Assistant editor, *New Age*. Editor *The Eye Witness*, 1912; *New Witness*, 1912–16. Member, Fabian Society Executive, 1906–7; later vehemently attacked Fabian socialism and 'The Party System'. Prominent in campaign relating to Marconi Scandal, 1912.

Father Brocard Sewell, Chesterton's biographer, states that all Mrs Chesterton's letters and papers relating to her husband were destroyed in World War II. Father Sewell has in his possession the holograph manuscripts of 15 poems by Chesterton, written c. 1900–5. A larger bundle of holograph poems is owned by Mr John Bourne of London, a nephew of Mrs Chesterton. He has a few miscellaneous manuscripts. The most detailed study, using available sources, is Brocard Sewell's *Cecil Chesterton* (St Albert's Press, Faversham, Kent, 1976).

CHESTERTON, Gilbert Keith (1874–1936)

Novelist, poet, journalist and social critic. Contributor to various national newspapers and journals. President, Distributist League. Editor, *New Witness*, 1916–23, and *G. K.'s Weekly*, 1925–36.

Miss Dorothy Collins, Top Meadow Cottage, Beaconsfield, Bucks, has a collection of manuscripts, letters and press cuttings. These are to be given to the British Library on her death. Mr Gregory Macdonald has relevant material on *G. K.'s Weekly* but this is not made available for research purposes. Miscellaneous MSS can be found in the Marie (Mattingly) Meloney Collection in Columbia University Library; while relevant material is available in the Sarolea papers in Edinburgh University Library, including letters and manuscripts.

CHEVINS, Hugh (1898–1975)

Journalist. On staff of *Daily Telegraph* from 1934, first as news editor and later as industrial and labour correspondent.

Mrs Chevins (widow) retained a collection of material, including albums containing press cuttings of all his articles from 1926; correspondence with various people including fellow journalists and prominent figures in the Labour movement; and an unpublished autobiography. These papers have been given to BLPES.

CHILDE, Vere Gordon (1892–1957)

Archaeologist and academic. Private Secretary to Prime Minister of New South Wales, 1919–21. Librarian to Royal Anthropological Institute, 1925–7. Professor of Prehistoric Archaeology, Edinburgh University, 1927–46. Professor of Prehistoric European Archaeology and Director of Institute of Archaeology, London University, 1946–56.

A number of Childe's notebooks, excavation report books and other material relating to his archaeological work are deposited in the Library of the Institute of Archaeology, London. It appears, however, that he destroyed the bulk of his papers shortly before his return to Australia just before his death. Any papers remaining with the family in Australia are not made available. Ms Sally Green, 40 High Street, Warwick, is preparing a biography.

CHILDERS, (Robert) Erskine (1870–1922)

Author and Irish politician. Author of works on military affairs and on Home Rule. Secretary to the Irish delegation at the Treaty negotiations, 1921.

Copies of letters and newspaper cuttings relating to Childers, 1889–1922 with obituary notices, are available in the National Library of Ireland. Correspondence regarding personal and Irish matters can be found in the Sir Horace Plunkett papers, and correspondence with Lloyd

George, 1917, may be consulted at the House of Lords Record Office. There is a biography by Andrew Boyle: *The Riddle of Erskine Childers* (1977).

CHIROL, Sir (Ignatius) Valentine (1852–1929)

Journalist, author and traveller. Director, Foreign Department of *The Times*, 1899–1912. Served on Royal Commission on Indian Public Services, 1912. Author of works on Middle and Far Eastern problems. Supporter of Zionist aspirations.

The archives of *The Times* have Foreign Department letterbooks up to 1910 which include, *inter alia*, out-letters to Chirol. The archivist of *The Times* stated that Chirol conducted the bulk of his professional correspondence from home and this has generally been lost. There are, however, two boxes of papers in *The Times* archive. A memorandum by Chirol on Egyptian nationalism is available in St Antony's College, Oxford, while notes on Indian Administration and provincial government, letters to and from Lord Hardinge, and certain other correspondence can be found in the Hardinge papers in Cambridge University Library. Further correspondence survives in the papers of L. S. Amery (see *Sources* Vol. 3, p. 11), while correspondence with Gertrude Bell can be found in Durham University, Oriental Section (84 letters in all), and with Sir Cecil Spring-Rice at Churchill College, Cambridge. Chirol–Morley correspondence is at the India Office Library, and Chirol–Tyrrell correspondence at the Public Record Office. Correspondence with Lord Sydenham is in the British Library (Add. MSS 50831–41).

CHUBB, Percival

Pioneer socialist. Founder-member of the Fellowship of the New Life.

Enquiries should be directed to Mr Robert Walston Chubb (son), c/o Lewis, Rice, Tucker, Allen and Chubb, Attorneys at Law, Suite 1400, Railway Exchange Building, 611 Olive Street, St Louis, Missouri 63101, USA, who has a collection of papers. Mr Basil Chubb (nephew), 9 Greyfriars, Eastgate Street, Winchester, also has relevant information. Relevant material can also be found in the Thomas Davidson collection in Yale University Library.

CITRINE, 1st B
Walter McLennan Citrine (1887–)

Trade union leader. Held union office in the Electrical Trades Union from 1914; Assistant General Secretary, 1920–3. Assistant Secretary, Trades Union Congress, 1924–5; General Secretary, 1926–46. President, International Federation of Trade Unions, 1928–45. Chairman, Central Electricity Authority, 1947–57.

Lord Citrine has deposited certain material in BLPES, including transcriptions of his Journals (including comments on visits to Russia in 1925 and his world tour of 1930), and some correspondence files. The collection is closed for the time being. Records of the Trades Union Congress are described in *Sources* Vol. 1, pp. 261–3.

CLAPHAM, Sir John Harold (1873–1946)

Economist. Fellow of King's College, Cambridge, 1898–1904, 1908–46; Dean, 1908–13; Vice Provost, 1933–43. Lecturer, Cambridge University, 1898–1902. Professor of Economics, Leeds University, 1902–8. Professor of Economic History, Cambridge University, 1928–38. President of the British Academy, 1940–5.

Certain papers are held at King's College, Cambridge, including a volume of notes and essays, 1894; 12 papers read to the King's College Political Society; eight letters to various correspondents, 1915–46; the manuscript of a fellowship dissertation; and two volumes of lecture notes.

A few other papers, consisting of typescript and MSS of two of his works, are held by Sir Michael Clapham. The Bank of England, Archives Section, holds the manuscript of the unfinished third volume of the *History of the Bank of England*. Sturges, *Economists' Papers* pp. 21–2, mentions these papers and material in other collections. The Oscar Browning papers, which were listed by the Historical Manuscripts Commission have a particularly useful group of letters relating to Clapham's early career.

CLARK, Lady
Barbara Keen

Feminist

The Bodleian Library, Oxford, has a collection of letters, miscellaneous papers, and notes, mainly concerned with women's trade union affairs and working conditions, comprising an introduction to the manuscripts, written by Lady Clark, 1971; eleven printed handbills of the National Union of Women's Suffrage Societies, c. 1912–13; some papers, including a financial statement, connected with a strike of women chairmakers at High Wycombe, 1913–14; correspondence and papers connected with the organisation of women workers in Bristol into trade unions, 1914; a handwritten report on an industrial dispute at the Bath Hygienic Laundry, 1914; four letters, one duplicated, in connection with the affairs of the National Federation of Women Workers, 1914–15; papers relating to the employment of women in the munitions trades, consisting mainly of two copies, one heavily annotated, of a report prepared for the Fabian Research Department by Barbara Clark, 1915–17; papers, correspondence and notes connected with the activities of the Central Committee on Women's Employment in organising women's workrooms in London during the war, 1914; a paper by J. A. Heaton on the payment of unemployment benefits during the war, n.d.; a paper by Barbara Clark on the employment of women during the war, n.d.; a letter and miscellaneous notes connected with the campaign to secure a minimum wage, 1914–19; drafts and notes about the history of women in industry; printed papers connected with the Sub-Committee on Women's Employment for the Reconstruction Committee, 1917; duplicated papers of the Joint Committee of Enquiry of the Fabian Women's Group and the Labour Research Department into women in trade unions, 1917–18; papers connected with the Women's Industrial League, 1919; a letter and miscellaneous papers about the Industrial Courts Act of 1919, 1920; and miscellaneous photographs, papers and newscuttings.

CLARKE, Sir Fred (1880–1952)

Educationalist. Professor of Education, Southampton, 1906–11; South African College and University of Capetown, 1911–29; McGill University, 1929–34. Adviser to Overseas Students, Institute of Education 1935–6. Professor of Education and Director of Institute of Education, London University, 1931–45. Educational Adviser to National Union of Teachers.

The London University Institute of Education has a collection of papers, 1910–50. The material includes articles, speeches and papers, and consists of offprints, typescripts and manuscripts. They cover topics such as modern secondary education, the Institute of Education, English Educational Institutes, religious education, the 1944 Education Act, education in the colonies etc. The papers of the Moot, a small private discussion group on the 'crisis in Western Civilization', set up in 1939, also in the Institute of Education Library, reflect Sir Fred Clarke's interests throughout.

CLARKE, Hilda Selwyn- (d. 1967)

Anti-colonialist. Secretary, Fabian Colonial Bureau.

Administrative and personal papers can be found throughout the archives of the Fabian

Colonial Bureau at Rhodes House Library, Oxford. These records are described in *Sources* Vol. 1, pp 94–5.

CLARKE, Thomas (1884–1957)

Journalist and author. On staff of Lord Northcliffe's newspapers. News Editor, *Daily Mail*, 1919. Assistant Editor, *The Herald*, Melbourne, 1923–6. Managing editor, *Daily News*, 1926, and then editor, *News Chronicle*, to 1933. Director of Practical Journalism, London University, 1935–46. Columnist, *Reynolds News*, 1936–42. Deputy Director, News Division, Ministry of Information, 1939–40.

Tom Clarke published two volumes of diaries, *My Northcliffe Diary* (1931) and *My Lloyd George Diary* (1939). Both describe his journalistic work, his meetings with fellow-journalists, writers and politicians. They cover the periods Jan 1912–June 1922, and Jan 1926–Oct 1933 respectively. His heirs were not contacted. The solicitors who acted in the estate knew of no papers.

CLARKE, William (1852–1901)

Socialist pioneer. Early member of Fabian Society.

Professor Norman Mackenzie, historian of the early Fabian Society, was unable to locate personal papers. Some correspondence can be found in the archives of the Fabian Society at Nuffield College, Oxford, while the Thomas Davidson papers in Yale University Library contain relevant material.

CLAUSEN, Hugh (1888–1972)

Naval armaments engineer. Chief Technical Adviser to Naval Ordnance Department of the Admiralty from 1936.

Clausen's technical papers, lectures and other material, are in Churchill College, Cambridge. These include technical papers, 1938–62; articles, 1940–60; lectures, 1947–70; miscellaneous material, including press cuttings and correspondence with Sir Roy Harrod; personal papers, including naval service records, 1914–18, and official papers about this service; his History of Branch 5 of the Electrical Engineering Department of the Admiralty; and Captain Roskill's correspondence on Clausen.

CLAY, Sir Henry (1883–1954)

Economist. Lecturer for Workers' Educational Tutorial Classes, 1909–17. Worked at Ministry of Labour, 1917–19. Fellow of New College, Oxford, 1919–21. Stanley Jevons Professor of Political Economy, Manchester University, 1922–7; Professor of Social Economics, 1927–30. Economic Adviser to Bank of England, 1930–44. Warden of Nuffield College, Oxford, 1944–9.

The papers of Sir Henry Clay are preserved at Nuffield College, Oxford. They include notebooks of lectures dating from Clay's student days; syllabuses and early essays by Clay; notes for courses and lectures, including W.E.A. material; papers relating to economic matters during and after World War I; articles and drafts of articles by Clay; material relating to his publications including his book, *Economics*, and correspondence relating to his *Life* of Lord Norman; papers concerning his work in South Africa and Rhodesia, and various other visits abroad; documents relating to the League of Nations; papers of various committees on which he served; manuscript notes and documents relating to economic and social welfare matters; and Board of Trade material, including financial and other memoranda. The collection also contains material relating to Nuffield College and other institutions with which Clay was involved; some correspondence 1933, 1951—3; and newspaper cuttings. Another important group of papers relates to his official studies of unemployment and certain industries during the 1930s, and to his work on various Government committees during World War II.

CLIFFORD, Frederick (1828–1904)

Journalist and newspaper proprietor. On staff of *The Times* in Jamaica, 1860s; later assistant editor of *The Times*. A founder of the Press Association. Joint Proprietor of the *Sheffield Daily Telegraph* and chairman of Sir W. C. Leng and Co (Sheffield Telegraph Ltd).

Papers can be found in the Bodleian Library, Oxford.

CLIFFORD, John (1836–1923)

Baptist leader and author. Minister of Praed Street and Westbourne Park Church, 1858–1915. President, Baptist Union, 1888, 1899; National Council of Free Evangelical Churches, 1898–9; Baptist World Alliance, 1905–1911. Campaigned against 1902 Education Act. President, National Brotherhood Council, 1916–19; World Federation of Brotherhoods, 1919–20.

Relevant material is held by the Westbourne Park Baptist Church. Rev. E. H. Robertson, 9 Porchester Gardens, London W2 4DB, states that some papers were destroyed when the church was bombed during World War II, but the congregation is building up a substantial collection. This includes a growing collection of letters; an incomplete collection of church publications, photographs, personalia; a more or less complete collection of minutes of church meetings and deacons' meetings (some of which are printed, others handwritten); and a complete collection of his published works. Available sources were used in M. R. Watts, 'John Clifford and Radical Nonconformity, 1836–1923', unpublished Oxford D.Phil. thesis, 1966.

COATES, Wells Wintermute (1895–1955)

Architect and industrial designer.

Mrs Laura Cohn (daughter), The Old Rectory, Chipping Warden, Banbury, Oxfordshire, has a large collection of material, which includes drawings, correspondence, press cuttings, photographs, diaries, offprints, typescripts of lectures and articles, outlines for various planning schemes, etc. The most extensive correspondence is about the formation of Unit One, and with one of his major clients, Jack Pritchard. There is also some correspondence about the MARS group, though the MARS group archive itself has disappeared. The diaries include an account of a voyage from Japan to Vancouver in 1913, and a diary of his war service, covering the years 1917–18. Of the press cuttings, the most interesting group concerns the early wireless designs for EKCO. These papers have been used, together with much other relevant material, in a forthcoming study by Sherban Cantacuzino.

A small group of further material can be found with the Royal Institute of British Architects, including miscellaneous sketches and designs, notes etc. A further relevant archive is that of Jack Pritchard, deposited in the University of Newcastle Library.

COBBE, Frances Power (1822–1904)

Philanthropist and writer on religious and moral issues. President from 1898 of the British Union for the Abolition of Vivisection.

The Huntington Library, San Marino, California, has a collection of papers, purchased in 1949 and consisting of 854 pieces, covering the period 1855–1902. The collection consists of letters to Frances Cobbe, from a wide range of correspondents, including H. E. Brown, Bishop of Winchester, Wilkie Collins, 7th Earl of Shaftesbury, Charles Robert Darwin, J. A. Froude,

Mrs Millicent Fawcett, Benjamin Jowett, W. E. H. Lecky, Cardinals Manning and Newman, James Martineau, Herbert Spencer, Helen Taylor, Hallam Tennyson, Mary Augusta Ward and A. B. O. Wilberforce. Topics covered include Frances Cobbe's social work at Bristol, women's suffrage and rights, anti-vivisection, and her writings. Some of these letters were printed in the two volumes of her *Life* (2 vols, 1894). Some letters to Edward Enfield are in Dr Williams' Library, and a few letters and documents are available at Boston Public Library, Mass.

COCKCROFT, Sir John Douglas (1897–1967)

Scientist and academic. Fellow of the Royal Society. Fellow of St John's College, Cambridge, 1928–46. Jacksonian Professor of Natural Philosophy, Cambridge, 1939–46. Chief Superintendent, Air Defence, Research and Development Establishment, Ministry of Supply, 1941–4. Director, Atomic Energy Division, National Research Council of Canada, 1944–6. Director of Atomic Energy Research Establishment, Ministry of Supply, 1946–58. Chairman, Defence Research Policy Committee, and Scientific Adviser, Ministry of Defence, 1952–4. Master of Churchill College, Cambridge, from 1959. President of Manchester College of Science and Technology from 1961.

Churchill College, Cambridge, has a substantial collection of papers. Cockcroft had the habit of leaving many of his papers in the establishment for which he worked, and this is reflected in the balance of his papers in this collection. The pre-1939 correspondence and papers, though not large in total, appears to be nearly complete. The World War II period is reflected in a few letters, while for the period 1946–59, though there are many papers, others were probably left in the AERE filing system. The period at Churchill College is fully documented. The collection includes Cockcroft's Cavendish notebooks, 1927–46; lectures, lecture notes, and speeches dating from the 1930s; MSS of articles and material relating to them, 1925–67; papers and correspondence about the Kapitza Club, an informal gathering of the Cavendish physicists, which met until 1958; files on the Maud Committee; and on visits abroad, dating from 1931. Material concerning Churchill College includes correspondence, drafts for the Charter and Statutes, minutes of the Governing Body and the Trustees and various committees, papers concerning appeals, the budget, construction, the chapel, the archives centre, conferences, etc. His work in the Manchester College of Technology is reflected in correspondence, drafts of speeches, minutes of Council, etc. There are also papers on his visit to Ghana, the Ghana Academy of Sciences, science in the Commonwealth, and scientific training and policy. Various papers and correspondence concern Atomic Energy, and include material on the Pugwash conferences, the nuclear deterrent, disarmament etc. Correspondence, 1921–67, is with various fellow-scientists and other colleagues, and topics covered include the Society for Anglo-Chinese Understanding, Britain in Europe, the Overseas Development Institute, the Metropolitan-Vickers Electrical Company (1930s), the Institute of Physics, the Royal Society, UNO, etc. Personal papers include his famous 'Black Book' dating from 1934, in which he recorded information and questions; plus diplomas and honours; biographical material includes press cuttings and correspondence about Ronald Clark's biography; autobiographical material; photographs and congratulatory letters. The collection also has material on the Liberal Party, amongst which is general correspondence, 1964–7, correspondence with East Anglian Liberal Associations, correspondence on the Presidency of the Party, offered to Cockcroft, and papers of the research and development committee and the science and technology panel. Finally, there are obituary notices of various colleagues of Cockcroft's, amongst which are papers concerning Lord Rutherford.

COCKERELL, Sir Sydney Carlyle (1867–1962)

Director of the Fitzwilliam Museum, Cambridge, 1908–37. Secretary to William Morris and the Kelmscott Press, 1892–8.

The British Library has a large collection of diaries and correspondence (Add.

MSS 52623–773). The 80 volumes of personal diaries extend from 1886 to 1962; diaries for the period from 1932 are closed until 1994. The correspondence is extensive and includes a long list of distinguished correspondents, including Sir Patrick Abercrombie, Sir Henry Acland, C. R. Ashbee, Lady Astor, Lord Attlee, Enid Bagnold, Isobel Baillie, Lord Baldwin, Sir Ernest Barker, A. C. Benson, F. F. Blackman, Sir Muirhead Bone, Robert Bridges, Sir Edward Burne-Jones, Lady Helena Carnegie, Sir Christopher and Lady Chancellor, Professor S. P. Chew, Sir Kenneth Clark, Leonard Clarke, T. J. Cobden-Sanderson, G. D. H. Cole, Frances Cornford, Sir Trenchard Cox, Walter de la Mare, Mrs C. M. Doughty, Geoffrey Dowding, F. S. Ellis, Albert Fleming, Sir J. W. and Lady Fortescue, Roger Fry, Dame Katherine Furse, Eric Gill, Sir E. Gosse, Sir Alec Guinness, Allan Gwynne Jones, Rupert Hart-Davis, Archibald Henderson, Mrs Caroline Hill and Octavia Hill, C. H. St John Hornby, Sir Gerald Kelly, Lord and Lady Kennett, Archbishop Lang, Sir Shane Leslie, W. R. Lethaby, Lady Lovelace, J. W. Mackail, Margaret Mackail, John Masefield, Eric G. Millar, Mrs Harold Monro, T. Sturge Moore, Mrs William Morris, Jenny and May Morris, A. N. L. Munby, Gilbert Murray, Hon. M. F. Napier, Lord Plymouth, Sir R. D. Powell, Professor G. F. Reynolds, Charles S. Ricketts, T. M. Rook, Edith Countess Russell, Charlotte Shaw, William Simmonds, Sir S. G. Tallents, D. V. Thompson, Janet Penrose Trevelyan, G. M. Trevelyan, Sir Emery Walker, Sir William and Lady Watson, P. S. Webb and W. Hale White ('Mark Rutherford').

Westminster City Libraries (Marylebone Library) has Cockerell correspondence, including letters from Octavia Hill. Some 112 items of correspondence, 1904–56, are available in Boston Public Library, Mass. Copies of correspondence 1894–6 can be found in the letterbook of the Kelmscott Press, in the William Morris collection, while other papers about his work with William Morris are available at the Victoria and Albert Museum. Letters to George Bernard Shaw are at the British Library (Add. MS 50531). There are 12 letters, 1937–49, in the Percival Serle collection, La Trobe Library, State Library of Victoria, Australia.

COHEN, Israel (1879–1961)

Author and lecturer. Zionist propagandist and fund raiser. English Secretary, Zionist Organization Central Office, Cologne, 1910–11, Berlin, 1911–14. Berlin correspondent of the *Glasgow Herald and Globe*, 1911–14. General Secretary, World Zionist Organization from 1922. Member of the Foreign Affairs Committee, Board of Deputies of British Jews from 1931; Vice-Chairman from 1952

The Central Zionist Archives, Jerusalem, have relevant material, 1919–48 (ref. A 213). There is correspondence from Balfour, MacDonald, Sykes, Mond and Samuel. The Board of Deputies archives (described in *Sources* Vol. 1, pp. 20–1) also contain relevant material.

COHEN, Joseph L. (d. 1940)

Economist and Zionist propagandist. Economist to Marks & Spencer Ltd. Hon. Secretary, Central Council for Jewish Refugees. On Executive Committee of International Association for Social Progress, Family Endowment Society and Labour Zionist Organisation.

There is some material in the Central Zionist Archives (ref. A 173), Jerusalem. Reference should also be made to the records of Marks & Spencer.

COHEN, Sir Leonard Lionel (1858–1938)

Banker and philanthropist. Member of the Stock Exchange Committee, 1896–1904. President, Jewish Board of Guardians, 1900–20; and of Jewish Colonisation Association. Member of the Central Committee on the Unemployed.

The archives of the Board of Deputies of British Jews (described in *Sources* Vol. 1, pp. 20–1) contain correspondence, both personal letters (ref. E 3/71) and miscellaneous correspondence on foreign affairs (ref.C 11).

COHEN, Sir Robert Waley- (1877–1952)

Businessman. Managing Director, Shell Transport and Trading Co. Ltd. Chairman, Palestine Corporation Ltd. President of the United Synagogue.

Sir Bernard Waley-Cohen (son) has various papers of his father, at present in store. The Anglo-Jewish archive in the Mocatta Library, University College London, includes an unabridged copy of Chapters I–IV of the biography of Waley-Cohen by Robert Henriques. Special conditions apply for accesss to this document. The published biography records the operations of the Palestine Corporation.

Further relevant material can be found in the archives of the Board of Deputies of British Jews (*Sources* Vol. 1, pp. 20–1), including correspondence, c. 1939.

COIT, Stanton (1857–1944)

Ethical reformer and author. Minister of Ethical Church, London. Founder, Moral Education League. Parliamentary candidate for the Labour Party, 1910.

Surviving personal papers, including some early letters, are retained by Lady Fleming (daughter), G3 Buxton Lodge, Portinscale Road, London, SW15. The Labour Party archive at Transport House has other relevant material, while a few letters can be found in the Bernstein collection, International Institute of Social History, Amsterdam.

COLBY, Reginald (d. 1969)

Freelance journalist, 1919–1939; served in Political Intelligence Department, Foreign Office, Mediterranean, 1943–5, Berlin, 1945–6. Freelance journalist and historian, 1947–68. A founder member of the Anglo-Malagasy Society.

A large collection of papers is held by the Imperial War Museum which includes correspondence, reports, journals, typescript articles and autobiographical accounts, press cuttings and transcripts of Colby's broadcasts. The papers cover his career as a propaganda officer in Madagascar (1943) and Berlin (1945–6), together with his work as a freelance journalist and broadcaster in Austria and Germany both before and after World War II.

COLE, George Douglas Howard (1889–1959)

Socialist writer and University teacher. Fellow of Magdalen College, Oxford, 1912–19. Worked for Fabian (later Labour) Research Department from 1913; later Hon. Secretary until 1924. Member of Fabian Society Executive (resigned 1915). Founder member of National Guilds League, 1915. Unpaid official of Amalgamated Society of Engineers, during World War I. Founder of Society for Socialist Inquiry and Propaganda and New Fabian Research Bureau, 1930. Chairman, Fabian Society, 1939–46, 1948–50; President from 1952. Fellow of University College, Oxford, and University Reader in Economics, 1925–44. Director of Nuffield College Social Reconstruction Survey, 1941–4. Chichele Professor of Social and Political Theory, Oxford, 1944–57. Research Fellow, Nuffield College, 1957–9.

A substantial collection of Cole's papers is preserved in the Library of Nuffield College, Oxford. The material covers the wide range of Cole's interests, although correspondence is sparse for the earlier part of his career. Some material survives relating to his schooldays and early introduction to Socialism. Various papers also survive concerning Cole's work for the Fabian Research Department, including a letter relating to its constitution in 1913, and documents relating to Barrow House conferences on the Control of Industry, 1913 and 1914. There is also useful material relating to the Guild Socialist movement including correspondence relating to the formation of the National Guilds League, 1915; various NGL documents, 1915–20; typescripts of lectures, 1920–1; papers relating to the Whitley Councils and trade unions, and notes for a study circle. The J. P. Bedford papers, also at Nuffield College, Oxford, complement this material. The Bedford collection includes six boxes of NGL papers: conference papers, documents on individual guilds, lectures, office papers, and some correspondence with Cole. Cole's later socialist activities are well represented in the main collection. There are papers, for instance, of the TUC and Labour Party Advisory Committees from 1920; miscellaneous material (correspondence and memoranda) on Easton Lodge meetings, 1920s; papers relating to the SSIP (memoranda, correspondence, typescript notes) and the New Fabian Research Bureau in the early 1930s; minutes of the Friday Group, 1932; material relating to the Fabian Society from the late 1930s, including a folder concerning the Socialist Propaganda Committee from 1941, documents relating to the Buscot conferences on 'Problems ahead' in the early 1950s, and papers concerning local Fabian groups from 1942. A number of papers concern the International Society for Socialist Studies, 1955–7, including draft rules, material relating to policy and organisation, agenda, bulletins, press cuttings, lists of people interested in joining, British and foreign correspondence. Other material in the collection relates to Cole's **university and teaching work,** and includes lecture and tutorial notes on economics and social theory, teaching notes to the Common Ground Film Strips, manuscripts, proofs and offprints of books, articles, philosophical papers, etc., papers concerning the Manpower Survey 1940, and material relating to the Social Reconstruction Survey (circulars, memoranda, reports and correspondence). Cole's public activities can also be traced, for example, in papers of the Economic Advisory Council, 1930; in documents relating to the Ministry of Economic Warfare; in LCC Education Committee papers from the 1940s; and in UNESCO papers of the 1950s. There is also an incomplete set of Cole's pocket diaries, 1925–55, and some personalia, including a copy of Cole's comic play 'The Striker Stricken'. A bibliography of the works of Cole compiled by H. P. Smith is also available in the collection. In addition there is a bound collection of Cole's articles in Nuffield College Library. A collection of trade union papers assembled by Cole is also housed in the Library.

The International Institute of Social History, Amsterdam, has another small collection of Cole papers, including correspondence, chiefly with publishers, 1913–35; some personal correspondence, 1954–7; correspondence about the World Socialist movement, 1955–7; and a number of typescripts of books and articles. The Braunthal Collection at the Institute also has relevant material.

The Labour Party archive has other papers relating to Cole, including material concerning the War Emergency Workers' National Committee (ref. LP/CO-ORD/20).

Other material can be found in the archives of the Fabian Society, also deposited in Nuffield College. Many of the Cole papers were used in the biography by M. I. Cole, *The Life of G. D .H .Cole* (1971).

COLLET, Clara E. (1860–1948)

Sociologist. Worked for Charles Booth, 1888–92. Assistant Commissioner to Royal Labour Commission, 1892. Labour Correspondent, Board of Trade, 1893–1903; Senior Investigator, 1903–20. Member of Council of Royal Statistical Society, 1919–35; and of Royal Economic Society, 1920–41; Fellow of University College London.

Copies of a number of personal papers are available in the Modern Records Centre, University of Warwick Library. They can be broadly divided into two categories. The first relates chiefly to Clara Collet's friendship with the novelist, George Gissing, covering the period of his break-up with his first wife. Most of their correspondence, 1893–1903, has survived and is included in this collection. It was used in Gillian Tindall's study of Gissing, *The Born Exile* (1974). The archive also includes a number of letters from Gissing's companion, Gabrielle Fleury, and from Gissing's sisters. The second category relates more closely to Clara Collet's work, and includes sections from her diaries, 1876–90, 1904–14. There are also documents on women's employment, especially in the textile or sewing-machine trades and domestic employment. Of particular interest are two letters received by Clara's father from Karl Marx in November and December 1866, relating to the activities of Gladstone and containing news of emigré Russians in London.

COLLET, Sir Mark Wilks, 1st Bt (1816–1905)

Director of the Bank of England from 1866. Governor, 1887–9.

Kent Archives Office has a collection of business papers, Bank of England material, personal diaries, and family accounts, 1830–1905.

COLLINGWOOD, Robin George (1889–1943)

Philosopher. Waynflete Professor of Metaphysical Philosophy, Oxford University, 1935–41.

The Bodleian Library, Oxford, has correspondence with H. A. Prichard and Gilbert Ryle.
    Dr P. Johnson, Department of Politics, Southampton University, has prepared a checklist of Collingwood letters.

COMFORT, Alexander (1920–)

Biologist; poet and novelist. Hon. Research Associate, Department of Zoology, 1951–73, and Director of Research, Gerontology, 1966–73, University College London. Senior Fellow, Center for the Study of Democratic Institutions, Santa Barbara, from 1973.

Some seven boxes of literary correspondence, 1930s–60, are in the Library of University College London.

CONNOLLY, James (1870–1916)

Socialist and Irish patriot. Author of *Labour in Irish History* etc.

The National Library of Ireland has much relevant material, 1888–1916. There is material relating to the 1913 strike in Dublin, MS 13,911, MSS 13,914–15, MS 13,921; material relating to the Easter Rising, 1916, MS 13,932, MSS 13,935–7, MSS 13,939–40, MS 15,000; and letters and associated papers, some of which are printed, MSS 15,688, MSS 15,700–2. The papers in the National Library include records of the early socialist parties in Ireland, including minutes of the Irish Socialist Republican Party and the Socialist Party of Ireland. The Marx Memorial Library in London has certain other material.
    C. Desmond Greaves, *The Life and Times of James Connolly* (1961), uses unpublished material and Samuel Leventon, *James Connolly: a biography* (1973) is based on private papers.

CONNOR, Sir William Neil (1909–67)

Journalist. Popular columnist as 'Cassandra' of the *Daily Mirror* from 1935.

Reference should be made to Lady Connor, who can be contacted via the *Daily Mirror*.

COOK, Arthur James (1885–1931)

Trade Union leader. General Secretary, Miners' Federation of Great Britain.

It is believed that Cook's personal papers no longer survive. The Labour Party archive at Transport House has some miscellaneous correspondence in its files on the miners, including material concerning the dispute with the Labour Party in 1928. Records of the MFGB are described in *Sources* Vol. 1, p. 195. The Horner papers at University College, Swansea, and the Mainwaring papers in the National Library of Wales are particularly relevant. A note on his career appears in the *Dictionary of Labour Biography* Vol. III, pp. 38–44, together with a comprehensive bibliography.

COOK, Sir Edward Tyas (1857–1919)

Journalist and author. Editor, *Pall Mall Gazette*, 1890–2; *Westminster Gazette*, 1893–6; *Daily News*, 1896–1901. Edited works of Ruskin, 1903–11. Joint Director, Official Press Bureau, 1915.

The British Library has a small collection of miscellaneous letters and papers bequeathed by Sir Edward Cook (Add. MS 39927). Included in this collection is some correspondence from A. C. Swinburne and W. E. Gladstone; letters replying to questions submitted by the *Pall Mall Gazette* on the subject of the Hundred Best Books (from amongst others Matthew Arnold, Lord Coleridge, Henry Irving, Benjamin Jowett, H. M. Stanley); two autograph letters which Cook used in his *Life* of Florence Nightingale; and some material relating to Cook's work on Ruskin. Also in the collection are poems by George Meredith and Sir William Watson.
    Some social correspondence, 1897–1900, can be found in the Sladen papers.

COOTE, William Alexander (1842–1919)

Social morality crusader. Secretary, National Vigilance Association, 1885–1919. Organiser of numerous National Committees for the Suppression of the White Slave Trade throughout the world.

No personal papers have been discovered but Coote's work as Secretary of the National Vigilance Association can be traced in the archives held by the Fawcett Library (see *Sources* Vol. I, p. 31).

CORBETT, Sir Julian Stafford (1854–1922)

Naval historian. Director of Historical Section, Committee of Imperial Defence.

A collection of papers survives with Mr Brian Tunstall, 34 Dartmouth Row, Greenwich, London SE10. A catalogue of the papers is available at the NRA. The material covers the period 1873–1922 and includes early writings and correspondence with publishers, publishers' agreements, and general correspondence concerning his books; family papers; papers concerning the Sudan; and correspondence with Sir Henry and Lady Newbolt, 1898–1920. A number of papers relate to naval matters, including material on naval manoeuvres and education, naval history, strategy and public policy, 1905–14 (especially on national service, and including letters to *The Times*). Another section of the collection concerns the War College, the Admiralty and the Committee of Imperial Defence, and includes a memorandum on 'invasion' written in Nov 1907, letters from Sir Edmond Slade to Corbett about the CID, papers concerning the sub-committee on invasion, copies of Fisher/Clarke (Sydenham) correspondence, press cuttings on 'invasion' scares, 1906–8, letters from Vice-Admiral P. H. Colomb, Lt.-Col. E. Y. Daniel, papers on war plans, a precis of a war game at Portsmouth Naval College, and articles. The section on the Great War includes notes in Corbett's handwriting on the War Council, 5/6 Aug 1914, official memoranda, letters to Sir Herbert Richmond, copies of correspondence with Sydenham, letters from Lord Jellicoe. Another important grouping within the collection consists of letters from Lord Fisher. It is very revealing of Fisher's methods and actions, and illustrates the degree to which Fisher used Corbett as an Admiralty propagandist. There are also letters from other naval officers, including Richmond, Beatty, Blake and Prince Louis of Battenburg. There are a number of family letters and papers, including letters from Corbett to his parents from 1873 and letters to Edith Rosa Corbett from 1897. Other correspondents include the Duke of Abercorn, Byng of Vimy, Edward Elgar, M.P.s, military and naval leaders, etc. Most of these are largely of autograph interest, though the Richmond correspondence relates to the Smoke Abatement Society, and the correspondence with Brig.-Gen. R. N. Smyth concerns South Africa. A deed box contains lecture notes, reviews, letterbooks and miscellaneous material.

CORNFORD, Leslie Cope- (1867–1927)

Journalist. Naval correspondent of the *Standard* and the *Morning Post*. Author of works on naval and maritime subjects.

A collection of papers, including letters from Rudyard Kipling, Sir Geoffrey Callender and others, is in the National Maritime Museum.

COULSON, Charles Alfred (1910–74)

Scientist. Fellow of Royal Society. Professor of Theoretical Physics, King's College, London, 1947–52. Professor of Mathematics, Oxford University, from 1952. Member of the Central Committee, World Council of Churches, from 1962. Vice-President, Methodist Conference, 1959.

The papers (comprising some 200 boxes in all) have been catalogued by the Contemporary Scientific Archives Centre, Oxford, and are to be placed in the Bodleian Library, Oxford. The collection covers all aspects of his scientific career and fully reflects his religious, pacifist and humanitarian activities. The collection is catalogued by the following categories: biographical and personal (including diaries and family letters), scientific lectures, working papers, publications, broadcasts, correspondence; non-scientific writings, sermons, addresses, speeches, broadcasts; scientific committees, societies, organisations, conferences; non-scientific committees, societies, organisations, conferences; further correspondence; and Oxford.

COULTON, George Gordon (1858–1947)

Historian. Fellow of St John's College, Cambridge, and University Lecturer in History. Temporary Professor of Medieval History, University of Toronto, 1940–3.

A collection of papers was purchased by the University of Chicago Library. The papers have been divided into two series. The first includes miscellaneous correspondence, notes and indexes; the second contains 271 British Museum notebooks. The correspondence is fairly sparse, none of the material relates to personal matters, and little of it is of direct scholarly importance. A few letters, however, relate to the National Service League during World War I, and this complements further NSL material in the notebooks. The bulk of the contents of the first series relate to Coulton's academic pursuits. The notebooks were originally extracts and notes made by Coulton at the British Museum, but they became wider in scope than this and include notes for most of his research, with the chief subject matter being medieval social, economic and religious history.

Letters to Sir Sydney Cockerell can be found in Boston Public Library, Mass. Letters to the *Church Quarterly Review*, 1905–6, are in Lambeth Palace Library.

COUPLAND, Sir Reginald (1884–1952)

Historian. Beit Professor of History of British Empire, Oxford, 1920–48. Fellow of All Souls, Oxford, 1920–48, and 1952. Fellow of Nuffield College, Oxford, 1939–50. Editor of *Round Table*, 1917–19, 1939–41. Member of Palestine Royal Commission (Peel Commission) 1936–7. Member of Mission to India, 1942.

Coupland destroyed most of his personal papers before his death. The surviving material has been placed in Rhodes House Library, Oxford. It consists of travel diaries and albums, 1913–42, and papers relating to the history of the British Empire and Commonwealth, 1904–48. There is a little printed material relating to the Peel Commission. Records of the

Round Table, now deposited in the Bodleian Library, Oxford, are described in *Sources* Vol. 1, p 224.

COURTNEY, 1st B
Leonard Henry Courtney (1832–1918)

Politician and journalist. Professor of Political Economy, University College London, 1872–5. M.P. (Lib.) Liskeard, 1876–85; (Lib. Un.) Bodmin, 1885–1900. Parliamentary Under-Secretary, Home Department, 1880–1; Colonial Office, 1881–2. Financial Secretary to the Treasury, 1882–4. Chairman of Committees and Deputy Speaker, 1886–92. Frequent contributor to *The Times* and *Nineteenth Century*, etc.

Some forty volumes of correspondence, papers and diaries relating to Leonard and Catherine (Kate) Courtney are housed in BLPES. The substantial collection of letters includes Leonard Courtney's correspondence with Mill and Cairnes, 1862–72; his correspondence with family and personal friends, 1857–79; letters relating to his engagement and marriage, 1881–3; political correspondence, 1880–1918, including letters relating to domestic affairs, the Boer War, World War I; letters of condolence addressed to Lady Courtney on the death of her husband, 1918; letters, memoranda and other material concerning a Life of Courtney, 1918–19; miscellaneous and undated letters of Leonard and Kate Courtney, 1864–1927; and a letterbook containing copies by Kate of letters written by Leonard Courtney, 1885–1910. Correspondents include many leading political and intellectual figures. The Courtney collection also includes miscellaneous papers of Leonard and Kate Courtney, arranged chronologically, 1864–1927; printed speeches, pamphlets, periodical articles, etc., by Leonard, 1880–1913; a notebook containing a list of leading and other articles written for *The Times*, 1864–80; the diaries of Kate Courtney, 1875–1919; and the autobiography and diaries of Rosalind Dobbs, 1914–1929.

Duke University, Durham, North Carolina, has a further collection of Courtney family papers. This includes correspondence and other papers relating to Leonard Courtney and J. M. Courtney; articles, books and other papers of William Prideaux Courtney; and papers of Richard Olivier.

Further correspondence can be found in other collections of papers, including the Asquith, Balfour and Joseph Chamberlain collections. Correspondence as a leader-writer of *The Times* is held in *The Times* archives.

COURTNEY, Dame Kathleen D'Olier (1878–1974)

Philanthropist. Hon. Secretary, National Union of Women's Suffrage Societies, 1911–14. A founder of the Women's International League. Relief work in Europe during and after World War I. On the Executive Committee, League of Nations Union, from 1928; Vice-Chairman, 1939. Chairman, United Nations Association, 1949. During World War II lectured in USA on behalf of the Ministry of Information.

Miss E. A. Furlong, Flat 42, 5 Sloane Court East, London SW3, literary executor to Dame Kathleen, has deposited the papers in the Fawcett Library.

The Imperial War Museum has some letters and diaries relating to her work with the Friends' Relief Service, and in Salonika and Eastern Europe, 1915–27.

There is correspondence 1930–46, with Lord Cecil in the British Library (Add. MS. 51141), and correspondence 1919–20, in the Labour Party archive at Transport House. Correpondence with Laura (Puffer) Morgan is in the Morgan-Homes family papers in the Schlesinger Library on the History of Women in America, Radcliffe College.

Records of women's suffrage organisations, including the NUWSS, are described in *Sources* Vol. 1, pp. 279–85. Papers of the League of Nations Union (deposited in BLPES) are described in *Sources* Vol. 1, pp. 144–5; and records of the Women's International League for Peace and Freedom (British Section), also in BLPES, are described in *Sources* Vol. 1, p. 278.

COURTNEY, William Leonard (1850–1928)

Journalist and author. Editor of the *Fortnightly Review*, 1894. On editorial staff of *Daily Telegraph*. Fellow of New College, Oxford, from 1876.

New College, Oxford, has no knowledge regarding the personal papers of Courtney. There are a few items of a domestic nature, relating to the state of his house and to his appointment as a Fellow.
    The Sladen papers contain social correspondence, 1893–1913; correspondence concerning the New Vagabonds Club, 1919–20; and letters relating to the After Dinners Club. There are eight letters from Courtney in the Escott papers.

CRAIG, Alec (1897–1973)

Libertarian. Campaigner for sexual freedom and against literary censorship. Author of *The Banned Books of England*, etc. Founder member of the Federation of Progressive Societies and Individuals, later the Progressive League.

A bequest of books and pamphlets was made to the Hampstead Public Libraries, now part of the Libraries and Arts Department, London Borough of Camden. These were distributed to various interested libraries. The few manuscript items, including a few letters from Craig to H. G. Wells, and Havelock Ellis and Wells items, have been incorporated in the autograph letters collection, Swiss Cottage Library, Camden.
    Washington University Library, St Louis, Missouri, has purchased a small collection of Progressive League material, 1935–63, including correspondence between Ashton Burrall and Alec Craig and various British authors and political figures. The correspondence concerns readings and lectures for the League, Poetry Circle readings, and conferences. Amongst the correspondents are W. H. Auden, Cecil Day Lewis, Ernest Gombrich, and Sir Julian Huxley.
    Other Progressive League papers are described in *Sources* Vol. 1, p. 216.

CRAWFORD, R. Lindsay

Irish nationalist. Editor of the *Ulster Guardian*. Irish Free State Consul in New York.

The National Library of Ireland has a small collection of letters to Crawford and some papers, 1904–22.

CRAWFORD, Virginia Mary (d. 1948)

Feminist and author. Co-respondent in the Dilke divorce case, 1886. Later a propagandist for women's suffrage, the Labour Party, Roman Catholicism and in anti-fascist activities.

Churchill College, Cambridge, has six boxes of material. They include her correspondence with the Catholic Social Guild; manuscripts of articles on religious and social topics, including fascism and the Spanish Civil War, 1897–1938; MS notes on Germany and Russia; Belgium and Rome; nursing in Soho (1886, 1888); notes on interviews with General Boulanger and Cardinal Manning, Louise Michel and others, 1889–99; notes on a visit to Dublin, 1920; press cuttings; and copies of published works by her, 1890–1940.

CRAWFURD, Helen (1874–1944)

Feminist and early member of the Communist Party of Great Britain. First Women's Organiser, CPGB.

Helen Crawfurd's unpublished autobiography is in private hands. Enquiries should be directed to the Marx Memorial Library.

CREIGHTON, Mandell (1843–1901)

Ecclesiastic and historian. Dixie Professor of Ecclesiastical History, Cambridge University, 1884–91. Bishop of Peterborough from 1891; Bishop of London from 1897.

Three volumes of his Visitation Returns are in Lambeth Palace Library. Cambridge University Library has various relevant items, including letters from Lord Acton, 1882–98. The Figgis collection at the Borthwick Institute of Historical Research, York, has five letters from Creighton. Correspondence can also be found in the Grey of Howick, Sladen and Churchill papers. There are 17 letters from Mrs Humphry Ward in Pusey House.

CREW, Francis Albert Eley (1886–1973)

Scientist. Fellow of the Royal Society. Professor of Animal Genetics, Edinburgh University, 1928–44. Professor of Public Health and Social Medicine, 1944–55. Professor of Social and Preventive Medicine, Cairo, 1956. Director of Medical Research, War Office, 1942–6.

A complete collection of offprint articles, in three volumes, 1919–46, is held by the History and Social Studies of Science Division, University of Sussex.

CROAL, John P. (1852–1932)

Scottish journalist. Editor of *The Scotsman*, 1905–24.

There are some 56 items of correspondence in the Bonar Law papers at the House of Lords Record Office. *The Scotsman* knew of no substantial collection of papers.

CROKE, Thomas W. (1824–1902)

Roman Catholic Archbishop of Cashel from 1875. Adviser to the Irish Nationalist Party.

The Cashel Diocesan Archives, Thurley, Tipperary, has a collection of papers, a microfilm of which is in the National Library of Ireland. The material includes letters and, particularly after 1875, correspondence with various ecclesiastical and political figures. Papers for an earlier period include a notebook, 1849–75, giving the full texts of his sermons, the majority preached in Auckland, New Zealand, together with a journal, letters of appointments, proofs, etc.

CROOK, William Montgomery (1860–1945)

Liberal journalist and politician. Liberal Parliamentary candidate in 1892. Editor of the *Methodist Times*, 1892–8; the *Echo*, 1898–1900. Secretary of the Eighty Club; and the Home Counties Liberal Federation, 1902–40.

A substantial collection of letters (approximately 1000 in number) has been purchased by the Bodleian Library, Oxford. The collection dates from the 1880s and extends to the late 1930s. It covers the range of Crook's interests, including material relating to the Eighty Club, the Home Counties Liberal Federation, general elections, Irish politics and the fight for Home Rule, as well as social occasions which he organised or participated in. The correspondents include members of the Crook family as well as a wide range of prominent persons, including politicians such as Winston Churchill, Lloyd George, Ramsay MacDonald, John Burns, Lord Harcourt, literary figures such as Hilaire Belloc, G. B. Shaw, H. G. Wells, W. B. Yeats, journalists like Sir E. T. Cook, Robert Donald, and many others.

CROWTHER, Baron
Sir Geoffrey Crowther (1907–72)

Economist and journalist. Editor of *The Economist*, 1938–56. Served during World War II at the Ministries of Supply and Information and as Deputy Head of Joint War Production Staff,

Ministry of Production. Chairman, Central Advisory Council for Education (England), 1956–60; Committee on Consumer Credit, 1968–71. Chairman, Royal Commission on the Constitution, 1969–72.

Lord Crowther's papers remain in the care of his family, while papers on the Royal Commission will become available under the Thirty Year rule at the Public Record Office.

CROZIER, William Percival (1879–1944)

Journalist. Joined *Manchester Guardian*, 1903; editor from 1932.

John Rylands University Library of Manchester has accounts, both typescript and holograph, of 230 interviews by W. P. Crozier with 62 statesmen and politicians, 1931–44, chiefly concerning European affairs and the Nazi threat, the Jewish National Home and the Far East (India and China). One hundred and seventy three are major interviews with 23 leading political figures and the remaining 57 (1931–44) relate to 39 other interviewees. About half of these were published by A. J. P. Taylor. (ed.), *Off the Record: Political Interviews by W. P. Crozier, 1932–44* (1973). The John Rylands University Library of Manchester also holds the records of the *Manchester Guardian* (see *Sources* Vol. 1, p. 104). Mrs Mary McManus (daughter) holds further records, of a private nature, and these are not made available.

CUMMINGS, Arthur John (d. 1957)

Journalist and author. Assistant editor, *Yorkshire Post*, 1919. Assistant editor, later deputy editor, *Daily News*, from 1920. Political editor and chief commentator, *News Chronicle*, 1932–55. President, Institute of Journalists, 1952–3.

Papers survive in the care of the family and are at present unsorted. The literary executor is Mr Michael Cummings (son), c/o the *Daily Express*, London.

CUNARD, Nancy (1896–1965)

Author and founder of Hours Press. Journalist in Spain during Civil War. Supporter of Black Rights in USA.

Southern Illinois University Library (Carbondale) has relevant material covering the period 1944–65, including miscellaneous papers, and letters from Nancy Cunard to Charles Burkhart regarding her books and her work with the Hours Press. Articles, poems and lectures by Nancy Cunard, and including correspondence with Janet Flanner, is available in the Library of Congress. The Humanities Research Center, University of Texas, Austin, has perhaps the largest single collection of manuscripts and correspondence.

CURTIS, Lionel George (1872–1955)

Historian and writer on imperial affairs. Served South African war, 1899–1902. Town Clerk of Johannesburg. Assistant Colonial Secretary to the Transvaal for local government. Secretary to the Irish Conference, 1921. Adviser on Irish Affairs in the Colonial Office, 1921–4. Fellow of All Souls, Oxford.

The papers of Lionel Curtis, together with some papers of the Round Table, were given to the Bodleian Library in 1973. Many of Curtis's papers were destroyed in a fire in the early 1930s so what remains of his own papers consists for the most part of about 150 boxes of correspondence dating from 1930 to his death in 1955, with some correspondence from the late nineteenth and early twentieth centuries. Virtually nothing survives for the World War I period and the immediate post-war years. A substantial collection of papers of the Round Table organisation came to the Bodleian with the Curtis papers. These consist of about 50 boxes of correspondence and papers for the period 1910–20, with a few similar papers for the 1930s and 1940s. They include many memoranda on various subjects and correspondence of the Round Table office.

Relevant published and manuscript material relating to the Federal Trust is in the University of Sussex Library. Correspondence can be found in the Lothian papers (Scottish Record Office), Selborne papers (Bodleian Library), the Creech-Jones papers (Rhodes House Library) and the Richard Jebb papers. Some letters from T. E. Lawrence are at Jesus College, Oxford. Letters to C. R. Ashbee, 1898–1916, are at King's College, Cambridge. Some 33 items of correspondence, 1910–48, are in the William Downie Stewart papers, Hoken Library, University of Otago, Dunedin, New Zealand.

DALLEY, Frederick William (b. 1885)

Trade unionist. Editor of *Journal* of Transport Salaried Staffs' Association, 1924–36. Member of Labour Party National Executive. Member of Labour Advisory Committee to Secretary of State for the Colonies. Vice President, National Peace Council.

Hull University Library has a collection of papers. They include material on Trinidad, 1927–52; Trinidad and British Guiana, 1947–54; Nigeria, 1946–60; Nigeria and West Africa, 1950–3; Malaya and Singapore, 1920–56 (press cuttings, correspondence, memoranda particularly on trade unions); the East Africa Royal Commission, 1952–5; Israel, 1956–60; Germany, 1950–3; Trade unionism (especially the World Federation of Trade Unions), 1945–50; articles and notes for lectures and miscellaneous papers.

DANIEL, David Robert (1859–1931)

Welsh Liberal publicist. General Secretary, North Wales Quarrymen's Union.

A collection of papers has been deposited in the National Library of Wales. It includes material relating to T. E. Ellis, comprising *inter alia* correspondence with Ellis; memoirs of public figures by Daniel; notes on conversations (e.g. with John Burns on the Marconi scandal); letters to and from various personalities, postcards, etc.; material relating to the North Wales Quarrymen's Union and Penrhyn Quarry Strikes; and material relating to Lloyd George, including letters to Daniel and Mrs Daniel from Lloyd George and his family, a memoir of Lloyd George, and copies of letters and newspaper cuttings.

DANIELS, Harold Griffith (1874–1952)

Journalist. Worked for *Daily Express, Reuters* and *Manchester Guardian*, 1903–14. Assistant Military Censor, Press Bureau, 1914–15; with News Department, Foreign Office, 1915–16. Director, British Wireless Service, 1916–18; at Admiralty 1918. On staff of *The Times* from 1919. Berlin correspondent, 1920–7; Paris correspondent, 1927–36; and League of Nations correspondent, Geneva, 1936–9. Worked at the Press Department, British Legation in Berne, 1939–45.

Miscellaneous items are in the archives of *The Times*.

D'ARCY, Charles Frederick (1859–1938)

Irish ecclesiastic. Priest from 1885. Chaplain to the Lord Lieutenant of Ireland,1895–1903. Bishop of Clogher, 1903–7; Ossory, Ferns and Leighlin, 1907–11; Down and Connor, 1911–19. Archbishop of Dublin, 1919–20. Archbishop of Armagh and Primate of All Ireland (Church of Ireland) from 1920.

Papers are at present held by the family. Further details were not available.

DARWIN, Leonard (1850–1943)

Eugenicist. M.P. (Lib. Un.) Lichfield, 1892–5. President, Royal Geographical Society, 1908–11. President, Eugenics Education Society, 1911–28. Chairman, Bedford College, London, 1913–20. Chairman, Professional Classes War Relief Council throughout World War I.

Correspondence and papers have been listed by the History and Social Studies of Science Division, University of Sussex.

Records of the Eugenics Society, in the Society's offices, are described in *Sources* Vol. 1, pp. 92–3.

DAVIDSON, 1st B
Randall Thomas Davidson (1884–1930)

Ecclesiastic. Dean of Windsor and domestic chaplain to the Queen, 1883–91. Clerk of the Closet to the Queen, and then King Edward VII, 1891–1903. Bishop of Rochester, 1891–5. Bishop of Winchester, 1895–1903. Archbishop of Canterbury, 1903–28.

Lambeth Palace Library has correspondence and miscellaneous papers. The correspondence is extensive, with leading churchmen and other prominent public figures. There is also complementary correspondence, with Blanche Sitwell, 1882–1929, Sir Almeric Fitzroy, 1910–21, amongst others. The correspondence with the Royal Family is also in Lambeth Palace Library but this is closed at present. Other items in Lambeth Palace include the Rochester Ordination Book, 1891–1925.

The National Library of Scotland has several items of correspondence, 1885–1929, while correspondence with A. J. Balfour concerning the Clergy Discipline Bill and the Church Enabling Bill is in the Balfour papers. Letters to Sir Thomas Barlow are in the Royal College of Physicians; and there is further correspondence in the Asquith and 2nd Earl Selborne papers at the Bodleian Library. Correspondence with Walter Frere can be found at the Borthwick Institute of Historical Research, York.

DAVIES, George M. Llewelyn

Pacifist and worker for the Fellowship of Reconciliation.

Records concerning the work of the Fellowship of Reconciliation in Wales can be found in the National Library of Wales. The material includes reports, bulletins and memoranda, and letters, 1916–47. Records of the Fellowship, in BLPES and elsewhere, are described in *Sources* Vol. 1, pp. 99–100.

DAVIES, Sir John Thomas (1881–1938)

Private Secretary to David Lloyd George from 1912. Director of the Suez Canal Company from 1922; and of the Ford Motor Company.

Letters to Lloyd George and miscellaneous secretarial papers can be found in the Lloyd George collection at the House of Lords Record Office. Correspondence, 1919–21, can also be found in the W. H. Dawson papers.

DAVIES, Margaret Llewelyn (1861–1944)

Co-operator and social reformer. General Secretary of the Women's Co-operative Guild, 1889–1921. Chairman of the Society for Cultural Relations between the USSR and Britain, 1924–8.

The BLPES has a collection of material, presented by Miss Lillian Harris, lifelong friend and companion of Margaret Llewelyn Davies. It consists of eleven volumes and appears to represent records accumulated by Miss Davies. The collection illustrates the aims and activities of the Women's Co-operative Guild during roughly the period 1890–1944, and reveals also the personal influence of Miss Davies and Miss Harris in encouraging the spread of co-operation among working-class women. Volume 1 consists of manuscript, typed and printed material covering the activities of the Guild, 1890–1944; Volumes 2–5 are concerned with a propaganda campaign organised by the Coronation Street branch of the Sunderland Co-operative Society, 1902–4, and include three scrapbooks, with letters, printed material and photographs; Volume 6 has records of the Sheffield enquiry, 1902, and the promotion of People's Stores in Bristol, 1905–6; Volume 7 contains photographs and prints of a visit to Belgian co-operators in 1906; Volume 8 consists of press cuttings and correspondence connected with the retirement of Miss Davies and Miss Harris from the Guild, Oct 1921; Volume 9 is a testimonial presented to Miss Davies at this time; Volume 10 includes drafts of a speech by her in June 1933, and material relating to the appearance of a new banner, 1933; and Volume 11 is a photograph album, covering the years 1903–38.

A larger collection of material, formerly in the possession of the Guild, is now housed in Hull University Library. Much of this again can be used to trace Miss Davies' work. Also in Hull University, in the *Dictionary of Labour Biography* collection, are two memoirs of Miss Davies, one by Mrs Vaughan Nash (8 pp.) and the second by a niece, Dr Katherine Davies (28 pp.). A biography appears in the *Dictionary of Labour Biography* Vol. 1, pp. 96–9. Correspondence with Bertrand Russell is at McMaster University, Hamilton, Ontario.

DAVIES, (Sarah) Emily (1830–1921)

Promoter of Higher Education for Women. Hon. Secretary, Girton College, Cambridge.

Girton College, Cambridge, has a considerable collection of material relating to Emily Davies, but it is not made available pending cataloguing. It mostly relates to women's rights and the foundation of the College.

DAVITT, Michael (1846–1906)

Irish revolutionary and Labour agitator.

The National Library of Ireland has much relevant material, including letters to William O'Brien, 1893–99 (MS 913); correspondence with J. F. X. O'Brien, 1892–1904 (MSS 13,420; 13,451; 13,457); letters to William Bulfin, c. 1890–1910 (MS 13,810); letters to John Redmond, 1891–1906 (MS 15,179); letters from John Dillon, 1899 (MS 15,741); letters to W. M. Colles, literary agent, 1890–1903 (12 letters, MS 18,575); and letters to Daniel Crilly, c. 1900 (microfilm no. 5992 p. 6,567). Reference should also be made to the Library of Trinity College Dublin.

There are some letters in the Terence Pourderly papers in the Catholic University of America, Washington D.C.

DAWSON, (George) Geoffrey
Geoffrey Robinson* (1874–1944)

Journalist. Fellow of All Souls, Oxford, 1898. Private Secretary to Lord Milner in South Africa, 1901–5. Editor, *Johannesburg Star*, 1905–10. Secretary to the Rhodes Trust, 1921–2. Editor of *The Times*, 1912–19, 1923–41.

Papers in the archives of *The Times* cover the period 1906–40 and include a press cutting book covering his career, and correspondence. The correspondence, relating chiefly to his second term as editor, is important in illustrating his relationship with public figures. Correspondents include Maxse, Northcliffe, and leading politicians, etc. He had the habit also of writing memoranda of events and interviews and these provide a useful guide to his attitude to major events, e.g. the Abdication. Certain private papers are in the possession of his family and a microfilm of these is in *The Times* archive. Correspondence with Cecil can be found in the British Library (Add. MS 51156), with Samuel and Bonar Law in the House of Lords Record Office and with Lothian in the Scottish Record Office. John Evelyn Wrench in *Geoffrey Dawson and Our Times* (1955) made use of personal papers in the care of the family.

* Adopted name.

DAWSON, William Harbutt (1860–1948)

Journalist and publicist. Author of numerous books and articles on Germany.

Birmingham University Library has a substantial collection of papers. The larger part of the material consists of correspondence, mostly addressed to Dawson, and dating from the 1870s to the 1950s. There is a large range of correspondents, many of them German, but including many people prominent in British public life. Amongst subjects covered are business matters, politics, and journalism (letters from editors and other journalists regarding articles, etc.). The collection also includes typescripts, including many of his works on Germany and Central Europe; two commonplace books from 1883; magazine and newspaper articles by Dawson, and by others, arranged chronologically by author; reviews of Dawson's books; press cuttings; obituary notices; notebooks containing press cuttings; and diaries from 1882–1932 (with gaps).

DEAKIN, Ralph (1888–1952)

Journalist. On the staff of *The Times* from 1919. Foreign News Editor from 1922.

Miscellaneous material can be found in the archives of *The Times*.

DE BLANK, Joost (1908–68)

Churchman. Priest from 1932. Chaplain to Forces, World War II. Assistant General Secretary, Student Christian Movement, 1946–8. Suffragan Bishop of Stepney, 1952–7. Archbishop of Cape Town, 1957–63. Canon of Westminster from 1964. Assistant Bishop, Diocese of Southwark from 1966. Chairman, Greater London Conciliation Committee from 1966.

York University Library has a collection of personal papers, correspondence, diaries, travel journals, sermons, photographs, manuscripts, articles and publications, covering his career as Bishop of Stepney, Archbishop of Cape Town, and Canon of Westminster (some 16 boxes in all).

DENBY, Elizabeth Marian (1893–1965)

Sociologist. Specialist on low-cost housing.

The Building Research Establishment, Garston, Watford, has an important collection of some 750 items. The main bulk of the collection consists of printed matter, and includes British Parliamentary papers, HMSO and local government publications; foreign government and other publications; journals and other documents of professional and similar organisations; trade literature; supplements and special issues of the daily press; and press cuttings.

DEVOY, John (1842–1928)

Fenian and Irish Nationalist.

Papers, 1867–1928, are in the National Library of Ireland (MSS 18,000–157). They consist of correspondence, circulars and press cuttings of or concerning him. There are about 350 political letters and a smaller group of family correspondence. The bulk of the material is for the period 1895–1905.

DIBDIN, Sir Lewis Tonna (1852–1938)

Ecclesiastical lawyer and administrator. Vicar-general, Province of Canterbury, 1925–31. First Church Estates Commissioner, from 1931. Ecclesiastical Commissioner, from 1931. Member of Royal Commission on Church Discipline, 1904–6, on Divorce, 1909–12.

Lambeth Palace Library has papers, including lectures and addresses, letters to C. Jenkins, and newspaper cuttings.

DICEY, Albert Venn (1835–1922)

Jurist; writer on the Constitution. Vinerian Professor of English Law, Oxford, 1882–1909. Fellow of All Souls, Oxford.

A few items of correspondence and a manuscript essay on 'History and Politics' is in Glasgow University Library. Correspondence can be found in a variety of collections. There are letters, 1886–93, in the Selborne papers at the Bodleian Library, and correspondence, 1882–1922, in the Bryce Collection, also in the Bodleian. Letters to J. H. Bernard, 1910–20, are in the British Library (Add. MS 52781), which library also has his correspondence with Macmillans, (Add. MSS 55084–5). Correspondence, 1894–1919, can also be found in the St Loe Strachey collection in the House of Lords Record Office.

DICKINSON, Goldsworthy Lowes (1862–1932)

Humanist, historian, philosopher and internationalist. Fellow of King's College, Cambridge. Author of works on French History, Greek civilization, international relations etc. Advocate of a League of Nations during World War I.

King's College Library, Cambridge, has Lowes Dickinson's papers. These include some correspondence from and to him; papers read at societies; articles; travel diaries; dialogues; dramatic works; and poems. There is also the typescript of his autobiography, 'Recollections', with autograph drafts of some sections. This was published as *The Autobiography of Goldsworthy Lowes Dickinson*, ed. Sir Dennis Proctor (1973). His correspondence with friends and colleagues such as J. M. Keynes, E. M. Forster, Clive and Vanessa Bell, C. R. Ashbee, N. Wedd and Roger Fry is well represented in collections at King's. Further correspondence can be found in the Edward Carpenter Collection, Sheffield City Libraries; the Marvin collection at the Bodleian Library, Oxford; the Sir Norman Angell collection at Ball State University; the Kingsley Martin papers at Sussex University Library. A few notes and press cuttings are in BLPES.

DIGBY, William (1849–1904)

Businessman and journalist. Journalist in Ceylon, 1871–6. Editor, *Madras Times*, 1877–9; *Liverpool and Southport Daily News*, 1880; *Western Daily Mercury*, 1880–2. Secretary, National Liberal Club from its foundation in 1882 to 1887. Founder and director, Indian Political Agency, 1887–92. Editor, *India*, 1890–2. Merchant and agent in India. 1888–1904.

The India Office Library has a collection of letters, papers and newspaper cuttings, 1888–92. The papers relate chiefly to Dadabhai Naoroji, consisting of letters from him to Digby about his candidature for Central Finsbury.

DILKE, Lady
Emily (Emilia) Francis Strong (1840–1904)

Trade unionist and art historian. Active in the Women's Protective and Provident League, she was on its committee from 1887, and later President.

The Library of the Trades Union Congress has relevant material, including her trade union notebook, records of the WPPL, later the Women's Trade Union League, and the Gertrude Tuckwell Collection (Gertrude Tuckwell was her niece and colleague). Records at the TUC are briefly described in *Sources* Vol. 1, p: 285. Some correspondence with Mark Pattison (her first husband) is in the British Library (Add. MS 44886) and in the Bodleian Library, Oxford (MS Patt 140, and MS Patt 139). Papers of Sir Charles Dilke, Bt (her second husband) are in the British Library (Add. MSS 43874–967, 49385–455); diaries, dating from the 1880s, are in Birmingham University Library. Churchill College, Cambridge, has nine boxes of family papers and correspondence.

The *Dictionary of Labour Biography* Vol. III, pp. 63–7, has a note on her career.

DOBB, Maurice Herbert (1900–76)

Economist. Lecturer and Fellow of Trinity College, Cambridge. Reader in Economics, Cambridge University.

Enquiries should be directed to the archivist, Trinity College, Cambridge, who will have current information.

DONALD, Sir Robert (1861–1933)

Journalist and newspaper proprietor. Founder and proprietor, *Municipal Journal*, 1893, and *Municipal Yearbook*. Editor, *Daily Chronicle*, 1902–18. Chairman and Managing Director, Everyman Publishing Co. Ltd. President, Institute of Journalists, 1913. Chairman, Empire Press Union, 1915–26. Director at the Ministry of Information, World War I. Chairman of Committee on Imperial Wireless Telegraphy, and Committee on Organisation of Imperial Wireless Services, 1924.

A collection of papers, assembled by Donald's biographer, H. A. Taylor, and presented by him to the Beaverbrook Library, is now housed in the House of Lords Record Office. The material is arranged according to subject matter in five folders, and consists of certain correspondence, articles written by or about Donald, and press cuttings. Folder 1, 1899–1933, contains a printed copy of an address by Donald to the West Scotland area of the Institute of Journalists, 1913; a few personal letters; an article by him on 'Labour and Liberalism', and various press cuttings about him. Folder 2, 1885–1933, contains material relating to Donald's association with the *Daily Chronicle*, including an account of his early journalistic work, and a long account by Donald of the negotiations concerning the control of the *Daily Chronicle* which led to his resignation in 1918. Also in this folder are some relevant press cuttings. Folder 3, 1893–8, contains articles and some notes concerning the establishment of the *Municipal Journal*, and some forty letters. Folder 4, 1908–17 contains some 30 letters, chiefly from Admiral Lord Fisher and mainly concerning the conduct of World War I. Folder 5, 1912–17, again concerns Lord Fisher, and includes copies of various memoranda and papers he sent to the Prime Minister and Winston Churchill about the Royal Navy, a copy of Churchill's evidence before the Dardanelles Commission, and a few copies of Fisher's correspondence with Lloyd George and others on this theme.

Correspondence, 1910–15, 1930–2, between Donald and W. H. Dawson concerning articles is available in the Dawson papers (NRA List 14020). Two letters plus documents relating to the cost of a proposed Labour newspaper can be found in the Labour Party archives (ref. LP/NEW/06/13–16).

DOTT, George

Scottish Nationalist.

The National Library of Scotland has various papers and correspondence (Acc. 5542 and Acc. 5927). The material includes some letters; documents, statements, and correspondence on behalf of the Forth Road Bridge Promotion Committee, 1936–7; printed items relating to the

National Party of Scotland, 1932–3, including statements, memoranda, some official correspondence and minutes, etc.; miscellaneous printed and manuscript items relating to Scotland and the Scottish; 13 issues of an information sheet provided by the National Party; a minute book, 1926–31, of the Scottish National Movement; press cuttings, 1928–58; and various pamphlets and books.

DRAGE, Geoffrey (1860–1955)

Conservative politician, publicist and writer. Secretary of the Royal Commission on Labour, 1891–4. M.P. (Con.) Derby, 1895–1900. President, Central Poor Law Conference, 1906. President, National Conference on Sea Training, 1910–14. Alderman, London County Council, 1910–19. Worked for War Office Military Intelligence Section, 1916. Vice President, Royal Statistical Society, 1916–18. Chairman, Finance Committee, Organisation for the Maintenance of Supplies, 1925–6. Author of works on Labour issues and trade unions, poverty, statistics and foreign issues.

Geoffrey Drage's papers are preserved at Christ Church, Oxford. They cover the wide range of his interests. Material relating to the Royal Commission on Labour dates from 1891, and includes documents dealing with staff matters as well as policy issues. Other aspects of the Labour question are also represented by papers on working-class housing, women's trade unions, public assistance, etc. A number of the documents relate to external affairs. Some fifteen packets of correspondence relating chiefly to Germany, Austria and Russia have been preserved. Imperial affairs are also represented, and there are letters from Sir Ernest Satow concerning the Russo-Japanese War. Another group of papers concerns the origins of the Boer War, and includes letters from Lord Windsor, President of the Imperial South African Association, and 16 letters from Miss Ethel Newman Thomas, daughter of the Sergeant at Arms in the Cape Parliament.

A number of papers relates to Germany, and particularly German internal politics during the 1920s. These include 55 letters from Ellis Loring Dresel, covering the period 1890–1925, and his years in Berne and Berlin during World War I and the subsequent peace negotiations. A final group of papers contains miscellaneous material, ranging from German propaganda during World War I to naval affairs. There are some 20 letters from Hankey, and 23 letters from Frank Pember, Warden of All Souls. In addition, there are three large volumes of press cuttings.

DRYSDALE, Charles Vickery (1874–1961)

Neo-Malthusian and scientist. Hon. Secretary, and later President, of the Malthusian League, and editor of its journal. President, International Neo-Malthusian Conferences, 1921, 1925. Director of Scientific Research, Admiralty, 1929–34.

A number of Drysdale's working papers are preserved at BLPES. The collection consists largely of documents, notes, drafts, etc., relating to Drysdale's publications on behalf of the Malthusian League and its advocacy of birth control. Two boxes contain the manuscript, two copies of the typescript and various drafts for incomplete chapters of *A Religion of Humanity*. Another box has material relating to the Royal Commission on Population, including evidence, rough diagrams and notes; also a typescript of *To All Who Desire Permanent Peace and Prosperity*, and the manuscript and typescript of *The Determination of Longevity*. Three folders have material concerning *The Malthusian Doctrine and the Criterion of Overpopulation*, and another file relates to Bessie Drysdale's *Wage Earners, Save Yourselves*. Another five folders contain drafts and notes for articles. A final box of material contains notes and a few letters relating to 'Vital Statistics', a file of Supplements to *The Malthusian* and various statistics.

Rosanner Ledbetter, *History of the Malthusian League 1877–1927* (Ohio State U.P., 1976) makes use of manuscript sources.

DUGDALE, Blanche Elizabeth Campbell
Mrs Edgar T. S. Dugdale (d. 1948)

Prominent supporter of Zionist aspirations. Head of the Intelligence Department, League of Nations Union, 1920–8. Member of British Delegation to the League of Nations Assembly, 1932. Biographer of her uncle, A. J. Balfour.

Her diaries are housed in the Weizmann Archives, Rehovot, Israel. They have been published, edited by Norman Rose.

DURBIN, Evan Frank Mottram (1906–48)

Socialist writer and politician. Senior Lecturer in Economics, London School of Economics. Joined the Economic Section of the War Cabinet Secretariat, 1940; Personal Assistant to the Deputy Prime Minister from 1942. M.P. (Lab) Edmonton from 1945. Parliamentary Secretary, Ministry of Works, from 1947.

Papers, c/o Mrs. A. M. Durbin (widow), 2 Eldon Grove, London NW3 5PS, include correspondence, manuscript and typescript drafts, diaries, lecture notes etc. Durbin's school days and period in university are reflected in material on Taunton School, in correspondence with his school friends, including Henry Phelps Brown, in correspondence and other papers on his undergraduate career; and in his journal, kept until 1932. The journal also has material on the general strike, his sister's marriage and an SCM conference. There is also a personal diary, 1918–19. There are typescript drafts of his early works, including papers on philosophy and economics; a typescript of parts of *Purchasing Power and Trade Depression* (with bibliographies and some notes); and notes for, reviews of, and correspondence relating to his other books. There is an interesting grouping of correspondence concerning his books, and especially *The Politics of Democratic Socialism*. Correspondents include Attlee, Beatrice Webb, Ivor Thomas, W. B. Forshaw, H. B. Lees Smith, Robert Fraser, E. D. Simon, Malcolm Murray, J. A. Spender, John Strachey, Arthur Greenwood, Hugh Dalton, D. R. Davies, Emmeline Cohn, Lance Beale, Christopher Yorke, W. E. Williams, L. G. Robinson, J. L. Hammond, D. J. Guy, R. H. Tawney and H. J. Laski. There is also material on *Personal Aggressiveness and War*, with his co-author John Bowlby. Other papers reflect his teaching career, and include lectures on socialism, economics and political theory. There is correspondence with colleagues and co-thinkers, such as Roy Harrod, R. G. Hawtrey, Dennis Robertson and Geoffrey Crowther; and material on his Rockefeller Research Project. Other material relates to his wartime career in the Cabinet Office, his period as an M.P. and in Government office. Correspondents here include Hugh Dalton, Attlee, Gaitskell, Tawney, Christopher Mayhew, Cripps, Reginald Bassett and John Bowlby. Additionally, there are personal papers, including personal account books, and family correspondence.

DURHAM, Mary Edith (1863–1944)

Balkan traveller and observer.

Sketches, photographs, journals, notebooks and paintings are in the possession of the Royal Anthropological Institute.

DUTT, (Rajani) Palme (1896–1974)

Communist journalist and theorist. Secretary, International Section, Labour Research Department, 1919–22. Chairman, Communist Party's Reorganisation Commission, 1922. Editor, *Labour Monthly* from 1921; *Workers' Weekly*, 1922–4; *Daily Worker*, 1936–8. Executive Committee Member, Communist Party, 1922–65. Author of works on socialism, imperialism, India etc.

The British Library, Department of Printed Books, has relevant papers (ref. Cup 1262 K.1/6). These include six volumes of offprints of his Notes of the Month, published in *Labour Weekly*, 1921–73; 26 volumes of typescript letters and articles, 1922–70; typescript memoranda and reports, 1934–50, chiefly relating to the policy of the CPGB; eight volumes of press cuttings, 1921–73, collected by Palme Dutt, largely on political issues; and pamphlets.

Other papers are believed to remain with the literary executor.

EAGAR, Waldo McGillycuddy (1884–1966)

Liberal publicist. Secretary, Garden Cities and Town Planning Association, 1921–3; Secretary, Liberal Land Enquiry, 1923–7; Liberal Industrial Inquiry, 1926–8. General Secretary, Land and Nation League, 1926–7. Editor, *The Boy*, 1927–43. Secretary-General, National Institute for the Blind, 1928–49.

Eagar's papers are preserved in the Library of the Reform Club. Much of the material emanates from Eagar's work in the 1920s for the Liberal Party. The collection includes minutes, and summaries of meetings, of the Rural Policy Committee, convened by Lloyd George from June 1923 to 1926, together with reports of conferences held at Lloyd George's home, August and Sept 1924, and a draft of *The Land and The Nation*, 1925, with annotations by Lloyd George, Eagar and others; minutes of the Land Committee, Urban Section, Dec. 1924 to Jan 1926; a file of papers (1925–6) relating to a conference held by the National Liberal Federation concerning the Land Enquiry; and transcripts of the proceedings of this conference, 17–19 Feb 1926. There are also papers relating to the Land and Nation League, Emergency Committee, and its meetings in March 1926. Part of the collection relates to the Liberal Industrial Inquiry, including various lists of committees and their members (1926–7), a draft preface by Asquith to *England's Industrial Future* (later deleted from the final version); and a file of miscellaneous papers, including memoranda on the establishment of an enquiry into industry, with notes by Lloyd George and others, and correspondence Aug–Sep 1927. Another file contains press cuttings about Lloyd George, 1910, 1913, 1925–33, 1945, 1959, 1963; miscellaneous notes and doodles by Lloyd George; and various pieces of Eagar correspondence, 1924–59, including correspondence with Tom Jones about the latter's biography of Lloyd George. There is also a miscellaneous collection of books and pamphlets preserved in the library.

The Royal National Institute for the Blind knows of no other personal papers.

EBBUTT, Norman (1894–1968)

Journalist. Second correspondent in Paris, Russia and Finland, 1911–13. Served on *The Times*, 1914, and from 1919. Chief correspondent in Berlin, 1927–37.

The archives of *The Times* has some relevant items, including management records and some correspondence and memoranda.

EDER, Montague David (d. 1936)

Author and psychiatrist. Zionist publicist. Member of the Socialist League, 1889; of the Independent Labour Party and Fabian Society; and of the Council of the Jewish Territorial Organization, 1905. Editor, *School Hygiene*, 1910–15; on the editorial staff of the *New Age*, 1907–25. Sat on the Zionist Commission, Palestine, 1918, on the Executive of the Zionist organisation, Jerusalem and London, until 1929. President of the Zionist Federation of Great Britain and Ireland, 1931–6. Director of the Psychoanalytical Institute. A governor of the Hebrew University, Jerusalem.

Papers can be found in the Central Zionist Archives, Jerusalem, (ref. 11/31). Further details of these will eventually be made available by the British Academy's Anglo-Palestinian Archives Project.

EDGEWORTH, Francis Ysidro (1845–1926)

Economist. Tooke Professor of Political Economy, King's College, London. Professor of Political Economy, Oxford. President of the Royal Statistical Society. Editor, *Economic Journal*.

Sturges, *Economists' Papers*, pp. 27–8, cites a collection of papers in the care of Dr D. E. Butler, Nuffield College, Oxford, including letters, 1875–1916 (mainly testimonials and congratulations); offprints of reviews on economics; and some press cuttings. Other letters can be found in the Bickerdike, Cannan, Keynes and Seligman Collections.

EDWARDS, Joseph (d. 1946)

Journalist. Editor of the *Labour Annual* and *Reformers' Yearbook*.

Nuffield College, Oxford, has one box of papers, containing chiefly proofs of articles from the *Labour Annual* and correspondence relating to the purchase of pamphlets and offprints.

EINZIG, Paul (1897–1973)

Journalist and economist. Paris correspondent of the *Financial News*, 1921. Foreign editor, 1923; political correspondent, 1939–45. Political correspondent, *Financial Times*, 1945–56. London correspondent of the *Commercial and Financial Chronicle*, New York, from 1945.

The papers of Paul Einzig have been deposited in the library of Churchill College, Cambridge. They consist of 132 files of correspondence and papers, covering the various aspects of his career, together with several manuscripts of his books. Of particular interest is the pre-war correspondence which includes letters from J. M. Keynes and Brendan Bracken, and concerns German penetration into the Danubian and Balkan states. Also of interest is the section covering his career with the *Financial Times*, which contains considerable material from Bracken.

ELLIS, (Henry) Havelock (1859–1939)

Psychologist and man of letters. Author of numerous works on sex psychology, marriage, men and women, art, literature, philosophy, travel. Editor, Contemporary Science series of books. A founder member of the Fellowship of the New Life, 1883. Member of the Committee, Eugenics Education Society. Hon. President, World Congress for Sexual Reform.

The University of Texas at Austin has a collection of Ellis correspondence and papers. Correspondents include J. A. Symonds, Arthur Symons, Olive Schreiner, Margaret Hinton, Emma Goldman, Radclyffe Hall, Edward Carpenter, J. W. Robertson Scott, Henry Salt, Winifred and A. E. Coppard, Clifford Bax, and 'John Gawsworth' (T. I. F. Armstrong). Yale University Library has a collection of 240 letters and three boxes of writings, 1871–1939. Correspondents include Thomas Hardy, Herbert Spencer, Rebecca West, Edmund Gosse and Sigmund Freud. There is further Ellis correspondence in the Malinowski papers, also at Yale. The Library of the University of California at Los Angeles has ten volumes of papers including typescript and annotated copies of published works. Amongst these is the original typescript of *Sex and Marriage*, with earlier chapters revised in Ellis's hand, and later chapters corrected by François Delisle, and including four chapters which were not published in the final work; 1st and 4th editions of *Man and Woman* with corrections; a work on genius by Lombroso which Ellis translated; marginal notes and corrections to Ellis's chapter in *The New Generation* (ed. V. F. Calverton and S. D. Schmalhausen, 1930); and proofs of an unpublished work on marriage law reform, with Ellis's correction notes.

The Menninger Foundation, Topeka, Kansas, has some 23 letters and 16 manuscripts or typescripts of Ellis's. Most of the letters relate to various publications, but there is a 36-page manuscript on 'Eleanor Marx', drafts of articles and reviews (e.g. on Freud) and drafts of sections of various books. Some 164 items, 1925–37, are in the Indiana University Library, and New York Public Library has a few items, several in an Ellis file, with some letters in the Mencken and Calverton collections. Fourteen letters from Ellis are in Boston Public Library, Mass.

Much Ellis material can be found in the papers of his friends and colleagues. The Edward Carpenter collection in Sheffield Public Library has correspondence from the 1880s, together with letters from his wife, Edith Ellis. There is some correspondence in the J. A. Symonds papers in the University of Bristol Library. The Emma Goldman collection at the International Institute of Social History has some correspondence, 1920s. Letters to G. B. Shaw, 1888, are in the British Library (Add. MS 50533), and the British Library also has the Society of Authors collection which contains correspondence, and material concerning Ellis's estate (Add. MSS 56701–2).

Havelock Ellis is the chief correspondent to be found in the papers of Jane Burr, a feminist journalist, housed in Smith College Library, Northampton, Mass. The collection has material relating to personal matters, sex reform, the position of women in marriage, divorce and birth control.

Correspondence can also be found in the John Gould Fletcher collection in the University of Arkansas Library; and correspondence with John Gawsworth is in Iowa University Library. The Norman Haire collection at the University of Sydney, Australia contains further correspondence. Letters also survive in the Galton papers at University College, London, and in the Malinowski papers at BLPES and in Yale University Library.

Phyllis Grosskurth is preparing an authorised biography of Ellis, and has access to all papers in family hands.

ELLIS, Thomas Iorworth (1899–1970)

Educationalist and publicist for the Welsh language and culture. Hon. Secretary, Undeb Cymru Fydd (New Wales Union), 1941–66.

Mrs Mary Ellis (widow) has a number of unsorted papers and correspondence which are not presently available for research purposes. Papers concerning T. I. Ellis's public activities, particularly his work for Undeb Cymru Fydd, are deposited in the National Library of Wales and are described in *Sources* Vol. 1, p. 267. The papers of Ellis's father, T. E. Ellis, the Liberal politician, are also in the National Library of Wales.

ELMY, Elizabeth C. Wolstenholme (fl. 1865–1920)

Feminist.

The British Library has seven volumes of letters and papers (Add. MSS 47449–55). These largely consist of letters concerning the organisation of the suffrage movement, and in particular material concerning the Women's Franchise League and the Women's Emancipation Union, exchanged between Mrs Elmy and Mrs Harriet McIlquham, 1889–1914.

ELTON, 1st B
Godfrey Elton (1892–1973)

Writer. Fellow of The Queen's College, Oxford, and lecturer in Modern History, 1919–39. Labour Parliamentary candidate, 1924 and 1929. Hon. Political Secretary, National Labour Committee, 1932. Editor, the *News Letter*, 1932–8. General Secretary, Rhodes Trust, 1939–59.

Shortly before his death Lord Elton wrote that he had a considerable number of personal diaries, letters from J. R. MacDonald and other prominent men and women, and other documents. It was his intention to leave these to his heirs.

ENSOR, Sir Robert Charles Kirkwood (1877–1958)

Historian, journalist and author. Leader-writer for *Manchester Guardian*, 1902–4; *Daily News*, 1909–11; *Daily Chronicle*, 1912–30. Member of Fabian Society. Lecturer, London School of Economics, 1931–2. Deputy for Gladstone Professor of Political Theory and Institutions, Oxford, 1933, 1940–4. Research Fellow, Corpus Christi College, Oxford, 1937–46. Member London County Council, 1910–13. Wrote under the pseudonym, 'Scrutator' for *Sunday Times*, 1940–53.

A collection of papers has been deposited by Ensor's family in the library of Corpus Christi College, Oxford. The whole range of Ensor's activities and interests is represented. A collection of letters, dating from 1898, and arranged chronologically, includes correspondence from Ben Tillett, Charles Dilke, the Webbs, Beveridge, George Lansbury, Bruce Glasier, Hubert Bland, Clifford Allen, H. N. Brailsford, Ramsay MacDonald, L. T. Hobhouse, J. A. Hobson and many others. A series of pocket diaries cover the period 1902–55, and in addition there are additional manuscript diaries for the years 1901, 1904. A number of personal papers cover a range of interests, from ornithology (Ensor's hobby), to his Winchester and Oxford essays and examination papers, a number of literary essays, guidebooks, etc. There are in addition a number of press cuttings, relating both to Ensor himself (obituary notices) and to general subjects. There is a substantial group of papers relating to foreign affairs, including material on World War I and papers of the Labour Party International Advisory Committee from 1919. Manuscripts and typescripts also cover various aspects of Home Affairs. A number of manuscripts, typescripts and cuttings cover Ensor's interests in political thought, and the arts and literature. Additionally, reports of various organisations in which Ensor was interested are retained. Copies of leaders by Ensor in the *Manchester Guardian*, the *Speaker*, the *Daily News* and *Daily Chronicle* also survive. A substantial part of the collection reflects Ensor's interest in the development of the socialist movement. This includes manuscript notes for lectures by Ensor; cuttings on the Labour and Socialist Movements; reports, circulars and papers relating to the Fabian Society; some material on the Social Democratic Federation; papers relating to the Independent Labour Party; reports, circulars, etc., of the Labour Party; and a great deal of miscellaneous material relating to the growth of the Labour movement in London. Other papers cover Ensor's work on the London County Council, 1910–13.

Letters from Ensor can be found in the Fabian Society archive in the Library of Nuffield College, Oxford.

ESCOTT, Thomas Hay Sweet (1844–1924)

Journalist and author. Lecturer in Logic, King's College, London; Deputy Professor of Classical Literature, 1866–73. Chief article writer for the *Standard* from 1866. Editor, *Fortnightly Review*, 1882–6.

A collection of papers is located in the British Library (Add. MSS 58774–801). It consists of over 2200 letters, and a number of enclosures, addressed to Escott, chiefly with regard to his editorship of the *Fortnightly Review*, but also including a small group of correspondence relating to the British School in Athens. There are also letters of a family nature, chiefly concerning the education of his children. The first letters date from 1879 and relate to the reception of the first edition of his book, *England, Its People, Polity and Pursuits*. Correspondents include prominent politicians, literary figures, military men, commentators on colonial and domestic current affairs, including a number of Frenchmen, such as Camille Barrère and Paul Best. One of the largest and most important groups of correspondence is that of Joseph Chamberlain, and relates in particular to the publication of the articles which eventually became *The Radical Programme*.Other correspondents include the 1st Marquess of Aberdeen, James Tynte Agg-Gardner, Grant Allen, Sir Arthur Arnold, Sir Edwin Arnold, Matthew Arnold, Arnold Forster, Alfred Austin, Lord Balfour of Burleigh, William Ballantine, Viscount Barrington, Lord Battersea, George Bentley, Lord Charles Beresford, J. S. Blackie, W. S. Blunt, T. G. Bowles, Sir Henry Brackenbury, Lord Brassey, John Bright, G. C. Brodrick, Oscar Browning, Robert Browning, Viscount Bryce, G. E. Buckle, William Burdett-Coutts, Sir Francis Burnand, Lord Burnham, 5th Earl Cadogan, 4th Earl Carnarvon, Lord Carnock, Thomas Catling, Viscount Chaplin, Thomas Chenery, Lord Randolph Churchill, Leonard Courtney, 1st Marquess of Dufferin and Ava, Lord Dunraven, Rev. Hay Sweet Escott (father), 1st Lord Farnborough (Sir T. Erskine May), Henry Fawcett, E. A. Freeman, J. H. Froude, Sir Francis Galton, Henry George, 1st Viscount Goschen, 2nd Earl Granville, Sir W. H. Gregory, Sir L. H. Griffin, A. G. F. Griffiths, Frederic Harrison, Sir Henry Irving, Ismail Pasha, Sir R. C. Jebb, Sir James Knowles, Henry Labouchère, S. Laing, Lord Lansdowne, Sir Wilfrid Lawson, Sir Louis Mallet, W. H. Mallock, Duchess of Marlborough, 8th Duke of Marlborough, F. Max-Muller, George Meredith, Lady Molesworth, John Morley, W. H. Mudford, A. J. Mundella, 1st Earl of Northbrook, Lawrence Oliphant, Violet Paget (Vernon Lee), Charles Kegan Paul, Sir Robert Peel, Sir F. Pollock, Lady Priestley, H. C. Raikes, 11th Baron Reay, 1st Baron Rothschild, 3rd Marquess of Salisbury, Francis Schnadhorst, Sir J. R. Seeley, Thomas Sexton, Goldwin Smith, Hon. Philip Stanhope, Sir H. M. Stanley, W. T. Stead, E. S. Talbot, Sir Richard Temple, W. T. M. Torrens, Sir G. O. Trevelyan, G. S. Venables, S. H. Walpole, Rev. Edmond Warre, 2nd Duke of Wellington, Oscar Wilde, Charles Williams, Sir C. R. Rivers, Sir C. W. Wilson, Sir Henry Drummond Wolff, Lord Wolseley and E. H. Yates.

Escott's letters to Wolseley, 1883–5, are in Hove Public Library, and his letters to Joseph Chamberlain are in Birmingham University Library.

EVANS, Sir (Evan) Vincent (1851–1934)

Welsh administrator and journalist. Secretary, National Eisteddfod Association, 1881–1934.

Correspondence relating to Welsh institutions and affairs is in the National Library of Wales.

EVANS, Griffith Ivor (1889–1966)

Medical doctor. Welsh Nationalist.

The National Library of Wales has papers, 1946–65, chiefly relating to the Welsh Economic Development Association Ltd, its operating subsidiary, Welsh Ventures Assistance Association Ltd, and Manton Association Ltd, including files of correspondence, accounts and printed matter.

EVANS, Howard (1839–1915)

Editor of the *Arbitrator*, organ of the International Arbitration League (of which he was Chairman). Chairman, London Congregational Union, 1909.

Some items relating to the International Arbitration League are with the Mondcivitan Republic, 27 Delancey Street, London NW1.

EVANS, Thomas Philip Conwell

Academic

A small collection of papers is in the care of Mr Martin Gilbert, and will in due course be given to the Bodleian Library, Oxford.

EVANS, Stanley George (1912–65)

Churchman and Christian Socialist. Parish Priest. University of Oxford Extra-Mural Lecturer. Canon Residentiary and Chancellor of Southwark Cathedral from 1960.

A collection of papers has been given to Hull University Library, and includes files of material on Canon Evans' wide range of interests, scrapbooks, notebooks, sermons and miscellaneous material. The files date from 1929 to his death, and cover personal matters (e.g. ordination, extra-mural lectures, 1929–36); church affairs; and other more political matters. Amongst the latter are files relating to the Thurloe Square Anti-Fascist demonstration, 1936, the International Peace Campaign, 1937–41, Industrial Christian Fellowship, 1937–44, and the German Church Struggle, 1937–8, Active Christian Democrats, 1939–40, the People's Convention, 1940–2, relations with the Soviet Union, Democracy in Greece, the Society of Socialist Clergy and Ministers, 1946–58, the British Peace Committee, the Christian Peace Group, the Movement for Colonial Freedom, the Christian Socialist Movement, 1961–5, and the Campaign for Nuclear Disarmament. The scrapbooks again cover a range of interests. One series, relating mainly to personal and local affairs, but also containing cuttings and items of interest on a wide variety of topics, dates from 1938. Other scrapbooks cover international affairs, particularly Russia and other Communist countries, and the position of the Church there (1940–62); the parish of Holy Trinity with St Philip, Dalston (1955–60); the Campaign for Nuclear Disarmament from 1958; and other miscellaneous topics. The diaries are fragmentary, and contain little detail. They date from c. 1937 to 1956. The notebooks cover a wide range of topics, particularly Christian Sociology, the Church and Politics, Economics and Marxism. The Evans collection also includes files and notes, texts, scripts of talks, essays, articles and longer works, dating from 1931; files of notes for sermons dating from 1934; and miscellaneous leaflets, pamphlets, reports, speeches, etc.; miscellaneous correspondence, 1940–65; broadcast scripts, 1963–5; and items relating to Dr Hewlett Johnson, 1952–7.

FARREN, Sir William Scott (1892–1970)

Aeronautical engineer. Deputy Director of Scientific Research, Air Ministry, 1937–9. Deputy Director, Research and Development, Aircraft, Air Ministry, and Ministry of Aircraft Production, 1939–40; Director of Technical Development, 1940–1. Director, Royal Aircraft Establishment, 1941–6.

Correspondence and papers are in Churchill College, Cambridge.

FAWCETT, Dame Millicent (1847–1929)

Leader of Women's Suffrage campaign. President, National Union of Women's Suffrage Societies, 1897–1918. Leader of Ladies' Commission of Inquiry into Boer War concentration camps.

Mrs Fawcett's collection of letters, largely addressed to her from feminists, politicians, writers, etc., forms the basis of the Fawcett Library autograph collection. The Fawcett Library also has her Boer War concentration camp inquiry notebook, and her interleaved copy of the resulting Commission Report (including some correspondence, printed ephemera and photographs). The Fawcett Library has other relevant material relating to the NUWSS, which is briefly described, together with other material on women's suffrage campaigns, in various libraries, in *Sources* Vol. 1, pp. 279–85. Manchester Central Library in particular has a substantial collection, a large part of which consists of papers held by Dame Millicent. These include in-correspondence, notes, her analyses of Parliamentary divisions, notes for speeches, correspondence and papers of the NUWSS, together with material (correspondence, papers, press cuttings) on the education, employment and the welfare of women, miscellaneous other papers relating to women, and papers on World War I (including material on the drink problem, the Parliamentary War Savings Committee, the British Women's Patriotic League). Some letters to Mme Bodichon are at Girton College, Cambridge, while Camden Public Libraries have several letters (kept at the Holborn Library) from Dame Millicent to various correspondents during the period 1880–1920, and largely of autograph interest.

FAY, Charles Ryle (1884–1961)

Economic historian. Professor of Economic History, University of Toronto, 1921–30. Reader in Economic History, Cambridge University, from 1930.

The University of Toronto Library has notes by Fay, and copies of documents, letters and photographs concerning his work *Adam Smith and the Scotland of his Times* and to do with Charles Townshend and David Hume. There is a typescript of Fay's unpublished work, 'Grenfell and the Moravian Mission to the Labrador', with a chapter on epidemic disease. There is correspondence with Vincent Wheeler Bladen and others.

Other papers are held in the Public Record Office of Northern Ireland.

FENBY, Charles (1905–74)

Journalist. On the editorial staff of the *Westminster Gazette*, 1926; *Daily News*, 1927. Helped found the *Oxford Mail*, 1928, and editor until 1940. Assistant editor, *Picture Post*, from 1940. Editor, *Leader Magazine*, 1944–8. Editor of the *Birmingham Gazette* from 1948; editor in chief, 1953–7. Editorial Director, Westminster Press Ltd, from 1957. Chairman, British Committee of the International Press Institute, and the Commonwealth Press Union.

The Modern Records Centre, University of Warwick Library, has a small grouping of material. Few papers relate directly to his journalistic career, and the chief portion of the material relates to his study of Oxford City politics and society in the early part of the century, *The Other Oxford* (1970). Papers relating to this include autobiographical drafts by Frank Gray, M.P. for Oxford, 1922–4 (see *Sources* Vol. 3, p. 183) which Fenby drew on. A few items concern his book *Anatomy of Oxford*, compiled by Fenby with C. Day Lewis in 1938. Other material includes some papers deriving from Fenby's work with the Commonwealth Press Union and the International Press Institute; the texts of articles and reviews by him, and a small group of material relating to his work on W. T. Stead.

FERGUSON, Allan (1880–1951)

Scientist. Editor, *The Philosophical Magazine*. Advisory editor, *Nature*, 1939–40. Assistant Professor of Physics, Queen Mary College, London. General Secretary, British Association, 1936–46. President, Hertford Divisional Liberal Association.

Relevant material can be found with the History and Social Studies of Science Division, Sussex University.

FEUCHTWANGER, Ludwig (1885–1947)

Anglo-German publisher. Editor and author.

The Leo Baeck Institute, New York, has papers, including correspondence with friends and business associates; manuscripts of lectures on the history of the Jews from the Middle Ages, and of plans to solve the refugee problem after World War II, articles, poems and short stories sent to him; circular letters relating to religious aspects of World War I; 37 sermons, 1934–8, by various rabbis; and articles.

FIGGIS, John Neville (1866–1919)

Historian, theologian and political theorist. Curate of Kettering, 1894–5; Great St Mary's Cambridge, 1895–8. Chaplain of Pembroke College, 1898–1900. Member of the Community of the Resurrection from 1909. Author of *Divine Right of Kings*, *Churches in the Modern State*, contributor to the *Cambridge Modern History*, etc.

Figgis's papers, formerly housed in the Community of the Resurrection, are now deposited in the Borthwick Institute of Historical Research, York. The material includes correspondence, and personal papers, lecture notes and notebooks. The correspondence includes letters from and relating to Lord Acton from the 1890s, consisting of letters to Figgis, encouraging his work, inviting him to contribute to the *Cambridge Modern History* and letters from F. A. Gasquet to Figgis concerning the publication of Acton's letters. Other correspondence includes letters from Bishop Creighton, 1889–95, and letters from Figgis's brother concerning his health. The lectures and sermons are chiefly on religious topics, and illustrate the range of Figgis's theological preoccupations. The notebooks again cover a range of subjects, and include drafts, articles and lectures on, among others, G. K. Chesterton, A. E. Housman, St Thomas Aquinas, William of Ockham, Marsilius of Padua, Dr Johnson, Bergson, Nietzsche, the Church of England, Constitutional History, Fundamental Christian concepts, notes on the relationship of Church and State, and Divine Office

FINERTY, John F. (1885–1967)

Irish-American lawyer and friend of Eamon de Valera.

Correspondence with many of the Irish Republicans, especially in the 1920s, as well as assorted documents, minutes of meetings, speeches, legal papers, clippings, photos and mementoes, are housed in the Library of the University of Michigan, Ann Arbor.

FISHER OF LAMBETH, Baron
Geoffrey Francis Fisher (1887–1972)

Ecclesiastic. Priest from 1913. Headmaster of Repton School, 1914–32. Bishop of Chester, 1932–9. Bishop of London, 1939–45. Archbishop of Canterbury, 1945–61.

Lambeth Palace Library has relevant correspondence and other material.

FLANDERS, Allan David (1910–73)

Expert on industrial relations. Senior Lecturer in Industrial Relations, Oxford University, 1949–69. Faculty Fellow, Nuffield College, Oxford, 1964–9. Industrial Relations Adviser to Prices and Incomes Board, 1965–8. Full-time member, Commission on Industrial Relations, 1969–71. Reader in Industrial Relations, Warwick University, from 1971.

Surviving\papers are in the care of his widow, Mrs Anne Marie Flanders and Professor George Bain of the University of Warwick. They include the manuscript of his unfinished 'Theory of Union Growth' together with related material.

FLÜGEL, John Carl (1884–1955)

Psychologist and author. Assistant Professor of Psychology, University College London, 1929–43. Secretary, British Psychological Society, 1911–20, Librarian, 1921–32, President, 1932–5. Secretary, International Psychoanalytical Association, 1920–2. President, Section J, British Association, 1950. Hon. Treasurer, Sex Education Society.

Mr Nicholas Bennett (grandson) states that all the family papers were destroyed after Professor Flügel's death.

FORD, Edmund (d. 1930)

1st Abbot of Downside.

The archives of the English Benedictine Congregation, St Gregory's, Downside, contain a large collection of papers, at present unsorted.

FORSHAW, John Henry (1895–1973)

Architect. Chief Architect, Miners' Welfare Commission, 1926–39. Deputy Architect of London County Council, 1939–41; Architect, 1941–6. Chief Architect and Housing Consultant to Ministry of Health and later of Ministry of Housing and Local Government, 1946–59.

Forshaw's papers are deposited with Liverpool University Archives.

FORSTER, Edward Morgan (1879–1970)

Novelist and critic. Fellow of King's College, Cambridge, 1927–33; Honorary Fellow from 1946.

Forster bequeathed his papers to King's College Library. These include the autograph manuscripts of *Marianne Thornton* and of all his novels except for *Where Angels Fear to Tread* (given to the British Library; Add. MSS 57472–3) and *A Passage to India* (which is in the University of Texas at Austin). Other material includes manuscripts and typescripts of essays, lectures and broadcast talks; his commonplace book; notebooks; letters received by Forster, and letters to members of his family. Further material relating to Forster can be found in other collections at King's College, such as the Charleston, Keynes, Dent and Lowes Dickinson papers, and in 1971 Rosamond Lehmann gave the College a large collection of letters from her friends and fellow-writers, including letters from Forster.

Besides the manuscript of *A Passage to India*, the University of Texas Library, Austin, has certain other relevant material, including letters to Hugh Walpole, 1908–39. Correspondence with the Society of Authors is in the British Library (Add. MS 56704), which also has correspondence with Marie Stopes.

FORTESCUE, Hon Sir John William (1859–1933)

Military historian and author. Librarian at Windsor Castle, 1905–26.

Twenty-six notebooks relating to Fortescue's *History of the British Army* (1899–1929), are in the care of the National Army Museum. Correspondence between Sir John and Lady Fortescue and Sir Sydney Cockerell, 1909–30, is in the British Library (Add. MS 52715), as is correspondence with Macmillans the publishers, 1894–1933 (Add. MSS 55064–5).

FOSTER, Sir (Thomas) Gregory, 1st Bt (1866–1931)

Academic. Professor of English Language and Literature, Bedford College. Secretary, University College London, 1900–4; Provost, 1904–29.

The Library of University College London has some six boxes of correspondence, lecture notes, working papers etc, c. 1887–1914.

FOXWELL, Herbert Somerton (1849–1936)

Economist. Professor of Political Economy, University College London, 1881–1928. President of the Royal Economic Society. Fellow and Director of Economic Studies, St John's College, Cambridge.

Sturges, *Economists' Papers*, pp. 31–3, found that Foxwell's papers, including a large correspondence on economic, bibliographical, personal and other matters, were in private hands, and not available pending the writing of a study of Foxwell. Enquiries should be directed to the Historical Manuscripts Commission.

The University of London Library has various papers, including notes on the Japanese Exchange Markets, and metal and paper currencies, made for him by Juichi Soyeda, 1884–6; letters to R. A. Rye, the Goldsmiths' Librarian, and other officers of the Library, 1903–16; and correspondence with Sir Walter Prideaux of the Goldsmiths' Company, 1906–16. Foxwell's large collection of books and tracts on social and economic matters was purchased by the Goldsmiths' Company in 1901, and presented by them to the University of London Library in 1903.

University College London, has correspondence and testimonials relating to his appointment as Professor there, 1881, in its College correspondence. The Baker Library, Harvard University, has further correspondence, including c. 400 letters to him from various correspondents, and 72 letters to W. R. Scott, 1889–1933, and a few to James Bonar. There are also manuscripts of two lectures given to the City of London, 1894. Some 35 letters, to C. C. Eaton, A. H. Cole and Wallace B. Donham, 1927–32, are also in the Baker Library.

Correspondence can be found in various collections. The Marshall Library, Cambridge, has three letters to H. R. Beeton, 1894; four to Sir George Darwin, 1901–3; eight to C. R. Fay, 1908–26; 23 to J. M. Keynes, 1910–32, and 34 to J. N. Keynes, 1877–1917. Cambridge University Library has letters to Francis John Henry Jenkinson, 1889–1922, and three letters, 1884, to Sedley Taylor. There is correspondence with Edwin Cannan and Graham Wallas at BLPES; with F. Y. Edgeworth; with George Howell, 1892–1906, at the Bishopsgate Institute; with Sir Joseph Larmor, 1893–1923, at St John's College, Cambridge; with E. R. A. Seligman, 1888–1928, in Columbia University Library, New York; and with Sir R. H. I. Palgrave, in private hands. There are 22 letters to Leon Walras, 1882–93, at the Bibliothèque Cantonale et Universitaire, Lausanne, while the Macmillan archive in the British Library has a substantial correspondence, 1885–1920 (Add. MS 55196).

FOYLE, William Alfred (1885–1963)

Bookseller. Managing Director of W. & G. Foyle Ltd. Founder, Right Book Club.

Miss Christina Foyle (daughter), Beeleigh Abbey, Maldon, Essex, states that her father's papers were stolen.

FRANCIS-WILLIAMS, Baron
(Edward) Francis Williams (1903–70)

Author, journalist and broadcaster. Editor, *Daily Herald*, 1936–40. Controller of News and Censorship, Ministry of Information, 1941–5. Adviser on Public Relations to Prime Minister, 1945–7. Regents' Professor, University of California, Berkeley, 1961. Kemper Knapp Visiting Professor, University of Wisconsin, from 1967.

Churchill College, Cambridge, has a collection of letters and manuscripts, in 45 boxes. The collection includes manuscripts, typescripts and material relating to *A Pattern of Rulers* (1965), *The American Invasion* (1962), *The Triple Challenge: The Future of Socialist Britain* (1948),

Nothing so Strange: an autobiography (1970); *Magnificent Journey: The Rise of the Trade Unions, A Prime Minister Remembers* (plus the tapes of his interviews with Attlee) the manuscript of his work on Ernest Bevin, and papers relating to his other various publications, amongst which are copies of his published articles, and reviews of his books. There are also papers on the Advertising Commission; a US Seminar on Freedom and Information; a Czech Film Experiment file; correspondence on a libel action resulting from his autobiography; some papers and cuttings concerning his work on the *Daily Herald*, and many about his work in connection with Fleet Street, including a draft of a lecture on government and the press; and two files concerning the Society of Authors. The collection also includes his files of press cuttings. Amongst the correspondence are letters from Attlee, from a variety of colleagues and friends, and about appointments; correspondence relating to the British Humanist Association, and with the BBC, and letters of congratulations on honours.

FRASER, David Stewart (d. 1953)

Journalist. Correspondent of *The Times* from 1904; covered the Russo-Japanese War; then served in Persia, Mesopotamia and Macedonia, and in Peking, 1912–39; correspondent in Siberia during the allied intervention in Russia, 1918.

The archives of *The Times* contain two boxes of papers. This material includes correspondence, from Peking and elsewhere, on his assignments, chiefly to Wickham Steed of *The Times*, c. 1904–30s, but also to others. This correspondence covers his business arrangements with the paper, but also contains many comments on political and economic circumstances in East Asia. Topics covered include the Russo-Japanese War, World War I, the allied intervention in Siberia, etc. The collection also includes the typescript of a draft for a projected autobiography, and this covers most aspects of his journalistic career.

FRASER, Lovat (1871–1926)

Journalist. Editor, *Times of India*. On staff of *The Times*, London, 1907–22. Chief Literary Adviser and Contributor, *Sunday Pictorial* and *Daily Mirror*.

The archives of *The Times* contain various items, 1907–22, Fraser's correspondence with Lord Hardinge, 1910–13, 1917, is in Cambridge University Library.

FRAZER, Sir James George (1854–1941)

Social anthropologist. Author of *The Golden Bough*, etc. Fellow of Trinity College, Cambridge.

The British Library has Frazer's notebooks, in 55 volumes (Add. MSS 45442–96). Vols I–XL are the 'Unclassified' notebooks, being anthropological extracts and notes, chiefly drawn from printed sources. Much of the contents were published in R. A. Downie (ed.) *Anthologia Anthropologica* (4 vols, 1938–9). Areas covered include America, East Asia, Australia and Oceania. The remainder of the volumes are the 'Classified' notebooks, which are references to printed anthropological sources, with some extracts and notes, arranged by subjects, e.g. marriage customs, classical myths, burial and mourning customs.

Cambridge University Library has a collection of letters to Frazer, and further letters, 1925–8, are in the National Library of Scotland. There is correspondence with Malinowski in Yale University Library; correspondence with Macmillans, 1884–1940, at the British Library (Add. MSS 55134–55), and further correspondence, 1895–1925, is in the Sir Edmund Gosse collection.

FRERE, Walter Howard (1863–1938)

Ecclesiastic and church historian. A founder member of the Anglican monastic order, the

Community of the Resurrection, and its superior, 1902–13, 1916–22. Bishop of Truro, 1923–35.

A substantial collection of papers is included in the Mirfield deposit at the Borthwick Institute of Historical Research, York. The papers reflect the variety of his work and interests, including not only his religious but also his musical interests and work. The papers include various documents arising out of the attempt at Prayer Book Revision, 1927–8; a large body of correspondence relating to the conversations held at Malines on church reunification, 1921–6, and to his work at Mirfield and as a bishop; manuscript notes on church history; notes for sermons, papers and articles; and an interesting corpus of family correspondence.

Papers of Dr Armitage Robinson, at Lambeth Palace Library, contain further material on the Malines conversations.

FRY, Roger Eliot (1866–1934)

Artist and critic. Slade Professor of Fine Art, Cambridge, 1933.

A large collection of his papers, including manuscripts of numerous lectures, articles and broadcast talks, together with some correspondence to and from him, are deposited in King's College Library, Cambridge.

FURNIVALL, Frederick James (1825–1910)

Scholar and editor. Worked in the Christian Socialist Movement and at the Working Men's College. Editor of the *Oxford English Dictionary*.

The British Library has correspondence, 1851–76 (Add. MSS 34813, 43798). They include letters to Furnivall from Elizabeth Gaskell, Charles Kingsley, Harriet Martineau, F. D. Maurice, J. S. Mill and others.

The Library of King's College, London, has papers relating to the *Dictionary*, including memoranda, notes for some of his editions of texts, etc.

The Henry E. Huntington Library, San Marino, California, has almost 1000 items of correspondence, 1843–1910.

FURSE, Dame Katherine (1875–1952)

Director, Women's Royal Naval Service, 1917–19. Director, World Bureau of Girl Guides and Girl Scouts, 1928–38.

Letters and papers are housed in Bristol University Library. The material includes drafts and correspondence relating to *Hearts and pomegranates* (autobiography); various miscellaneous papers; papers concerning the WRNS, the growth of the German Youth Movement, the Girl Guide Movement, Mrs T. H. Green, R. Vaughan Williams and J. A. Symonds; miscellaneous correspondence from a variety of persons, plus correspondence and papers concerning Marion North, Charles Furse and Symonds, amongst others. There is also a collection of photographs. The collection is a substantial one and has not yet been fully catalogued.

FYFE, Henry Hamilton (1869–1951)

Journalist and author. On the staff of *The Times* from 1889. Editor, *Morning Advertiser*, 1902–3; *Daily Mirror*, 1903–7. Dramatic critic, *The World*, 1905–10. Special correspondent for *Daily Mail*, 1907–18. Hon Attaché, British War Mission to USA, 1917. In charge of British propaganda in Germany, July–Nov 1918. Editor, *Daily Herald*, 1922–6. Political writer, *Reynolds News*, 1930–42. President, League against Cruel Sports, 1934–46.

No personal papers have been traced but some correspondence can be found in the Sir Norman Angell collection, Ball State University.

FYFE, Sir William Hamilton (1878–1965)

Academic. Headmaster, Christ's Hospital, 1919–30. Principal and Vice Chancellor, Queen's University, Kingston, Ontario, 1930–6; University of Aberdeen, 1936–48. Chairman, Scottish Advisory Council on Education, 1942–6.

A small collection of papers is preserved in the Douglas Library, Queen's University, Kingston, Ontario. This includes sermons, 1919–38; broadcasts and speeches, 1930–65; correspondence, 1950–2.

GALLAGHER, Frank (fl. 1920–60)

Irish journalist. Editor, *Irish Press*.

Various papers are deposited in the National Library of Ireland. They include *The Four Glorious Years* by David Hogan (Gallagher's pseudonym), with author's corrections and additions; an anonymous letter to Hogan, with a warning of Black and Tan activities, 1920; and miscellaneous letters and papers, many relating to the anti-Partition literature written, or edited, by Gallagher, c. 1918–56.

GALTON, Sir Francis (1822–1911)

Scientist; founder of study of eugenics. Secretary, British Association,1863–8. President, Anthropological Institute, 1885–8. Author of studies on biology and heredity. Inspirer of Eugenics Movement.

A large collection of papers is deposited in the Library of University College London. Amongst material relating to his personal history and that of his family are family papers and correspondence dating from 1612, including various Darwin papers; family books and genealogical tables, personalia etc., correspondence between Francis Galton and his parents, brothers and sisters, 1830–1905, and acquired papers and books. Other material concerns Galton's scientific work. This includes papers in connection with apparatus and instruments, meteorological material; notes and letters concerning *The Reader*, 1864–5; and papers on heredity in man, 1865–1909, including correspondence, Galton's notes, family trees, press cuttings and reviews. The material relates to his books *Hereditary Genius*, *Englishmen of Science, their nature and nurture, Twins* and his study of longevity, etc. A variety of papers relate to the Galton Laboratory and the Eugenics Record Office. These include copies of Galton's will on the endowment of the Laboratory, notes, newspaper articles, draft schedules, and agenda for the Eugenics Record Office, the Laboratory and the Research Fellowship, together with data, notes, etc., collected by Galton. Amongst the related themes covered in notes and papers are anthropology and anthropometry, eugenics, heredity in plants and animals, the Evolution Committee (Animals and Plants) of the Royal Society, pedigree dogs and horses, statistical material, psychometry, photography and portraiture, fingerprints etc. There are miscellaneous scientific papers by Galton, 1853–1907, together with miscellaneous notes, lists and notebooks, including material on discontinuous variation, dispersion of families, and minutes and other papers of the Philosophical Club, 1847–79. There are 66 offprints of Galton's published papers, plus printed matter and a folder labelled 'memoirs by F. Galton Vol. VI', which includes newspaper cuttings and three letters. There are also lists and indexes of Galton's published papers, proof copies of various of his books and notes by Galton from books read. There are also various press cuttings. Correspondence is varied. A letterbook contains 97 letters to Galton from notable Victorian scientists, travellers, and others. A further 58 letters, formerly in a letter book, display the same range. Some 40 letters and 15 sets of notes are in the Galton Bequest books in three bookcases in the Galton Laboratory, while 83 letters, notes, statistical tables, pamphlets and press cuttings are in the letterbook of the Anthropometric Laboratory. A further set of correspondence arranged alphabetically, reflects the range of Galton's interests. Correspondents include Charles J. Andersson, Havelock Ellis, Karl Pearson, members of the Darwin and Galton families, Frederic Merrifield, Conwy Lloyd Morgan, Frank H. Perrycoste, Ernest Rhys, Caleb Williams Saleeby, C. E. Spearman and E. R. Spearman, James Sully, E. B. Titchener, Sir E. B. Tylor, John Venn, A. R. Wallace, Lady Welby and W. F. R. Weldon (179 letters). The Karl Pearson papers, also at University College London, contain further relevant material.

The Museum of the History af Science, Oxford, has miscellaneous papers relating to his work and to the anthropometric laboratories in South Kensington and Cambridge. There are letters to Charles Darwin and other members of the family in Cambridge University Library.

The British Library has correspondence in the Macmillan archive (Add. MS. 55218).

Amongst relevant works which have used manuscript material are Francis Galton, *Memories of My Life* (1908), Karl Pearson, *Life, Letters and Labours of Francis Galton* (Cambridge, 1914–30); and D. W. Forrest, *Francis Galton: The Life and Work of a Victorian Genius* (1974).

GALTON, Frank Wallis (1867–1952)

Fabian socialist. Secretary to Beatrice and Sidney Webb, 1892–8. Secretary, London Reform Union, 1899–1918. Editor, *Municipal Journal*, 1918–20. Secretary of the Fabian Society, 1920–39.

A typescript unpublished autobiography is in BLPES. Reference should also be made to the Passfield papers there. Records relating to the London Reform Union are described in *Sources* Vol. 1, pp. 157–8, and papers of the Fabian Society, in Nuffield College, Oxford, are described in *Sources* Vol. 1, pp. 95–6.

GARBETT, Cyril Forster (1875–1955)

Churchman. Bishop of Southwark, 1919–32; Winchester, 1932–42. Archbishop of York, 1942–55.

Archbishop Garbett bequeathed his papers to York Minster Library. The material includes correspondence, diaries, sermons and addresses (many of which refer to social issues) and press cuttings. Access is restricted. The permission of the literary executor, Dr Gerald Ellison, Bishop of London, is necessary before any papers may be consulted.

Letters from Garbett to A. C. Don, 1946, are available in Lambeth Palace Library.

GARDINER, Baron
Gerald Austin Gardiner (1900–)

Lawyer and politician. Lord Chancellor, 1964–70. Chairman, National Campaign for the Abolition of Capital Punishment.

The British Library has nine volumes of correspondence, relating chiefly to his activities in various campaigns for the abolition of capital punishment, 1946–69 (Add. MSS 56455–63).

GARDINER, Alfred George (1865–1946)

Journalist and author. Editor, *Daily News*, 1902–19. President, Institute of Journalists, 1915–16.

BLPES has the Gardiner papers, which are currently being sorted and listed. They were extensively used and quoted from in Stephen Koss, *Fleet Street Radical: A. G. Gardiner and the Daily News* (1973). Letters to Asquith are in the Bodleian Library, Oxford.

GARRETT, Fydell Edmund (1865–1907)

Journalist. Editor, *The Cape Times*, from 1895. Member of Cape Legislature, 1895–9.

The British Library has a collection of papers (Add. MS 45929), including letters to Miss Agnes Garrett (cousin), 1896–8, which include some account of events in South Africa following the Jameson Raid; and letters, 1897, to Garrett from Sir Alfred Milner relating to a proposal to appoint the former as Imperial Secretary.

GARVIN, James Louis (1868–1947)

Journalist and author. Editor of the *Outlook*, 1905–6; *Pall Mall Gazette*, 1912–15; *The Observer*, 1908–42. Editor-in-Chief, *Encyclopaedia Britannica* (14th ed.), 1926–9. Writer for *The Daily Telegraph*. Author of the *Life* of Joseph Chamberlain.

The University of Texas, Austin, has an extensive collection of papers, amounting to approximately 100 boxes of manuscript material. They cover the whole span of Garvin's career, and include notebooks, personal papers and correspondence with major political figures, from World War I to his death.

Letters to Captain Gerard Garvin, 1915–16, including letters from J. L. Garvin, are on loan to the Liddell Hart Centre for Military Archives, King's College, London.

There are letters to the editorial staff of *The Times* in the archives of that newspaper.

There is correspondence in the Chamberlain papers and the Parker Smith papers about his *Life*. There are letters to Lloyd George, 1913–15, 1925–43, in the House of Lords Record Office.

GASTER, Moses (1856–1939)

Sephardi Chief Rabbi (Haham), 1887–1919. Vice President, Zionist Congress, 1898–1900. Vice President, Anglo-Jewish Association; English Zionist Federation.

A substantial collection of correspondence and papers is held in the Mocatta Library, University College London. The collection includes incoming correspondence and copies of outgoing mail, 1874–1939, as well as original letters from him; notes and manuscripts; photographs; notices of lectures, circulars, bills, greetings, notes of condolence and visiting cards. Subjects represented include Rabbinica, Judaica, Philology, Slavonic and Oriental Studies, Folklore, especially of gypsies, Samaritans, Zionism (the Anglo-Palestinian Company, Zionist Congress reports, Jewish Colonial Trust). There are notebooks; lectures, especially on Anglo-Jewry; and autobiographical notes. Press cuttings cover the period 1867–1939. Correspondents include Sir Moses Montefiore, Dr Herzl, Weizmann and N. Mayer, and members of his family. Diaries remain in private hands.

The Central Zionist Archives, Jerusalem, has photocopies (ref. A203) of Gaster's correspondence in 1917 with Weizmann, Sokolov, Sacher and Leo Simon. This relates to the finalisation of the Balfour Declaration.

GATES, (Reginald) Ruggles (1882–1962)

Biologist, geneticist and anthropologist. Professor of Botany, King's College, London, 1921–42. On Consultative Council of Eugenics Society; Advisory Council, Monarchist League.

There are papers in the Library of King's College, London. Records of the Eugenics Society are described in *Sources* Vol. 1, pp. 92–3.

GEDDES, Sir Patrick (1854–1932)

Biologist, sociologist, educationalist and town planner.

The National Library of Scotland has a collection of correspondence and papers. The material includes letters from Geddes to his wife and children, 1863–1932; other family business and personal papers; miscellaneous correspondence of other members of the Geddes family; letters of his children, 1916–19; biographical material, including a family tree, biographical notes, obituary notices, press cuttings concerning Geddes and a script of a BBC broadcast on him, notes on his life by Anna Geddes, wills, etc. Papers by Geddes include material on his early life; a folder of pamphlets and leaflets by him; a report on the proposed Hebrew University in Jerusalem, 1919; typescripts of lectures on civics, sociology, biology, social geography etc; press cuttings collected by Geddes, mainly 1919–20; notes on botany and geography. His correspondents include Charles Darwin, 1880–2, John Ruskin, 1877–85, James Mavor, 1899–1925, H. V. Lanchester, 1914–26, Patrick Abercrombie, Sir Jagadis C. Bose, Sir Frank Mears, William Sharp ('Fiona Macleod'), Gilbert Slater, R. Tagore, Paul and Elisée Reclus, G. S. Stuart Glennie, Edward McGegan, John Ross, Joseph Fels, Lewis Mumford, Raymond Unwin, J. Arthur Thomson and Victor Branford. There are miscellaneous letters of Geddes, 1880–1932; a folder of verse and verse letters by Geddes, 1925–32; letters to Geddes and colleagues, 1878–1932; letters relating to T. R. Marr; miscellaneous business papers; 'Outlook Tower' papers, including correspondence with Mrs Craigie Cunningham and F. C. Mears, and miscellaneous other papers and pamphlets.

Edinburgh University Library has relevant material in the Sarolea and Sir Donald Tovey papers.

Original sources were used in Paddy Kitchen, *A Most Unsettling Person: An Introduction to the Ideas and Life of Patrick Geddes* (1975). A further study of Sir Patrick Geddes has been prepared by H. E. Meller of Nottingham University.

GEDGE, Ernest (1862–1935)

Businessman, with interests in Africa and Asia. Special correspondent for *The Times* during Matabeleland campaigns.

Rhodes House Library, Oxford, has a collection of papers and correspondence. There is correspondence, 1890–2, including letters from traders, from *The Times* and from Sir Frederick Jackson and F. D. Lugard. Correspondence, 1893–5, covers the religious disputes in Uganda and his relations with *The Times*. There is correspondence, 1895–7, between Sir Henry Stanley and Gedge, and there is assorted correspondence, 1900–20. There are reports on East African development, 1902–3; letterbooks, 1892–1905; account books, 1898–1912; notes on expeditions, 1888–98; notes for articles; miscellaneous undated writings on Uganda; maps, etc; press cuttings of Gedge's reports for *The Times*; miscellaneous press cuttings, 1888–1929. Gedge's journals and diaries, 1878–1919, form an important grouping. They include notes on his life, 1862–79; diaries of the Jackson–Gedge expedition in Uganda; a diary of his work for *The Times*; a Yukon diary, 1898–9; a journal of travels in Malaya, Borneo and Java, 1911–12; in Iraq, 1919; and biographical notes.

GEDYE, George Eric Rowe (1890–1970)

Journalist. Served in World War I and on the Rhine, 1919–22. Special correspondent for *The Times* in the Rhineland and the Ruhr, 1922–5. Central Europe correspondent of *The Times*, 1925–6, *Daily Express*, 1926–8, *Daily Telegraph*, 1929–39. Moscow correspondent of *New York Times*, 1939–40; Turkey correspondent, 1940–1. Employed on Special Military Duties in Middle East, 1941–5. Correspondent for the *Daily Herald* in Central Europe, 1945–50; for *The Observer*, 1950–2; *Manchester Guardian* correspondent for Central and South East Europe, 1953–4. Vienna correspondent of Radio Free Europe and Special Correspondent for *The Guardian*, 1956–61.

An extensive collection of papers covering the whole of George Gedye's military and journalistic career is held at the Imperial War Museum. The core of the collection is formed by newspaper articles and typescripts of books, written by Gedye, including propaganda articles and his autobiographical work *Curtain Raiser*. The papers also include some of Gedye's correspondence, and articles, books and photographs collected by him together with papers relating to his service in Army Intelligence during and immediately after World War I. Part of the collection is officially restricted under the Thirty Year Rule.

GELL, Philip Lyttelton (1852–1926)

Businessman. Director, British South Africa Company, 1899–1925; Chairman, 1917–20; President, 1920–3. First Chairman, Toynbee Hall, 1884–96.

Papers are in the care of Mrs A. E. Gell, OBE, Hopton Hall, Wirksworth, Derbyshire DE4 4DF. The papers have been listed by the Historical Manuscripts Commission. The collection is a major source for the British South Africa Company, whose own records were destroyed in World War II. There are official minutes, agenda, and circulated papers and much relevant correspondence. There is a voluminous correspondence with colleagues in the office and on the board, including Sir L. S. Jameson, Sir Lewis Michell, Sir Henry Birchenough, H. Wilson Fox, Sir Otto Beit, and Dougal Malcolm. The papers and correspondence are also revealing of Gell's activities in other companies, such as the Rhodesian Lands Co. and the Rhodesia Cold Storage Co., and of his interests in Siberian goldfields and Spanish·copper mines; and in publishing, Liberal Unionist politics, the co-operative movement, Toynbee Hall, and the Church of England. Gell's close friendship with Lord Milner, 4th Earl Grey, and Benjamin Jowett (of whom he was literary executor) is well illustrated by extensive runs of correspondence, that with Milner running from 1870 to his death.
　Gell's letters to Milner are in the Bodleian Library, Oxford.

GIFFEN, Sir Robert (1837–1910)

Economist, statistician and journalist. Assistant editor, *The Economist*, 1868–76. Chief of Statistical Department, Board of Trade, 1876–82. Assistant Secretary, Board of Trade, and later Controller-General of Commercial, Labour and Statistical Departments, 1882–97. President of Statistical Society, 1882–4.

BLPES has a collection of letters and papers. Letters, largely personal and arranged chronologically, date from 1861 to 1910, and amongst the correspondents are Gladstone, Lord Avebury, the 3rd Earl Granville, H. Roscoe, Edwin Chadwick, C. M. Bell, Mundella, Spring-Rice, Sidney Webb, R. H. Mead, Henry Chaplin, Sydney Hall, Earl of Selborne, Muir-Mackenzie, Lord Goschen, Lord Farrer, Maxse, E. R. Russell, J. E. Buckle, J. R. Thursfield, the Earl of Northbrooke, W. J. Ashley, A. J. Balfour, Lady Dudley, Lord Hillingdon, Lords Morley, Revelstoke, Brassey, Newton, Welby, Geoffrey Drage, Spenser Wilkinson, Lord Rosebery, 1st Lord Eversley and Monk Bretton. There are also letters of congratulation and miscellaneous cards and undated letters. The collection also includes articles by Giffen, miscellaneous papers, letters and papers concerning various organisations, and press cuttings of articles.
　Correspondence with Joseph Chamberlain is in the Birmingham University Library, and correspondence on financial affairs is in the St Aldwyn papers in Gloucestershire Record Office. Nine letters and memoranda, 1879–86, are in the Gladstone papers at the British Library (Add. MSS 44256–666).

GILL, Stanley (1926–1975)

Computer expert. Fellow of St John's College, Cambridge, 1952–5. Worked with Computer Department of Ferranti Ltd, 1955–63. Professor of Automatic Data Processing, College of Science and Technology, Manchester University, 1963–4. Professor of Computing Science, 1964–70, and Director of Centre for Computing and Automation, 1966–70, Imperial College, London. President, British Computer Society, 1967–8.

A large collection of papers is being listed by the Oxford Contemporary Scientific Archives Centre, and it is expected that the papers will be deposited with the Science Museum.

GILL, Thomas Patrick (1858–1931)

Irish Nationalist politician. M.P. (Irish Nat.) South Louth, 1885–92. Secretary, Irish Recess Committee, 1895–8. Secretary, Department of Agriculture and Technical Instruction for Ireland, 1900–23. Commissioner for Intermediate Education, 1909–23. President, Irish Technical Instruction Association, 1925–9.

A collection of letters and papers is preserved in the National Library of Ireland (ref. MSS 13478–526). The material, comprising some 5000 documents, 1871–1931, relates, *inter alia*, to the Plan of Campaign, 1886–90; the Parnell Crisis, 1889–91; the co-operative movement; the Irish Convention of 1917; and the Government of Ireland Bill, 1920. Correspondents include Archbishop Croke and Horace Plunkett (500 letters, 1891–1923). Further correspondence between Plunkett and Gill (six letters in all) can be found in the Plunkett papers.

GINSBERG, Morris (1889–1970)

Sociologist. Editor of *British Journal of Sociology* and *Sociological Review*. Professor of Sociology in the University of London, London School of Economics, 1929–54. Author of *The Psychology of Society*, *On Justice in Society* etc.

BLPES has a collection of papers, correspondence and printed material (some 12 boxes). There are pamphlets and papers on trade unions, AUT, anthropology, casual labour, eugenics, women in industry, social evolution, colour and inequality. Correspondence is chiefly from the 1940s to the 1960s, though a few letters, especially concerning L. T. Hobhouse, date from the 1920s. Other material includes notebooks, questionnaires, examination papers, manuscript notes for some of his works, and university and school papers.

GLADSTONE, Helen (1849–1925)

Educationalist. Vice Principal, Newnham College, 1882–96. Warden, Women's University Settlement, 1901–6.

Family correspondence, miscellaneous letters and papers concerning her educational work, devotional writings, etc., may be consulted at Clwyd Record Office.

GLASIER, John Bruce (1859–1920)

Socialist publicist. Chairman, Independent Labour Party, 1900. Editor, *Labour Leader*.

Mr Malcolm Bruce Glasier (son), of West Kirby, has a large collection of papers, including correspondence and a diary, 1900–19. These were extensively used and quoted from in Lawrence Thompson, *The Enthusiasts. A Biography of John and Katherine Bruce Glasier* (1971). They will eventually be deposited in a suitable library.
    The records of the ILP, to be deposited in BLPES, contain relevant material. A catalogue of the papers is available at BLPES.
    The William Morris papers, at the William Morris Gallery, Water House, Lloyd Park, Forest Road, Walthamstow, London E17, and in the British Library, contain relevant items.
    The Labour Party archive at Transport House has miscellaneous letters and other material.

GLOVER, Terrot Reaveley (1869–1943)

Classical scholar and historian. Professor of Latin, Queen's University, Kingston, Ontario,

1896–1901. Classical Lecturer, St John's College, Cambridge, 1901–39. President of the Baptist Union, 1924.

Cambridge University Library has two boxes of material; one contains some correspondence and obituary notices, the other letters to Glover. The bulk of the material refers to his classical interests.

GODFREY, Cardinal William (1889–1963)

Roman Catholic leader. Archbishop of Liverpool, 1953–6. Archbishop of Westminster from 1956.

Papers are with the Westminster Diocesan Archives.

GOLDING, Louis (1895–1958)

Anglo-Jewish novelist, essayist, traveller, lecturer and broadcaster.

No personal papers have been traced. Golding left a large number of his own books to The Queen's College, Oxford, but no papers. Some correspondence can be found in the Brett Young collection and in the Creech Jones papers, Rhodes House Library, Oxford.

GOLLANCZ, Sir Victor (1893–1967)

Publisher. Founded firm of Victor Gollancz Ltd in 1928. Launched Left Book Club in 1936. Organised the 'Save Europe Now' campaign in 1945. A founder of the Jewish Society for Human Service, 1948. Founder of 'War on Want' in 1951. Chairman, National Campaign for the Abolition of Capital Punishment, from 1955.

A substantial collection of papers has been given to the Modern Records Centre, University of Warwick Library. The papers reflect, to a greater or lesser degree, the wide range of his interests in political and humanitarian matters. Recurrent correspondents include Sir Richard Acland, Daphne du Maurier, Canon Collins, Harold Laski, Vera Brittain, Liddell Hart, Peggy Duff, and Gilbert Murray. Material survives on the Left Book Club, the United Europe Movement, and various pacifist and Jewish organisations. At the time of writing the collection had not been fully catalogued.

Some material is in the Hugh Harris collection, in the Anglo-Jewish Archives, Mocatta Library, University College London, while some correspondence can be found in the Anna Graves papers, Swarthmore College Peace collection. Reference should also be made to the John Strachey papers which contain material on the Left Book Club (*Sources* Vol. 4, p. 188). The Kingsley Martin papers, Sussex University Library, contain further correspondence.

A study of the firm is being prepared for its 50th Anniversary in 1978 by Sheila Bush.

GONNE, Maud (1866–1953)

Irish patriot and philanthropist.

Papers concerning Maud Gonne can be found in the Public Record Office (CO 904). Further sources are detailed in Samuel Levenson, *Maud Gonne* (1977).

GOODE, Sir William Athelstane Meredith (1875–1944)

Journalist and Financial Adviser. News and Managing Editor, the *Standard*, 1904–10. Joint News Editor, *Daily Mail*, 1911. Director, Ministry of Food Cable Department, 1917–19. British Director of Relief in Europe, 1919–20. Unofficial financial adviser to Hungarian Government, 1923–41. Director of Communications, Ministry of Food, 1941.

Messrs Clayton, Leach, Sims and Co, solicitors who acted in the estate, knew of no relevant material.

GOODMAN, Paul (1875–1949)

Historian and Zionist publicist. Hon. Secretary, first Zionist Political Committee in London, 1916. Vice President of the English Zionist Federation, 1919–27. Hon. Treasurer and Chairman of the Political Committee, Zionist Federation of Great Britain and Ireland. Hon. Treasurer of the International Confederation of General Zionists. Editor of *The Jewish National Home* and *Zionist Review*.

A few papers are to be found in the Central Zionist Archives, Jerusalem (ref. K11/6).

GORDON, Harry Pirie- (1883–1969)

Journalist and naval intelligence officer. Member of the Foreign Department, *The Times*, 1911–14, 1919–39. Served in Royal Navy Volunteer Reserve, and on political mission to Palestine, 1914–19. Served in Admiralty, Naval Intelligence, 1939–55.

The Middle East Centre, St Antony's College, Oxford, has a few items, including xerox copies of proposals for an offensive against the Baghdad and Palestine Railways, 1917; and a biographical note written by his son, 1972.

Some further material is available in the archives of *The Times*. This consists of a large envelope of correspondence, dating from 1922, covering his service with the newspaper.

GORE, Charles (1853–1932)

Churchman and theologian. Librarian of Pusey House, Oxford, 1884–93. Vicar of Radley, 1893–4. Canon of Westminster, 1894–1902. Editor of *Lux Mundi*. Bishop of Worcester, 1902–4; of Birmingham, 1905–11; of Oxford, 1911–19.

The Community of the Resurrection believed that Gore's personal papers were destroyed. The Community's papers, now deposited at the Borthwick Institute of Historical Research, contain certain relevant material, including correspondence with Walter Frere. Lambeth Palace Library has correspondence between Gore and C. Cheshire, T. Tatlow, B. Webb and others, 1917; plus a critique of 'God the Invisible King'. The papers of Joseph Armitage Robinson, Dean of Wells, concerning the Conversations at Malines (about the reunion of the Anglican and Roman Catholic Church, in which Gore participated) are also relevant. The Asquith papers, at the Bodleian Library, contain correspondence 1908–11, regarding Church appointments, while further correspondence can be found in the Sladen, Selborne and Ponsonby collections.

GOULD, Sir Francis Carruthers (1844–1925)

Political cartoonist. Regular contributor to the *Pall Mall Gazette*, and later to the *Westminster Gazette*.
A draft autobiography is in the House of Lords Record Office.

GRAHAM, Robert Bontine Cunninghame (1852–1936)

Traveller, scholar, socialist pioneer and Scottish Nationalist.

A collection of papers has been deposited in the National Library of Scotland, including correspondence and literary manuscripts. The letters are mainly to Cunninghame Graham, with some letters to his wife, Gabrielle. They cover the period 1874–1936. Correspondents include A. J. Balfour, Max Beerbohm, Wilfrid Scawen Blunt, Sir Roger Casement, Edward Garnett, John Galsworthy, Thomas Hardy, T. M. Healy, M. A. S. Hume, Professor J. F. Kelly,

Prince Kropotkin, T. E. Lawrence, John Masefield, Lord Rosebery, G. B. Shaw and W. T. Stead. The other material includes manuscripts and typescripts of books, essays, prefaces, reviews and miscellaneous writings. Amongst these are manuscripts and typescripts of *Progress* (1905), *His People* (1906), *Faith* (1909), *Redeemed and other Sketches* (1927), *The Horses of the Conquest* (1930), *Writ in Sand* (1932), *Portrait of a Dictator* (1933), *Mirages* (1936), *Rodeo* (1936).

Further papers, part on microfilm, are in the Baker Library, Dartmouth College, USA. These include political and literary correspondence, literary MSS, and photographs.

The British Library has correspondence with G. B. Shaw, 1888–1913 (Add. MS 50531) and John Burns, 1888–1928 (Add. MS 46284). Some other papers (415 items) are available in the University of Texas Library, Austin.

GRAVES, Alfred Perceval (1846–1931)

Educationalist and author. H.M. Inspector of Schools, 1875–1910. Chairman of the Representative Managers of London County Council Schools, 1911–19. Closely involved in Irish literary renaissance and in Pan Celtic Movement.

Letters, 1909–12, are in the National Library of Wales. Correspondence, 1900–21, with the Society of Authors, is in the British Library (Add. MS 56715).

GRAVES, Philip Perceval (1876–1953)

Journalist and author. Pro-Zionist publicist. Correspondent for *The Times*, Constantinople, 1908–14. Temporary army officer in Egypt, Palestine, Arabia and Turkey, 1915–19. Helped expose the forged 'Protocols of the Elders of Zion'. On staff of *The Times* until 1946.

The archives of *The Times* contain a box of correspondence, dating from 1919. It contains material on Turkey from 1919, material covering his visit to Palestine, 1921–2, and on Ireland in the 1930s.

GRAVES, Richard Massie (1880–1960)

Consular official. Entered Levant Consular Service, 1903; Egyptian Civil Service, 1910. Inspector of the Interior, 1910–22; Assistant Director General, European Department, Ministry of the Interior, 1924. Director, Labour Department, Egyptian Ministry of Commerce and Industry, 1930–9. Major in the Intelligence Service, 1939–40. Labour Adviser to the Palestine Government, 1940–2. Director, Department of Labour, Palestine Government, 1942–6. Chairman, Municipal Commission, Jerusalem, 1947–8. Adviser on Social Affairs, International Administration, Tangier, 1949–51.

Enquiries should be directed to the Middle East Centre, St Antony's College, Oxford. It is believed that some material may survive with Mr Simon Gough, Howe Farm House, Wood Dalling, near Reepham, Norfolk.

GRAY, Sir Alexander (1882–1968)

Economist. Served at Local Government Board, 1905–9; Colonial Office, 1909–12; Insurance Commission, 1912–19; Insurance Department, Ministry of Health, 1919–21. Jaffrey Professor of Political Economy, University of Aberdeen, 1921–34. Professor of Political Economy and Mercantile Law, University of Edinburgh, 1935–56. Writer of verse.

A collection of material, chiefly, it appears, relating to Gray's literary interests, is available in the National Library of Scotland. The material includes three notebooks containing 'Jottings for Rhymes', 1920–7; 'The Beastie Book, or Some Recreations of a Hand Loom Weaver', by Gray's grandfather; 'Kith and Kin' and 'Recollections' by his father, John Young Gray; a Register of the Gray family; 'Posthumous Ballads', consisting of 42 ballads, comprising three volumes of typescript; folders of the manuscripts and typescripts of often unpublished poems; notebooks containing notes for and revisions of poems; and miscellaneous letters, usually referring to his literary work, and press cuttings, including obituary notices.

Some material, 1924–54, is also housed in Edinburgh University Library, including five letters to Charles Sarolea, 1942–7 (with four replies) and three letters from F. J. de Jong, 1951–2.

GREEN, Alice Sophia Amelia Stopford (1847–1929)

Historian and writer on Ireland. Member of the Irish Senate from 1922.

The National Library of Ireland has various papers, including letters to A. S. Green from various correspondents, 1870–1928; amongst these letters from Mrs D. de Villiers in South Africa, 1901–14 (c. 70 letters) and from Roger Casement (81 letters plus associated documents, 1904–16) are particularly prominent. Some correspondence is contained in papers chiefly relating to her husband, J. R. Green, the historian, at Jesus College, Oxford. These include, *inter alia*, correspondence relating to the publication of Sir Leslie Stephens' *Life and Letters of J. R. Green* (1901) and also typescript copies of letters from J. R. Green to Mrs Green before their marriage. Correspondence with Macmillans the publishers, 1877–1928, can be found at the British Library (Add. MSS 55059–061), while a little correspondence regarding the Irish Question is available in the Sir Horace Plunkett papers. Reference should be made to a biography, R. B. McDowell, *Passionate Historian* (Dublin, 1967).

GREENBERG, Ivan Marion (1896–   )

Journalist. Editor, *Jewish Chronicle*, 1936–46.

There is a collection of papers in the Anglo-Jewish Archives, Mocatta Library, University College London. It comprises correspondence, notes, pamphlets, reports relating to the *Jewish Chronicle*, communal correspondence, material on Palestine, Israel, Zionism, Herut, Irgun, Shelach, Refugees, resettlement, articles, newspaper cuttings and other material. Correspondents include M. Trau, Lord Nathan, N. J. Laski, Leonard Stein, M. Gordon Liverman, Leonard Montefiore, H. H. Roskin, Sir R. Waley-Cohen, Florence Greenberg, L. Kostoris, D. Francis Kessler, Cecil Roth, South African Jewry, Anglo-Palestine Club, A. M. Hyamson, Maurice Rosette, the Chief Rabbi, Hertz, the Board of Deputies, the Council of Christians and Jews. A great deal of material relates to Palestine, the establishment of the State of Israel and Zionism. There are also articles on various subjects, mostly submitted for publication to the *Jewish Chronicle* 1938– c. 1947.

GREENBERG, Leopold J. (d. 1931)

Journalist. Founder of the *Jewish Year Book*, 1896. Vice President, Zionist Congress, 1907. Editor of the *Jewish Chronicle* and the *Jewish World*.

It is believed that papers survive in private hands. Reference should be made to the findings of the British Academy's Anglo-Palestinian Archives Project.

GREENIDGE, Charles Wilton Wood (1889–1972)

Colonial administrator and campaigner against slavery. Chief Justice of British Honduras, 1932–6: Solicitor General, Nigeria, 1936–41. Secretary, Anti-Slavery Society, 1941–56; Director, 1957–68.

A collection of papers is available at Rhodes House Library, Oxford. The bulk of the papers date from 1941, though there are some miscellaneous items from the Nigerian period which show his interest in judicial and legal reform, and in refugee resettlement. Boxes 3–7 reflect his work for the Anti-Slavery Society, and complement the Society's own records, also in Rhodes

House Library, and his other interests in liberal and humanitarian concerns. These boxes contain a heterogeneous collection of papers and correspondence, arranged on a territorial basis, some related to the work of the society, some to Greenidge's work with other organisations. Of this material, only the items concerning South Africa, S.W. Africa, the Protectorates and the Seychelles is at all comprehensive. Boxes 8–12 illustrate most fully the range of Greenidge's preoccupations and activities. Between 1941 and 1958 he sat on the committees of some 13 organisations and was associated with the activities of nearly 50 other groups, chiefly dealing with the reorganisation of the post-war world, race relations, human rights, colonial policy, etc., and his work can be traced in these papers. Box 11 contains material relating to his membership of the Fabian Colonial Bureau, and Box 12 to his involvement with the Labour Party Advisory Committee on Imperial Affairs. Boxes 13–25 relate to his interest in the Caribbean area and his membership of a Commission to examine the economic potentialities of this area. These papers include Committee documents, background material, correspondence with M.P.s, officials, and private individuals in both the UK and the West Indies, and drafts of the report. Box 26 contains lectures and articles by Greenidge, mainly on Colonial matters, 1942–57. Box 28, covering the period 1947–58, contains correspondence relating to his help to private individuals, while Boxes 27, 29 and 30 contain a mixture of printed material and personal papers. Boxes 31–3 contain papers concerning Lord Olivier, and consist mainly of alternative draft versions of an incomplete published work, *The Dual Ethic of Empire*, with related material for appendixes. The collection ends in 1959, with Greenidge's departure for the West Indies.

Records of the Anti-Slavery Society and the Fabian Colonial Bureau are also in Rhodes House Library, and are described in *Sources* Vol. 1, pp. 9–10, and pp. 94–5 respectively. The Creech Jones papers in Rhodes House Library also contain relevant material.

GREENING, Edward Owen (1836–1923)

Co-operator and social reformer. Founder and editor of *Industrial Partnership Record*, later *Social Economist* from 1868. He was instrumental in convening the Co-operative Congress of 1868, out of which the Co-operative Union developed; he helped found the Co-operative Institute in London in 1874; the Co-operative Productive Federation in 1882; and in 1895 he was a founder of the International Co-operative Alliance.

The Co-operative Union Library, Manchester, has a collection of papers. This consists of some 11,000 letters and documents, covering the period 1860–1920. At the time of writing the papers had not been catalogued.

GREGORY, Sir Richard Arman (1864–1952)

Scientist and Fellow of the Royal Society. Professor of Astronomy, Queen's College, London. Joint editor of *The School World* and of the *Journal of Education*, with which it was amalgamated, 1899–1939. Editor, *Nature*, 1919–39. President, British Association for the Advancement of Science, 1940–6. President, Ethical Union, 1947–50.

A collection of papers and correspondence is currently being catalogued in Sussex University Library. It includes about 200 letters to Sir Richard, chiefly 1940s; and notes and typescripts of lectures, articles and addresses. W. H. G. Armytage, *Sir Richard Gregory: His Life and Work* (1957), used private papers in the possession of Lady Gregory.

GREGORY, Sir Theodore Emanuel Gugenheim (1890–1970)

Economist. Lecturer, London School of Economics, from 1913. Cassel Reader in International Trade, 1920. Professor of Economics in the University of London, 1927–37. Member of the Macmillan Committee on Industry and Finance, 1929–31. Economic adviser, Niemeyer Mission to Australia and New Zealand, 1930. Economic Adviser to the Government of India, 1938–46.

BLPES has a group of papers dating from c. 1910 to the 1930s. These include a MS notebook on the history of currency and banking (probably his notes from lectures); MS notes on public finance and taxation (probably notes on lectures by Cannan); a few letters from F. Hayek, I. Fisher, and D. H. Robertson; and material concerning Edwin Cannan. The latter material includes letters and postcards from Cannan, and includes many comments on economic matters, especially concerning currency and banking, 1920–34. There are in addition two typescript memoranda, one headed 'Cannan's notes on the Gold Standard', c. 1929–31, probably written before the devaluation of 1931; and the other concerning the editing of Ricardo's work for the Royal Economic Society. The collection also has copies of articles on the economic situation, 1920s.

GREIG, Teresa Billington- (1877–1964)

Feminist. Advocate of women's suffrage. Founder of the Women's Freedom League, 1907.

The Fawcett Library has much relevant material. This includes a volume of letters in its autograph collection; various feminist articles, published and unpublished; biographical material, including cuttings; correspondence, notes on politics and suffrage, 1903–7; papers on the ILP and WSPU covering her break with the latter in 1907; material for a biography of Mrs Charlotte Despard (never completed) plus some relevant correspondence; papers of the Women's Freedom League, including official papers and drafts on its organisation by Teresa Billington-Greig; and official and her own papers relating to the later 'Women for Westminster' group. The records of the Women's Freedom League, both at the Fawcett Library amd the Museum of London, are described in *Sources* Vol. 1, p. 283; while material relating to 'Women for Westminster' is mentioned on p. 235.

GRENFELL, Sir Wilfred Thomason (1865–1940)

Medical missionary and author. Founded and developed the Labrador Medical Mission, 1893–1935. Founder of the International Grenfell Association, for which he lectured and wrote.

Yale University, Medical Library, has a collection of papers which are currently being organised and indexed.

GREY, Maria Georgina Shirreff (1816–1906)

Promoter of women's education. Initiated Girls' Public Day School Company, 1872, which had 25 schools by 1929. Founded Maria Grey Training College for Women Teachers, 1878. Author of works on women's education and enfranchisement.

Cambridge University Library has a few items only.

GRIER, (Mary) Lynda Dorothea (1880–1967)

Economist. Fellow and Lecturer, Newnham College, Cambridge. Acting Head of Economics Department, University of Leeds, 1915–19. Member, Consultative Committee, Board of Education, 1924–38. President, Economics Section, British Association, 1925; Education Section, 1946. Principal, Lady Margaret Hall, Oxford, 1921–45.

Apart from the College records during Miss Grier's Principalship, Lady Margaret Hall, Oxford, has a number of unsorted personal papers. These include miscellaneous early letters, and correspondence while at Lady Margaret Hall; sermons preached in the college chapel; a *Life* of the Rev. Richard Grier; further letters, reports, notebooks relating to her first visit to China; miscellaneous material concerning Newnham, Leeds, China, etc.; plus speeches by and about Miss Grier, 1945; and obituary notices.

GRIERSON, John (1898–1972)

Documentary film producer. Associated with formation of the Empire Marketing Board and GPO Film Units. General Manager, Canadian Wartime Information Board, 1942–3. Director of Mass Communications, UNESCO, 1946–8. Controller, Films, Central Office of Information, 1948–50. Professor of Communications, McGill University.

The University of Stirling has a large collection of papers. These include manuscripts and typescripts of correspondence, lectures, speeches, memoranda and policy papers relating to his work with a large number of national and international agencies. The papers form the core of the John Grierson Archive, opened in late 1977.

McGill University, Montreal, Canada, also has John Grierson material, especially covering the latter part of his career.

GRIEVE, Christopher Murray
Hugh McDiarmid* (1892–   )

Poet and journalist. Active in communist politics, and a founder of the Scottish Nationalist Party.

Grieve has retained the bulk of his papers but various items can be found in a number of libraries. Some 200 letters, 1922–64, are in Edinburgh University Library, as are typescripts of books and articles by him. Miscellaneous items are in the National Library of Scotland including assorted letters and the manuscripts of an article, 'Injustice to the Scottish National Library' and of 'The Raucle Tongue'. The University of Texas, Austin, also has various items.

* Pseudonym.

GRUBB, Edward (1854–1939)

Author and lecturer on Biblical and Religious History. Secretary of the Howard Association (for Penal Reform), 1901–6. Proprietor and editor of *The British Friend*, 1901–13. Treasurer of the No-Conscription Fellowship, 1915–19.

Friends' House Library, London, has correspondence (chiefly 1918–19) and an autobiography. Records of the Howard Association (now Howard League for Penal Reform) are briefly described in *Sources* Vol. 1, p. 106, and are now housed in the Modern Records Centre, University of Warwick Library. Papers relating to Grubb include an MS notebook, recording inspections of prisons, interviews, notes on conferences; a notebook recording a visit to the USA, describing visits to prisons and interviews with prominent individuals; a chronicle covering the period 1900–4, partly compiled by Grubb, recording important correspondence, interviews, lectures, prison visits, issue of annual reports etc; a further chronicle, 1904–6, with similar material. Records relevant to the No-Conscription Fellowship are described in *Sources* Vol. 1, pp. 206–7.

GUEDALLA, Philip (1889–1944)

Historian and essayist. Liberal Parliamentary candidate. Secretary, Flax Control Board, 1917–20.

A few papers are held at the Central Zionist Archives, Jerusalem (ref. A 159). Reference should also be made to the records of the Board of Deputies of British Jews (described in *Sources* Vol. 1, pp. 20–1), and there is relevant material in the Anglo-Jewish archives, Mocatta Library, University College London.

The manuscript of *The Duke* and other works by Guedalla are in the Bodleian Library. The Lloyd George papers contain letters from Guedalla, 1928–42, relating to the persecution of the Jews.

GWYNNE, Howell Arthur (1865–1950)

Journalist. Reuter's correspondent in Romania, Sudan, Greece and South Africa. Foreign Director of Reuter's Agency, 1904. Editor, the *Standard*, 1904–11; *Morning Post*, 1911–37.

A collection of material is available in the Bodleian Library, Oxford. The material is arranged in four sections: A. Subjects; B. Major correspondents; C. Miscellaneous correspondents; D. Miscellaneous papers. Amongst the subjects covered are the Marconi Company, 1912–24; the Jane Mieville Trust, 1924–34; censorship in World War I; wartime Press Bureau releases, 1914–18; the prosecution of the *Morning Post*, 1918; the Protocols of the Elders of Zion, 1919; the sale of honours; the General Dyer Fund, 1920–8; the 'Diehard Fund', 1922–33; India, 1933–7; the finances and eventual collapse of the *Morning Post*, 1937. The major correspondents represented cover a wide range, and include Sir Max Aitken (Lord Beaverbrook), 1912–31; L. S. Amery, 1913–30; H. H. and Margot Asquith, 1914–31; Baden-Powell; J. L. Baird, 1st Baron Stonehaven; A.J. Balfour; Stanley Baldwin; Lord Charles Beresford, 1907–17; Sir Edward Carson, 1912–30; Robert Cecil, 1913–23; Austen and Neville Chamberlain; Winston Churchill, 1922–31; Sir James Craig; Lord Curzon; Sir John Fisher, Lord French; Sir Edward Grey; Lord Kitchener; Andrew Bonar Law; David Lloyd George, 1915; Walter Long, 1911–16; Ramsay MacDonald, 1924–31; Sir John Reith, 1935–7; Lord Derby, 1912–24; Wickham Steed, 1921; H. G. Wells; Younger of Leckie, 1922–7. Other miscellaneous correspondence is filed in alphabetical order. The miscellaneous papers include drafts of speeches, legal documents, diary pages, correspondence and papers, chiefly of a business nature; and miscellaneous printed material, including material relating to the sale of the *Daily Chronicle*, 1918.

Some correspondence, 1914–16, can be found in the Kitchener papers, and further letters are in the Edward Carson papers. Letters, 1905–12, to R. J. Marker are in the British Library (Add. MS 52278).

HADDON, Alfred Cort (1855–1940)

Anthropologist. Professor of Zoology, Royal College of Science, Dublin, 1880–1901. Lecturer in Ethnology, Cambridge, 1900–9; Reader, 1909–26.

Some 136 boxes of field notes and correspondence are deposited in Cambridge University Library.

HADOW, Grace Eleanor (1875–1940)

Educationalist and social reformer. Tutor and lecturer in English, 1906–17. Sub-section Director, Extra-Mural Department of Ministry of Munitions, and later the Ministry of Labour, 1917–20. Secretary of Barnett House, Oxford, 1920–9. Principal of the Society of Oxford Home-Students.

Papers on educational matters are in Worcester College, Oxford. H. C. Deneke, *Grace Hadow* (1946) uses papers and journals.

HADOW, Sir (William) Henry (1859–1937)

Academic, educationalist and music critic. Principal of Armstrong College, Newcastle, 1909–19. Vice-Chancellor, Sheffield University, 1919–30.

Papers survive in Worcester College, Oxford.

HAGGARD, Sir Henry Rider (1856–1925)

Novelist and traveller. Writer and propagandist, on imperial, agricultural and social conditions.

Correspondence, notebooks and diaries, 1874–1925, are in the Norfolk Record Office. The 22 volumes of Rider Haggard's 'Great War Diaries', 25 July 1914 to 22 April 1925 are particularly valuable as a guide to public reaction to the war. Columbia University Library has letters to Haggard from C. J. Longman, Joseph Chamberlain, Andrew Lang, Marie Corelli and others, which are concerned with literary, publishing, social and personal affairs.

The Royal Commonwealth Society Library has papers and correspondence relating to his journey through the Dominions on behalf of the Royal Commonwealth Institute, to determine what facilities they were prepared to give to British ex-servicemen who wished to emigrate and settle on the land after the war. The material includes minutes of the committee and press notices, correspondence from Earl Grey, Lord Sydenham, Bonar Law, Obed Smith, G. McLaren Brown; papers concerning the journey, and subsequent action.

Correspondence, 1880–1925, mainly letters to Haggard, is in the Henry E. Huntington Library, San Marino, California. The Hastings Museum has various letters.

The Society of Authors archive at the British Library has correspondence, 1909–20 (Add. MS 56720). There are letters to Herbert Samuel, 1901–9, in the House of Lords Record Office.

HAIGH, Mervyn George (1887–1962)

Ecclesiastic. Chaplain and Private Secretary to Archbishop Davidson, 1924–8, and to Archbishop Lang, 1928–31. Chaplain to the King, 1929–31. Bishop of Coventry, 1931–42. Bishop of Winchester, 1942–52.

Lambeth Palace Library has letters to Haigh from Davidson, Lang, Temple, Fisher and other clergy.

HAIRE, Norman (1892–1952)

Sexologist, gynaecologist and obstretician. Involved in birth control movement during 1920s; Medical Officer-in-Charge of the Walworth Welfare Centre, a pioneering contraception advice centre, 1921. President, Contraceptive Section, 5th International Birth Control Conference, 1922. President, World Congress for Sexual Reform; Sex Education Society. Councillor for British Society for the Study of Sex Psychology.

Norman Haire's library was bequeathed to the University of Sydney, Australia, which now has the bulk of his surviving papers. His diaries and other papers referring to intimate details of his patients and friends were destroyed by his executors. Correspondence at the University of Sydney includes letters to newspapers and journals, etc., amongst which are the *Hurstville Propeller*, 1943, *Daily Telegraph*, 1940–4, *Australian Highway*, 1944–5, *Daily Mirror*, 1947–51; the *Woman*, Sydney, 1941–6, the *Sydney Morning Herald*, 1942–4; and correspondence with societies, including the Australian Cultural Society, 1943–5, the New South Wales Medical Co-ordination Committee, the British Medical Association, 1943–9, and the National Society for the Retention of Corporal Punishment, 1951–2. There is also correspondence relating to the *Journal of Sex Education*, together with copy for articles, book reviews and a postage book. Amongst the personal correspondence are letters from Dr Henry T. Gillett, 1929–31, Aldous Huxley, 1936, Terence Millin, 1937, Mervyn Findlay, anonymous correspondence, 1947–9, Kegan Paul & Co, 1934–6, the UK Minister of Health, 1939, and miscellaneous correspondence, 1919–53. There is also correspondence with Havelock Ellis, 1921–39, consisting of some 97 letters and cards; most of them are of a social nature or referrals of patients to Haire, but they are often revealing of Ellis's preoccupations and character. Correspondence with Magnus Hirschfeld, some 50 letters in all, chiefly relates to the World League for Sexual Reform, and is in German. Amongst the personal papers in this collection are financial papers, material concerning his home, Nettleden Lodge, biographical papers, etc., photographs and personalia. Other material in the collection includes lectures, on sex education, the falling birthrate, the anatomy of sex; articles, including three folders of material published in *Woman*, Sydney, and various MSS; and press cuttings, on population, birth control, etc., 1944–5; cuttings from a press agency, 1931–2, and cuttings from the *Newcastle Morning Herald* on the church, education, etc. There is extensive correspondence in the Marie Stopes collection at the British Library.

A study of Norman Haire is being prepared by Dr F. M. Forster, East Melbourne, Australia.

HALDANE, John Burdon Sanderson (1892–1964)

Geneticist; author. Fullerian Professor of Physiology, Royal Institution, 1930–2. Professor of Genetics, London University, 1933–7; of Biometry, 1935–57. Research Professor, Indian Statistical Institute; Head of Genetics and Biometry Laboratory, Government of Orissa, India, from 1962. President, Genetical Society, 1932–6. Chairman, Editorial Board of *Daily Worker*, 1940–9.

Dr Helen Spurway Haldane (widow), c/o Habshiguda 16, Hyderabad 500007, Andhra Pradesh, India, has various papers. Naomi (Lady) Mitchison (sister) also has a mass of family papers, which she hopes to use for a study of her father and brother. University College London has letters from Haldane, 1935–64, but this collection is closed.

There are letters to J. M. Keynes in King's College Library, Cambridge, and further correspondence is in the David Lack papers (NRA 18780). There is a biography by Ronald Clark.

HALL, Sir (Alfred) Daniel (1865–1942)

Agriculturalist. First Principal, South-Eastern Agricultural College, Wye, 1894–1902. Director of the Rothamsted Experimental Station, 1902–12. Director, John Innes Horticultural Institution. Chief Scientific Adviser, Ministry of Agriculture.

Reading University Library has correspondence and material, 1902–42, collected for the biography by H. E. Dell.

There is correspondence, 1915–30, about wartime food production and agricultural co-operation in the Plunkett papers at the Plunkett Foundation, Oxford. There are 17 letters to Lloyd George, 1939–41, concerning food production, in the House of Lords Record Office.

HALL, Margeurite Radclyffe (1880–1943)

Poet and novelist. Member of the Council of the Society for Psychical Research. Fellow of the Zoological Society. Author of *The Well of Loneliness*, etc.

Mr Lovat Dickson, who owns the copyright in all Radclyffe Hall's work, has relevant material, including letters to her from friends and contemporaries with some 21 letters from Havelock Ellis to her. Mr Dickson also has the diaries of Una, Lady Troubridge, long-time companion of Radclyffe Hall. These cover the years 1911–33. There is also a letter file of Una Troubridge's, which includes correspondence with Lord Fisher, letters from the Board of Admiralty, correspondence about her meeting with Radclyffe Hall, plus an unpublished manuscript of sketches and essays, autobiographical in intent. Lovat Dickson, *Radclyffe Hall at the Well of Loneliness* (London and Toronto, 1975) makes use of these sources.

Her correspondence with Havelock Ellis is in the University of Texas Library, Austin. There is a little general and literary correspondence, 1892–1916, in the Sladen collection; and there are some letters from her in the Arnold Bennett collection.

HAMILL, John Molyneux (1880–1960)

Nutritionist. Inspector of Foods, Local Government Board, from 1907. Senior Medical Officer in charge of Foods Division, Ministry of Health, 1934.

His reports, 1937–9, with Sir John Boyd-Orr, on nutrition and housing conditions in Germany are in the Public Record Office (MH 79/358). The Boyd-Orr papers are in the National Library of Scotland.

HAMILTON, Sir Frederic Howard (1865–1956)

Journalist and businessman. Editor, *Johannesburg Star* during 1890s. Chairman of the Executive Committee of the Liberal National Council.

Rhodes House, Library, Oxford, has papers relating to the Transvaal, including correspondence with the Transvaal Responsible Government Association, 1894–1906 (MSS Afr. S.139), and a typescript letter to Howell Wright concerning Cecil Rhodes and the Jameson Raid, London, 1937 (MSS Afr. S.19).

HAMMOND, John Lawrence Le Breton (1872–1949)

Historian and journalist. Editor of the *Speaker*, 1899–1906. Leader writer on *Tribune*, 1906–7; *Daily News*, 1907. Secretary, Civil Service Commission, 1907–13. Employed at Ministry of Reconstruction, World War I. Special correspondent for the *Manchester Guardian* at the Peace Conference, 1919. On editorial staff of the *Manchester Guardian* from 1939. Co-author with Lucy Barbara Hammond of various studies of social history (*The Village Labourer*, *The Town Labourer*, etc.).

The papers of J. L. and Lucy Barbara Hammond are available at the Bodleian Library, Oxford. The collection includes correspondence, diaries, drafts of publications, working papers, newspaper cuttings, family papers and some printed material. There is a considerable quantity of correspondence exchanged between the Hammonds, with the earliest letter dated 1901. There is also a large amount of general correspondence to both J. L. and L. B. Hammond, covering the period 1895–1951. In addition there are important groups of letters from various correspondents, e.g. letters from Gilbert and Mary Murray, 1901–57, letters from Florence Halévy, 1939–56, and letters connected with newspapers, particularly the *Manchester Guardian* (letters from C. P. Scott, W. P. Crozier). A large number of 'day diaries' and 'pocket diaries', both containing appointments only, cover the period 1902–52. There are a number of drafts for publications and scripts of broadcasts, 1909–38, including 'Recollections of Peace Conference 1918–1919' by L. B. Hammond, reviews of books and a script for a BBC broadcast on 'The Village' (1936). The working notes are largely contained in notebooks, and include a number of notebooks relating to Gladstone. The press cuttings again chiefly relate to the Hammonds' historical writings, and include cuttings of review articles, obituaries, etc. The family papers include two typescripts (dated 1938) of a history of the Hammond family by J. L. Hammond, cuttings, school certificates, etc. In addition to the above, there are various miscellaneous items, including drafts and notes, proofs, accounts, etc., and a diary of two visits the Hammonds paid to Ireland, Feb and Oct 1921. The printed material in the collection, a small group, largely consists of pamphlets and reports.

HAMMOND, Lucy Barbara (1873–1961)

Historian.

See above.

HANCOCK, Sir (William) Keith (1898–   )

Historian. Professor of Modern History, University of Adelaide, 1924–33. Professor of

History, Birmingham University, 1934–44. Chichele Professor of Economic History, Oxford, 1944–9. Supervisor of Civil Histories, War Cabinet Office, from 1941. Director of Institute of Commonwealth Studies and Professor of British Commonwealth Affairs, London, 1949–56. Professor of History, Australian National University, 1957–65.

The Institute of Commonwealth Studies, London University, has items relating to Africa, including his correspondence while working on the Smuts papers and his report after the deportation of the Kabaka of Buganda. Papers relating to General Smuts, collected by Sir Keith Hancock are in the National Library of Australia (MS 2886). Included are copies of letters by Gen. Smuts, a draft of Sir Keith's biography of Smuts, and Sir Keith's correspondence with various people while collecting material for his book. Correspondents include Lord Trenchard, Professor P. G. H. Boswell, Piet Beukes, Sir Dougal Malcolm, Professor D. W. Kruger, Dr W. J. de Kock, Professor K. Kirkwood, Lord Reith, Alan Paton, Mrs Gillett, Professor G. Elliott, Sir V. C. H. R. Brereton, Lord Brand, J. C. Smuts and Clark Bancroft.

HANNAY, David (1853–1934)

Journalist and man of letters. Worked on *Pall Mall Gazette, Saturday Review, St James's Gazette*. A founder of the Navy Records Society.

There is correspondence in the Library of University College London. Correspondents include C. F. Moberly Bell, 1897; Walter Besant, 1884–94; George William Blackwood, 1898–9; Sir Cyprian A. G. Bridge, 1894–8; Austin Dobson, 1906–12; Frederick Greenwood, 1896–1907; Sir Henry Rider Haggard, 1895; W. E. Henley, 1891–4; Rev. William Hunt, 1892–1907; Rudyard Kipling, 1895–1906; G. E. B. Saintsbury, 1896–1907; A. M. M. Stedman, 1893–8; E. D. J. Wilson, 1894–1906.

HANNINGTON, Walter (d. 1966)

Communist publicist and organiser. National organiser, National Unemployed Workers' Movement during 1920s.

The Marx Memorial Library has a collection of Hannington's papers relating to the National Unemployed Workers' Movement. They are described in *Sources* Vol. 1, p. 190. Some papers also survive with the Communist Party of Great Britain.

HARLEY, John Hunter (1865–1947)

Journalist and socialist propagandist. Press representative of Labour Party in House of Commons press gallery, 1908. President, National Union of Journalists, 1911, 1912. Editor, *Polish Review*, 1915; *New Poland*, 1917. General editor, Polish Press Bureau and the Polish Economic *Bulletin*, 1920.

The Modern Records Centre, University of Warwick Library, has a small collection of letters and papers relating to Harley, including two from Rev. Joseph Parker, two from G. B. Shaw and one from Dr Alfred Salter.

HARMSWORTH, Sir Alfred Charles William, 1st Bt, see NORTHCLIFFE, 1st Vt

HARRINGTON, T. R.

Irish journalist. Chief Reporter of *The Nation*, 1897–1904. Editor of *The Irish Independent*, 1904–30.

The Public Record Office of Ireland has a collection of papers. The material includes items of correspondence relating to his work for *The Nation*, including letters inviting him to apply for the position of Chief Reporter, as well as material concerning *The Irish Independent*. There are items relating to the first issue of the journal and Harrington's appointment, 1904–5, including comments from Michael Davitt, Alfred Harmsworth and J. Malcolm Fraser, News Editor of the *Daily Express*. Several letters refer to the 1906 General Election. They include correspondence about T. M. Healey, concerning the paper's attitude to his candidature in North Louth. A fairly extensive correspondence with William Murphy covers the years 1915–18. The subjects covered include Home Rule, the 1916 rebellion, Lloyd George's plan to pacify American feelings, the *Independent's* plans for an Irish settlement, reactions to Henry Duke's appointment as Chief Secretary, conscription, Sinn Fein, the Irish Convention, partition. Several letters from E. M. Murphy, Managing Director of the journal, 1916–17, relate to the rebellion, the alleged pro-German tone of the *Independent*, its attitude to Sir Roger Casement, and the 'evil influence of an unnamed person'. Correspondence with Dr. W. Lombard Murphy, Chairman of Independent Newspapers, covers the period 1919–29. It relates chiefly to the organisation of the paper. Miscellaneous correspondence and papers 1904–30, cover topics such as Home Rule, and the alleged anti-Republican tone of the paper.

HARRIS, Frank (1856–1931)

Journalist and author. Edited the *Fortnightly Review*, *Vanity Fair*, *Saturday Review* and *Candid Friend*.

New York Public Library has a collection of letters and papers, the bulk of them dating from c. 1907. Amongst the correspondence are 11 letters to Ouida (Marie Louise de la Ramèe) and letters to Martin Secker, Abraham Frankel, Einer Lyngklip, Theodore Fraser, H. L. Mencken and others. There are also letters in the Macmillan company records, H. L. Mencken and John Quinn Collections. Amongst the other Harris papers are typescripts of 'A Gambler's Luck', 'Jesus, the Christ', and 'Morning'.
    Correspondence with G. B. Shaw, 1898–1924, and letters to Shaw from Harris's widow are in the British Library (Add. MS 50538). Correspondence with A. C. Swinburne is in the University of Texas Library, Austin.

HARRIS, Walter Burton (1866–1933)

Journalist, traveller and explorer. On the staff of *The Times* from 1906. Correspondent in Morocco.

The archives of *The Times* contain three boxes of material. It includes correspondence, both family and professional, and was given to *The Times* by his family.

HARRISON, Agatha Mary (1885–1954)

Pacifist. From 1921 to 1924 worked in Shanghai with National Committee of YWCA; then to 1927 with American YWCA as an industrial welfare worker in New York. Secretary of the Indian Conciliation Group from 1931. Served on the Friends' Peace Committee, Friends' Service Council and East West Committee; and was a member of the Quaker international team at the United Nations from 1954.

The Library of Friends' House, London, has various papers, presented to it after Miss Harrison's death by her family. These chiefly relate to her work for the Indian Conciliation Group, and include correspondence with Carl Heath, 1938–9, 1940–9; papers on visits to India, 1934–50; notes on various countries and visits by Agatha Harrison; correspondence with Nehru, Desai, Krishna Menon, Jinnah, Cripps; Lords Mountbatten, Sankey, Halifax, Allen, Linlithgow, Pethick-Lawrence and Wavell; George Lansbury, Eleanor Rathbone, General Smuts; communications to and articles in the press; papers on the origins and funds of the

ICG; office correspondence, and with the India Office, Commonwealth Relations Office and M.P.s; material on 'Important Meetings, 1932–52'; pamphlets and other printed material.

HARRISON, Austin (1873–1928)

Author and journalist. Editor of *The English Review*.

Harrison's correspondence with George Bernard Shaw is in the British Library (Add. MS 50538), while correspondence with Thomas Hardy is in the University of Texas Library, Austin. See also below (father).

HARRISON, Frederic (1831–1923)

Author and positivist. Member of Royal Commission on Trade Unions, 1867–9. Secretary, Royal Commission for Digesting the Law, 1869–70. Professor of Jurisprudence and International Law to Inns of Court, 1877–89. Alderman, London County Council, 1889–93. President of English Positivist Committee, 1880–1905.

BLPES has a collection of correspondence, papers and press cuttings. Harrison's general correspondence includes letters from Acton, Charles F. Adams, L. Alma-Tadema, Joseph Arch, 8th Duke of Argyll, Asquith, Louis Baradin, Canon Barnett, letters to E. H. Beesly, 1852–70, letters from Beesly to Harrison, letters from C. Moberly Bell, A. W. Benn, Walter Besant, Professor J. S. Blackie, P. J. Blok, Paul Blouet, W. S. Blunt, G. G. Bradley, 1st Earl Brassey, John Burns, J. H. Bridges, G. Buckle, Edward Burne-Jones, Edward Caird, Andrew Carnegie, Joseph Chamberlain, Frances Power Cobbe, Lord Coleridge, Leonard Courtney, Mandell Creighton, Lord Curzon, Lord Davey, Austin Dobson, Edmund Fitzmaurice, Herbert Gladstone, Viscount Goschen, P. A. Wright Henderson, Fanny Hertz, Lord Hobhouse, Thomas Hodgkin, G. J. Holyoake, T. H. Huxley, H. A .Jones, William Knight, Lord Lytton, Muir Mackenzie, Sir H. S. Maine, Cardinal Manning, Gilbert Murray, letters to John Morley, 1870–1897, and letters from Morley, Francis Newman, Mark Pattison, Theodore Roosevelt, Lord Rosebery, John Ruskin, Lord Russell of Killowen, 3rd Lord Sheffield, Goldwin Smith, Herbert Spencer, W. T. Stead, William Stebbing, Leslie Stephen, W. R. Sullivan, Harold Thorneycroft, H. Beerbohm Tree, W. W. Vernon, Mrs Humphry Ward, Beatrice Webb, H. G. Wells, A. D. White, W. J. Collins and others about the University of London Parliamentary seat; other letters on appointments.

Other material includes diary notes of a visit to Lancashire, 1860–3, speeches, essays, autobiographical writings, drafts of writings on positivism, addresses given in honour of Harrison, printed programmes, invitations etc., proofs.

There is also a series of family correspondence, including that of his wife. Her correspondents include Emily Beesly, Stanton Coit, S. C. Cronwright-Schreiner, Rosalind Howard, later Countess of Carlisle, F. S. Marvin, J. W. Overton, Mrs Humphry Ward. There are also letters to Frederic Harrison, from his father and mother, with some to them, letters from Lawrence Harrison, letters exchanged between Frederic and his wife, letters to their son, Godfrey, and letters to and from other members of the family. There is also a collection of autograph letters. Press cuttings cover the period 1875–1923.

Records of the London Positivist Society, also at BLPES (and described in *Sources* Vol. 1, p. 157) contain further relevant papers.

Correspondence can be found in a number of other collections. At the British Library there are letters in the Macmillan archive (Add. MSS 55035–7) and in the Escott papers. The Bodleian Library, Oxford, has letters in the Asquith and Marvin papers. There is correspondence, 1876–88, in the Joseph Chamberlain collection in Birmingham University Library, while there are some letters to Beesly in University College Library, London. There are letters to Lord Rendel in the National Library of Wales, and letters in the Sir Edmund Gosse papers. The University of Texas at Austin has Harrison's correspondence with John Ruskin, Henry James and Thomas Hardy.

HARRISSON, Tom (1911–76)

Biologist, anthropologist and pioneer of social surveys. Founder (with Charles Madge) of Mass-Observation. Radio critic, *The Observer*, 1941–4. Government Ethnologist and Curator of the Museum, Sarawak, 1947–66. Visiting Professor, Cornell University, 1967–8. Visiting Professor and Director of the Mass-Observation Archive, University of Sussex.

Tom Harrisson's Mass-Observation papers form the core of the Mass-Observation Archive, Sussex University. It is briefly described in *Sources* Vol. 1, p. 163. The collection consists of diaries, observations, surveys and reports contained in over 700 boxes and four filing cabinets. Harrisson's books were also donated to the Archive.

The National Archives of Malaysia, Bangunan Rersekutan, Jalan Sultan, Petaling Jaya, Malaysia, have Harrisson's books and papers relating to his anthropological studies in Asia.

The International Union for Conservation of Nature and Natural Resources, 1110 Morges, Switzerland, has the papers concerning Harrisson's long-time interests in conservation.

Mme Isabelle Forani Welsh (daughter) retains certain papers but these will eventually be deposited.

HART, Sir Basil Liddell (1895–1970)

Military theorist, writer and publicist. Military correspondent, *Daily Telegraph*, 1925–35; *The Times*, 1935–9.

The Liddell Hart Centre for Military Archives, King's College, London, has a large collection of papers and correspondence. The correspondence is grouped in six sections: individual, general, literary, official bodies, clubs and organisations, and letters to the press. Correspondents are wide-ranging and include Sir Richard Acland, the Aga Khan, L. S. Amery, Noel Annan, Lord Attlee, Baden-Powell, Vernon Bartlett, Sir Raymond Beazley, Bishop Bell, Hilaire Belloc, Aneurin Bevan, Lord Boothby, John Buchan, Lord Byers, Lord Chalfont, Sir Winston Churchill, John Connell, Aidan Crawley, A. J. Cummings, General Eisenhower, Michael Foot, E. M. Forster, J. L. Garvin, Sir Ian Hamilton, Alastair Hetherington, Sir Samuel Hoare, Michael Howard, Sir Ian Jacobs, Canon King Salter, Jack Lee, Bernard Levin, Lloyd George, Douglas Macarthur, Donald McLachlan, J. Maisky, Kingsley Martin, James Maxton, Viscount Montgomery, Gilbert Murray, Nehru, Philip Noel-Baker, Sir Bernard Paget, Sir F. Pile, Arthur Ransome, Sidney Rogerson, Sir John Salmond, General E. L. Spears, Sylvia Stevenson, Richard Stokes, Nigel Tangye, Arnold Toynbee, G. M. Trevelyan, Hugh Trevor-Roper, Lord Wavell, W. T. Wells, Spenser Wilkinson, Michael Young and Lord Zuckerman.

The second broad category of papers in the collection is Liddell Hart's military papers. These include manuscripts, proofs, and reviews of his books; articles, books, reviews, forewords etc; his papers as journalist for *The Times* (over 200 items in all); unpublished notes, reflections, records of conversations, memoranda; and lectures, speeches, broadcasts and interviews.

The third broad category of papers includes his material on military affairs, politics and society, arrang d by subject. Finally there are papers of a more personal nature, and material on his 'non-m litary' interests, including religion, sport and fashion.

There is a b x of material in the archives of *The Times*. It includes correspondence with Barrington-War and Geoffrey Dawson, and topics covered include defence plans, the Spanish Civil War, Palesi ne, and the onset of war.

The University of Texas, Austin, has his papers concerning T. E. Lawrence.

HARTOG, Sir Philip Joseph (1864–1947)

Educationalist. Academic Registrar of the University of London, 1903–20. Vice-Chancellor of University of Dacca, Bengal, 1920–5. Member of Indian Public Service Commission, 1926–30.

The India Office Library has a collection of Hartog papers. It includes a draft bill and correspondence on the reform of Calcutta University, 1917–36; correspondence, reports, press cuttings concerning Dacca University, Sir Philip's tenure as Vice-Chancellor, etc.; papers relating to the Public Service Commission, 1922–9, including correspondence with W. R. Barker, Sir John Simon, Michael Sadler and Lord Irwin, 1926–32; personal correspondence, 1926–9; working papers, 1926–30, case files, 1920–30, and correspondence and memoranda on the Committee of Inquiry on Aligash University, 1927–31. There is a group of correspondence and papers concerning the Auxiliary Committee on Education, Indian Statutory Commission, including answers to the questionnaire issued by the Education Committee, 1927–8, notes on various subjects, papers on women's education, reports, etc. There is also a collection of publications: calendars, annual reports, minutes, budget estimates, pamphlets, university bulletins, speeches etc.

Autograph drafts of his novel *The Hireling* are in the British Library (Add. MS 57769 A–G) while letters, 1908–12, are in the Karl Pearson papers in University College London

HARVEY, John Wilfred (1889–1967)

Philosopher. Professor of Philosophy, Armstrong College, Newcastle on Tyne, 1927–32; University of Leeds, 1932–54.

The Imperial War Museum has a collection of papers, particularly relating to his work with the Friends' Ambulance Unit in World War I.

HASLETT, Dame Caroline (d. 1957)

Engineer. Director of the Electrical Association for Women, 1924–54; Secretary, Women's Engineering Society, 1919–29; editor, *Woman Engineer*.

The National Archive for Electrical Science and Technology at the Institution of Electrical Engineers has a collection of papers which reflect the range of her career.

HASTON, Jock (1912–)

Socialist publicist. An early member of the Communist Party of Great Britain, he became a Trotskyist in 1934. A founder of the Workers' International League, 1937, he became its secretary. Secretary of the Revolutionary Communist Party from 1944. He left the Trotskyist movement in 1949. Tutor/organiser, National Council of Labour Colleges, 1950–63. National Education Officer of the Electrical Trades Union and head of Esher College, 1964–73. National Education Officer of the General and Municipal Workers' Union and Head of Woodstock College, 1974–6.

The Haston collection of printed material, typescripts and correspondence was acquired by Hull University Library in 1967. It contains about 3500 pamphlets, covering a very wide range of subjects, published by a large number of left-wing organisations, mainly British. There are also many sets (of varying completeness) of periodicals, mainly in the 1930s and 1940s, but some going back very much earlier (*Plebs*, 1913–67, *Labour Monthly* 1922–65, *Communist International*, with gaps, 1919–39). Among the more important are perhaps *New International* (NY), 1934–58, and *Fourth International* (NY), 1940–54; American newspapers are represented by *Labour Action, Militant, Socialist Appeal*; English by *Daily Worker* (1930–66), *Workers International News* (1938–49), *Socialist Appeal* (London, 1941–9), all except the *Daily Worker* incomplete. There are also a large number of short and/or very incomplete runs of periodicals produced by smaller and often short-lived groups.

There is a quantity of duplicated typescript material and some correspondence from Trotskyist groups, mainly the Revolutionary Communist Party, c. 1944–50, the Workers' International League, c. 1938–44, and the Revolutionary Socialist League, c. 1938–43; there is a very little material from other Trotskyist groups of the 1930s. The RCP files include correspondence with groups and individuals abroad, among them the International Secretariat, the International Executive Committee of the Fourth International, and Natalia Trotsky.

The library also has a collection of xerox copies of duplicated typescript material originally belonging to D. D. Harber, and lent for copying by his son. This covers the years 1939–45, concerning the RSL mainly, including material from three conferences and some material of the Militant Group of the RSL; some WIL material, especially concerning fusion; and a file of RCP material from the years 1944–5. The Modern Records Centre, University of Warwick Library, has the originals of this material.

HAWTREY, Sir Ralph George (1879–1974)

Economist. On staff of Treasury, 1904–45. Director of Financial Inquiries, 1919–45. President of the Royal Economic Society, 1946–8. Price Professor of International Economics, 1947–52.

Churchill College, Cambridge, has an important collection of papers, covering his work from his early days in the Treasury to his death. Treasury papers date from 1915, and cover policy as regards America, Germany, India, the gold reserves, land values, navy estimates, unemployment and public works, inflation and deflation, subsidies, the cost of living, foreign trade, the gold standard, the Bank for International Settlements, the Committee on Finance and Industry, the 'Henderson Scheme', the Danubian currencies, fiscal policy during the depression, and various other papers, including 'The Treasury History of the Second World War', an unpublished typescript in two parts. Papers concerning Chatham House include correspondence and reports dating from 1929. There is also material, papers and correspondence on the Radcliffe Committee, 1957–8. The collection also includes official publications, dating back to 1894, but most dating from 1910, and largely concerning Financial Statements, together with articles by Hawtrey, published and unpublished, and copies of reviews by him. Additionally, some material concerns his dealings with his publishers, and includes correspondence and papers. There are also press cuttings and correspondence relating to newspapers and journals, including *The Economist* (1947–61, 1968), the *Observer, Sunday Times* and *Spectator*. Correspondence is extensive, and among the correspondents are Olive Armstrong, Lords Boothby and Brand, Edwin Cannan, Gustav Cassel, Sir Henry Clay, the Committee on Economic Development, 1957–8; the Council on Prices, Productivity and Incomes, 1957–9; C. H. Douglas, Evan Durbin, Irving Fisher, Sir Roy Harrod (this is an extensive correspondence, 1937–62); Frederick von Hayek, Paul de Hevesy, Sir J. R. Hicks, the Industrial Christian Fellowship, Lord Kaldor, Sir Frank Lee, Roger Makins, J. A. C. Osborne (extensive correspondence, 1923–64), Lord Robbins, Bertrand Russell, F. W. Taussig, Philip Wernett, and W. H. White. There is an important correspondence with J. M. Keynes, dating from 1922, including letters, papers and press cuttings. This grouping includes papers on the Committee on Finance and Industry, 1930–1, correspondence on *Treatise on Money*, 1930; the *General Theory*, 1935–6, other Keynes publications, and his *Proposals for an International Currency Union*, 1941. Finally, the collection also contains MS proofs of works by Hawtrey, and miscellaneous material on broadcasting, newspapers and research.

HAYLER, Guy (1850–1943)

Temperance reformer. Agent of the United Kingdom Alliance from 1874. General Secretary, North of England Temperance League from 1889. President of the World Prohibition Federation, 1909–39.

Papers are in the Memorial Library, University of Wisconsin, Madison. The Rare Book Department has three bound volumes of MS materials. Other material included in the original deposit has been dispersed within the Library. Records of British Temperance organisations are described in *Sources* Vol. 1, pp. 253–7. A memorial note by his son gives biographical details: Mark H. C. Hayler, *The Man from Battle* (Birmingham, 1950).

HEADLAM, Arthur Cayley (1862–1947)

Churchman. Editor, *Church Quarterly Review*, 1902–21. Principal of King's College, London, 1903–12; Professor of Dogmatic Theology, 1903–16. Regius Professor of Divinity, Oxford University, 1918–23. Bishop of Gloucester, 1923–45.

Lambeth Palace Library has an important collection of papers, covering many aspects of developments in the Church as well as Headlam's various activities. Amongst the files are the following: Kikuyu Controversy, 1914; Westminster Abbey Advent Lectures on Reunion; Correspondence on Bampton Lecture, 1920; Oxford Conference on Reunion and Lambeth, 1920; Eastern Churches, 1919–26; Oxford University – Reform of the School of Theology and Divinity Degrees; Tour of America and Canada, 1924; Church of South India 1913–46; Anglican–Free Church discussions on Unity; Prayer Book Revision, 1925–8; Faith and Order Movement; Lambeth Conference, 1930; Anglican–Old Catholic relations, 1930–9; Papers on relations between the Church of England and Sweden, Finland, Iceland, Latvia and Estonia, Yugoslavia, Romania; Council on Foreign Relations (including Germany and 1940 Balkan Tour); King's College, London.
A gift to Lambeth Palace Library by Mrs D. F. Buxton of papers concerning the Church struggle in Germany during the Nazi regime complements the relevant material in the Headlam papers and also in the Bishop Bell papers. Other relevant material in Lambeth Palace Library includes Headlam's papers and correspondence as editor of the *Church Quarterly Review*.
A biography of Headlam has been prepared by the Rev. R. C. D. Jasper, using the above papers.

HEADLAM, Stewart Duckworth (1847–1924)

Christian socialist and churchman. Curate in East End of London from 1870. Member, London School Board, 1888–1904. Member of London County Council from 1907.

A small amount of correspondence, 1915, is in the War Emergency Workers National Committee papers, in the archives of the Labour Party at Transport House. No personal papers are known to survive in Britain. *Stewart Headlam: a biography* by F. G. Bettany (1926) contains extracts from correspondence, autobiographical writings and contemporary reminiscences, but these do not appear to be extant. For biographical details, see *Dictionary of Labour Biography* Vol. II, pp. 172–8.

HENRIQUES, Sir Basil Lucas Quixano (1890–1961)

Author and publicist. Leader of the Anglo-Jewish community and Zionist supporter. Founder and warden of Bernhard Baron St George's Jewish Settlement, 1914–47.

Papers of Sir Basil survive in the Anglo-Jewish Archives collection in the Mocatta Library, University College London. The material includes original diaries, copies of correspondence with his mother, addresses and articles and miscellaneous other material. The Archives also have papers of Sir Basil's wife, Rose, in connection with her biography of her husband (over 50 files). Lady Henriques' 'Questionnaire to a cross-section of the Jewish community' in 1947–8 is also in the Anglo-Jewish Archives (ref. AJ/30). Other papers at present remain in the care of Mr Basil Henriques (son).

HENSON, Herbert Hensley (1863–1947)

Churchman. Bishop of Hereford, 1918–20; of Durham, 1920–39. Canon of Westminster Abbey, 1940–1.

Lambeth Palace Library has miscellaneous correspondence, including letters to Archbishop Davidson and the Bishop of Winchester. His sketches at meetings of the Prayer-Book Revision

Committee, 1926–8, are also in Lambeth Palace Library. Correspondence with the 2nd Lord Selborne is in the Bodleian Library, Oxford.

HERBERT, Sir Robert George Wyndham (1831–1905)

Administrator and civil servant. Premier of Queensland, 1860–5. Assistant Secretary, Board of Trade, 1868. Assistant Under-Secretary, Colonial Office, 1870. Permanent Under-Secretary for the Colonies, 1871–92. Agent-General for Tasmania, 1893–6. Chairman of the Tariff Commission, 1904.

Correspondence, 1863–91, is in the John Oxley Library, Brisbane, Australia. Records of the Tariff Commission are housed in BLPES and are currently being catalogued. Transcripts of his letters home, c. 1865–70, are in the Im Thurn collection at the Royal Anthropological Society.

HERTZ, Joseph Herman (1872–1946)

Rabbi, author and Zionist. Chief Rabbi of the United Hebrew Congregations of the British Empire from 1913. Professor of Philosophy, Transvaal University College, 1906–8. President of the Jews' College, London, from 1913; Acting Principal, 1939–45. Vice President of the League of Nations Union, the National Council of Public Morals, etc.

Mr Samuel Hertz (son) has a wide range of papers covering the various aspects of Hertz's interests. Further details will be published by the British Academy's Anglo-Palestinian Archives Project.

HICKS, Edward Lee (1843–1919)

Ecclesiastic. Bishop of Lincoln from 1910. Temperance advocate; Hon. Secretary, United Kingdom Alliance.

Correspondence and a diary are in the Diocesan records, Lincolnshire Archives Office. The Honnold Library, Claremont, California, has correspondence, 1865–1912, addressed to Edwin Palmer and Edward Lee Hicks. Records of the United Kingdom Alliance are described in *Sources* Vol. 1, pp. 255–6

HIGGINBOTTOM, Samuel (1874–1958)

Educator, missionary and agricultural economist. Founder of Allahabad Agricultural Institute in India.

The University of Virginia Library, Charlottesville, has a collection of some 20,000 items, 1874–1958.

HIGGS, Henry (1864–1940)

Economist and Civil Servant. Private Secretary to Sir Henry Campbell-Bannerman. Lecturer in Economics, Toynbee Hall, 1887–94. Secretary to the Royal Economic Society and joint editor, *Economic Journal*, 1892–1906. Fellow of University College. Special Commissioner to Natal, 1902–3. Inspector-General of Finance, Egypt, 1912–15. Principal Clerk, H.M. Treasury, to 1921. Lecturer in Economics, University College, Bangor, 1925–9. Author and editor of various books on economics.

Sturges, *Economists' Papers*, p. 4, was unable to trace any personal papers. There are letters, however, in other collections. The Campbell-Bannerman collection at the British Library (Add. MSS 41240–2) has relevant correspondence, with enclosures, 1906–19. At BLPES some 12 letters, 1896–33, can be found in the Cannan papers. The Baker Library, Harvard University, has some material in the Cole and Foxwell papers, while some 12 letters to J. M. Keynes,

1930–6 are in the Marshall Library, Cambridge. The Seligman papers, Columbia University Library, contain 28 letters, 1895–1910, and the Ponsonby papers include 10 letters, 1907–8 (NRA 18634).

HILL, Octavia (1838–1912)

Philanthropist. Worked with Charity Organisation Society, Kyrie Society, Women's University Settlement. Member of the Royal Commission on the Poor Law, 1905, etc.

Westminster City Libraries (the Marylebone Library, Local History Room) have a collection of Octavia Hill material, manuscript and printed. There are some 26 letters from her to Paula Schuster, who gave her financial backing, concerning the 'open-space' schemes, housing prospects (especially the Notting Hill scheme), the Poor Law Commission and the Charity Organisation Society. There are also three letters from Harriot Yorke and Miranda Hill to Miss Schuster. There is also extensive correspondence with Sir Sydney Cockerell and his family, 1887–1912. This includes a bound volume containing 257 letters to Sir Sydney, with mainly personal details and some information about housing prospects and 'open-space schemes' and the Red Cross Hall, Southwark. Another bound volume contains 63 letters from Octavia Hill to Sydney J. Cockerell (Sir Sydney's father) and Alice Cockerell, and 12 letters to Olive Cockerell. The letters are mainly personal, with general points about her work. There are also other assorted letters relating to Octavia Hill. The printed material includes some press cuttings, and also works by and about Octavia Hill.

There is further correspondence with Sir Sydney Cockerell (some 70 letters) in the British Library (Add. MS 52722). Letters from Octavia Hill to Canon and Mrs S. A. Barnett are in the care of BLPES, and further correspondence can be found in the Barnett papers in the Greater London Record Office. Some nine letters to Lady Wolseley, 1883–1903, are in Hove Public Library

HINDEN, Rita (1909–71)

Socialist journalist and anti-imperialist. Secretary of the Fabian Colonial Bureau, 1940–50. Secretary, Socialist Union. Editor of *Socialist Commentary* from 1948.

On her death, Rita Hinden's papers passed to Dr E. Hinden (husband), 20 West Heath Drive, London NW11. Apart from purely personal and private material, he now has a complete file of her published works, together with a press-cuttings book, 1940–8, which contains cuttings of her articles. Papers, 1940–50, concerning Rita Hinden's work for the Fabian Colonial Bureau, are in Rhodes House Library, Oxford. These records are described in *Sources* Vol. 1, pp. 94–5. Rhodes House Library also has the papers of Arthur Creech Jones with whom Rita Hinden worked closely. Reference should also be made to the records of *Socialist Commentary*. A biographical note on Rita Hinden appears in the *Dictionary of Labour Biography* Vol. II, pp. 179–82.

HIRSCH, Samuel Abraham (1843–1923)

Hebraist. Theological tutor of the Jews' College. Editor of the *Jewish Standard* and *Palestine*. President of the Joint Zionist Council, 1914.

The Anglo-Jewish Archives, at the Mocatta Library, University College London, contain papers of Samuel Hirsch and his son Julian. Most of the collection relates to Hirsch's work at the Jews' College, Hebraic Studies, the Jewish Dictionary and the *Jewish Standard*. Correspondents include Professor Flinders Petrie, Alfred Adler, Norman Bentwich, Dr J. H. Hertz, Claude G. Montefiore, staff at the College of Preceptors and the Jews' College, etc. Other material includes drafts of published and unpublished works, lectures, essays etc, many on Zionist themes; and various notes and press cuttings. Julian Hirsch's papers include manuscript and typescript essays and notes relating to the early history of Zionism.

97

HIRST, Francis Wrigley (1873–1953)

Economist and journalist. Editor of *The Economist*, 1907–16. Hon. Secretary, Cobden Club. Author of works on Liberalism, Political Economy, Free Trade etc.

According to Sturges, *Economists' Papers*, p. 42, the bulk of the Hirst collection was destroyed or dispersed as a result of successive moves, and more papers were destroyed following his death. Most of the surviving material was placed in the care of Mr A. F. Thompson of Wadham College, Oxford, and is not currently available. This grouping consists of drafts for books and articles, a mass of press cuttings, and a miscellaneous collection of correspondence.

Some lectures and notes by Hirst on Viscount Morley, with five letters to Hirst from Morley, 1928–30, are in the Morley papers at the India Office Library. Correspondence can also be found in the James Truslow Adams papers, Columbia University Library, New York (42 letters, 1930–48); the Beveridge papers at BLPES (1925–33); the Sir John Brunner papers, Liverpool University Library (29 letters, 1909–17); the John Stewart Bryan papers, Virginia State Library, Richmond (c. 175 items, 1924–43); the J. M. Keynes papers, Marshall Library, Cambridge (11 letters, 1909–20); and the Oswald Garrison Villard papers, Houghton Library, Harvard University (80 items, 1921–49).

Certain records of the Cobden Club, briefly described in *Sources* Vol. 1, p. 44, are now deposited in West Sussex Record Office.

HIRST, William Alfred (1870–1948)

Author and traveller. In India from 1894. First Professor, Meerut College, 1896–1902. Principal, Gujerat College, Ahmedabad, 1902–7.

No personal papers have been traced. Some notes for lectures on Viscount Morley are in the India Office Library, while the papers of his brother Francis Wrigley Hirst, are described above.

HOBHOUSE, Leonard Trelawney (1864–1929)

Social theorist. On editorial staff of the *Manchester Guardian*, 1897–1902; of *Tribune*, 1906–7. Secretary of the Free Trade Union, 1903–5. Professor of Sociology, London University, from 1907.

A small quantity of material, including letters from Hobhouse to Margaret Llewelyn Davies, is in the Ginsberg collection at BLPES. The *Manchester Guardian* archive at the John Rylands University Library of Manchester has certain relevant material, including correspondence with C. P. Scott, 1896–1925. Some further letters are in the Marvin collection. *L. T. Hobhouse: His Life and Work*, by J. A. Hobson and Morris Ginsberg, was published in 1931.

HOBSON, Bulmer (d. 1969)

Irish nationalist. Founder of the *Republic*, assistant editor of the *Peasant* and editor of *Irish Freedom*. Member of the Irish Republican Brotherhood; a leading figure in the Irish Volunteers.

The National Library of Ireland has a collection of letters and papers, consisting of some 600 items. The material relates to the Irish volunteers, the 1916 rising, and related topics and includes letters from Sir Roger Casement, Eoin MacNeill, Alice Stopford Green, Alice Milligan, Padraic O'Conaire, Brinsley MacNamara and P. H. Pearse.

HOBSON, John Atkinson (1858–1940)

Economist and publicist. Lecturer in English Literature and Economics for the Oxford University Extension Delegacy, 1887–97. Author of numerous works on economics, social science, politics.

A small collection of material has been given to Hull University Library. This includes a volume of press cuttings (indexed), 1894–1914, which also includes letters from Peter Kropotkin, Frederic Harrison, W. Sinclair, J. H. Whitehouse, W. E. Collingwood, Patrick Geddes, Albert Fleming and William White. There is in addition a single letter from Herbert Spencer on Hobson's book *The Psychology of Jingoism*. The collection also includes a folder of typescript works of Hobson's, mostly talks delivered in the 1930s to the South Place Ethical Society; a few obituary notices; and a number of Hobson's printed pamphlets and articles, dating from 1895. Hobson's notes on a League of Nations, 1915, can be found at the Bodleian Library, Oxford (ref. MSS Eng. Hist. C402).

The J. M. Keynes papers at the Marshall Library, Cambridge, contain some 13 relevant items, while the Gilbert Murray papers at the Bodleian Library contain 17 letters, 1900–18. Correspondence, 1901–8, can also be found in the Samuel papers at the House of Lords Record Office, and some letters to Henry Demarest Lloyd are in the State Historical Society, Madison, Wisconsin. A microfilm of some of these is in BLPES.

Hobson published his *Confessions of an Economic Heretic* in 1938, and H. N. Brailsford *The Life-Work of J. A. Hobson* in 1948. Reference should also be made to Sturges, *Economists' Papers*, pp. 43–4, which mentions relevant material.

HOCKING, Silas Kitto (1850–1935)

Novelist, Methodist preacher and social reformer. His special interests included temperance and the education of children.

The Modern Records Centre, University of Warwick Library, has a collection of some 800 sermons and other texts by Hocking, covering the period 1871–96. The bulk of the collection consists of sermons preached at Burnley, Liverpool, Southport, Manchester, Northampton, London, Llandudno, etc. There is also a memorial sermon for John Bright, 1883; a 19-page essay on Socialism; various speeches and addresses concerning the National Children's Home, the training of children, disestablishment, etc.; a 15-page diary of a journey to Ireland, 1874; a short story; and notes for lecture tours abroad, etc.

HODGE, Harold (1862–1937)

Journalist, with particular interest in social problems. Editor, *Saturday Review*, 1898–1913. Edited series of pamphlets on Reconstruction Problems for the Ministry of Reconstruction, 1918–19.

No personal papers have been traced but a few letters, 1907–9, to the *Church Quarterly Review* are in Lambeth Palace Library.

HODGKIN, Henry Theodore (1877–1933)

Quaker missionary and pacifist. Medical missionary in China, 1905–10. Secretary of the Friends' Foreign Mission Association, 1910–20. Chairman of the Fellowship of Reconciliation, 1915–20. First Director of Pendle Hill College, Pennsylvania.

His papers are preserved in the Library of Friends' House, London. Material relating to his early life and work includes letters to his mother, 1899, 1901, 1907–9; correspondence from China; letters received, 1907–8; and drafts and correspondence relating to the Chengtu Union University Constitution. A group of material relates to the FFMA Secretaryship, 1910–17, and includes material relating to China, Anglo-Chinese friendship, Quakerism and issues of peace. More personal papers for the same period, including correspondence with E. Jay Hodgkin, also survive. There are several files concerning the Fellowship of Reconciliation and of matters relating to peace, and a number of letters deal with China during the early 1920s. For the same period there is a group of papers concerning the National Christian Council Secretaryship. Material for the Pendle Hill period, 1928–33, includes letters on leaving China, 1928–9; American Quaker and educational duplicated and printed material, 1930–3; and miscellaneous correspondence, 1929–33. The collection also includes miscellaneous lectures; printed and duplicated material on peace and China; and obituary notices and letters of condolence; typescript drafts of early chapters of H. G. Wood, *Life of H. T. Hodgkin*; and personalia.

Records of the Fellowship of Reconciliation are described in *Sources* Vol. 1, pp. 99–100.

HODGSON, (John) Stuart (1877–1950)

Journalist. Editor, *Daily News*, 1921–31. Publications include *A Summary of the Liberal Industrial Report*.

No personal papers have been traced. The National Westminster Bank, Trustee Department, who acted in the estate, had no present contact with the family. A few letters to Lloyd George, 1926–7, are in the House of Lords Record Office.

HOGARTH, David George (1862–1927)

Archaeologist and Arabist. Director, British School at Athens, 1897–1900. Keeper of the Ashmolean Museum from 1909. Director of the Arab Bureau, 1916–18.

An important collection of papers is housed at the Middle East Centre, St Antony's College, Oxford. The material includes World War I papers and records relating to the peace settlement.

Correspondence with Sir Sydney Cockerell concerning his biography of C. M. Doughty is in the British Library (Add. MS 52722).

HOGBEN, Lancelot (1895–   )

Scientist. Fellow of the Royal Society. Professor of Zoology, University of Cape Town, 1927–30; Professor of Social Biology, London University, 1930–7; Regius Professor of Natural History, University of Aberdeen, 1937–41; Mason Professor of Zoology, Birmingham University, 1941–7; Professor of Medical Statistics, 1947–61. Vice Chancellor, University of Guyana, 1963–5.

A complete offprint collection, in five volumes, dating from 1922, is held by the History and Social Studies of Science Division, University of Sussex.

HOLE, Hugh Marshall (1865–1941)

Businessman and colonial administrator. Joined British South Africa Company, 1890; onetime Secretary. Entered Civil Service of Rhodesia, 1891, as Secretary to the Administrator, Sir L. S. Jameson.

Papers are at Yale University Library.

HOLFORD, Baron
Sir William Graham Holford (1907–75)

Architect and planner. Professor of Civic Design, Liverpool University, 1936–47. Professor of Town Planning, University College London, 1948–70. President, Royal Institute of British Architects, 1960–2. Director, Leverhulme Trust Fund, 1972–5.

A collection of papers has been deposited with Liverpool University Archives. The papers comprise some 700 files, box files and boxes, and cover most aspects of Lord Holford's career and work, both with and for public and professional bodies in Britain and abroad, 1924–75. The papers are being catalogued, and no decision has yet been made regarding access. Further material, relating to his work in the University, is in the archives of the University itself. Other personal papers are being retained for the moment by Sir William Holford and Partners and by Lord Holford's family.

HOLLAND, Henry Scott (1847–1918)

Theologian. Canon of St Paul's, 1884–1910. Regius Professor of Divinity, Oxford, from 1910. Founder of the Christian Social Union. Editor of *The Commonwealth*.

The Rev. Canon John H. Heidt, who has prepared a study of Scott Holland, was unable to trace any general collection of papers, and believes they may have been destroyed. He did, however, use a number of papers in other collections. The Bodleian Library has various items, including letters in the Asquith collection, chiefly relating to Holland's appointment to the Regius Professorship; three letters fron Thomas K. Cheyne (Eng. Lett. c. 28); several letters to William Sanday and miscellaneous letters to J. M. Thompson, Sidney Lee, etc. (Eng. Misc. d. 126 and 140). Over 70 letters to R. C. Moberley are also on deposit in the Bodleian Library. At the British Library there is correspondence with Mary Drew, 1876–1918 (Add. MSS 46247–8); letters to R. W. Church and E. S. Talbot (Add. MSS 44127 and 44476); letters to Herbert Gladstone (Add. MSS 46050, 46051 and 46055), and letters to Sir Charles Dilke (Add. MS 43919). At Lambeth Palace Library several letters from Holland can be found in the E. W. Benson, Frederick Temple and Randall Davidson papers, and in MSS 1773, 1617, 1620 and 1750. At the National Library of Scotland, there are letters in the Rosebery and R. B. Haldane collections, and St Andrews University Library has the Lilley papers which contain relevant material. There are letters from Holland and Stephen Freemantle to W. H. Ady and Cecilia Ady in the Cartwright (Edgcote) collection, Northamptonshire Record Office. The Working Men's College Archives, London, has over 20 letters from Holland to H. R. Jennings and MS notes taken from Holland's address on St Paul's Cathedral in the College. Reference should be made to Stephen Paget, *Henry Scott Holland, Memoir and Letters* (1921), and *A Forty Years' Friendship: letters fron the late Henry Scott Holland to Mrs Drew*, ed. S. L. Ollard (1919). Records of the Christian Social Union, including papers of the Oxford University branch in Pusey House Library, are briefly described in *Sources* Vol. 1, p. 37.

HOLMES, Walter (1892–1973)

Communist journalist.

Enquiries should be directed to the Communist Party of Great Britain.

HOLT, John (1841–1915)

Businessman. Trader in West Africa. Chairman, John Holt & Co Ltd. Chairman of African Association. Advocate of the development of West Africa.

Papers are housed in Rhodes House Library, Oxford. They include business and personal correspondence and diaries. Correspondents include Mary Kingsley and E. D. Morel. Many of the papers concern the firm, John Holt & Co, 1863–1923, and include correspondence with other businessmen and with the Foreign and Colonial Offices and the French Government. There are also four boxes of correspondence and papers relating to the Lagos Marina Case, 1909–21.

The Picton Library, Liverpool, has a collection of diaries, 1858–1900, press cuttings, 1876–1933, John Holt letterbooks, 1861–1914, trade diaries, 1875–1905, and business papers, maps, photographs, etc.

HOLTBY, Winifred (1898–1935)

Novelist and author. Director of *Time and Tide* from 1926.

A collection of material is housed in the local history libraries of Hull and Bridlington (Humberside Public Libraries). The collection is in two parts, the first consisting of all printed editions of Winifred Holtby's work, including first and later editions, foreign language translations, etc., and bibliographies, biographies and criticisms; the second consists of a large collection of original material. Most of this original material was given by her literary executor, Vera Brittain, with further additions from various sources. This part of the collection consists of several thousand separate items, including letters (particularly correspondence with Vera Brittain, q.v.), notebooks, diaries, manuscripts of various writings, and photographs. Winifred Holtby's output as a journalist is reflected in a large number of articles and newscuttings, many of which reflect her own views on current affairs. The political material is particularly interesting, chiefly relating to South African affairs. This includes letters from F. S. Livie-Noble of the London Group on African Native Affairs, W. C. Ballinger of the Industrial and Commercial Workers' Union of Africa, Miss M. L. Hodgson and Archdeacon W. E. Owen, and correspondence on the early history of the ICU, consisting mostly of letters written by Clements Kadalie and A. Creech Jones.

The Creech Jones collection in Rhodes House Library, Oxford, has some 29 letters and postcards from Winifred Holtby relating to her work in South Africa and the beginning of the Friends of Africa Society, and letters concerning her death and memorial service.

HOLYOAKE, George Jacob (1817–1906)

Co-operator and secularist. Editor of the *Reasoner*, 1846–66. Author of histories of the Co-operative Movement, and of works on secularism.

A collection of letters and papers (3000 in all) covering the period 1835–1903 is deposited in the Library of the Co-operative Union, Manchester. A catalogue is available there which fully describes the collection. It was given to the Library in the form of bundles, many of which had been roughly assembled for autobiographical purposes. The material has now been catalogued in chronological order, though the outline of the original grouping is included in the catalogue. The letters are from a wide number of correspondents and cover the range of his interests.

A further collection of diaries and other papers is available at the Bishopsgate Institute, London. This collection includes a muster roll of Garibaldi's British Legion (of which Holyoake was secretary) with related correspondence, 1860–1; a Central Garibaldi Committee minute book, Aug 1860–Mar 1861; MS and press-cutting minutes of the Travelling Tax Abolition Committee, 1877–98; London Atheistical Society, rules, 1842–3, and index of c. 5000 letters from Holyoake, 1845–8; a notebook containing brief notes of lectures, etc., 1838–9; odd pages of a diary for 1845, and diaries, 1849, 1850, 1853–63, 1865–77, 1879–81, 1882–1905; Holyoake's 'Cash Book of the Fleet Street House', 1858–61; letters relating to Collett's *History of the taxes upon knowledge*, 1898–9; copy of an article entitled 'Self-Culture – Use of Books'; 'logbooks' (i.e. chronological autobiographical notes), 1831–40, 1845; and a diary-cum-notebook, 1847–52.

Further minor items can be found in the Local History Collection, Birmingham Central Library. The Library of Duke University, North Carolina, has a collection consisting mostly of letters from Holyoake to William H. Duignan. The material covers a range of interests, including working class conditions, reform in Ireland, Home Rule, a journey to the USA in 1882, and religion.

Miscellaneous correspondence on Robert Owen, including copy letters to him, and printed ephemera on co-operation, collected by Holyoake, are in the Robert Owen Memorial Museum, Newtown, Powys.

HORN, David Bayne (1901–69)

Historian. Lecturer, Edinburgh University, 1927–54. Professor of History, Hull University College, 1935–6. Professor of Modern History, Edinburgh University, from 1954. Hon. President, Edinburgh Workers' Education Association.

Edinburgh University Library has a collection of Professor Horn's papers. These have not been fully catalogued. There are six boxes of papers relating to the history of Edinburgh University which were intended for a large-scale history; and there are also eight boxes of papers, containing manuscripts and offprints of articles, lectures etc.

HORNER, Arthur Lewis (1894–1968)

Trade unionist and leading member of the Communist Party of Great Britain. President, South Wales Miners' Federation, 1936–46. General Secretary, National Union of Mineworkers, 1946–59.

A collection of material has been deposited in the Library of the University College of Swansea. It includes a small number of letters, chiefly to Horner, 1932–59, but also correspondence relating to the Maerdy Distress Committee, 1929 (together with its minute book) and the Maerdy Defence Committee, 1931–2; miscellaneous postcards; two telegrams to Horner, 1933; leaflets; election material for the Rhondda East Parliamentary by-election, 1933; the copies of a script for a BBC talk by Horner, Oct 1945; a transcript of discussion between Horner and M. M. Postan, 1938; cuttings from the press; reports, addresses and speeches by Horner to the NUM; pamphlets; miscellaneous printed material; and a collection of personalia (birthday cards, membership cards, pay slips, photographs, etc.).

HORRABIN, Winifred (1887–1971)

Feminist and socialist writer.

The papers of Winifred Horrabin are preserved in Hull University Library. The collection includes a series of diaries, 'Journals' and 'Notebooks' dating from 1922. The diaries are basically day-to-day accounts of events, while the 'Journals' are fuller, containing descriptions of major events and journeys interspersed with comment, literary notes, observations and self-analytical jottings. The 'Notebooks' contain notes and jottings intended for extension or use at a later date in written work, or are related to personal matters. Amongst matters covered in the 'Journals' are journeys to Russia (1926), Poland (1927–52), and the USA (1949). The 'Notebooks' contain, *inter alia*, material relating to Thomas Carlyle, Olive Schreiner (several 'Notebooks'), the Spanish Civil War, notes for stories, personal and autobiographical notes, comments on Frank Horrabin, on 'Oxford', and a variety of other matters. There is also a collection of literary MSS and typescripts, dating from 1916. Amongst these are seven folders of typescript of 'This Year . . . Next Year . . . ? A War-time story' (1916); several folders of notes, press cuttings, MSS and typescripts relating to 'Citizen of the World, Olive Schreiner' (1937); 'A Collage' of articles (c. 1965); and folders of drafts and jottings for articles, 1920s–60s. The correspondence ranges from personal to literary and political matters. There is a considerable amount of correspondence with and relating to her husband, Frank Horrabin, dating from 1907, covering his political involvements as well as their personal relationship, and culminating in their separation and eventual divorce in the 1940s. There is also correspondence from members of her family, and from H. G. Wells, Vera Brittain, William Mellor, G. R. Strauss and others. Other material in the collection includes volumes of press cuttings, 1926–63, photographs, miscellaneous family material and personalia.

HORTON-SMITH, Lionel Graham Horton (1871–1953)

Naval propagandist. Secretary of the Imperial Maritime League, which pressed for a stronger naval policy, 1908–13.

The National Maritime Museum has 28 volumes of pamphlets and press cuttings on naval policy and the Imperial Maritime League.

HOUSMAN, Laurence (1865–1959)

Author and artist. Supporter of women's suffrage. One-time Chairman of the British Society for the Study of Sex Psychology.

There is a collection of books and papers in Street Library, 1 Leigh Road, Street, Somerset. Apart from copies of his published works and drawings, the major element consists of some 200 letters, chiefly from Housman to Roger and Sarah Clarke, 1908–52. There are also a number of autograph letters and poems by Max Beerbohm, Lawrence Binyon, G. K. Chesterton, John Masefield, G. B. Shaw, 'Q', Oscar Wilde and A. E. Housman. The collection also includes a tape of a radio programme about Housman, first broadcast in November 1965, a scrapbook of production photographs of *Victoria Regina*; obituary notes etc. A *Brief Catalogue* has been published by the Library.

The University of Texas, Austin, also has some 30 years of correspondence between Housman and George Ives, 1916–46, chiefly concerning their endeavours for changes in attitudes towards homosexuality, as well as records of the British Society for the Study of Sex Psychology.

The Special Collections at Colby College, Waterville, Maine 04901, USA have letters from Housman to various correspondents. They include Granville Bantock, Harley Granville Barker and Grace M. Martin. Iowa University Library has correspondence, especially with Harry Quilter, the art critic. Columbia University Libraries have a collection of letters from Housman.

The Library of University College London, has correspondence on the literary estates of Laurence and A. E. Housman (the Robert E. Symons collection).

At the British Library there is an autograph draft of his introduction to the diaries of A. E. Housman (Add. MS 45861) and correspondence with Sir Sydney Cockerell, 1936–7 (Add. MS 52726).

There is extensive correspondence in King's College Library, Cambridge, in the C. R. Ashbee Journals, 1902–41. Correspondence can also be found in the Russell archive at McMaster University.

Housman edited a series of his letters: *What Can We Believe? Letters exchanged between Dick Sheppard and Laurence Housman* (1939).

HOWARD, Sir Ebenezer (1850–1928)

Town planner. Founded the Garden City Association, 1899. Director of First Garden City Ltd and Welwyn Garden City Ltd.

Manuscripts, books, correspondence and miscellaneous papers are deposited in Hertfordshire Record Office. They include notes in manuscript and typescript for *Tomorrow: a peaceful path to real reform*; miscellaneous documents concerned with Howard's work as a town planner, including correspondence on the purchase of land for Welwyn Garden City and other papers on Welwyn; biographical and autobiographical material, including pages of a desk diary, notes and miscellaneous papers; and correspondence. Correspondents include Sir Jesse Boot (Lord Trent), James Bryce, Edward Cadbury, Lord Robert Cecil, Cecil Harmsworth, Henry Holiday and Sir Ralph Neville. There are also press cuttings, obituary notices; papers on his estate, etc.

HOWELL, George (1833–1910)

Trade union leader and radical politician. M.P. (Lib.) Bethnal Green N.E., 1885–95.

The Bishopsgate Institute has a collection of material. It includes letterbooks, 1865–79, 1883–4; industrial notes on engineering, 1909–10; Howell's personal diaries, 1864–73, 1875–83, 1885–9, 1895–7, 1899, 1900, 1902, 1903, 1908, and diaries of Howell's son, George Washington Taviner Howell, 1873–80; George Howell's autobiography (six volumes). Trades Union Congress records include: TUC Parliamentary Committee minutes and reports,

1872; notes on the 3rd annual TUC, 7–11 March 1871; notes on the 4th and 5th TUCs, 1872 and 1873; TUC Parliamentary Committee, financial reports and balance sheets, 1871–6. The Plimsoll Seamen's Fund Committee reports, correspondence, etc., also in the collection, cover the years 1873–5. Reform League papers include Executive Committee minute books, 1865–9; Executive agenda book, 1867–9; Council minutes, 1866–9; Finance Committee minutes, 1866–8; cashbook, 1865–9; account book, 1865–8; Secretary's petty cash book, 1865–6; ledger, 1865–7; Bazaar Committee, 1866; notes, 1865–6; list of departments and branches; branch election reports, 1868.

Other papers include Howell's incoming correspondence, 1865–1910; School Board Election Committee, minute book and letters, 1879; Crystal Palace, Mansion House Committee, minutes, notes, miscellaneous letters, 1877; biography of Ernest Jones, the Chartist; personal diaries of Ernest Jones with notes by Howell, 1840–7; box file of MS notes, cuttings and other material for the biography of Jones. Also in this collection are minutes of the International Workingmen's Association, 1866–9, and a history of the Association dated 1900.

Copies of a selection of items from this collection are at the International Institute of Social History, Amsterdam. Correspondence can be found in the George Holyoake and Thomas Huxley collections, while items concerning Howell are in the Labour Party archive at Transport House.

HUDSON, Sir Robert Arundell (1864–1927)

Political organiser. Worked with National Liberal Federation, Birmingham, from 1882. Secretary of the Federation, and of Liberal Central Association, 1893.

No personal papers are known but correspondence survives in other collections. The Bodleian Library, Oxford, has various items, including correspondence with Asquith, with Sir Donald Maclean, 1919–25, and with Lord Ponsonby of Shulbrede, 1907–10. There are seven letters in the Sir Edward Evans papers (NRA 18343).

HUGHES, Ernest Richard (1883–1956)

Missionary and scholar in Chinese history and philosophy. Mission work in China, 1911–29. Reader in Chinese Religion and Philosophy, Oxford, 1934–47. Visiting Professor in Graduate School, Claremont, California, 1949–52.

A collection of papers and correspondence in connection with efforts to encourage greater cultural and intellectual co-operation between Oxford and Chinese universities and including letters of various Oxford and Chinese scholars, 1939–47, is deposited in the Bodleian Library (MS Eng. Misc. c. 516).

HUGHES, John (d. 1950)

Australian freelance journalist in London during World War II. He wrote for newspapers, including the *Daily Express* and the *Sydney Morning Herald*.

The Imperial War Museum holds a small collection of manuscript letters written by Hughes to his family in Australia during the war.

HULME, Thomas Ernest (1883–1916)

Philosopher and poet. Worked on the *New Age* from 1908. Hon. Secretary, 'The Poet's Club', 1908.

Hull University Library has a collection of papers relating to Hulme. They include photostats of three letters and two cards from Hulme to Edward Marsh; several other letters from Hulme, and reminiscences of him by Ramiro de Maeztu; five letters from Michael Roberts to Katherine

Lechmere concerning his book on Hulme; letters to A. R. Jones about Hulme, 1955–61; notes and photographs; and an album of photographs of Jacob Epstein's work, with MS notes on them by Hulme.

Other items relating to Hulme can be found in the University of Texas, Austin.

HURST, Charles Chamberlain (1870–1947)

Biologist and pioneer in genetics.

Cambridge University Library has a collection of papers, at present not listed, chiefly relating to his biological work.

HUXLEY, Aldous Leonard (1894–1963)

Novelist and critic.

A fire in 1961 which destroyed his home in Los Angeles destroyed Huxley's files of manuscripts and his correspondence with his first wife, Maria Nys Huxley, and his early letters to his second wife. A sample of his later letters to her has been published: Laura Archera Huxley, *This Timeless Moment* (1968). Further letters were reproduced in *Aldous Huxley: A Memorial*, ed. Sir Julian Huxley (1965). A large collection of his letters has been published: *Letters of Aldous Huxley*, ed. Grover Smith (1969). These letters and other manuscript material, oral testimony and BBC transcripts were used in Sybille Bedford, *Aldous Huxley: A Biography* (2 vols, 1973–4).

There are various Aldous Huxley papers at the Libraries of the University of California at Los Angeles and at Santa Barbara.

HUXLEY, Sir Julian Sorell (1887–1974)

Biologist and writer. Fellow of New College, Oxford, 1919–25. Professor of Zoology, King's College, London, 1925–7. Fullerian Professor of Physiology at the Royal Institution, 1926–9. President, National Union of Scientific Workers, 1926–9. Secretary, Zoological Society of London, 1935–42. Director-General, UNESCO, 1946–8. Fellow of the Royal Society from 1938.

Sir Julian's papers, a substantial collection, are in the care of his widow, Lady Huxley, 31 Pond Street, London NW3. No further details are available at present.

His correspondence can be found in a number of other collections. There is correspondence with Sir Oliver Lodge, 1924–30, at Birmingham University Library; and with Lord Lothian, chiefly concerning African affairs, 1929–39, in the Scottish Record Office. Correspondence with Arthur Creech Jones, 1944–63, is in Rhodes House Library, Oxford. Correspondence with the World Education Fellowship is in the Institute of Education Library, London, and there are letters in the Morton M. Hunt Collection, Temple University Library, Philadelphia, USA. There is correspondence with Edward Roux in the University of the Witwatersrand Library, Jan Smuts Avenue, Johannesburg. His early Bird-Observation Diaries are in the Edward Grey Institute of Field Ornithology, Oxford.

HYNDMAN, Henry Mayers (1842–1921)

Socialist pioneer and propagandist. Founded Social Democratic Federation, 1881. Chairman, International Socialist Congress, London, 1896. Member of International Socialist Bureau, 1900–10. A founder of the British Socialist Party, 1912. Member, War Emergency Workers' National Committee, 1914–19. Helped establish the pro-war National Socialist Party, 1916. Member of Consumers' Council, 1918–19.

The BLPES has microfilms of Hyndman correspondence in American repositories, including correspondence with Charles E. Russell during World War I (originals in the Library of Congress); letters to Algernon M. Simons (with originals in the State Historical Society, Madison, Wisconsin); correspondence with Thomas Davidson (in Yale University Library); correspondence with Henry George (in New York Public Library); and correspondence with H. Gaylord Wilshire (University of California, Los Angeles, and in private hands). BLPES has also purchased two letters to Douglas Sladen, dated 8 Nov 1917 and 9 Mar 1919, which reflect on the War Emergency Workers' National Committee, Italy, the Russian Revolution and Clemenceau (Coll. Misc. 492).

There is further social and literary correspondence in the Douglas Sladen papers. The Labour Party Archive has correspondence with Hyndman throughout, while the G. B. Shaw papers in the British Library contain correspondence 1884–1920 (Add. MS 50538). Letters to do with Socialism can be found in the C. E. Russell papers (NRA 19082) and there are 22 letters to Mrs Cobden Sanderson on International Socialist Affairs, 1900–21, at McGill University, Montreal. A photocopy of the manuscript of an article on 'Socialism, Trade Unions and Political Action' (the original of which is in the Moscow Institute of Marxism–Leninism) can be found at the Marx Memorial Library, while the International Institute of Social History has letters in the Kautsky collection (six letters, 1902–11) and the Kleiner collection (15 letters, 1895–7).

Records of the Social Democratic Federation; in BLPES, the National Library of Scotland, the International Institute of Social History and the Marx Memorial Library, are described in *Sources* Vol. 1, pp. 236–7.

INGRAM, John Kells (1823–1907)

Economist. Professor of Oratory and English Literature, Trinity College Dublin, 1852; Regius Professor of Greek, 1866; Librarian, 1879; later Vice-Provost. President, Royal Irish Academy and Statistical Society of Ireland. Author of works relating to political economy, slavery, positivism, etc.

A collection of correspondence, 1850–1906, with members of his family, with fellow-economists, positivists, etc., together with miscellaneous papers can be found in the Public Record Office of Northern Ireland. Trinity College Dublin has other papers covering his work for the Irish Academy, together with notebooks and lectures. Sturges, *Economists' Papers*, pp. 53–4, mentions these and relevant material in other collections.

IVES, George Cecil (1867–1950)

Author and criminologist. Leading member of the British Society for the Study of Sex Psychology and of the Howard Association.

The University of Texas, Austin, has diaries, notebooks, correspondence and ephemera. The diaries cover the years 1886–1950, and fill some 122 quarto volumes, and over 20,000 pages.

The University of Texas, Austin, has further relevant material, including his records of the British Society for the Study of Sex Psychology and an extensive correspondence between Ives and Laurence Housman concerning their joint work for the reform of attitudes towards homosexuality.

JACKS, Lawrence Pearsall (1860–1955)

Clergyman, philosopher and writer. Principal of Manchester College, Oxford, 1915–31. Editor of the *Hibbert Journal* from 1902.

Efforts to contact a member of his family proved unsuccessful. There is correspondence in the Lodge and Marvin papers, and letters, 1936–8, in the Lothian papers at the Scottish Record Office.

JACKSON, Sir Cyril (1863–1924)

Educationalist. At Toynbee Hall, 1885–95. Inspector-General of Schools, Western Australia, 1896–1903. Chief Inspector, Board of Education, 1903–6. Expert Investigator on Unemployment, Poor Law Commission, 1906. Member of London County Council, 1907–13; Chairman, Education Committee, 1908–10, 1922. Member of various Government committees and Royal Commissions.

No personal papers have been traced but a few letters can be found in the Marvin papers.

JACKSON, Holbrook (1874–1948)

Author and editor. Joint editor of the *New Age*, 1907. Editor, *The Beau*, 1910. Acting editor, then editor, of *T.P.'s Magazine* (later *T.P.'s Weekly*) from 1911–16. Editor, *Today*, 1917–23.

Some 14 letters from Edward Thomas are in the Lockwood Memorial Library, State University of New York, Buffalo, while 12 items, in holograph draft, are in the University of California, Los Angeles Library. Correspondence with Edward Blunden can be found in the University of Iowa Library. A bound volume containing manuscripts by Jackson for *Appreciations of William Morris*, published by the Walthamstow Antiquarian Society, is in the William Morris collection.

JAMES, Lionel (1871–1955)

Journalist and author. On staff of *The Times*, 1899–1913.

Papers as correspondent of *The Times* are in the archives of that newspaper.

JAMESON, Sir Leander Starr, 1st Bt (1853–1917)

Imperial politician and businessman. Member of South African Legislature, 1910–12. President, British South Africa Company.

Rhodes House Library, Oxford, has papers relating to his trial, 1896. Correspondence and papers concerning Jameson are in the P. L. Gell collection, while correspondence on the Jameson raid is in the Houstoun of Johnstone papers. The National Archives of Rhodesia has other material.

JEBB, Richard (1874–1953)

Traveller and author of works on Imperial affairs. Member of Round Table Group.

The Institute of Commonwealth Studies, University of London, has a collection of material, consisting of three box-files of papers, mainly concerning imperial defence, 1906–18. Correspondents include Colonel James Allen (1913); L. S. Amery (1910–18); A. R. Atkinson (1906–7); Lionel Curtis (1908–13); J. S. Ewart (1912–13); Edward Grigg (1906–12); Philip Kerr, later Marquess of Lothian (1908); Viscount Milner (1906–14); Geoffrey Robinson (1906–12); Fabian Ware (1907–17); Sir Harry Wilson (1908–18); and Evelyn Wrench (1916–17).

The National Library of Australia has a small collection of correspondence with Australians for the period 1905–23 (MS 813).

The Bodleian Library holds the papers of the Round Table, which are briefly described in *Sources* Vol. 1, p. 224.

JEFFREYS, W. Rees (1871–1954)

Road administrator. Served at the Board of Trade, 1891–1903. Organised the Motor Union of Great Britain and Ireland, 1903–10, and the Commercial Motor Users Association and the Institution of Automobile Engineers. Secretary of the Road Board, 1910–18. Organised and endowed a Road Trust to encourage building of new roads and bridges.

BLPES has a collection of papers. It includes biographical material; bibliographies; correspondence; press cuttings and offprints; notes on foreign visits; material concerning 'The King's Highway', the history of roads, roads and transport (including road safety, designs, etc.); statistics on roads, etc.; material on arterial roads, bridges, London, foreign roads; roads and railways; the Road Board; post-war planning; finance; Road Congresses and the International Road Federation; the Ministry of Transport and other official bodies; papers concerning the RIA, the Automobile Association and the Royal Automobile Club; and other road and transport organisations; miscellaneous material; and articles on subjects other than roads.

JENKINS, Claude (1877–1959)

Churchman. Professor of Ecclesiastical History, King's College, London, 1918; and in University of London, 1931–5. Canon of Christ Church, and Regius Professor of Ecclesiastical History, Oxford, from 1934. Joint Editor, *Church Quarterly Review*, 1921–7. Chairman, Central London Federation of Working Men's Clubs. Lambeth Librarian, 1910–29. Curator of the Bodleian Library, 1936–52.

The Library of Christ Church, Oxford, has one volume of papers, consisting of letters to him, drafts by him, official notices, bills, etc., 1934–59. Lambeth Palace Library has an extensive collection of correspondence, lecture notes and sermons, 1877–1958. The Bodleian Library has further material.

JEVONS, Herbert Stanley (1875–1955)

Economist. Lecturer and later Fulton Professor of Economics and Political Science, University College, Cardiff. Professor of Economics, University of Allahabad, 1914–23; University of Rangoon, 1923–30. Editor, *Indian Journal of Economics*, 1916–22. Hon. Secretary, Abyssinia Association. Treasurer, Anglo-Ethiopian Society, 1952–4. Adviser to the Ethiopian Embassy from 1942. Chairman, Bombing Restrictions Committee, 1943–5.

Papers have been deposited in the National Library of Wales by Jevons' daughter. The collection includes material for, and correspondence relating to, the following books published by him – *The British Coal Trade* (1915), *Money, Exchange and Banking in India* (1922), and *Economic Equality in the Co-operative Commonwealth* (1933); drafts of works which do not appear to have been published, including 'The Social Revolution' (1919), 'The Problem of War' (1932), 'Utopia' (1935), and 'Why Federation Means Peace' (1940); numerous articles and lectures, and a large number of files containing articles, correspondence, etc., on various subjects including 'Agriculture in Central India' (1914–18), 'The Bombay Cotton Industry' (1926), 'The British Heavy Steel Industry' (1931–2), 'The Burma Agricultural Society' (1929), 'Coal and Mining' (1909–49), 'Economic Development of Great Britain' (1934–5), 'Housing in Wales' (1912–14), 'Indian Economic Enquiry Committee' (1925–6), 'Indian Economics Professorships' (1914), 'Indian Exchange and Currency' (1924–5), 'Proposed Society for Economic and Cultural Relations with Germany' (1946–7), 'Rangoon University: memorandum on the Co-ordination of Industrial Research' (1928); 'Rhiwbina Garden Village' (1951–2), 'Merthyr Co-operative Garden Village Society' (1954); 'Royal Commission on Agriculture in India' (1927), and 'The Royal Statistical Society' (1933–41). There are numerous files containing articles, correspondence, pamphlets, etc., relating to the Abyssinian Association, of which H. S. Jevons was the first Secretary, and to the Anglo-Ethiopian Society, of which he was the first Treasurer, 1935–55; plus correspondence with Haile Selassie I, Emperor of Abyssinia, 1937–53. The collection also includes correspondence with Sir Richard Acland, Lord Cecil, Sir Stafford Cripps, Hugh Dalton, Anthony Eden, Cyril Garbett (Archbishop of York), Patrick Geddes, Sam Higginbottom, D. Caradoc Jones, Kebede Makonnen, Sir John Simon, Madam Genevieve Tabouis, and Dr John Thomas, 1918–55.

Printed material deposited in the Library includes books, pamphlets, and periodicals containing articles by H. S. Jevons, a large number relating to Abyssinia.

JOAD, Cyril Edwin Mitchinson (1891–1953)

Philosopher and author. Head of Department of Philosophy, Birkbeck College, London, from 1930.

No substantial collection of papers is known to be available. The archives of Birkbeck College, London, have various letters relating to Joad, but they do not form a substantial grouping. Mr John Beaumont, c/o Faculty of Law, The University, Leeds 2, is undertaking research into his career. Some correspondence can be found in other collections, including the Vera Brittain papers at McMaster University, Hamilton, Ontario. Records of the Federation of Progressive Societies and Individuals, now the Progressive League, with which Joad was associated for a time, are described in *Sources* Vol. 1, p. 216.

JOHNSON, Francis (d. 1970)

Socialist organiser. Secretary of the Independent Labour Party.

The papers of the Independent Labour Party, to be deposited in BLPES, contain much relevant material. A catalogue is available in BLPES.

JOHNSON, Hewlett (1874–1966)

Churchman. Dean of Manchester, 1924–31; of Canterbury, 1931–63. Founder of *The Interpreter*, and its editor, 1905–24. Author of *The Socialist Sixth of the World, Christians and Communism*, etc.

Mrs Nowell M. Johnson (widow), The Red House, 24 New Street, St Dunstans, Canterbury, Kent CT2 8AU, has a collection of her husband's papers, together with copies of *The Interpreter*. The papers include sermons, diaries, correspondence and press cuttings covering the range of his career up to his death. A biography by Robert Hughes (1977) made use of these papers. Some correspondence, 1932–5, with C. Jenkins and others, is in Lambeth Palace Library.

JOHNSON, Tom (d. 1960)

Irish Labour leader. Secretary of the Irish Trades Union Congress and one-time Chairman, Irish Labour Party.

The National Library of Ireland has a collection of material, including papers, articles and assorted manuscripts, 1896–1960. Most relate to the Irish Labour Party.

JOHNSTON, Sir Harry Hamilton (1858–1927)

Explorer and colonial administrator. Commissioner and Consul-General, British Central Africa Protectorate, 1891. Consul-General, Regency of Tunis, 1897–9. Special Commissioner, Commander-in-Chief and Consul General, Uganda Protectorate, 1899–1901. Author of works on the empire, racial questions etc.

Papers are in the National Archives of Rhodesia. Six reels of microfilms of this collection, used for Roland Oliver's *Sir Harry Johnson and the Scramble for Africa* (1957) are in the Royal Commonwealth Society Library. The material includes letters received by Sir Harry and Lady Johnston, 1894–1928; sketchbooks (including Tunis and Congo); notes for various publications and of unpublished material; diaries, 1878, 1879–1881, 1887, 1888, and a Report on the Cross River (Uganda), June–Aug 1900; a diary of the Congo Expedition of 1883 and African notebook no. 3 (including linguistic and ethnological entries); early drawings, photographs, illustrated articles by Johnston; letters to and from him concerning the British South Africa Company, Cape Town (Kimberley) office; miscellaneous letters to him, 1879–1902. Amongst the correspondents are Lord Salisbury, Lord Rosebery, Joseph Chamberlain, Sir Henry and Lady Stanley, Rudyard Kipling, Edmund Gosse, Sir Charles Dilke, Lord Lansdowne and W. C. Oswell.

Letters, 1888–91, are in the Sir William Mackinnon collection (NRA 10515), and there are eight letters, 1888–91, in the Edmund Gosse collection.

JONES, (Alfred) Ernest (d. 1958)

Pioneer of psychoanalysis. Professor of Psychiatry, University of Toronto. Hon. President, International Psycho-Analytical Association and British Psycho-Analytical Society. Author of various works on Neurology, Psychology and Anthropology. Founder of the *International Journal of Psycho-Analysis*. Author of three-volume study of Freud.

Papers have been deposited with the British Institute of Psycho-Analysis, 63 New Cavendish Street, London W1. They include six box files of notes, cuttings, MSS for the *Life and Work of Freud*; reviews of this biography; and letters concerning it; material and proof copy of *The Nature of Genius*; lecture notes and addresses; various typescripts; numerous letters from prominent psycho-analysts; and biographical material. Access to the papers is restricted.

JONES, Sir Cadwaladr Bryner (1872–1954)

Agriculturalist. Professor of Agriculture, University College of Wales, Aberystwyth, 1907–12. Chairman of Welsh Agricultural Council, 1912–19. Welsh Secretary, Ministry of Agriculture, 1919–44.

A small collection of papers, including literary and historical papers, lectures, papers relating to research into the history of cattle, and biographical material, is deposited in the National Library of Wales.

JONES, D. Caradoc (1883–1974)

Sociologist. Lectured in the Universities of Bristol, Durham, Manchester. Senior Lecturer, later Reader, in Social Statistics, Liverpool University, 1924–44. Directed the Social Survey of Merseyside, and edited its report, 1934.

Liverpool University Archives have a collection of papers. It includes autobiographical notes, and the manuscript and typescript drafts of his autobiography; printed material by him; papers and reviews, some of which were not published; memoranda, typescripts, press cuttings, publishers' handouts etc., on the *Social Survey*; papers on peace proposals, world unity proposals, etc., 1937–43; documents on the Proposed Advisory Committee for Reconstruction, 1942 and 1946; unpublished poetry, 1902–22; religious notes, 1948–c. 1970, particularly concerning his work with the Society of Friends; and miscellaneous material, including letters to the editor, etc. The final draft of his autobiography has been deposited with the National Library of Wales.

JONES, Sir John Edward Lennard- (1894–1954)

Scientist. Fellow of the Royal Society. Professor of Theoretical Physics, Bristol University, 1930–2. Professor of Theoretical Chemistry, Cambridge, 1932–53. During World War II served successively as Key Scientist, Chief Superintendent of Armament Research, Chief Scientific Officer, and Director-General of Scientific Research (Defence), Ministry of Supply. President, Faraday Society, 1948–50. Chairman, Scientific Advisory Council, Ministry of Supply, 1947–53. Principal of the University College of North Staffordshire from 1953.

Churchill College, Cambridge, has a collection of papers. Very little of the collection is of directly scientific importance, though some of the lectures and correspondence deal with scientific subjects. The bulk of the material is personal or to do with his general career. The collection includes memoirs, and other personal material, including correspondence, honours, etc.; scientific and personal correspondence, 1922–54, to correspondents such as Dr P. R. Manning and A. C. Hurley; personal daily journals, 1942–54; lectures, sermons and addresses, 1921–54, including 'The Nonconformist Conscience', 1921, 'The Organisation of Scientific Workers in Peace and War', 1938; and private correspondence, much of which is under restriction.

A collection of lecture notes, taken in 1928–32, has been placed by Professor C. A. Coulson in Cambridge University Library. They include careful notes of lectures given by Lennard-Jones in Cambridge.

JONES, Sir Roderick (1877–1962)

Principal proprietor of Reuters, and Chairman and Managing Director, 1919–41. Chief Executive and Director of Propaganda, Ministry of Information, 1918. Member of Council of the Royal Institute of International Affairs, 1927–55.

Enquiries should be directed to Lady Jones (widow), North End House, Rottingdean, Sussex BN2 7HA. Relevant material, including correspondence, is reproduced in Sir Roderick's autobiography, *A Life in Reuters* (1951).

JONES, Thomas (1870–1955)

Public servant. Deputy Secretary to the Cabinet, and Secretary of the Economic Advisory Council. Special Investigator, Poor Law Commission, 1906–9. Secretary, National Health Insurance Commissioners (Wales), 1912–16. Secretary of the Pilgrim Trust, 1930–45.

The Thomas Jones collection at the National Library of Wales comprises over 30,000 documents bound into 221 volumes, which in turn are subdivided into 25 classes. There is a comprehensive guide and index. This collection cannot be consulted without the prior agreement of Mr Tristan Jones and Lady White, son and daughter of Thomas Jones.

The diaries of Tom Jones have been published. Tom Jones himself published *A Diary with Letters, 1931–1951* (Oxford, 1954) and Keith Middlemas edited the *Whitehall Diary* in three volumes (1969–71).

JONES, (William) Ernest (1895–1973)

Trade unionist. General Secretary, Yorkshire Miners' Association, 1939. Regional Labour Director, Ministry of Fuel and Power, 1942–4. President, National Union of Mineworkers, 1954–60. Member of the General Council, Trades Union Congress, 1950–60. Secretary, Miners' International Federation, 1957–60. Chairman, Southern Regional Board for Industry, 1961–6.

Hull University Library has a collection of papers. They include notes for, and texts of, speeches, articles and reviews by Jones, covering topics such as mining, religion, defence, the United Nations, the trade union movement and the EEC, 1930s–50s; press cuttings, 1935–61, congratulatory letters from 1939, and general correspondence from Sir Herbert Houldsworth, G. Lloyd-George, Philip Noel-Baker, Lady Cripps, Harold Wilson, Peter Thorneycroft, Selwyn Lloyd, John F. Kennedy, Christopher Soames, Lord Pilkington and others, 1940–68; letters on his retirement from the NUM, 1960; papers on the Southern Regional Board for Industry, the EEC; correspondence, statements, offprints, programmes, etc., concerning the miners' union.

JOSEPH, Horace William Brindley (1867–1943)

Philosopher. Fellow of New College, Oxford. Oxford University Lecturer in Philosophy, 1927–32. Author of works on logic, the labour theory of value, ethics, etc.

A collection at New College, Oxford, includes some 13 boxes of material. Amongst the material are a number of notebooks, with notes, comments and reflections on various philosophical topics, technical problems, mathematics, etc., as well as more social topics such as concepts of intelligence, psychology, etc. There is occasional correspondence, including philosophical correspondence with J. C. Wilson and occasional letters to colleagues such as Roy Harrod, A. D. Lindsay, J. A. Smith. There are notes on socialism, and the Douglas social credit schemes, etc.; but the bulk of the material relates to philosophical topics.

KEEN, Frank Noel (d. 1957)

Lawyer. A founder of the League of Nations Union.

Correspondence and lecture notes, 1914–57, can be found at BLPES.

KEITH, Arthur Berriedale (1879–1944)

Political scientist and Sanskrit scholar. In Colonial Service from 1901. Regius Professor of Sanskrit and Comparative Philology, Edinburgh University, from 1914. Lecturer on the Constitution of the British Empire from 1927.

Edinburgh University Library has a substantial collection of papers, especially concerning his interest in the colonies. The Scottish Record Office has correspondence with Lothian, 1932–3, concerning India.

KELLY, Herbert Hamilton (1860–1950)

Theologian. Director of the Society of the Sacred Mission, 1893–1910. Professor of the Theological College, Ikebukuro Tokyo, 1913–19.

Miscellaneous correspondence, 1906–12, including his letters to the *Church Quarterly Review*, is in Lambeth Palace Library.

KENNEDY, Aubrey Leo (1885–1965)

Journalist. Correspondent of *The Times* 1910–42; BBC, 1942–5.

The archives of *The Times* contain relevant material, including a file relating to his appointment, etc.; letters, 1927–42, many again relating to his position; and a photocopy of his journal, 1936–9.

KESSLER, Leopold (1864–1944)

Journalist. Leading British advocate of Zionism. Head of Zionist Congress, El-Arish Committee, 1903. Editor, *Jewish Chronicle*.

All Kessler's papers concerning his Zionist activities, including some material on his leadership of the 1903 expedition to Sinai, are in the Central Zionist Archives, Jerusalem. The Middle East Centre, St Antony's College, Oxford, has a duplicate set of the 1903 material, including copies of his photographs and the logbook of the journey. Rhodes House Library, Oxford, has recently acquired further photographs of a journey made in 1895 from Durban to Port Said.

KEYNES, 1st B
John Maynard Keynes (1883–1946)

Economist. Fellow of King's College, Cambridge. Civil Servant from 1906; Treasury 1915–19. Principal Treasury Representative, Paris Peace Conference. Member of Committee on Finance and Industry, 1929–31. Editor of *Economic Journal*, 1911–44. Economic adviser to the Government during and immediately after World War II.

The Marshall Library, Cambridge, has Keynes' professional papers, arranged in subject groupings, each with relevant correspondence. The material includes papers on official work, manuscripts of books, articles, lectures, broadcasts, etc.; papers relating to his work for various societies, business organisations and educational institutions.

King's College Library, Cambridge, has a collection of personal papers, including juvenilia; family letters and papers; papers concerning the Bursarship of King's College; book collecting, the Arts Theatre, Cambridge; CEMA, the Arts Council, the National Gallery, the Fine Arts Commission, etc.; picture-collecting. There are also letters from about 100 people to Keynes, including correspondence with the National Council for Civil Liberties and others on the Bertrand Russell case, 1916. The British Library has other relevant material, including correspondence with Keynes, 1910–46 (Add. MSS 55201–4); and his letters to Duncan Grant (Add. MSS 57930–1). BLPES has letters from Keynes and others to Professor Hayek as editor of *Economica*, and 65 letters of Keynes to E. Rosenbaum, with eight replies.

Correspondence can also be found in other collections. There is a memorandum on the Depression, and correspondence, in the Lothian papers at the Scottish Record Office. The Chamberlain papers at Birmingham University Library have his correspondence with Austen Chamberlain, 1924, concerning L. L. Klotz's book *De La Guerre à La Paix*. There are two memoranda on the financial situation in the Asquith papers.

Papers were used in R. F. Harrod, *The Life of John Maynard Keynes* (1951). Papers and correspondence are used in Elizabeth Johnson and Donald Moggridge (eds), *The Collected Works of John Maynard Keynes* (25 vols, 1971–   ).

KEYNES, John Neville (1852–1949)

Political economist and university administrator. University Lecturer in Moral Science, Cambridge, 1884–1911. Registrar, University of Cambridge, 1910–25.

Cambridge University Library has a collection of material, including diaries, 1864–1917, in 40 volumes, dealing with academic and family affairs, and including some correspondence; two volumes of collected examination questions on logic, mainly from the 1870s and 1880s; and about 250 letters in the J. M. Keynes Collection. The Marshall Library, Cambridge, has about 400 letters to J. M. Keynes, 1891–1942, though most are before 1900. Pembroke College, Cambridge, has a collection of notebooks; c. 1875, and post-1884, while King's College, Cambridge, has seven volumes of notes, mainly from Henry Sidgwick's lectures on philosophy and ethics, 1874–6. References to material in other collections can be found in Sturges', *Economists' Papers*, pp. 57–8.

KIDD, Benjamin (1858–1916)

Sociologist. Clerk in the Inland Revenue Department, 1877–94. Author of *Social Evolution* (1894), which attacked Socialist ideas, *Principles of Western Civilisation* (1902) and *Science of Power* (1918).

A collection of papers, including correspondence and press cuttings, is in Cambridge University Library.

KIDD, Ronald (d. 1942)

Libertarian. Founder in 1934 and first General Secretary, National Council for Civil Liberties.

Records of the National Council for Civil Liberties are in Hull University Library.
    Mr Barry Cox, author of *Civil Liberties in Britain*, has some relevant material. So has Mrs Sylvia Scaffardi, a former colleague of Kidd.

KING, Edward (1829–1910)

Ecclesiastic. Principal of Cuddesdon College, 1863–73. Canon of Christ Church and Regius Professor of Pastoral Theology, Oxford, 1873–85. Bishop of Lincoln from 1885.

Lincolnshire Archives Office has many letters to Canon Bramley and Rev. Larken, 1863–1903, together with the manuscripts of sermons, etc.; and official correspondence of the Registry of the Bishop.

KINLOCH, John L. (d. 1968)

Labour politician and Scottish Nationalist.

Miscellaneous manuscripts and papers relating to Kinloch are in the custody of Alexander D. Craig, 110 Maxwell Avenue, Westerton, Bearsden, Scotland, and have been listed by the NRA (Scotland). The political papers include MSS relating to his term of office as political agent for Josiah Wedgwood, M.P.; miscellaneous political correspondence, especially before, during and after World War I; MSS regarding his stand as a conscientious objector; his various local and parliamentary campaigns; and papers on the Scottish National Party. There are also papers concerning the Educational Institute of Scotland; youth movements and work for peace; papers concerning the various organisations and committees with which he was involved; items on the kilt and dress reform; miscellaneous typescripts and lecture notes; religious manuscripts; autobiographical material; press cuttings; and miscellaneous material including family correspondence, articles, etc.

KIPLING, Rudyard (1865–1936)

Author. Awarded the Nobel Prize for Literature, 1907. Advocate of Empire.

A major collection of papers formerly in the care of his daughter is now deposited in Sussex University Library. The British Library has relevant items, including two volumes of prose and verse, (Add. MS 44840–1); autograph drafts of poems, stories, articles (Add. MS 45100, Add. MSS 45540–2, Add. MS 45680, Add. MS 45982). Also at the British Library there is correspondence in the Society of Authors archive (Add. MS 56734) and in the Macmillan archive (Add. MS 54940).
    Cornell University Library, Department of Rare Books, has correspondence, 1866–1935, concerning Kipling's works, sketches, press cuttings, poems, articles and literary MSS.
    Dalhousie University Library, Halifax, Nova Scotia, has correspondence, manuscripts and notes on his works. Letters on literature, politics, family affairs are with the State Historical Society of Wisconsin, Madison. Syracuse University Library has correspondence, papers,

poetry, 1890–1956. The Houghton Library, Harvard University has letters, 1885–1935. Columbia University Libraries has various items, including letters and manuscripts.

There are letters in the Rosebery collection, National Library of Scotland; in the Tovey collection, Edinburgh University Library; in the Bensusan archive, University of Essex Library. The Fitzwilliam Museum, Cambridge, has a few items, including the manuscript drafts of the preface to *Life's Handicap*. There is literary and social correspondence in the Sladen collection.

KIRK, Sir John (1832–1922)

Naturalist and administrator. Fellow of the Royal Society. Chief Officer of Livingstone's expedition to Africa, 1853–64. H.M. Agent and Consul-General, Zanzibar, 1886. Special Commissioner to Niger, 1895. Foreign Secretary, Royal Geographical Society.

The National Library of Scotland has various letters, including correspondence with David Livingstone. There are also letters, 1873–93, in the William Mackinnon papers (NRA 10515).

KLEIN, Viola (1908–73)

Sociologist. Came to Britain as a refugee from Czechoslovakia, 1939. Employed at the British Foreign Office; Research Officer, London School of Economics; Simon Research Fellow and Senior Research Associate, Manchester University; Lecturer in Sociology, Reading University. Author of *The Feminine Character, History of an Ideology* (1946), *Women's Two Roles* (with Alva Myrdal) (1956), *Working Wives* (1960), etc.

Papers are housed in Reading University Library. They include notes for articles and books, correspondence, offprints, etc. There are, *inter alia*, notes for an article on 'Some theories on feminine attitudes and so-called character trends', c. 1950; papers relating to an International Seminar on the role of women in a changing society, 1961; papers concerning meetings of experts organised by the Youth Institute of UNESCO, 1959–63; correspondence and notes on a research project relating to ageing; correspondence relating to *The Feminine Character*; general correspondence on research projects; a collection of press cuttings on women's organisations, 1969–73; correspondence, cuttings and excerpts relating to the study of the family, 1944–8; correspondence with Karl Mannheim relating to the publication of Viola Klein's Ph.D. thesis; correspondence on research projects, 1960–5; correspondence relating to a survey of women's employment, 1960–2; correspondence relating to the employment of women graduates, 1962–4; correspondence relating to conferences and courses addressed by Viola Klein; press cuttings of reviews of her books; notes on marriage and the family in the Soviet Union, 1950; notes and statistics on the employment of married women; papers relating to the International Council of Social Democratic Women, 1962; papers on international sociology conferences; and copies of questionnaires, etc., mostly relating to the status of women.

KNIGHT, William Angus (1836–1916)

Philosopher. Professor of Moral Philosophy, University of St Andrews, 1876–1902.

Boston Public Library, Mass., has certain papers, including 90 letters from him and some documents.

KNOWLES, Lilian Charlotte Anne (d. 1926)

Economist. Lecturer in Modern Economic History, London School of Economics from 1904; Reader from 1907; later Professor of Economic History, University of London. Author of various economic articles and of *The Economic Development of the Overseas Empire, 1763–1914*. A supporter of imperialist policies. Member of the Departmental Committee on the rise of the cost of living to the Working Classes, 1918. Member of the Royal Commission on the Income Tax, 1919–20.

Papers are preserved in BLPES. These include typescript drafts and proofs of books by Lilian Knowles, including her works on the industrial and commercial revolutions in Great Britain and the development of the Empire, plus works based on her lecture notes and published after her death. There are also manuscript lecture notes, with relevant typescript syllabuses, press cuttings and other printed material. The collection also includes letters, from William Cunningham, W. R. Dunlop, Wyndham R. Dunstan, A. H. Millar and others which appear to refer to bibliographical enquiries; together with other bibliographical material and miscellaneous notes (including MS notes of William Cunningham's lectures, taken by Lilian Knowles at Girton College).

KNOX, (Edmund Francis) Vesey (1865–1921)

Irish politician. M.P. (Irish Nat.) West Cavan, 1890–5; Londonderry, 1895–9. Fellow of All Souls, Oxford, 1886–93.

The Public Record Office of Northern Ireland has a small collection of c. 70 letters received by Knox, 1890–1920. (ref. D 1222). The correspondence discusses his political and nationalist preoccupations, and includes letters from Thomas Sexton, Michael McCartan, John Dillon, Archbishop Walsh, A. W. F. Knox, F. D. (Lord) Lugard, William Murphy and T. M. Healey.

KNOX, Sir (Thomas) Malcolm (1900–   )

Academic. Professor of Moral Philosophy, University of St Andrews, 1936–53; Principal, 1953–66.

Dundee University Library has papers and correspondence. There are letters to Knox from various persons on miscellaneous topics, philosophical, cultural and social, 1918–63. There are also miscellaneous printed and other papers, including cuttings of book reviews, 1907–53.

LACEY, Thomas Alexander (1853–1951)

Churchman and theologian. Canon of Worcester from 1918.

Lambeth Palace Library has correspondence chiefly relating to proposals for reunion with the Roman Catholic Church, 1892–1906; and letters to the *Church Quarterly Review*, 1904–7. Correspondents include the 2nd Viscount Halifax, 1894–8; the Rev. Frederick William Puller of the Cowley Mission, 1895–1921; the Abbè Fernand Portal, 1895–1923.

LANDMAN, Samuel (1884–1967)

Zionist publicist.

Papers can be found in the Central Zionist Archives, Jerusalem (ref. A 226). They cover the 'Committee of Delegates'; immigration; the 'National Military Organisation'; and protocols and circulars of the Zionist executive meetings.

LANE, Sir Allen Lane Williams (1902–70)

Publisher. Founder of Penguin Books, 1936.

The archives of Penguin Books Ltd, Harmondsworth, Middlesex, contain papers relating to Sir Allen. These include correspondence and press cuttings. They are not generally available for research purposes.

LANE, John (1854–1925)

Publisher. Joint founder of the Bodley Head publishing firm. Founder of the *Yellow Book*.

The Sir Hugh Walpole manuscripts at the Bodleian Library, Oxford, contain a collection of letters received by Lane, including letters from Lord Alfred Douglas. The Elkin Matthews collection at Reading University Library contains relevant material. The British Library has correspondence and notes on Prince Moore (Add. MS 50857).

LANE, Joseph

Socialist publicist, involved in the Labour Emancipation League and the Socialist League in the 1880s.

The British Library has letters to Lane, mainly from political sympathisers, 1881–1905, in the J. E. Burns collection (Add. MS 46345). Several letters are from William Morris, 1887–9, and his daughter May, 1887.

LANG OF LAMBETH, 1st B
Cosmo Gordon Lang (1864–1945)

Ecclesiastic. Bishop of Stepney, 1901–8. Archbishop of York, 1908–28. Archbishop of Canterbury, 1928–42.

Lambeth Palace Library has relevant miscellaneous material. This includes minutes of committees appointed by Lang; letters to the Rev. R. A. Rawstorne, 1915–45; letters from the Rev. T. Tatlow, 1918–37, and letters to the Rev. C. Jenkins, 1917–42. There is a memorandum of the conference with the Dean and Chapter of Canterbury, 1934, and papers concerning Lockhart's biography. Also at Lambeth Palace Library are verbatim reports of his sermons as Bishop of Stepney, 1906; and papers of Alan Campbell Don, Dean of Westminster, 1912–46, and one-time Chaplain to Archbishop Lang. Lang is featured amongst the correspondents in this collection, which contains other items relating to Lang.

The Borthwick Institute of Historical Research has two boxes of miscellaneous material, including correspondence, 1909–28. Certain letters are in the British Theatre Museum collection at the Victoria and Albert Museum, while some letters to George Thomson are in Huddersfield Public Library. Correspondence with Lord Cecil, 1909–44, is in the British Library (Add. MS 51154) as is correspondence with Sir Sydney Cockerell (Add. MS 52729). Letters to Asquith, 1908–25, are in the Bodleian Library, Oxford.

LARKIN, James (1876–1947)

Irish Trade Unionist and socialist activist. Leader of the Irish Transport and General Workers Union.

The National Library of Ireland has correspondence and associated papers, 1915–36 (MSS 15,678–79; 17,231; 17,616). The Labour Party archive at Transport House has letters and papers, 1907, 1913 (ref. LP/PA/07/1/16–17, 114–66; LPGC 17/183; LP/Dub/13).

LASKI, Harold Joseph (1893–1950)

Political scientist, socialist theorist and politician. Journalist on *Daily Herald*, 1914. Lecturer in History, McGill University, 1914–16; Harvard, 1916–20. At the London School of Economics from 1920; Professor of Political Science, University of London, from 1926. Member of the Fabian Society Executive, 1922–36. Member of Labour Party Executive, 1936–49.

Hull University Library has a small collection of letters, mainly to Harold Laski, with some to Mrs Frida Laski. Correspondents include H. A. L. Fisher, H. W. Nevinson, George Lansbury, J. L. Paton, Morley, Ernest Barker, the Webbs, J. R. MacDonald, H. G. Wells, Clement Attlee. Hugh Dalton, F. D. Roosevelt, Stafford Cripps, Winston Churchill, Carr Saunders, with single letters from Felix Frankfurter, Bertrand Russell, Ellen Wilkinson, and others. There are some letters to Mrs Laski from c. 1950, including two from Jawaharlal Nehru, and one from R. H. Tawney. The collection also includes the transcript of 'Justice Felix Frankfurter's Contribution to the BBC's Harold Laski Programme', 15 Nov 1961, and a script for a BBC programme on Laski, 1962.

The International Institute of Social History, Amsterdam, has some correspondence, 1910–50, including letters to Laski from G. B. Shaw, Graham Wallas, Beatrice and Sidney Webb, H. G. Wells, plus a letter from Laski to the Academic Registrar of the University of London about the chair of political science at LSE; and some manuscripts of books, articles and lectures. Also at the International Institute, some correspondence can be found in the Emma Goldman and Julius Braunthal collections.

Laski family papers at University College London include some documents, press cuttings and writings. A further small collection of Laski material was purchased by Syracuse University Library, New York, in 1966. It includes correspondence and a few other papers. Among correspondents are Lord Bryce, John Dewey, May Follett, E. M. Forster, Felix Frankfurter, Harold Macmillan, Bertrand Russell and H. G. Wells. The Labour Party archive at Transport House has a file of his correspondence, 1938–50.

Some letters can be found in the Percy Redfern collection in Manchester Central Library (MS Fo. 91 5Re 1) while the Angell Collection in Ball State University contains further correspondence. Correspondence with Creech Jones, concerning Colonial universities and Palestinian affairs is in Rhodes House Library, Oxford. The British Library has correspondence with Sir Sydney Cockerell (Add. MS 52729). A few letters, 1914, are in the Lansbury papers, BLPES. The David Soskice papers in the House of Lords Record Office contain letters from Laski.

Correspondence with Governor John Gilbert Winant can be found in the Franklin D. Roosevelt Library, Hyde Park, New York, while letters to Benjamin W. Huebsch are included in the latter's papers in the Library of Congress, Manuscript Division. Copies of some 141 of these letters are in the BLPES. The Library of Congress also holds correspondence between Laski and Felix Frankfurter. Occasional letters can also be found in the Herman Deutsch collection in the State Historical Society of Wisconsin, Madison.

Over 100 volumes from Laski's library were presented to Lady Margaret Hall, Oxford, after his death.

LASKI, Neville Jonas (1890–1969)

Lawyer. A leader of the Anglo-Jewish community. Recorder of Burnley, 1935–56; of Liverpool, 1956–63. Vice President, Anglo-Jewish Association. President, London Committee of Deputies of British Jews, 1933–40. Author of *Jewish Rights and Jewish Wrongs*, etc.

Papers in the Anglo-Jewish archives, the Mocatta Library, University College London, include material on the Laski family; biographical material on N. J. Laski; papers relating to Jewish Defence, 1936–41; a small grouping of correspondence; press cuttings; and various other items. Further papers are available in Manchester Central Library. There are also relevant papers in the archives of the Board of Deputies of British Jews (described briefly in *Sources* Vol. 1, pp. 20–1). A memorandum by Laski on the position of Jews in Czechoslovakia, 1938, is in the archives of Hill, Samuel and Co Ltd, merchant bankers, 100 Wood Street, London EC2.

LAWRENCE, Thomas Edward (1888–1935)

Author and Arabist. Served in Arabia, 1914–18. Attached to staff of General Sir F. Wingate, Hejaz Expeditionary Force, 1917; served on General Allenby's staff, 1918; on British Delegation to Peace Conference, 1919. Adviser on Arab Affairs, Colonial Office, 1921–2. Author of *The Seven Pillars of Wisdom* (1926, 1935) etc.

The British Library has Lawrence's diaries (Add. MSS 45914–5, 45983); correspondence with G. B. and Charlotte Shaw (Add. MSS 45903–4, 45916, 45922); literary works (Add. MSS 45912–3, 45916–7, 45930) and the autograph MS of his 'Confession of Faith' (Add. MS 46355). There is further Lawrence correspondence with Shaw, 1922–4, and material on Lawrence (Add. MS 50540) and correspondence with Charlotte Shaw (Add. MSS 56495–9). The Bodleian Library, Oxford, has a collection of manuscripts and correspondence presented by Mr Bayard K. Kilgour. They include letters from Lawrence to Edward Garnett, Robert Graves, James Hanley, Wilfred Merton, Bruce Rogers and others. There are also notes, drafts, notebooks on *The Seven Pillars of Wisdom*, etc. The Bodleian Library also has other assorted letters and papers including the manuscript of *The Seven Pillars* and *The Mint*.

The Imperial War Museum has a Lawrence of Arabia collection, the fruits of research that produced the biography by P. Knightley and C. Simpson, *The Secret Lives of T. E. Lawrence* (1969). The collection contains the typescript of the book, including an unpublished chapter, numerous photocopies of official and other documents, copies of letters from Lawrence and those concerned with his activities in the Arab revolt and in the subsequent history of the Middle East, and relevant press cuttings from publications of the past fifty years. The National Library of Scotland has certain papers for 1918.

The University of Texas, Austin, has a collection including correspondence with E. H. Kennington, a collection of photographs of the Arab campaign, notes and literary manuscripts, correspondence with Edward Garnett, and Liddell Hart's papers for a biography. Letters and papers are at the Houghton Library, Harvard University, while the typescript of *The Passionate Pilgrim* is in Dartmouth College, New Hampshire. Correspondence can also be found in the Astor papers, Reading University Library. The Middle East Centre, St Antony's College, Oxford, has a card index to all known Lawrence material.

LAYTON, 1st B
Sir Walter Thomas Layton (1884–1966)

Economist. Member, Munitions Council, World War I. Director of Economic and Financial Section, League of Nations. Financial Adviser, Indian Statutory Commission, 1929–30. Editor, *The Economist*, 1922–38. Served Ministry of Supply and Ministry of Production, World War II. Leader of Liberal Party, House of Lords, 1952–5. Director of Reuters Ltd, 1945–53.

A substantial quantity of papers, including fragments of an unpublished autobiography, survive in the care of the present (2nd) Lord Layton, 45 Westleigh Avenue, Putney, London SW15.

LEE, Henry William (1865–1932)

Socialist propagandist. Secretary, Social Democratic Federation, 1885–1911; British Socialist Party, 1911–13. Helped found pro-war National Socialist Party, 1916. Editor, *Justice*, 1913–24.

No personal papers have been traced, but some letters from Lee are available in the International Institute of Social History, Amsterdam: in the Socialist League, Kautsky and Kleiner collections. Material pertaining to the Social Democratic Federation (in BLPES, National Library of Scotland and elsewhere) is described in *Sources*, Vol. 1, pp. 236–7.

LEE, Vernon, see PAGET, Violet

LENNARD, Reginald Vivian (1885–1967)

Historian, specialising in history of agriculture. Lecturer to Workers' Educational Association, 1908–15. Worked at Labour Section, Ministry of Munitions, 1915. Member of Royal Commission on Agriculture, 1919. Lecturer in Agricultural History, Oxford School of Agriculture, 1919–32; University Lecturer in Modern History, 1930–2. Reader in Economic History, Oxford, 1932–51.

The Bodleian Library, Oxford, has a collection of material, including papers relating to the Royal Commission of 1919 and papers of the Oxford Agricultural Wages Commission, miscellaneous correspondence and various other items.

LENNOX, Victor Charles Hugh Gordon- (1897–1968)

Journalist. Political correspondent, *Daily Mail*, 1923–9. On staff of *Daily Telegraph* from 1930; diplomatic correspondent from 1935.

Some papers are believed to be with the family, but no details are available.

LESLIE, Sir (John Randolph) Shane, 3rd Bt (1885–1971)

Writer.

Churchill College, Cambridge, has four boxes of miscellaneous unsorted material. Papers concerning a biography of Mahaffy are in Trinity College Dublin.

LE STRANGE, Guy (1854–1933)

Orientalist, chiefly interested in the historical geography of the Middle East. Author of *Palestine Under the Moslems* (1890) and *The Lands of the Eastern Caliphate* (1905).

The Fitzwilliam Museum, Cambridge, has a collection of some 90 letters to Le Strange from G. Bentley, Doughty, Albert Grey, Henry James, A. W. Kinglake, and Laud A. Oliphant.

LETHABY, William Richard (1857–1931)

Architect and author. Principal, Central School of Arts and Crafts. Professor of Design, Royal College of Art. President, Arts and Crafts Exhibition Society.

The North Devon Athenaeum, Barnstaple, Devon, has a collection of Lethaby's books and three tin boxes of manuscript and typescript material. A large part of this material consists of notes by Lethaby on a variety of topics, from education to ritual, architecture to embroidery; also drafts, often incomplete, of articles or lectures, sketches, press cuttings, reprints of articles, etc. The collection has been roughly catalogued by the Institute of Advanced Architectural Studies, York.

The Royal Institute of British Architects has a variety of relevant papers, including letters to Charles Hadfield, Rev. S. Wheatley, H. H. Peach, W. W. Begley and Lord Manners. The RIBA also has a folder containing two carbon copies of a collection of aphorisms and rhymes, and two brief draft memoirs of Lethaby, possibly by H. H. Peach; and a binder of slips for a bibliography.

Correspondence with Sir Sydney Cockerell, 1894–1931, is at the British Library (Add. MSS 52730–2), and some letters are at the Victoria and Albert Museum. Further letters are in the Ashbee Journals, King's College Library, Cambridge.

LEWIS, John Spedan (1885–1963)

Businessman. Founder of the John Lewis Partnership.

J. S. Lewis's papers are currently in the archives of the John Lewis Partnership. They are not available for research purposes.

LEWIS, Percy Wyndham (1884–1957)

Author and artist.

Cornell University Libraries (Department of Rare Books) has a collection of correspondence and papers. Papers include MSS and typescripts of books and articles, galley proofs, drawings, personal documents, notebooks, scrapbooks, press cuttings. Correspondents include Wyndham Lewis's parents and family, T. S. Eliot, Augustus John, T. S. Moore, Ezra Pound, and many other artists, writers, publishers, admirers and personal friends.
    Some 60 letters to Sidney and Violet Schiff are in the British Library (Add. MS 52919). Some 60 letters to Thomas Sturge Moore are in London University Library. A few letters to Naomi, Lady Mitchison are in the National Library of Scotland.

LEWIS, Sir Willmott Harsant (1877–1950)

Journalist. Worked in East Asia in 1900s during the Boxer Rebellion, the Russo–Japanese War, etc. On the staff of *The Times* from 1919; correspondent in Washington, 1920–48.

The archives of *The Times* have a box of relevant material, including a management file; and correspondence with colleagues in London such as Wickham Steed, Geoffrey Dawson, Barrington-Ward etc. Topics covered include Woodrow Wilson and the League of Nations, Anglo–American relations, Franco–American relations, the New Deal, Roosevelt and Japanese naval power.

LEYS, Norman (1875–1944)

Critic of British colonial policy in East Africa. Member of the Colonial Medical Service. Author of numerous books and articles on colonial questions, including *A Last Chance in Kenya* (1931) and *The Colour Bar in East Africa* (1941).

A collection of correspondence between Leys and J. H. Oldham has been published. There are letters in the Leonard Woolf papers in Sussex University Library, in the Winifred Holtby papers, and in the W. M. Macmillan papers. Diana Wylie has written an unpublished M.Litt. thesis, Edinburgh University, 1974, dealing with the role of Leys and McGregor Ross as critics of British colonial policy.

LILLEY, Alfred Leslie (1860–1948)

Churchman and theologian. Canon Residentiary of Hereford Cathedral, 1911–36.

The papers of Canon Lilley are preserved in the Library of St Andrews University. The collection includes correspondence, and miscellaneous material, consisting largely of the manuscripts of lectures and publications by Lilley. Correspondents include Oscar Browning, Sir J. G. Fitch, H. Scott Holland, Baron von Hugel, J. R. MacDonald, J. Murray, Dean H. Rashdall, Lord Stanley and G. Tyrrell, S.J. Most of the material relates to the Catholic Modernist Movement.

LINDSAY OF BIRKER, 1st B
Alexander Dunlop Lindsay (1879–1952)

Political theorist. Fellow of Balliol College, 1906. Jowett Lecturer in Philosophy, 1911. Professor of Moral Philosophy, Glasgow University, 1922–4. Master of Balliol College, 1924–49. Vice Chancellor of Oxford University, 1935–8. Principal of the University College of North Staffordshire (Keele) from 1949.

Keele University Library has a collection of family and personal papers, at present unsorted. The family papers include 30 box-files of correspondence (some of it written from India) during the second half of the nineteenth century; journals; albums of photographs; notebooks; and some printed matter. The majority of the later material concerns Lord Lindsay, and includes letters and copy letters, memoranda, lectures, sermons, diaries, articles (including printed broadcasts) and newspaper cuttings, roughly sorted into files, not all identified by subject or date. Lindsay's daughter has used much of this material in her biography: Drusilla Scott, *A. D. Lindsay: A Biography* (Oxford, 1971).

Lindsay's involvement in adult education can be traced in records of the Workers' Educational Association, at Temple House, London, and Rewley House, Oxford. These are described in *Sources* Vol. 1, p. 286.

LIVINGSTONE, Dame Adelaide Lord (d. 1970)

Administrator. Hon. Secretary, Government Committee on the Treatment of British Prisoners of War, 1915–18. Head of Public Meetings Department, League of Nations Union, 1923; Director of Special Activities, 1928–34. Secretary, National Declaration Committee, 1934–5. Secretary, International Peace Campaign, 1936–40. Member, Executive Committee, United Nations Association, 1945–55.

Messrs Crane and Hawkins, solicitors in the estate, state that on Dame Adelaide's instructions a filing cabinet full of papers was destroyed after her death. Correspondence, 1935–44, with Lord Cecil is in the British Library (Add. MS 51142).

LLOYD, Edward Mayow Hastings (1889–1968)

Civil Servant, economist and expert on nutrition. Served in the Inland Revenue from 1913; in the Contracts Department, War Office, 1914–17; and the Ministry of Food, 1917–19. Worked in the Economic and Financial Section of the League of Nations Secretariat, 1919–21. Assistant Secretary, Empire Marketing Board, 1923–33. Secretary, Market Supply Committee, 1933–6. Assistant Director, Food (Defence Plans) Department, 1936–9. Principal Assistant Secretary, Food, 1939–42. Economic Adviser to the Minister of State, Middle East, 1942–4. UNRRA Economics and Financial Adviser for the Balkans, 1945; at the Food and Agriculture Organisation, UNO, 1945–7; Permanent Under-Secretary, Food, 1947–53.

A collection of papers at the BLPES, at present being catalogued, contains material relating to Lloyd's two central concerns: general questions of economic management; and nutritional problems. The collection includes War Office material for World War I, including papers on state control and strategic raw materials. There are also papers on the problems of economic organisation and management which he prepared for the ILP during the 1920s. Other material relates to the Empire Marketing Board, the Food Defence Plans, the Ministry of Food during World War II; his service with Harold Macmillan in the Middle East; and his work for UNRRA.

LLOYD, James Henry (b. 1883)

Ethical reformer and trade unionist. Chairman, Association of Public Health Lay Administrative Officers. President of the National Union of Clerks and Administrative Workers.

Hull University Library has a collection of manuscript and printed material. The collection includes a notebook of essays and papers by Lloyd; a book of press cuttings; a file of circular letters, correspondence on China, material on ethics, local government, notes for lectures on Marxism, the Labour Party, beauty, post-war Europe, poems; applications for jobs; notes for lectures on humanism, religion, the Labour Party, town planning, pacifism etc; a bundle of correspondence on Lloyd's possible Parliamentary candidature, 1921–7; a portfolio relating to Karel and Josef Capek; notes for lectures, articles by Lloyd on 'The Clerk in Literature', 'Trade

Unionism for Clerks', letters to the editor on morals, humanism, socialism, 1947–58; a group of papers relating to the Clerical and Administrative Workers Union, and articles in *The Clerk*; material relating to the International Federation of Commercial, Clerical and Technical Employees; papers on the Health Service; material on the Co-operative Movement; papers on humanism and the Ethical Association, including correspondence (including a letter from Shaw) and lecture notes; and miscellaneous other papers on trade unionism, wages, road safety etc. The printed material includes pamphlets, reports etc.

LLOYD-GEORGE, Countess
Frances Louise Stevenson (1888–1972)

Secretary to David Lloyd George.

Papers are in the House of Lords Record Office. Lloyd George's letters to her have been published, edited by A. J. P. Taylor, *My Darling Pussy* (1975).

LOCH, Sir Charles Stewart (1849–1923)

Social worker. Secretary to the Council of the London Charity Organisation Society, 1875–1914. Tooke Professor of Economic Science and Statistics, King's College, London, 1904–8.

London University Library has a diary, 1876–92 (MS 801). It is largely in typescript with manuscript corrections, and is in 3 sections: (*a*) 14 Sept 1876–5 Nov 1887, concerned mainly with his work as secretary to the Charity Organisation Society, and including some statistics; (*b*) two leaves n.d.; (*c*) 26 Sep 1892: an entry concerning a visit to Rouen. Correspondence can be found in the Booth papers, also in London University Library.

    Records of the Charity Organisation Society are in the Greater London Record Office, and are described in *Sources* Vol. 1, pp. 97–8.

LOCKYER, Sir (Joseph) Norman (1836–1920)

Scientist. Fellow of the Royal Society. Director of Solar Physics Observatory, South Kensington, 1885–1913. Director, Hill Observatory, Salcombe Regis, Sidmouth. President of the British Association for the Advancement of Science, 1903–4. Founder of the British Science Guild.

Papers with the Norman Lockyer Observatory, Salcombe Regis, Sidmouth, Devon, include letters to Lockyer, from Airy, Spencer, Huxley, Frankland and Rider Haggard; extensive files of solar observations; spectroscopic plates; and photograph albums.

LODGE, Sir Oliver Joseph (1851–1940)

Scientist. Professor of Physics, University College, Liverpool, 1881–1900. President of the Physical Society of London, 1899–1900. President of the Society for Psychical Research, 1901–4, 1932. President of the British Association, 1913–14. Principal of Birmingham University, 1900–19.

Correspondence and papers are deposited in the Library of University College London. Correspondents include W. G. Adams, Edward Neville da Costa Andrade, Henry Edward Armstrong, W. E. Ayrton, Sir R. S. Ball, .Frank Stanton Carey, A. P. Chattock, William Henry Eccles, Sir Arthur Stanley Eddington, Sir James Alfred Ewing, George Francis Fitzgerald, Sir John Ambrode Fleming, George Carey Foster, Sir Douglas Strutt Galton and Sir Francis Galton, Richard Tetley Glazebrook, W. G. Gregory, Oliver Heaviside, Heinrich Hertz, Adam Hilger, Sir William Huggins, Sir James Hopwood Jeans, Sir Joseph Larmor, George Minchin, Sir Peter Chalmers Mitchell, Alexander Muirhead, John Henry Poynting, Sir

William Henry Preece, Sir William Ramsay, Sir Arthur William Rücker, Arthur Schuster, Arthur Smithells, J. W. Strutt, 3rd Baron Rayleigh, Silvanus Phillips Thompson, William Thomson, 1st Baron Kelvin, George Walker Walker and Pieter Zeeman.

Lodge's correspondence relating to psychical research is in the possession of the Incorporated Society for Psychical Research, 1 Adam and Eve Mews, London W8 6VQ. Correspondents include W. W. Baggally, G. W. Balfour, W. F. Barrett, Henri Bergson, A. C. Bradley, Lord Bryce, Sir William Crookes, A. Conan Doyle, Lord Dunraven, Edmund Gurney, Rev. Henry Higgins, L. P. Jacks, William James, Andrew Lang, Dame Edith Lyttelton, J. H. Muirhead, F. W. H. Myers, J. G. Piddington, Professor Charles Richet, W. H. Salter, Rev. Dick Sheppard, Mrs Sidgwick, Professor E. A. Sonnenschein, Mrs Coombe Tennant, Professor R. J. Tillyard, Lady Troubridge and Mrs Vervall.

Other correspondence, and miscellaneous papers concerning the University are in Birmingham University Library. This library also has the Fiedler-Harding letters, which contain miscellaneous Lodge correspondence, 1902–3. Scientific notebooks and letters to Lodge, 1874–1912, are in Liverpool University Library.

There is correspondence, 1909–16, in the Society of Authors archive at the British Library (Add. MS 56739); and in the A. J. Balfour, Sladen and Rayleigh papers. W. P. Jolly, *Sir Oliver Lodge* (1974), uses all the available archival material.

LONG, Basil Kellett (1878–1944)

Journalist and South African politician. Editor, *The State*, 1909–12. Dominions editor, *The Times*, from 1913. Foreign and Dominions editor, 1920–1. Editor, *Cape Times*, 1921–35. Member of the South African legislature from 1938.

The Times archives contain a folder of letters to Geoffrey Dawson, written after Long had left the staff of the newspaper, chiefly from South Africa.

LOVEDAY, Alexander (1888–1962)

Economist. Lecturer in Political Philosophy, Leipzig University, 1911–12. Lecturer in Economics, Cambridge University, 1913–15. At the War Office, 1915–19; League of Nations Secretariat from 1919. Director of Financial Section and Economic Intelligence Department, 1931–9; of the Economic, Financial and Transit Department, 1939–46. Warden, Nuffield College, Oxford, 1950–4.

Nuffield College, Oxford, has a collection of some 50 boxes of papers, at present not fully catalogued. There is a considerable collection of correspondence, including miscellaneous correspondence, c. 1912–17; general correspondence, 1930–40; personal correspondence, 1930–40, including letters about articles, especially 'Britain and World Trade'; broadcasts, and elections to membership of various societies; a file containing personal correspondence prior to 1930, private family matters, correspondence with Eric Butt; personal correspondence, 1941–57, chiefly dealing with Loveday's time in the USA; a box-file marked 'strictly private', 1934–5, containing correspondence from 1931, and including details of the financial situation in Hungary and Bulgaria; letterbook containing League of Nations correspondence, 1940; personal and family correspondence from 1940 on, including letters to Loveday, Mrs Loveday, Thomas Loveday; correspondence with Hector McNeill, 1946–7, correspondence, 1951, about *The Only Way*; correspondence concerning the Wardenship at Nuffield College, and the 'Letter Books' of the Warden's personal correspondence, 1949–53; correspondence about European economic problems from the 1930s; correspondence on the Common Market; correspondence with the Central Office of Information, 1948–9; and miscellaneous correspondence of an earlier period, including correspondence between Loveday and B. P. Blackett; League of Nations Union correspondence, etc. Other material in the collection includes copies of articles and speeches; papers relating to Nuffield College, its building and administration; diaries dating from 1908 to 1962; copies of reviews; papers on European economic affairs, 1930s; notes and minutes, 1933–42, on various related topics: the peace settlement, European Union, Bulgarian external loans, public finance, the need to maintain League of Nations activities; papers relating to Loveday's trip to the USA in 1934 (correspondence, memoranda, pamphlets) to study the recovery programme; minutes and correspondence concerning the composition of the League of Nations Financial committee; International Chamber of Commerce papers; material on the Mont Perelin Society; material concerning the European Movement; financial correspondence and articles on GATT; and more personal papers, including lecture notes, and personal documents such as passports, address books, photographs, sketchbooks, invitations etc.

LOVERIDGE, Arthur John (1904–   )

Colonial official and educationalist. Member of the Colonial Administrative Service from 1929. Chief Commissioner, Gold Coast Colony, 1950; Northern Territories, 1953; Ashanti, 1954. Lecturer on Education in Tropical Areas, London University Institute of Education, 1959–72.

Tapes and transcripts concerning his work on the Gold Coast, 1930–56, are in Rhodes House Library, Oxford.

LUBBOCK, Sir John, 4th Bt, see AVEBURY, 1st B

LUCAS, Edward Verrall (1868–1938)

Journalist, essayist and publisher. Chairman of Methuen & Co., publishers.

Columbia University Libraries has a small collection of correspondence, 1908–38, chiefly with Arnold Bennett, relating to Lucas' work at Methuen's.
    There is correspondence, 1910–29, in the Galsworthy papers and in the Sladen papers. Correspondence with Sir Edmund Gosse is in the University of Texas, Austin.

LUDLOW, John Malcolm (1821–1911)

Social reformer and Christian Socialist. Secretary to Royal Commission on Friendly and Benefit Building Societies, 1870–4. Chief Registrar of Friendly Societies, 1874–91. Editor of *Politics for the People, Christian Socialist, Journal of Association, Reader*; author of works of history and numerous articles.

A collection of Ludlow family papers, including papers of John Malcolm Ludlow, is preserved in Cambridge University Library. Ludlow went through his own papers in old age and destroyed many. As a result, little of his correspondence survives after 1874. However, there are a considerable number of letters surviving, with a number of correspondents represented. Among these are Charles Kingsley and his wife, Thomas Hughes, Norman Macleod and Donald Macleod, F. D. Maurice, Charles B. Mansfield, F. D. Dyster, Harold Westergaard. In addition there are occasional letters from a range of people, including French and German correspondents. There are also various letters and papers relating to Ludlow's application for the post of Registrar of Friendly Societies, and much correspondence with members of his family. The collection also includes the autograph manuscript of Ludlow's autobiography, together with (an occasionally inaccurate) typescript copy; diaries, 1838–40, 1840–5 (in French); original poems, translations of poems, drafts of articles and reviews; periodicals containing articles by Ludlow, and biographical and obituary notices of him; proposals and letters concerning the foundation of the 'F.D.M. Club', 1882–91; and miscellaneous papers, including notes of Ludlow's earnings. Amongst the family papers are many relating to the Des Graz family. A number of papers about the Ludlow family history include correspondence of J. M. Ludlow with H. H. Ludlow-Bruges and others; correspondence of Edwin Liot on his change of name to Ludlow; a Ludlow pedigree, compiled in 1890; and various other material.

About 20 letters to Ludlow from Charles Kingsley, 1851–61, the property of the Institute of Agricultural Economics, are deposited in the Bodleian Library, Oxford.

LYTTELTON, Dame Edith (d. 1948)

Author and administrator. Deputy Director of Women's Branch of Ministry of Agriculture, 1917–19. British substitute delegate, League of Nations, 1923, 1926–8, 1931. President, Society for Psychical Research, 1933–4.

At Churchill College, Cambridge, there are 15 boxes of correspondence and memoirs, including letters from G. B. Shaw and W. B. Yeats, 1888–1945. Correspondence, 1908–46, with the Society of Authors is in the British Library (Add. MS 56741).Reference should also be made to the records of the Society for Psychical Research.

MACALISTER, Sir John Young Walker (1856–1925)

First Librarian, Gladstone Library, 1887. Hon. Secretary, Library Association, 1887–98; President, 1914–19. Secretary, Royal Society of Medicine.

Miscellaneous correspondence files can be found in the archives of the Royal Society of Medicine.

M'CARTHY, Justin (1830–1912)

Irish novelist, journalist and politician. Journalist in Ireland from 1848, Liverpool, 1852–60, London 1880. Editor, *Morning Star*, 1864–8. Leader writer on *Daily News* from 1871. M.P. (Irish Nat.) Longford County, 1879; Derry City, 1886–92; Longford North, 1892–1900. Chairman, Irish Parliamentary Party, 1890–6. Author of various works of fiction and history.

The National Library of Ireland has 37 volumes of manuscript diaries. The University of Kansas City Library (Snyder collection of Americana) has correspondence of M'Carthy and his daughter, Charlotte, chiefly with Chatto and Windus, concerning his books and articles.
   The autograph MS of 'Our Sensation Novel' is in the British Library (Add. MS 47468); as is his correspondence with the Society of Authors, 1908–31 (Add. MS 56742).
   There are letters in the William Conant Church collection, New York Public Library; in the Ada Rehan papers, University of Pennsylvania Libraries (Philadelphia); and in the O'Gorman Mahon collection, University of Chicago Library.
   Correspondence can also be found in the Chamberlain papers (1882–6), the Sladen papers; and the Rendel papers.

MACCOLL, Rene (1905–71)

Journalist. *Daily Telegraph* correspondent during the Spanish Civil War (Franco side), 1939. Director of Press and Radio Division, British Information Services, New York, 1941–5. Washington correspondent, *Daily Express*, 1946–8; Paris correspondent, 1949–50; Chief American correspondent, 1951–2. Chief Foreign correspondent, *Daily Express*, 1959–69.

The Imperial War Museum has a collection of correspondence and newspaper cuttings concerning the compilation and reception of MacColl's book on Roger Casement together with press clippings about Casement's 'Black Diaries'. The collection also contains a small number of typescript synopses for articles written in Spain, 1939, and reports on his tour of American States, 1943.

McDIARMID, Hugh, see GRIEVE, Christopher Murray

MACDONAGH, Michael (1860–1946)

Journalist and author. On staff of *The Times* from 1894, as a parliamentary correspondent. President, Irish Literary Society of London. Author of works on Ireland and Irish history.

Reference should be made to the archives of *The Times*. He published a diary, *In London during the Great War* (1935).

McFADYEAN, Sir Andrew (1887–1974)

Economist and Liberal politician. Entered Treasury, 1910; thereafter private secretary to various ministers. Treasury representative, Paris, 1919–20. Secretary to British Delegation, Reparation Commission, 1922–4; Secretary to Dawes Committee, 1924. Member of the Executive, National Liberal Federation, 1933–6. Joint Treasurer, Liberal Party Organisation, 1936–48; President, 1949–50. President, Free Trade Union, 1948–59.

BLPES has papers on international monetary problems, c. 1924–31; and personal papers, especially relating to the period after his retirement.

MACFALL, Haldane (1860–1928)

Soldier and author.

Papers are in Yale University Library.

MACGREGOR, David Hutchison (1877–1953)

Economist. Professor of Political Economy, Oxford University. Joint editor, *Economic Journal*, 1925–37.

R. P. Sturges was unable to trace MacGregor's daughter. There are letters in the Beveridge and Cannan papers (BLPES), the Keynes papers (Marshall Library) and the W. H. Dawson collection. The latter relate to various articles and their publication.

MACGREGOR, James (1832–1910)

Scottish church leader. Moderator of the General Assembly, Church of Scotland, 1891.

Diaries, 1892–8, are in the National Library of Scotland.

McLACHLAN, Donald Harvey (1908–71)

Journalist and author. On the editorial staff of *The Times*, 1933–6. Assistant Master, Winchester College, 1936–8. Editor, *Times Educational Supplement*, 1938–40. In Naval Intelligence, 1940–5. Assistant Editor (Foreign), *The Economist*, 1947–54. Deputy editor, *Daily Telegraph*, 1954–60. Editor, *Sunday Telegraph*, 1961–6.

Churchill College, Cambridge, has one box of material relating to McLachlan's *History of Naval Intelligence*.

MACLEAN, John (1879–1923)

Scottish socialist propagandist and agitator.

Material relating to the work and influence of John Maclean can be found in the National Library of Scotland. Many items relate to his educational work, including letters, cuttings, relating to Maclean's dismissal by Govan School Board, 1915–16, and his attempts at reinstatement, and material concerning the organisation of the Scottish Labour College, 1923. Various papers relate to his imprisonment for political activity, including papers relating to his trials, 1916–18; his imprisonments, 1916–18, 1921, with letters from prison. There are also papers relating to his appointment as Russian Consul in Glasgow, 1918. Amongst the correspondence are letters from his family, 1909, 1921–3, and miscellaneous correspondence, 1920–3. There are also letters of sympathy after his death, 1923, and obituary notices, plus articles about him and memoirs by colleagues and friends. The National Library of Scotland also has, on microfilm, notes of lectures on economics given by Maclean; minutes of the Townhead Branch of the Scottish Workers' Republican Party, 1923–6 and other items of correspondence and recollection. Papers emanating from James Clunie, M.P., also in the National Library of Scotland, include letters from Maclean, plus commentaries on them from Clunie. The most comprehensive study, using much original material, is by his daughter, Nan Milton: *John Maclean* (1973).

MACMILLAN, William Miller (1885–1974)

Historian. Specialist in African affairs. Professor of History, University of Witwatersrand, Johannesburg, 1917–34. Member of the Advisory Committee on Education in the Colonies, 1938–41; Empire Intelligence Section, BBC, 1941–3. Senior Representative of the British Council in Africa, 1943–6. Member, Colonial Labour Advisory Committee, 1946–52. Director of Colonial Studies, University of St Andrews, 1947–54. Author of works on the colour question in South Africa, *Warning from the West Indies*, *Africa Emergent*, etc.

Enquiries should be directed to his widow, Mrs. W. M. Macmillan, Yew Tree Cottage, Long Wittenham, Abingdon, OX14 6HB, who has correspondence with, for example, McGregor Ross, Winifred Holtby, Lord Lothian; drafts of speeches, broadcasts, diaries and press cuttings. Mrs Macmillan is using the material for a biographical study. In due course the papers may be deposited in Rhodes House Library.

McNEILL, Florence Marian (1885–1972)

Scottish author, journalist, lecturer and broadcaster.

Papers and correspondence have been given to the National Library of Scotland. Engagement and personal diaries date from 1902, with gaps, and there is also an address book and personalia. There are letters from a range of correspondents, including George Blake, Ivor Brown, C. M. Grieve, A. S. Wallace, Willa Muir, with occasional letters from J. M. Barrie, John Buchan, Aldous Huxley, Compton Mackenzie, Naomi Mitchison, Lewis Spence and others; and letters of sympathy. Other items include reviews, newspaper cuttings, etc.

MACKMURDO, Arthur Heygate (1851–1942)

Architect, designer and social theorist. Associate of William Morris.

The William Morris Gallery, Water House, Lloyd Park, Forest Road, Walthamstow, London E17, has a collection of papers. These include designs for furniture, architecture, textiles, etc.; drawings, and books. There are letters to Mackmurdo from Ernest Rhys, Sir William Blake Richmond, Lawrence Binyon, Walter Crane. There are also autobiographical notes by Mackmurdo, together with his system of monetary reform; notes on William Morris; and illustrated poems.

MAGILL, Andrew Philip (d. 1941)

Civil Servant. Secretary to Augustine Birrell, M.P. Later Assistant Secretary, Ministry of Home Affairs, Northern Ireland.

The Bodleian Library, Oxford, has various items, such as his memoirs and some correspondence, including several letters to Birrell from his contemporaries, and 29 letters from Birrell to Magill.

MAHAFFY, Sir John Pentland (1839–1919)

Provost, Trinity College Dublin. Member of the Irish Convention, 1917–18.

Trinity College Dublin holds a collection of papers, including a group of autograph letters, largely from his correspondence, and selected by his daughter; an account of a journey to Bayreuth by his daughter Elsie, illustrated with letters and photographs; and a variety of papers relating to his academic, personal and political interests. Amongst these are notebooks on Egypt, Greece, the Hebrews and Kant. There are also papers relating to the Irish Convention, 1917, including his diary.

MAITLAND, Frederic William (1850–1906)

Historian. Downing Professor of English Law, Cambridge, from 1888.

Cambridge University Library has various papers including materials for his book, *Life and Letters of Leslie Stephen*, drafts of his *History of English Law* and *Constitutional History*, various lectures and some correspondence, 1868–1906. Gloucestershire Record Office has the diaries of his wife, 1889–99.

There are letters to Rendel in the National Library of Wales. His correspondence with Munroe Smith is in Columbia University Libraries, and with M. M. Bigelow in Boston University Library, Mass.

Correspondence has been published. C. H. S. Fifoot (ed.), *The Letters of Frederic William Maitland* (1965), sought to use all the letters then known to exist. They are addressed to some 40 people, the most regular correspondents being H. A. L. Fisher, Henry Jackson, Fossett Lock and R. L. Poole. Further letters were published as E. L. G. Stones (ed.) *F. W. Maitland, Letters to George Neilson* (Glasgow, 1976). In *Frederic William Maitland, A Life* (Cambridge, Mass., 1971) Fifoot used and quoted from family papers.

MALINOWSKI, Bronislaw Kasper (1884–1942)

Anthropologist. At the London School of Economics from 1910. Professor of Anthropology, University of London from 1927. Visiting Professor of Anthropology, Yale, from 1939.

BLPES has a collection of correspondence, fieldwork journals, notes and research materials. The correspondence is varied, and includes letters from colleagues and co-thinkers, such as Seligman, Westermarck, Havelock Ellis; letters from publishers; and letters of condolence. There are also business and personal files, including papers relating to his appointments. There are a number of typescript articles and reviews, drafts of lectures, talks and speeches, with relevant notes. His field notes are extensive, and are complemented by various other research notes.

Yale University Library has other Malinowski papers. The correspondence series is composed of letters received and carbon copies of his letters to others. There is also a small amount of correspondence of his mother and wife. It appears that most of the correspondence for the later years of his life is in BLPES, and the remaining files have been weeded where there was originally extensive correspondence with organisations and individuals. The correspondence is wide-ranging, and includes letters to and from scholars in many disciplines, but principally anthropologists, psychologists and sociologists throughout the world. The correspondence is in various languages, German, Polish, French and Italian as well as English. Correspondents include Felix Gross, J. Huizinga, Wilhelm Reich, Bertrand Russell, Edward Westermarck, D. H. Westermann, Elton Mayo, M. F. Ashley Montagu. There are some 50 items of correspondence with Brenda and C. G. Seligman, some 45 items of correspondence with Sir James Frazer and Lady Frazer, and about 40 letters exchanged between Malinowski and Havelock Ellis. There are 47 letters from the Princess Marie Bonaparte, and 15 letters to her, 1932–8; and there is an important grouping of correspondence with former students, including Edith Clarke, Ian Hogbin, Raymond Firth, S. F. Nadel, Lucy Mair, Margaret Read, Audrey Richards and Godfrey Wilson. Finally, there is correspondence with scholarly journals and reviews, with publishers, with the London School of Economics and the BBC, as well as personal correspondence.

A second series in Yale University includes lectures, interviews, articles, reviews, notes and fieldwork material and books. The notebooks and notes date from Malinowski's period in New Guinea. There are two boxes of notes on anthropological and sociological topics, including critiques of the theories and work of other scholars.

The third series, 'Writings of Others', consists primarily of books, articles and papers written by students and colleagues of Malinowski. A final series, 'Special Files', consists of memorabilia, including notes of lectures, tributes, photographs, advertisements for his works, travel permits, etc.

Some Malinowski correspondence concerning African affairs is in the archives of the London Group on African Affairs, Rhodes House Library, Oxford; while a memorandum by Malinowski on the teaching of practical anthropology in connection with colonial studies is in the Lothian papers at the Scottish Record Office.

MALLOCK, William Hurrell (1849–1923)

Author, chiefly of works attacking Radicalism and Socialism.

No private papers are known. A few letters, 1884–5, on work in progress, are in the Escott papers.

MANN, Arthur Henry (1876–1972)

Journalist. Editor, *Evening Standard* and *Yorkshire Post*, 1919–39. Trustee of *The Observer*, 1945–56. Governor of the BBC, 1941–6.

Mr Peter Wright, 3317 Dent Place, N.W. Washington, D.C. 20007, USA, has an assortment of papers relating to Mann's career, including letters to his wife and other members of his family, a number of letters received from leading political figures of the day (Baldwin, Eden, etc.), various papers connected with the *Yorkshire Post* (particularly during the appeasement period) and *The Observer*, BBC documents and related correspondence, articles and pamphlets written by Mann, press cuttings and photographs, etc.

MANN, Thomas (Tom) (1846–1941)

Trade unionist and Communist. Socialist propagandist from 1880s; joined Social Democratic Federation, 1885. President, Dockers' Union, 1889–93. Secretary, Independent Labour Party, 1894–7. A founder and first President, International Federation of Ship, Dock and River Workers, 1896. Helped found Workers' Union, 1898. Labour organiser in Australia, 1902–10. Editor, *Industrial Syndicalist*, 1910–11. General Secretary, Amalgamated Society of Engineers (later AEU), 1919–21. Founder member, Communist Party of Great Britain. Chairman, National Minority Movement, 1924–32.

It is believed that papers may survive in private hands, but no information is available at present. The Communist Party of Great Britain has a few papers of Dona Torr, chiefly in connection with her biography of Mann.

Letters and photographs relating to Tom Mann are in the J. P. Jones papers in La Trobe Library, State Library of Victoria, Melbourne, Australia. Letters, 1888–95, are in the Herbert Samuel collection at the House of Lords Record Office; while correspondence with John Burns, 1887–1939, is in the British Library (Add. MS 46285).

Records of the old ASE/AEU are describe in *Sources* Vol. 1, pp. 6–8.

MANNHEIM, Karl (1893–1947)

Sociologist. Lecturer in Sociology, University of Heidelberg, 1926–30. Professor of Sociology, Frankfurt, 1930–3. Lecturer in Sociology, London School of Economics, 1933–45. Professor of Education, London University, 1945–7. Editor, International Library of Sociology and Social Reconstruction.

Various relevant items are in the records of the Moot, in the Library of the Institute of Education, London.

MANNING, Adelaide (d. 1905)

Hon. Secretary to the National Indian Association. Editor of *Indian Magazine and Review*.

A small folder of letters to Miss Manning, including some correspondence and miscellaneous papers on India, is in Cambridge University Library.

MANSBRIDGE, Albert (1876–1952)

Educationalist. Founded Workers' Education Association, 1903; Secretary, 1903–15. Founded National Central Library.

The main collection of Mansbridge papers is in the custody of the British Library. Correspondence with Leonard Clark is in McMaster University Library.

The WEA records, described in *Sources* Vol. 1, p. 286, at Temple House, 9 Upper Berkeley Street, London W1H 8BY, and at the Oxford University Department of External Studies, Rewley House, Oxford, contain much relevant information. The Rewley House archives, to be deposited in the Bodleian Library, cover the development of the WEA and the tutorial class movement. The Cambridge Extra-Mural Archives, now in Cambridge University Library, have some relevant information. A few items of correspondence with Lord Lothian, 1936–40, are in the Scottish Record Office.

Professor Bernard Jennings, Department of Adult Education, University of Hull, is preparing a study of Mansbridge which has made use of the available sources.

MARKHAM, Sir Clements Robert (1830–1916)

Geographer and historical writer. Secretary of the Royal Geographical Society, 1863–88. Secretary to the Hakluyt Society, 1858–87. Assistant Secretary in the India Office, 1867–77.

The British Library has a manuscript of his *History of Peru* (Add. MSS 46216–8), and manuscripts on Peru (Add. MSS 48197–200). The Royal Geographical Society has his private journals, notebooks and some letters. The Scott Polar Research Institute has some letters and a notebook on the British Antarctic Expedition. One volume of papers is in the William L. Clements Library, University of Michigan, Ann Arbor.

MARKHAM, Violet Rosa
Mrs Violet Carruthers (d. 1960)

Politician and administrator. Member of the Executive Committee, National Relief Fund. Chairman, Central Committee, Women's Employment. Deputy Director, Women's Section, National Service Department, 1917. Member Industrial Court, 1920–46. Member, Unemployment Assistance Board, 1934–46; Deputy Chairman, 1937–46. Chairman of the Advisory Council, National Institute of Houseworkers, 1946. Founder and President, Chesterfield Settlement.

The BLPES has a collection of papers, largely relating to the numerous committees on which Violet Markham sat. The material covers a range of work, from the National Relief Fund, 1914–23, to war babies, National Register, Women's Volunteer Reserve, canteens, Luxury Tax, the Rhineland High Commission, factory inspection, miners' welfare, unemployment and the Assistance Board (including minutes, reports and correspondence), domestic service, postwar organisation of women's employment, as well as drafts, correspondence, lectures and articles, and press cuttings. Some correspondence with her brother, Sir A. B. Markham, Bt, remains with the family (*Sources* Vol. 3, p. 45).

MARKS OF BROUGHTON, 1st B
Sir Simon Marks (1888–1964)

Businessman. Chairman and Joint Managing Director, Marks & Spencer Ltd. Supporter of Zionist aspirations.

Papers are in the Central Zionist Archives, Jerusalem (ref. A247), while other papers are in the archives of Marks and Spencer Ltd.

MARLOWE, Thomas (1868–1935)

Journalist. Editor, *Daily Mail*, 1899–1926. Chairman, Associated Newspapers Ltd, 1918–26.

Neither Sir Geoffrey Harmsworth, Bt, the biographer of Lord Northcliffe, nor the Associated Newspaper Group Ltd, knew of relevant personal papers. A few letters from Marlowe are in the Blumenfeld collection at the House of Lords Record Office, and there are three volumes of correspondence in the Northcliffe papers in the British Library.

MARSHALL, Alfred (1842–1924)

Economist. Principal of University College, Bristol, 1877–82. Lecturer, Balliol College, Oxford, 1883–4. Professor of Political Economy, Cambridge, 1885–1908.

The Marshall Library, Cambridge, has the largest collection of material. There are some 17 boxes of notes, lectures and some other material, covering the whole of Marshall's work. In addition, there are letters to him, 1877–1923, and some letters from him to others, chiefly Foxwell and Edgeworth. Sturges, *Economists' Papers*, pp. 71–2, lists a number of letters in other collections, including nine letters to E. A. Benians, 1904–13, at St John's College, Cambridge; nine letters to H. S. Foxwell at Harvard University; 15 letters to W. A. S. Hewins, Sheffield University Library; 39 letters to J. M. Keynes, and 117 letters to J. N. Keynes in the Marshall Library. There are some 45 letters in the Cannan collection, BLPES, which also has a small group of letters exchanged between Marshall and Francis Ysidro Edgeworth, 1880–93 (coll. Misc. 470); and there are some correspondence and notes relating to Marshall's Theory of Consumer Rent, including letters from Marshall and Edgeworth, in the small Sir Leslie Stephen collection, also at BLPES.

MARSHALL, Catherine E. (1880–1961)

Feminist, pacifist and internationalist. Between 1910 and 1914 worked full time for women's suffrage. Parliamentary Secretary, National Union of Women's Suffrage Societies. Helped found the Women's International League for Peace and Freedom, 1915; from 1916 worked full time for the No-Conscription Fellowship as Parliamentary and later Hon. Secretary. After the war, she was active in the international peace movement and the Labour Party.

Papers are preserved, in the Cumbria Record Office: They cover the whole span of Catherine Marshall's life and political activities, from the 1880s to the 1950s. Various correspondence, chiefly personal and family, dates from 1885 to 1914, and reflects her early life and activities. A number of boxes of correspondence and papers from 1909 onwards concern her work for women's suffrage and her involvement in the NUWSS; and various other papers relate to the Women's International League from its foundation to 1937. The largest grouping in the collection concerns the Great War and the various organisations with which she was concerned. Correspondence and papers (1914–18) of the No-Conscription Fellowship offer a very full account of her work, and include organisational material, reports, etc., and files relating to cases of conscientious objection, and include material concerning Clifford Allen and Bertrand Russell. Overlapping with this, and extending into the inter-war years are papers and correspondence concerning the Labour and Socialist movement, Communism, Parliament and elections, the Liberals and the National Council of Women. There is also material concerning the League of Nations (1920s), refugees (she was particularly concerned with the issue of Jewish refugees from the Nazis) and Czechoslovakia. Some three boxes of material concern personal and local issues; while another seven contain unsorted material.

Sources Vol. 1, pp. 206–7, contains a note on papers which relate to the No-Conscription Fellowship, particularly the Clifford Allen papers (University of South Carolina) and the Bertrand Russell papers (McMaster University). Papers of the Women's International League (British Section, now in BLPES) which contain material relating to Catherine Marshall, are described briefly in *Sources*, Vol. 1, pp. 278–9. Extensive relevant material can also be found in the archives of the Women's International League for Peace and Freedom (International Section), held by the Western History collections, University of Colorado, Boulder, Colorado 80302, USA, and in the papers of the American Section in the Swarthmore College Peace collection.

A biographical study of Catherine Marshall is being prepared by Dr Jo Vellacott Newberry, Lucy Cavendish College, Cambridge.

MARTIN, (Basil) Kingsley (1897–1969)

Socialist journalist. Assistant Lecturer, London School of Economics, 1923–7. Co-founder and joint editor, *The Political Quarterly*. On the editorial staff of the *Manchester Guardian*, 1927–31. Editor, *New Statesman and Nation*, 1930–60.

Sussex University Library has a large collection of papers and correspondence. Early and personal papers in the collection include school papers; files on World War I (including diary notes, peace statements); Cambridge (including press cuttings, notes, theatrical papers, and a notebook on archaeology and architecture, 1918); Princeton; reading notes; reviews, 1920–7; news cuttings, 1920–6; family correspondence; autobiographical papers; personalia; obituary letters; papers of Rev. D. B. Martin; diaries, notebooks, correspondence and press cuttings of Olga Martin; and miscellaneous papers and correspondence of Dorothy Woodman. Martin's diaries and notebooks date from 1913–14, with a notebook and diary of a visit to South Africa, and extend to his death. They include not only pocket diaries with brief notes but notebooks on his various visits abroad. The correspondence files (28 in all) reveal the range of his interests. Correspondents include Lord Aberdeen, Sir Richard Acland, Clifford Allen, Norman Angell, C. R. Attlee, M. Ayrton, Sir Gerald Barry, Lord Beaverbrook, A. C. Benson, S. L. Bensusan, J. Berger, Aneurin Bevan, Lord Blackett, Lady Violet Bonham-Carter (Lady Asquith), Lord Boothby, Brendan Bracken, H. N. Brailsford, Ritchie Calder, G. D. H. Cole, Margaret Cole, R. H. S. Crossman, Basil Davidson, G. L. Dickinson, Wilfrid Eady, L. Fielden, E. M. Forster, Victor Gollancz, J. M. Keynes, Liddell Hart, Harold Laski, David Low, Desmond MacCarthy, Walter Monckton, Herbert Morrison, D. N. Pritt, W. A. Robson, Bertrand Russell, C. P. Scott, G. B. Shaw, R. H. Tawney, Lord Vansittart, A. P. Wadsworth, G. Wallas, H. G. Wells, Dorothy Woodman, Leonard and Virginia Woolf and Konni Zilliacus. Various files relate to Martin's journalistic work, including articles and cuttings concerning his work for the *Manchester Guardian*, and above all his editorship of the *New Statesman*. The latter includes files (with correspondence, cuttings, papers on various topics) on Africa, America, Animals, Asia, Australia, Campaign for Nuclear Disarmament, Censorship, Cold War, Cuba, *Evening Standard*, Germany, India (including correspondence with Indian leaders, notes of visits, reports from Indian correspondents, periodical articles, cuttings, etc.), Ireland, Labour, Libel, Middle East, the Monarchy, *New Statesman* diary, Political Essays, the Press, Profiles, Propaganda, Religion and Ethics, Russell, Russia, Shaw (some five files of miscellaneous material, letters to the *New Statesman*, etc.), The Sixties, 'Tate Gallery Affair', The Thirties, Union of Democratic Control, Henry Wallace, H. G. Wells, World War II, Yugoslavia and the Balkans.

The collection also contains papers and material concerning Martin's books, broadcasts and lectures, and particularly concerning his autobiographical works. There are also recordings by Martin, on Harold Laski, the *New Statesman*, the Spanish Civil War; and recordings about him, taped by C. H. Rolph for *Kingsley: the Life, Letters and Diaries*. Amongst those interviewed were Janet Adam Smith, Walter Allen, Asa Briggs, Richard Crossman, John Freeman, Edward Hyams, Paul Johnson, Arthur Koestler, Ivor Montagu, Raymond Mortimer, Malcolm Muggeridge, J. B. Priestley, V. S. Pritchett, Tom Harrisson, W. A. Robson, A. J. P. Taylor, Dame Rebecca West, and Lady Wootton.

His library was given to the Nehru University, New Delhi. Letters, 1934–43, can be found in the Lloyd George papers at the House of Lords Record Office.

MARVIN, Francis Sydney (1867–1943)

Educationalist and positivist writer. Divisional Inspector and Inspector of Training Colleges in Yorkshire, 1903–13; East Central Division, 1914. Staff Inspector, Board of Education, until 1929. Professor of Modern History in the University of Egypt, 1929–30.

The Bodleian Library, Oxford, has a collection of letters, chiefly to Marvin and to his wife. The letters to Marvin cover the period, 1884–1936. Amongst the correspondents are Samuel Barnett, J. H. Bridges, G. L. Dickinson, A. J. Carlyle, Joseph Chamberlain, H. A. L. Fisher, J. L. Hammond, Frederic Harrison, Sir Patrick Geddes, Viscount Hewart, L. T. Hobhouse, C. L. Kingsford, H. W. Massingham, A. S. Peake, Sir Michael Sadler, Sir Cyril Jackson, Sir Herbert Llewellyn-Smith, Graham Wallas, H. G. Wells, Sir Paul Vinogradoff. Letters to Edith Mary Deverill Marvin cover the period 1896–1937, with a similar range of correspondents, including Beatrice Webb, Agnes Catherine Maitland, Eleanor Sidgwick, Eleanor Rathbone, Sir Robert Morant, J. R. MacDonald, J. M. Keynes, Sir John Eldon Gorst. In addition, there are letters from Marvin to Mrs Elsie Franklin, 1929–30, and papers of Edith Marvin relating to family matters.

MASON, Charlotte Maria Shaw (1842–1923)

Educationalist. Founded the Parents' National Education Union, 1887; the Ambleside House of Education, and the Parents' Union School; 1891; the *Parents' Review*, 1890.

Papers of Charlotte Mason, as well as the records of the Parents' National Education Union, are preserved in the University of London Library. The personal papers consist of letters to and from Charlotte Mason, papers on constitutional affairs, conference material, press cuttings, memoirs; the manuscripts of Charlotte Mason's writings; proofs and printed copies of her writings; and teaching materials. The PNEU papers include minutes, correspondence, accounts, and other administrative records, correspondence on schools and courses, lecture notes, questionnaires etc. They are described in *Sources* Vol. 1, pp. 209–10.

Correspondence can also be found in the Oscar Browning papers, at Hastings Public Library.

MASSINGHAM, Henry William (1860–1924)

Journalist and author. Editor at various times of the National Press Agency, the *Star*, *Daily Chronicle*. Editor, the *Nation*, 1907–23.

A. E. Havighurst has written the most comprehensive study, *Radical Journalist: H. W. Massingham* (Cambridge University Press, 1974). He reports that Massingham kept no journal, no appointment diaries, and almost no correspondence before 1914, and very little thereafter. The Massingham material that Havighurst amassed he proposes to give to the Norwich Central Library (p. x). Correspondence can be found in a number of other collections including the W. H. Dawson papers, the Shaw collection at the British Library (Add. MS 50543), the Ponsonby papers, the Norman Angell papers, the Fabian collection at Nuffield College, Oxford, and in the papers of Gladstone, John Burns, H. W. Nevinson, J. L. Hammond, Arnold Bennett (the Berg collection, New York Public Library), Edward Garnett (in Texas University Library), Northcliffe and J. R. MacDonald.

MAUDE, Aylmer (1858–1938)

Author and translator. Expounder of the works of Tolstoy; editor of Tolstoy translations in the World's Classics Series, and of the Centenary Edition of his works.

Columbia University Libraries has a collection of letters, 1897–1937, from Tolstoy to Aylmer Maude, dealing with subjects such as Tolstoy's health, art, censorship, John Ruskin, the 'Resurrection' fund, the banishment of the Doukhobors to Siberia, Jewish pogroms, peasant distress and famine and Tolstoy's doctrine of non-resistance.

At the British Library correspondence of Maude can be found in the Marie Stopes papers (Add. MSS 58487–90) and in the Society of Authors collection (Add. MSS 56746–49). The Fabian Society archive at Nuffield College, Oxford, has relevant correspondence.

MAXSE, Leopold James (1864–1932)

Journalist and political writer. Editor, *National Review*.

Family papers at the West Sussex Record Office contain miscellaneous papers and correspondence. Correspondence can also be found in various other collections. The Bonar Law papers in the House of Lords Record Office contain 28 letters, 1906–17. There are also letters in the Blumenfeld papers, 1911–15, and the St Loe Strachey papers, 1893–1918, both at the House of Lords Record Office. Letters to Lord Hardinge, 1898–1903, 1916, are in Cambridge University Library, while correspondence with Lord Croft, 1908–18, is in Churchill College, Cambridge.

MAXWELL, Sir William (d. 1947)

Conservative journalist. Editor, *Aberdeen Journal* and *Aberdeen Press and Journal*, 1910–27. President, Scottish Unionist Association, 1935–6.

Duke University, Durham, North Carolina, has a group of papers, 1915–39. There are some 29 items in all, including letters relating to political issues.

MAYHEW, Arthur Innes (1878–1948)

Educationalist. In the Indian Educational Service, 1903–22. Director of Public Instruction, Central Provinces, and Education Commissioner, Government of India. Master at Eton College, 1922–8. Secretary, Education Committee, Colonial Office, 1929–39.

Minutes and memoranda by Mayhew, 1937–9, concerning education and teacher training in the Commonwealth, are in the Creech Jones papers at Rhodes House Library, Oxford.

MAYO, Katherine (1868–1940)

Writer.

Yale University Library has a collection of some 20,000 items covering the period 1895–1961, and including correspondence, diaries, scrapbooks and manuscripts of writings. Many prominent British men and women corresponded with her, and her diaries contain comments from her British friends on Nazi Germany. Much of the correspondence is concerned with the British Apprentices Club organised by Katherine Mayo in 1921, and with the publication of *The Face of Mother India*.

MEADE, James Edward (1907–)

Economist. Fellow and Lecturer in Economics, Hertford College, Oxford, 1930–7; Bursar, 1934–7. Member, Economic Section of League of Nations, Geneva, 1938–40. Economic Assistant, 1940–5, and Director, 1946–7, Economic Section, Cabinet Office. Professor of Commerce, with special reference to International Trade, London School of Economics, 1947–57. Professor of Political Economy, Cambridge, 1957–68. Member of Council of the Royal Economic Society, 1945–62 (President, 1964–6); and Council Member of Eugenics Society, 1962–8.

Material deposited at BLPES, and not currently made available, includes correspondence; MS notes and papers on various topics, including Government economic policy, economic growth, inflation; and correspondence relating to his various books and studies.

MEARS, Sir Frank Charles (1880–1953)

Architect and town planner. Designed the National Library, Jerusalem.

Sketchbooks and notes are in the National Library of Scotland. See also the entry for Sir Patrick Geddes, his father-in-law.

MEINERTZHAGEN, Richard (1878–1967)

Soldier, traveller, ornithologist and writer. Supporter of Zionism. Chief Political Officer in Palestine and Syria, 1919–20. Military Adviser, Middle East Department of the Colonial Office, 1921–4. Served at the War Office, 1939–40.

Papers can be found at Rhodes House Library, Oxford. These include his intelligence reports, despatches and memoranda while in government service, 1902–24, and 76 volumes of his diaries, 1899–1965, which reflect his varied interests and activities. Correspondence can be found in the David Lack papers (NRA 18780), while a corrected typescript of his Kenya Diary, 1902–6, is in the National Library of Scotland.

MELLOR, William (1888–1942)

Journalist. Secretary, Fabian Research Department, 1913. Worked for *Daily Herald* from 1913; its Industrial Correspondent during World War I; editor, 1926–31. Assistant Managing Editor, Odhams Press Ltd, 1931–6. Editor, *Tribune*, 1937–8; *Town and County Councillor*, 1936–40.

It is believed that no papers survive with Mellor's son. Records of *Tribune* were destroyed during World War II and no relevant material survives. Some letters from Mellor, 1935–7, are in the Labour Party archive at Transport House (ref. LP/SL/35).

MERCER, Thomas (1883–1972)

A founder member of the Communist Party of Great Britain. Assistant editor, *Automobile Engineering*.

Miss Sarah Gilby (granddaughter), 15 Speer Road, Thames Ditton, Surrey, has a collection of papers.

MEYNELL, Sir Francis (1891–1975)

Book designer, publisher and poet. A director of the *Daily Herald*, 1918–20. Founder of the Nonsuch Press, 1923. Contributor to the *News Chronicle* from 1934. Adviser on Consumer Needs, Board of Trade, from 1940. Royal Designer for Industry, 1945. Director-General, Cement and Concrete Association, 1946–58. Typographic adviser to H.M. Stationery Office, 1945–66.

A large collection of letters is in the Boston Public Library, Boston, Mass.

MICHELL, Sir Lewis Loyd (1842–1928)

Banker and businessman. General Manager, Standard Bank of South Africa. Chairman, De Beers Consolidated Mines. Minister without portfolio, Cape Colony. Member of South African Legislature.

There is extensive relevant material in the P. L. Gell (q.v.) records of the British South Africa Company.

MIDDLETON, James Smith (1878–1962)

Labour politician. Assistant Secretary, and later General Secretary of the Labour Party.

Mrs Lucy Middleton (widow) has a number of papers which she is gradually transferring to the Labour Party archive at Transport House. At Transport House there is a large group of papers, called the 'J. S. Middleton papers', and formerly in his possession. The group consists of some 31 boxes: 16 General (ref. LP/JSM), 13 International (ref. LP/JSM/INT) and two Research Department-Conference decisions since 1918 (ref. LP/JSM/(RES)). It would seem, however, that apart from a small amount of personal material, including a box of picture post-cards from Labour notables, these papers are effectively extensions of Labour Party files. The Labour Party archive as a whole is described in *Sources* Vol. 1, pp. 127–32. The International Institute of Social History, Amsterdam, has a few relevant items, including a letter (and a reply) to J.R. MacDonald, Aug 1931; correspondence with Max Beer (11 letters, 1929–40), a letter from R. H. Tawney, and an internal note on the Labour Party, 1943. Other relevant material may be found in the J. R. MacDonald papers at the Public Record Office.

MIDDLETON, Mary

Socialist publicist. Secretary, Women's Labour League, 1907–11.

The archives of the Labour Party contain correspondence, 1906–8, deposited by Mrs Lucy Middleton, widow of J. S. Middleton, whose first wife was Mary Middleton. The archive also has the surviving records of the Women's Labour League. These are described in *Sources* Vol. 1, p. 279.

MILNER, Viscountess
Violet Georgina Milner (d.1958)

Champion of Imperial policies. Editor, *National Review*, 1932–48.

Papers in the Milner collection at the Bodleian Library include family material, with correspondence, and there is relevant material in the Cecil-Maxse papers in Kent Archives Office.

MITCHISON, Naomi Margaret (1897–   )

Author. Member, Highland and Island Advisory Panel, 1947–65; Highlands and Islands Development Council from 1966. Tribal adviser to Bakgatla, Botswana, from 1963.

The National Library of Scotland has certain of her papers, including some correspondence between herself and her husband Gilbert (Lord) Mitchison. Other papers remain in her care, while a further collection is in the University of Texas, Austin.

MITRANY, David (1888–1975)

Political economist. Worked on the *Manchester Guardian*, 1921–2. Assistant European editor, *Economic and Social History of the World War*, 1922–9. Visiting Professor at Harvard University, 1931–3. Professor in School of Economics and Politics at Princeton, Institute of Advanced Study, from 1933. Attached to the Foreign Office during World War II. Adviser on International Affairs to Unilever from 1943. Professor at Smith College, 1951.

BLPES has a collection of papers, which cover the range of Mitrany's interests. There is material on the following topics: the causes of war, World Community, International Organisation, Federalism, Regionalism, Functionalism, Nationality and Nationalism, Human Rights, International Law, Sovereignty, Peaceful Change, Security, International Administration, Voting and Representation, Equality of States, League of Nations and Proposals leading up to 1944, the United Nations, UN Specialised Agencies, Technical Assistance, Non-Government Organisations, International Economics, Planning, 'Marx against the peasant', the USA, Pacificism, the Study of International Relations, Psychology, Political Theory, Working Democracy, Political Science, Sociology and Methodology, Philosophy of History. The collection also includes other working files, book reviews, letters to the press, correspondence, press cuttings, and working notes.

MOFFAT, John (d. 1973)

General Staff Publications Officer, Northern Command, 1940–5. Press Chief, British Sector, Berlin, 1945–6. Started *Der Berliner*, in Berlin; editor, *British Zone Review*, 1946–9. Press Officer, War Office, 1951–8.

The Imperial War Museum holds a typescript of Moffat's unpublished autobiography covering his post-war work in Germany.

MONTAGUE, Charles Edward (1867–1928)

Author. Director of the *Manchester Guardian*.

At the British Library (Add. MS 45910) there are letters from Montague to his friend Francis Dodd, 1905–28; and letters from Mrs Montague and Oliver Elton to Dodd relating to the publication of the *Memoir*, 1929. Archives of the *Manchester Guardian*, in John Rylands University Library of Manchester, are described in *Sources* Vol. 1, p. 104.

MONTAGUE, Francis Charles (1858–1935)

Historian. Professor of History, University College London, 1893–1927.

Four volumes of notes on French history, c. 1897, are deposited in the Library of University College London.

MOODY, Sydney (b. 1889)

Colonial Civil Servant. Assistant, later Deputy Chief, Secretary in Palestine in the 1920s and 1930s. Colonial Secretary, Mauritius, 1939–48.

Correspondence and papers are deposited in Rhodes House Library. The bulk of the material emanates from Moody's wife, Flora, and includes her Palestine diaries, 1921–39; her Mauritius diaries, 1940–8; notebooks about visits to Israel and Jordan, 1957–8; and further notebooks on travels 1951–60; letters from Flora Moody to her husband and daughters, 1921–51; letters from Flora to relatives and friends. There are also letters from Sydney Moody to his wife, family and friends; the Palestine diaries of Dr William Ewing, 1888–92; letters from Dr Ewing and his wife to Sydney and Flora Moody; letters from Dr Ewing and other relatives to Sydney and Flora Moody, and a few letters to the Ewings; letters from various correspondents to the Moodys and miscellaneous papers about Palestine.

MOORE, George Edward (1873–1958)

Philosopher.

Moore's letters to J. M. Keynes can be found at King's College, Cambridge, and further letters are in the Thomas Sturge Moore papers (NRA 17929).

MOORE, Maurice George (1854–1939)

Soldier and Irish patriot. Commander of Irish and National Volunteers. Senator, Irish Free State, 1922–36.

Papers and correspondence can be found in the National Library of Ireland. There are about 800 letters to Colonel Moore from various correspondents, c. 1905–33, many with copies or drafts of replies. These relate to the Irish National Volunteers and other political issues. The collection also includes documents on various aspects of the war of independence – the Black and Tan and other outrages, the Irish National Aid Society, political prisoners, etc. (some 300 items, 1918–21).

MORRIS, Sir William Richard, 1st Bt, see NUFFIELD, 1st Vt

MORRISON, George Ernest (1862–1920)

Journalist. Correspondent of *The Times* in Indo-China and China, 1895–1912. Adviser to the President of the Chinese Republic from 1912.

Papers are in the Mitchell Library, Sydney, New South Wales, Australia. They include an important diary kept over many years in China and also a mass of correspondence, including copies of his own letters. Correspondents include members of successive British governments, the Diplomatic and Consular Service in China, and colleagues on *The Times* in London. The archives of *The Times* contain correspondence with Wickham Steed, Mrs Moberly Bell and others.

Papers have been used in Cyril Pearl, *Morrison of Peking* (1970) and letters are being published: Lo Hui Min (ed.), *Correspondence of G. E. Morrison* (Vol 1, 1976).

MOULE, Handley Carr Glyn (1841–1920)

Theologian. Principal of Ridley Hall, Cambridge, 1881–99. Norrisian Professor of Divinity, Cambridge, 1899–1901. Bishop of Durham from 1901.

Cambridge University Library has three boxes of material, which includes diaries, 1878–1920, and miscellaneous papers (lectures, sermons, biblical commentaries, etc.).

MOUNT STEPHEN, 1st B
Sir George Stephen, 1st Bt (1829–1921)

Financier and philanthropist. President of the Bank of Montreal. Head of Canadian Pacific Railway till 1888.

It is believed that Mount Stephen destroyed most of his papers before his death. Correspondence, especially letters to Lady Wolseley, are in the Wolseley papers in Hove Public Library. Letters from Sir J. Macdonald, 1881–9, concerning Canadian railways and politics, are in the Public Archives of Canada.

MUIRHEAD, Roland Eugene (1868–1964)

Leading Scottish Nationalist. Founder and Director of the Scottish Secretariat.

The National Library of Scotland has various papers relating to Muirhead. These include diaries and notebooks, 1893–1953; correspondence with various supporters and colleagues, including Lewis Spence (12 letters to Muirhead, 1927–30, and six carbons of letters from Muirhead), Douglas Young (15 letters from Young, 1940–59), G. B. Shaw (one letter, ?1920), plus business letters. There are also various other items, including miscellaneous notes by Muirhead, transcripts of speeches made at a meeting of the Scottish National Party, which Muirhead chaired, in 1929; membership cards of various organisations; collections of bills and receipts; copies of a draft bill; and other leaflets and memorabilia. The records of the Scottish Secretariat (described in *Sources* Vol. 1, p. 234) contain both general correspondence (about 1400 files), and personal correspondence of the Director, Muirhead (800 files). This collection is at present uncatalogued. *Sources* Vol. 1 also describes other relevant material for the Scottish Nationalist Movement (see pp. 233–4, pp. 308–9).

Edinburgh University Library has correspondence between C. M. Grieve (Hugh MacDiarmid) and Muirhead dating from the 1920s, plus a diary of Muirhead's visit to the USA, 1900, and certain other items. Muirhead's own personal library, together with Guy Aldred's, formed the basis of the Baillie's Library, Glasgow. This has a number of letters from Archibald MacLaren to Muirhead, and these include references to Edward Carpenter, Bruce Glasier, Socialist League activities, and the Trafalgar Square demonstration of 13 Nov 1887 ('Bloody Sunday'). There are also 23 items of correspondence and other material, largely addressed to Muirhead, from Jean Lambie, 1906–21. Much of the correspondence relates to the activities of the WSPU, of which she was for a time 'Organising Secretary'. In a 42-page letter/memorandum dated 30 Mar 1921, Jean Lambie discusses the affairs of the Scottish Home Rule Association and her own position in the Association as editor of its news-sheet and Edinburgh 'organiser'.

MULCAHY, Richard (1886–1960)

Irish general and politician.

University College, Dublin, has a collection of material, amounting to some 70 boxes. This includes much official material from the period as Chief of Staff and Commander in Chief of the Irish Republican Army and Free State Army, 1919–24; material relating to his political career as a member of Dail Eireann, 1922–60; and draft articles and taped discussions on aspects of Irish history, mainly for the period 1916–24, compiled in the 1960s. The National Library of Ireland has certain other relevant items for the period 1916–25.

MÜLLER, Ernest Bruce Iwan- (1853–1910)

Journalist.

Correspondence of Iwan-Müller can be found in the British Library (Add. MSS 51316 52914).

MURRAY, (George) Gilbert Aimé (1866–1957)

Classical scholar and internationalist. Fellow of New College, Oxford, 1888. Professor of Greek, Glasgow University, 1889–99. Regius Professor of Greek, Oxford University, 1908–36. Founder Member of League of Nations Union; Chairman of its Executive Council, 1923–38. President, United Nations Association, 1945–9. Delegate at the League of Nations, Geneva, for South Africa, 1921–3. Member of the League Committee on Intellectual Co-operation from 1922. Liberal Parliamentary candidate for Oxford University.

A substantial collection of the papers of Gilbert Murray is located in the Bodleian Library, Oxford, and provides a comprehensive guide to his career and interests. Murray had a wide range of correspondents, including leading politicians (Asquith, Attlee, Balfour, Eden, MacDonald); fellow-publicists and academics (Norman Angell, the Coles, J. L. and B. Hammond, H. J. Laski, A. E. Zimmern) and literary figures such as Galsworthy, Granville-Barker, Rose Macaulay, G. B. Shaw, H. G. Wells, W. B. Yeats. Murray's political correspondence and papers range from the questions of women's suffrage and conscientious objection in World War I to the General Strike and general elections in the 1950s; and internationally, from Austria and Germany to China and Japan. Murray's League of Nations work is also fully represented, and the papers (correspondence, memoranda, speeches, etc.) cover the establishment and activities of the League of Nations Union as well as his work for the League itself at Geneva. The academic papers include material relating to Glasgow and Oxford, correspondence with fellow-scholars, journalists and artists, correspondence and papers relating to his various publications, copies of lectures, and papers relating to various academic committees. The collection also includes personal and family papers, correspondence with close relatives, congratulatory letters, personal notebooks and scrapbooks, miscellaneous biographical material and obituary notices. In addition to MSS there is a quantity of printed material, mainly consisting of Gilbert Murray's publications. There is also a bibliography of his major works; and fourteen volumes of press-cuttings relating to his various activities.

The National Library of Australia has a further collection of family correspondence, lectures, translation notes, speeches, 1885–1957 (ref. MS 565). The League of Nations Union papers at BLPES are useful for tracing aspects of Murray's internationalist activities. Four volumes of his correspondence are available in the Cecil of Chelwood papers at the British Library (Add. MSS 51071–51204), while correspondence, 1932–8, can also be found in the Lothian papers at the Scottish Record Office. The British Library has correspondence in the Society of Authors archive (Add. MS 56761) and the Shaw collection (Add. MS 50542). The Russell Archive at McMaster University also has correspondence. Relevant items can be found too in the Norman Angell papers, the Kautsky collection at the International Institute of Social History, and in the Asquith papers at the Bodleian Library.

MURRY, John Middleton (1889–1957)

Author.

Some correspondence, 1921–55, from Joyce Cary, William Gerhardi, Samuel S. Kotelansky, Herbert Read and others is in the University of Calgary Library. Some 70 papers, 1916–48, are in the University of Cincinnati Library. Letters to Violet and Sidney Schiff are in the British Library (Add MS 52921).

NADEL, Siegfried Ferdinand (d. 1956)

Anthropologist. Senior Lecturer, London School of Economics. Professor of Anthropology, Australian National University, and at Durham University.

BLPES has a collection of papers and field notebooks and diaries. Many of the papers concern his investigation of the Nupe in Nigeria in the late 1930s, and the Nuba of the Sudan in the early 1940s. The diaries also recount Nadel's experiences in Eritrea after the liberation in the early 1940s. There are also lecture notes, photographs etc.

NAMIER, Sir Lewis Bernstein (1888–1960)

Historian. Worked in Information Department, Foreign Office, 1917–18; Political Intelligence Department, 1918–20. Lecturer in Modern History, Balliol College, Oxford, 1920–1. Political Secretary of the Jewish Agency for Palestine, 1929–31. Professor of Modern History, Manchester, 1931–53. Member, Editorial Board, *History of Parliament*.

The papers of Sir Lewis Namier as Political Secretary of the Jewish Agency, and all his other papers concerning the Zionist Movement, have been deposited in the Central Zionist Archives, Jerusalem. Most of the remaining papers are in the care of Mr John Brooke, and include two box-files of correspondence, mostly relating to his historical work, and including drafts and proofs of essays and reviews; press cuttings of articles and reviews, c. 1915–24, mostly on East European affairs; four box-files of transcripts of historical documents relating to the eighteenth century, most of which were made in American archives before 1914. There are also papers relating to Namier's biography of Charles Townshend, which was completed by John Brooke after his death. These include transcripts of documents; Namier's drafts for the work; correspondence between Lady Namier and John Brooke; and the final version of the book, with Lady Namier's comments. There are also about 50 notebooks, all in Namier's shorthand (a modified form of Pitman's) which contain the material on which he based his *Structure of Politics* and *England in the Age of the American Revolution*. It is proposed that these papers will eventually be deposited in the Lewis-Walpole Library, Farmington, Connecticut 06032, USA. A small number of personal papers, relating to Namier's naturalisation, change of name, service in the Army and the Foreign Office, etc., have already been deposited there.

The Bodleian Library, Oxford, has several items, including papers for Namier's Waynflete Lectures, 1946–7: typescript drafts, notes, calculations and tables, card bibliographies of members of the Frankfurt and Austrian parliaments, etc. Two letters from Winston Churchill about his *Life* of Marlborough are in Churchill College, Cambridge.

NAOROJI, Dadabhai (1825–1917)

Indian political leader. Prime Minister, Baroda, 1874. M.P. (Lib.) Finsbury Central, 1892–5 (first Indian Member of Parliament). President, Indian National Congress, 1886, 1893, 1906. President, London Indian Society. Life governor, University College London.

The National Archives of India has a collection of papers, 1870–1917, consisting of Naoroji's correspondence with his eminent contemporaries, both English and Indian; and members of his family; press cuttings; his notes and notices for meetings; posters and circular letters relating to clubs and organisations with which he was associated. Correspondents include D. E. Wacha, William Digby, W. S. Cains, Alfred Webb, W. Douglas Hall, and R. E. Paget.

The Digby papers at the India Office Library have correspondence on Naoroji's candidature for Finsbury Central.

Correspondence, 1914–15, can be found in the Hardinge papers at Cambridge University Library.

NEILL, Alexander Sutherland (1883–1973)

Educationalist and child psychologist. Founded Summerhill School, 1921, using part of the International School, Hellerau, Dresden. The School moved to Leiston, Suffolk, in 1924.

Enquiries should be directed to Summerhill School, Leiston, Suffolk. Some correspondence can be found in the World Education Fellowship collection at the Institute of Education, and the Bertrand Russell collection at McMaster University contains some 25 letters, 1926–32.

NEVINSON, Henry Woodd (1856–1941)

Journalist and essayist. Leader-writer, *Daily Chronicle*, 1897–1903; *Daily News*, 1908–9. On staff of *The Nation*, 1907–23. Correspondent for *Manchester Guardian*, and writer for *Daily Herald*. Campaigned for women's suffrage and on various social issues.

Nevinson s papers are housed in the Bodleian Library, Oxford. They include 18 volumes of journals, 1893–1941, which reflect the range of Nevinson's interests; a book of lecture notes, 1889; a notebook of poems, 1891; the typescripts and MSS of poems and articles, 1940–1; press cuttings and printed articles by Nevinson, 1892–1940, including press reviews of his books, 1901–49, with cuttings about his honorary degrees, and memoirs and obituary notices; and photographs of Nevinson. A further deposit, of the papers of Nevinson's wife, Evelyn Sharp, has other relevant material, including correspondence with John Masefield. Correspondence, 1895–1945, can be found in the British Library (Add. MS 57040). In addition, there are letters in the Edward Carpenter collection.

NEWALL, Dame Bertha Surtees
Bertha Phillpotts (1877–1932)

Educationalist. Attached to the British Legation, Stockholm, 1916–19. Principal of Westfield College, 1919–21. Mistress of Girton College, Cambridge, 1922–5.

Girton College, Cambridge, has certain papers, including a few letters to Dame Bertha; notes for three or four lectures, and a small quantity of notes on general subjects. The College also has some material relating to various obituaries and to her *Dictionary of National Biography* entry.

NEWBOLT, Sir Henry John (1862–1938)

Barrister, poet and author. Editor, *Monthly Review*, 1900–4. Controller of Wireless and Cables, World War I. Professor of Poetry, 1911–21. Official Naval Historian from 1923. President of the English Association, 1927–8.

Certain papers are available at the Ministry of Defence Library (Navy). These include correspondence and minutes relating to Admiralty Vetting of Naval Operations. Various letters, 1917–32, are in the National Library of Scotland, while correspondence can be found in the papers of Sir Julian Corbett, Sir Edmund Gosse, A. J. Balfour and Thomas Hardy (at the University of Texas Library).

NEWSHOLME, Sir Arthur (1857–1943)

Chief Medical Officer, Local Government Board, 1908–19. Prolific writer and lecturer on public health.

Dr G. A. Newsholme (son) states that no diaries or correspondence are known to survive with the family.

NICHOLSON, Joseph Shield (1850–1927)

Economist. Professor of Political Economy, Edinburgh University, 1880–1925.

Sturges (*Economists' Papers*, p. 81) was unable to locate any private papers. However, a number of letters can be found in the following collections: William Blackwood & Sons (National Library of Scotland); Edwin Cannan (BLPES); C. R. Fay and J. N. Keynes (Marshall Library).

NICOLL, Sir William Robertson (1851–1923)

Journalist and author of works on religion and literature. Editor of *British Weekly* from 1886, *Bookman* from 1891, *Expositor* from 1895.

Papers have been retained by the family. No further details are available.

NOBLE, Frederick S. Livie-

Anti-colonialist. Hon. Secretary, London Group on African Affairs from 1930.

Papers of the London Group on African Affairs, at Rhodes House Library, Oxford, contain relevant files. The material is described in *Sources* Vol. 1, p. 156.

NOEL, Conrad le Despenser Roden (1869–1942)

Christian Socialist. Vicar of Thaxted from 1910. Writer and journalist, and lecturer to various socialist bodies.

Various papers are available in Hull University Library. Amongst these are papers of Hon. Roden Noel (father), including a bound volume, 'In Memoriam. 1894', including letters and cuttings, with additional items. The files of Conrad Noel himself cover the wide range of his interests. There are files on Thaxted Church; Imperialism; Boy Scouts; Militarism; Life after Death; the Oxford Group Movement; his sermons, and publications; and certain correspondence. His notebooks are similarly wide-ranging. There are copies of correspondence relating to the refusal of the Bishops of Exeter and Chester to ordain him, 1893–4; a journal of a visit to Venice, 1898; notes for articles and short stories; notes on 'The Church'; and on medieval art and architecture. There are also notes, drafts and typescripts of various publications, both articles and books, plus a collection of printed material collected by Noel. Amongst other, miscellaneous material, are leaflets; notes and correspondence relating to his debate with Hilaire Belloc, 1909; travel material; and photographs.

NORTHCLIFFE, 1st Vt
Sir Alfred Charles William Harmsworth, 1st Bt (1865–1922)

Newspaper proprietor. Founder of *Answers*; *Daily Mail*, etc. Proprietor of *The Times*. Chairman of the British War Mission to the USA, 1917. Director of Propaganda in Enemy Countries, 1918; and of the Civil Aerial Transport Committee, 1917.

The British Library has a major collection of papers, in 229 volumes. No Add. MSS numbers have yet been assigned. There are some 19 volumes of correspondence with statesmen and other public figures. Correspondents include Balfour, Curzon, Onslow, Rosebery, Churchill, Stamfordham, Lloyd George, F. E. Smith, L. S. Amery, Lord Fisher, Philip Sassoon, Lord Beaverbrook, H. G. Wells and John Buchan. A volume of papers relates to the Committee for Propaganda in Enemy Countries, 1917–18, including a minute book, 1917–18. There is extensive correspondence with newspaper proprietors, writers and journalists; and papers and letters concerning his newspapers and companies: the Amalgamated Press, Associated Newspapers, the *Evening News*, *Weekly Dispatch*, *Daily Mirror*, *Observer*, *The Times*, *Daily Mail*, *Manchester Courier*, the Anglo-Newfoundland Developments Company, etc. Another group of correspondence is with bankers, solicitors, accountants, etc. There are 88 volumes of miscellaneous and general correspondence, arranged chronologically; and two volumes of miscellaneous papers. There are also diaries, 1891–1906; and a record of his journey round the world, 1921–2. This was published as *My Journey Round the World* (1923). Also at the British Library (Add. MS 58850) there are letters to Sophia Mary, wife of Lt-Col. Sir John Richard Hall, Bt, 1915–22, being chiefly typewritten circular letters, written by Northcliffe as Chairman of the British War Mission to the USA.

The Bodleian Library has typescript copies, in chronological order, of Northcliffe's communiqués to the staff of the *Daily Mail*, 1915–22. They are bound in three volumes (MSS Eng. Hist. d. 303–5).

The archives of *The Times* contain a substantial grouping of papers. The major constituent of this is the large number of notes headed 'communiqué', 'memoranda' or 'messages' which began in 1912 in the form of typewritten letters to the editor. The surviving 'messages' cover all aspects of journalism: ink, paper, typography, printing, advertising, style, as well as political issues.

Northcliffe's papers were used in R. Pound and A. G. A. Harmsworth, *Northcliffe* (1959).

NORTHCOTE, Dudley Stafford (1891–1955)

Soldier and cleric.

The British Library has a collection of papers (Add. MSS 57559–61). The three volumes of papers chiefly relate to work in Mesopotamia and Armenia, where he was relief officer for the Armenian Refugees Fund. They include correspondence and papers, 1918–26, including letters to his family; and an account of events in Armenia, c. 1920–5.

NUFFIELD, 1st Vt
Sir William Richard Morris, 1st Bt (1877–1963)

Motor manufacturer and philanthropist. Chairman, Morris Motors Ltd, 1919–52. President, British Motor Corporation Ltd.

The most recent biography, R. J. Overy, *William Morris, Viscount Nuffield* (1976) states that Nuffield left 'few records for the historian' (p. xlv). A few items of a more or less personal nature are deposited at Nuffield College, Oxford, including personalia such as honorary degrees and cheque-book stubs. These papers are not generally available. There are published records in Oxford Central Library. The archives of the Cowley and Longbridge works, formerly owned by Nuffield, contain little of relevance. Some papers were lost during air raids, others during the reorganisation of the firm in the late 1960s, when over 300 boxes of material were destroyed.

There is correspondence with Lord Weir at the Air Ministry, 1935–6, in Churchill College, Cambridge.

Reference should be made to the study by R. J. Overy and to P. W. S. Andrews and Elizabeth Brunner, *The Life of Lord Nuffield: A Study in Enterprise and Benevolence* (1955).

O'BRIAIN, Art Patrick (1872–1949)

Irish patriot. President of Gaelic League of London, 1914–35; Sinn Fein Council of Great Britain, 1916–23; Irish Self Determination League of Great Britain, 1919–25. Irish Republican Official Envoy and Representative in Great Britain, 1919–24. Irish Minister Plenipotentiary to France and Belgium, 1935–8. Director and Deputy-Chairman, Minerals Exploration and Development Co. Ltd.

The National Library of Ireland has a substantial collection of papers. These include correspondence, financial accounts, miscellaneous material of the Gaelic League, Sinn Fein and the Irish Self Determination League; correspondence relating to Irish political prisoners in Great Britain, to the Irish Prisoners Dependants' Fund, to the hunger striker, Terence MacSwiney, and to Roger Casement's execution; correspondence, minutes of meetings and other documents relating to the Irish National Relief Fund, 1916–22; miscellaneous papers dealing with Irish politics, including a statement by De Valera on the shooting of Sir Henry Wilson, press notices relating to the Peace Negotiations and the Treaty, draft and final copies of the Declaration of Irish Independence, etc.; correspondence with O'Briain as envoy of the Dáil Eireann in London, his correspondence as Envoy, and other official papers of the Dáil; and a miscellaneous collection of other material, including four volumes of press cuttings relating to the Irish independence movement, 1916–23.

O'BRIEN, Dermod (1865–1945)

President, Royal Hibernian Academy of Arts from 1910. Organised Irish Conference Committee from which emerged the Irish Convention.

Trinity College Dublin has various papers. These include material relating to the Irish Conference Committee, 1916, and his correspondence as Secretary of this Committee, 1916–17; papers concerning the Irish Reconstruction Association, the Irish Dominion League and the Irish Peace Conference, 1919–21; his business letters, 1909; and his library catalogues and list of subscribers to the Dublin Modern Art Gallery, 1905–8; papers on public and family affairs, about the Cahirmoyle estate and financial affairs, and the Inchiquin trust.

O'KELLY, Seán T.
Seán T. O Ceallaigh

Irish Nationalist leader.

The National Library of Ireland has original and copy letters, mainly concerning the Gaelic League, and his activities as representative of the Dáil Eireann in Paris, from members of the Dáil and other people prominent in the National Movement, 1903–23.

OLDHAM, Joseph Houldsworth (1874–1969)

Missionary. Secretary of the Student Christian Movement, 1896–7. Secretary, World Missionary Conference, 1908–10; of its Continuation Committee, 1910–21; of the International Missionary Council, 1921–38. Editor, *International Review of Missions*, 1912–27. Administrative Director, International Institute of African Languages and Cultures, 1931–8. Member of the Advisory Committee on Education in the Colonies, 1925–36; and of the East Africa Commission on Closer Union, 1927–8. Editor, *Christian Newsletter*, 1939–45. Author of *Christianity and the Race Problem*, etc.

Edinburgh House, 2 Eaton Gate, London SW1, has papers, chiefly memoranda and correspondence between Oldham and Norman Leys, W. M. Ross and others concerning African questions.

OLDMEADOW, Ernest James (1867–1949)

Journalist and author. Editor of *The Dome*, 1897–1900; *The Tablet*, 1923–36.

The Westminster Diocesan Archives contain various papers, including Bourne Pastorals, 1897–1903, and correspondence concerning his resignation as editor of *The Tablet*.

OLIVER, Frederick Scott (1864–1934)

Man of business and publicist. Entered the firm of Debenham & Freebody (1892) and made it a major business. Author of *Federalism and Home Rule* (1910) and *Ordeal by Battle* (1915).

Relevant material at the British Library includes correspondence with Lord Cecil, 1912–18 (Add. MS 51090) and with Macmillans (Add. MSS 55027–8). Correspondence, 1911–18, concerning the Irish Question is in the papers of Sir Horace Plunkett, and there are further letters in the Edward Carson collection. Correspondence, 1915–22, can also be found in the Austen Chamberlain papers in Birmingham University Library.

ORAGE, Alfred Richard (1873–1934)

Journalist. Editor of the *New Age*, 1907–22; *New English Weekly* from 1931. From 1919 an enthusiastic exponent of Social Credit ideas.

No personal papers are known, but reference should be made to the M. B. Reckitt collection, the A. J. Penty papers and the papers of F. W. Dalley in Hull University Library. Some correspondence can be found in the Peter Neagoe collection in Syracuse University Library, and in the Mary Johnston papers in the University of Virginia. Some 32 letters are in the Herbert Read collection, University of Victoria, British Columbia. The fullest study of Orage's influence is in Wallace Martin, *'The New Age' under Orage* (Manchester, 1968).

ORWELL, George*
Eric Arthur Blair (1903–50)

Journalist and novelist. Author of *The Road to Wigan Pier, Homage to Catalonia, Animal Farm, Nineteen Eighty-four*, etc.

University College Library, London, has a major collection of material. It includes over 700 letters written by Orwell, many of which have been published in *The Collected Essays, journalism and letters of George Orwell*, and are available for public inspection. The remainder are closed at present. In addition, there are over 400 letters to Orwell, most of which are again closed. There are also two boxes of manuscripts and typescripts of poems, articles, and reviews, dating back to Orwell's days at Eton; two boxes of political and domestic diaries dating from the 1930s; one box of literary notebooks, lists of articles, etc; personalia relating to Orwell and other members of the Blair family, background material, and letters relating to Orwell; and two albums of photographs of Orwell. University College Library also has various editions and translations of Orwell's works, critical studies and theses, background material, books from his own library, and copies of all his known published journalism. The Library attempts to collect or locate all articles and reviews on Orwell.

Also at University College, the Sir Richard Rees collection includes material concerning his literary estate, legal and general correspondence, material on the George Orwell Archives Trust (including correspondence and records of Trust meetings); and a folder of Orwell material, including some press cuttings, mostly obituary notices and typescript transcripts of six poems by Orwell contributed to the *Adelphi*, 1933–6.

Orwell's pamphlet collection was presented to the British Library, and copies of letters (chiefly on literary topics) found in the pamphlets are now collected as Add. MS 49384.

The Berg Collection, New York Public Library, has additional material.

The Collected Essays, journalism and letters of George Orwell (edited by Sonia Orwell and Ian Angus, 4 vols, 1968) is a valuable source of information. The forthcoming authorised biography of Orwell by Professor Bernard Crick has used all the available material.

* Pseudonym.

OSBORN, Sir Frederic James (1885–   )

Town planner. Estate Manager, Welwyn Garden City, 1919–36. Hon. Secretary and Chairman, Town and Country Planning Association, 1936–61. Editor, *Town and Country Planning*. 1949–65.

Sir Frederic Osborn has retained a collection of documents and correspondence. No decision has yet been made about their future preservation. Enquiries may be directed to the Divisional

Librarian, Central Library, The Campus, Welwyn Garden City, who is assisting in sorting the papers.

The Letters of Lewis Mumford and Frederic J. Osborn, A Transatlantic Dialogue, 1938–70 (ed. Michael R. Hughes) have been published (Bath, 1971).

OWEN, Sir Hugh (1835–1916)

Civil Servant. Assistant Secretary, Local Government Board, 1876–82; Permanent Secretary, 1882–98. Chairman of the Commissioners under the London Government Act, 1899–1907.

A small group of letters to Sir Hugh Owen, 1879–1910, is in Cardiff Public Library.

OWEN, John (1854–1926)

Leading Welsh Churchman. Principal of St David's College, Lampeter. Bishop of St David's from 1897.

The papers of Bishop Owen are deposited on permanent loan in the National Library of Wales. The collection includes correspondence, memoranda, diaries, press cuttings, pamphlets, concerning his family and his career, and relating to the compilation of a biography by his daughter, Eluned E. Owen. The papers also relate to education in Church schools, the Welsh Church Commission, the Disestablishment campaigns, etc. The manuscript material is not currently available.

PAGE, Sir Frederick Handley (1885–1962)

Businessman. Founder and Managing Director, Handley Page Ltd; Chairman from 1948. Officer of the Society of British Aircraft Constructors Ltd; Chairman, 1929–31, 1937–8; President 1938–9.

The Royal Air Force Museum, RAF Hendon, The Hyde, London NW9 5LL, has Handley Page records, 1909–71. They include correspondence and papers of the Managing Director's Office, mainly relating to Sir Frederick's period with the firm.

PAGET, Violet
Vernon Lee*(1856–1935)

Author and novelist.

A collection of papers was deposited in the library of Somerville College, Oxford, after Violet Paget's death with the stipulation that the material was not to be made available for 50 years (i.e. until 1985). It appears that the papers cover the period 1881–1934 but no further details are presently available.

Colby College, Waterville, Maine, USA, has a collection of family and personal papers, including correspondence with William Gosse, Daniel Halévy, Karl Hillebrand, Aldous Huxley, Henry·James, J. S. Sargent, J. A: Symonds, Mary Augusta Ward and H. G. Wells.

Letters to Lady Wolseley can be found in the Wolseley papers at Hove Central Library (64 in number), while 12 letters to E. J. Dent, 1904–33, are available in the Fitzwilliam Museum, Cambridge. The J. A. Symonds papers in Bristol University Library also contain relevant letters while other items of correspondence are in Ball State University. A selection of her letters was published privately in 1937 by Miss Irene Cooper Willis. Private papers were used in Peter Gunn's *Vernon Lee: Violet Paget, 1856-1935* (1964).

*Pseudonym.

PALGRAVE, Sir (Robert Harry) Inglis (1827-1919)

Economist. Editor of *The Economist*, 1877-83; *Dictionary of Political Economy* (3 vols, 1894-1914).

The Palgrave family papers, c/o Mr G. P. Barker, 15 Neville Court, Abbey Road, London NW8 9DD, contain much correspondence of Sir Inglis with members of the family, 1847-1903, together with five bundles of correspondence with economists and bankers (c. 1880s, 1890s) together with a few other items. Some 27 letters to Palgrave, 1873-1882, are in King's College, Cambridge, while the British Library has a journal of a tour in France, 1847 (Add. MS 45738). Sturges, *Economists' Papers*, pp. 83-4, lists these and correspondence in other collections (e.g. Cannan, Ingram, J. N. Keynes, Seligman).

PANKHURST, Dame Christabel (1881-1958)

Propagandist for Women's Suffrage. A founder and leader of the Women's Social and Political Union. Later a religious propagandist.

The Museum of London has important collections of material relating to Christabel and Emmeline Pankhurst and to their work with the Women's Social and Political Union. The Suffragette Fellowship collection includes correspondence of the Pankhursts together with a mass of material concerning the WSPU: diaries, autobiographical notes of various suffragettes, organisational and agitational material, press cuttings, papers concerning the WSPU's constitution and policy, etc. The David Mitchell collection represents material collected by him for his works on the suffragettes, *Women on the Warpath* and *The Fighting Pankhursts*. It includes photocopies of material gathered by Mr Mitchell from various parts of the world – Canada, the USA, Australia and Ethiopia. It also contains considerable correspondence from Sylvia Pankhurst's son, Dr Richard Pankhurst.

The autograph collection in the Fawcett Library collection of suffrage records is another major source of correspondence from the Pankhursts.

Manchester Central Library has material concerning the relations of the ILP and WSPU in its suffrage collection, and some letters from Mrs Pankhurst.

The British Library has correspondence between Christabel and Henry Harben (Add. MS 58226). Also at the British Library, the Balfour collection (Add. MSS 49683-962) contains correspondence with Christabel Pankhurst. The Henry Nevinson journals and the letters to Evelyn Sharp at the Bodleian Library, Oxford, contain further correspondence, including a few letters from Christabel in Paris, c. 1912-13.

At the House of Lords Record Office the Lloyd George collection has relevant material, as does the George Lansbury collection at BLPES. Correspondence with Inez Irwin is in the Radcliffe College Library Women's Archives.

David Mitchell has had access to other Christabel Pankhurst material in private hands, including correspondence with Dame Ethel Smyth. He has used this material in his biography of Christabel. Jill Craigie has further material in her care, which is to be used in a forthcoming study of the suffragette movement. Andrew Rosen's *Rise up Women!* (1974) made use of much unpublished material.

PANKHURST, Emmeline (1858-1928)

Suffragette leader. Founder and leader of the Women's Social and Political Union.

The Sylvia Pankhurst collection at the International Institute of Social History contains much relevant material. The oldest part consists of papers of Dr R. M. Pankhurst. There are books of newspaper clippings (1863–96, 8 vols.), some letters from Lydia Becker about suffrage matters and a few personal and family documents (late 1860s, early 1870s). There are a few letters from Mrs Jacob Bright to Mrs Emmeline Pankhurst about suffrage matters for the early 1890s. To this period also belong a number of family photographs, some of them unidentifiable, birth certificates, certificates of burial, school reports and diplomas of several members of the family, and some correspondence about legacies. There is hardly any personal correspondence. Correspondence with Adelaide Johnson is in the Library of Congress, Manuscripts Division.

Other relevant material is described above.

PANKHURST, (Estelle) Sylvia (1882–1960)

Propagandist for women's rights and for socialism. One time Hon. Secretary, Women's Social and Political Union. Founded East London Federation of Suffragettes, later the Workers' Socialist Federation. Edited *Workers' Dreadnought*, 1914–24. During 1920s and 1930s an active fighter against Fascism in Italy. Foundation member, Abyssinia Association. Editor, *New Times and Ethiopia News*, 1936–56; *Ethiopia Observer* from 1956.

The International Institute of Social History, Amsterdam, has a collection of material, relating both to the Pankhurst family and to Sylvia Pankhurst. The material of Sylvia Pankhurst herself can be divided roughly into three parts. Firstly, there are the notes, manuscripts, typescripts, printed material and photographs used for her books and articles, some of them unpublished; and some correspondence connected with the collecting of material for them; as well as some material put together in connection with a lawsuit about *The Home Front*. Secondly, there is a collection of correspondence, leaflets, minute books, etc., connected with her various activities: e.g. the minute books of the East London Federation of Suffragettes, later Workers' Suffrage Federation, still later Workers' Socialist Federation; correspondence about her membership of the Communist Party of Great Britain; notes about international congresses, material (mostly printed) about her involvement in various anti-fascist activities, in particular her support of Ethiopia and its emperor and the publication of the *New Times and Ethiopia News*. Finally, there is a small amount of personal correspondence, with J. Keir Hardie, Emmeline Pethick-Lawrence, Dora Russell, Adela Walsh (née Pankhurst) and others; some sketches and designs and photographs. The collection is being catalogued, but may be consulted by writing in advance to the England-North America Department of the Institute.

Certain material concerning the East London Federation, 1914, is in the Labour Party archives at Transport House, while the Watford ILP files and the George Lansbury collection at BLPES contain some letters from Sylvia Pankhurst. The British Library has her correspondence with the Society of Authors, 1931–60, (Add. MSS 56769–71). Correspondence with Ada Lois James is in the State Historical Society of Wisconsin collections. Reference should also be made to the Keir Hardie papers, National Library of Scotland.

PARES, Sir Bernard (1867–1949)

Historian. Reader in Modern Russian History, University of Liverpool, 1906–8; Secretary to the School of Russian Studies, Liverpool, 1907–17; Professor of Russian History, Language and Literature, Liverpool, 1908–17; and in London University, 1919–36. Director of the School of Slavonic and East European Studies, 1922–39. Editor, *Russian Review*, 1912–14. Temporary Civil Servant, 1939–40. Lectured in USA for Ministry of Information, 1942–4.

The Library of the School of Slavonic and East European Studies has 44 boxes of papers, at present not sorted in detail. These contain correspondence, mainly to Pares from a variety of correspondents, and on a range of different topics; manuscripts and notes for books and writings, notes for lectures; notes for despatches from the Russian front, 1915–18; press cuttings from different periods; papers relating to relief and educational organisations and activities from 1918; and papers relating to the School of Slavonic Studies at King's College, London.

Correspondence relating to Russian affairs, 1918, can be found in the Lothian papers at the Scottish Record Office. Some correspondence is also available in Chicago University Library.

PARKES, James William (1896–   )

Advocate of Christian Jewish reconciliation. Supporter of Zionism. Chairman, National Committee, Commonwealth, 1942–3. President, Jewish Historical Society, 1949–51. Director, The Parkes Library, 1956–64.

The Parkes Library, University of Southampton, has much relevant material. This includes press cuttings dating from the 1920s on Arab attitudes, Israel, the Holy Places, Suez, and Zionism generally. Various papers, including minutes of committees and correspondence, concern organisations with which he was involved: the Anglo-American Committee for a Jewish Army, Anglo-Israel Association, the British Association, the Jewish National Home in Palestine, the Council of Christians and Jews, Jewish Historical Society, National Committee for Rescue from Nazi Terror, Socialist Christian League, Society of Christians and Jews, World Council of Churches, World Jewish Congress, Zionist Federation, and the Zionist Information Office. There is also correspondence with the Israeli Embassy and with publishers. Among the individual correspondents are Bishop Bell, D. L. Edwards, Maurice Eisendrath, A. Freeman, C. L. Horn, S. A. Morrison, David Polish, Else Rosenfeld, J. Seaver, Chaim Wardi and Paul Winter. Special topics covered in the collection include relations between Jews and Presbyterians, Palestine, Missions to the Jews, Anti-Semitism, Fascism in Britain, visits to the USA and Israel, etc.

PARKIN, Sir George Robert (1846–1922)

Propagandist for Imperial Federation. Principal of Upper Canada College, Toronto, 1895–1902. Organising Representative of Rhodes Scholarship Trust from 1902.

Papers and correspondence are in the Public Archives of Canada. The correspondence includes letters from L. S. Amery, 1900–22; Arnold Forster, 1892–1906; Asquith, 1897–1918; 2nd Earl Brassey, 1891–1919; Viscount Bryce, 1891–1920; G. E. Buckle, 1893–1922; Moreton Frewen, 1886–1920; J. L. Garvin, 1905–9; Rudyard Kipling, 1907–20; Lee of Fareham, 1898–1922; Lord and Lady Minto, 1899–1922; Vaughan Morgan, 1898–1922; Gilbert Parker, 1897–1920; Sir Thomas Raleigh, 1889–1918; Lord Rosebery, 1888–1912; Sir Michael Sadler, 1903–20; W. T. Stead, 1893–1909; Henry, Lord Thring, 1888–1906. There is also correspondence with various organisations, both religious and imperialist (e.g. League of the Empire, British Empire League). Family correspondence covers the period 1884–1922, and there are also copies of letters sent by Parkin, 1874–1922. Diaries date from 1872 to 1922. Other material includes files of papers on a wide range of subjects, together with miscellaneous items, from the early nineteenth century to 1922. Press cuttings date from 1870.

PARRY, Sir David Hughes (1893–1973)

Academic and administrator. Lecturer in Law, Aberystwyth, 1920–4; London School of Economics, 1924–8. Editor, *Solicitors' Journal*, 1925–8. Reader in English Law, London University, 1928–30; Professor of English Law, 1930–59. Vice Chancellor, University of London, 1945–8. Director of University of London Institute of Advanced Legal Studies, 1947–59. President, University College, Aberystwyth, 1954–64. Chairman, Inter-Departmental Committee on the Legal Status of the Welsh Language, 1963–5.

An extensive collection in the National Library of Wales reflects Sir David's varied activities as a university teacher and administrator, author of works on law, member of government committees, Welsh patriot, leader of the Welsh Calvinistic Methodist Connexion, etc. The collection includes papers relating to the universities of Wales, London, Cambridge (student at Peterhouse), and Birmingham, Exeter and Hull (honorary graduate); the committee of Vice-Chancellors and Principals (chairman, 1947–8); and the University Grants Committee (vice-chairman, 1951–4). These papers also show that his advice was often sought in connection with senior appointments in several other universities and in the formation of the University of Essex.

The collection also contains papers relating to the Committee of Enquiry on New Zealand University (chairman, 1959); Canadian universities (visiting lecturer and honorary graduate); the Hebrew University of Jerusalem (Lionel Cohen lecturer, 1956); Colonial Universities Grants Committee (member, 1948–52); and Colonial Social Science Research Council (chairman, 1951–5). Other papers concern the committees and societies of which he was a member or official, including the Advisory Council on Post-War Reconstruction in Wales; the War Works Commission (member, 1944–64); Royal Commission on Remuneration of Doctors and Dentists, 1957–60; Inter-Departmental Committee on Business of Criminal Courts, 1958–60; Inter-Departmental Committee on the Legal Status of the Welsh Language (chairman, 1963–5); the Society of Public Teachers of Law (president, 1948–9); and the Selden Society (vice-president, 1956–9). The collection also includes proof sheets, etc., of some of his publications and papers relating to the Caernarvonshire Quarter Sessions (deputy chairman, 1950–66). The following organisations are also represented: the standing conference of National Voluntary Youth Organisations (chairman, 1944–5); the 18–30 Conference (chairman, 1947–9); and the National Council of Social Service.

Papers are also to be found relating to Welsh cultural movements, including Urdd Gobaith Cymru; the Royal National Eisteddfod; the Pantyfedwen Trust; the Honourable Society of Cymmrodorion, and other London Welsh societies; the National Petition for the recognition of the Welsh Language in the Law Courts of Wales ('Y Ddeiseb Genedlaethol am Gydnabyddiaeth Gyfreithiol i'r Gymraeg yng Nghymru'); the Lleyn Defence Committee; and the Council for the Protection of Rural Wales.

The collection includes a large number of letters, many congratulating Sir David on his knighthood, 1951. Approaches to be considered as a parliamentary candidate, 1924–51, may also be mentioned.

Papers relating to Sir David Hughes Parry's family include the papers of his wife Lady Hughes Parry, consisting mainly of correspondence. Letters, 1883–99, to T. D. Jones, a solicitor from Llanuwchllyn who afterwards settled in London, include a group from her uncle, Professor Edward Edwards. The Welsh Calvinistic Methodist Connexion or Presbyterian Church of Wales also figures prominently in the deposit with papers relating particularly to churches in the London and Bala areas, to financial matters, and to his period as moderator, 1964–5. A collection of photographs is mainly of family interest.

PARRY, William John (1842–1927)

Welsh trade union leader and author.

The National Library of Wales has a substantial collection of speeches, addresses, diaries, letters and miscellaneous papers. They include material on the North Wales Quarrymen's Union, the Penrhyn Strike, the Bethesda Strike etc.; notes on the Welsh Church commission; addresses by Parry; reminiscences; copies of essays; extracts from books, newspapers; lectures; a journal, 1907; his autobiography; notebooks, on religious and political topics; correspondence, including letters on the Royal Commission on Labour, 1892; election material; press cuttings, etc.

PATON, John Brown (1830–1911)

Nonconformist divine. First Principal of the Congregational Institute, Nottingham, 1863–98. Joint-editor, the *Eclectic Review*, 1858–61. Associate editor, *Contemporary Review*, 1882–8.

The Labour Party archive at Transport House has letters from Paton, including some to Ramsay MacDonald.

PAUL, (Maurice) Eden (1865–1944)

Medical practitioner and socialist author. Founder member of Communist Party of Great Britain. Author of works on Marxism, eugenics, birth control, etc.

Efforts to trace papers proved unsuccessful. Routledge & Kegan Paul, publishers, knew of no material, and there are no relevant papers with the Communist Party of Great Britain.

PEARSE, Patrick H. (d. 1916)

Irish nationalist. Supporter of Sinn Fein. Member of the Irish Republican Brotherhood Military Committee. Executed in 1916 following the Easter Rising.

Papers of and concerning Pearse, c. 1890–1930s, are in the National Library of Ireland.
    Reference should be made to R. Dudley Edwards, *Patrick Pearse: The Triumph of Failure* (1977).

PEARSON, Sir (Cyril) Arthur, 1st Bt (1866–1921)

Newspaper proprietor. Founded C. Arthur Pearson Ltd. President, National Institute for the Blind and Fresh Air Fund. Vice-President, Tariff Reform League and Vice-Chairman, Tariff Commission, 1903.

Sir Neville Pearson, Bt (son), states that he has no papers which would be of assistance. Reference should be made to the study of his life by Sidney Dark (1922).
    A few letters from Pearson and his wife, concerning personal and newspaper matters, are in the Blumenfeld papers at the House of Lords Record Office. Papers of the Tariff Commission are at BLPES.

PEARSON, Karl (1857–1936)

Biologist and eugenicist. Fellow of the Royal Society. Professor of Eugenics and Director of the Francis Galton Laboratory for National Eugenics, University of London. Editor of *Biometrika*, 1900–36.

There is a collection of papers in the Library of University College London. The collection, which is fully catalogued, reflects the whole range of his career and interests. Papers relating to Pearson's personal history include early essays; testimonials, correspondence about professional posts and bodies with which he was involved, e.g. the Association for Promoting a Professional University for London (correspondents here include T. H. Huxley, Sir E. R. Lankester, Sir George Young); press cuttings on the London University; income tax returns; honours; after-dinner speeches; a Commemoration Fund; letters from G. M. Morant concerning a bibliography of his writings; obituary notices; photographs and personalia. Pearson's lectures and lecture notes date from 1877 and are very comprehensive. In addition to these, there are extensive notes and papers concerning his work, including his notes on literature dating from 1882; offprints of early papers and articles; papers on various books; concerning his work in the fields of mathematics, heredity, mosquitoes, astronomy, the feeble-minded and statistics. Many papers concern the history of the Department of Applied Statistics at University College, including correspondence, proposals for laboratories, management and staffing questions, minutes, etc. Other material concerns the work of the Department and of Pearson's colleagues, including W. F. R. Weldon (a substantial grouping), G. V. Yule, F. Howard Collins, David Heron, A. C. Houston, W. S. Gossett, Ethel M. Eldeston, W. F. Sheppard, etc. Another group of material concerns the publication of *Biometrika*, including correspondence with potential printers, editorial material, notebooks, and papers prepared for publication. There are a number of papers relating to Pearson's *The Life, Letters and Labours of Francis Galton*, including the manuscript of the volumes, personalia collected by Pearson, copies of letters used in a biography including copy-letters from Galton, extracts from reviews; and letters to Pearson, particularly after the publication of the work. A number of papers in the collection relate to Pearson's wartime research, 1914–18, and include material on the employment figures, the 'aeroplane blade problem' and on bomb trajectories. In addition to this material, there is a substantial grouping of correspondence and personal items concerning various topics from family and personal issues and the Men and Women's Club of the 1880s to biometry, plus speeches, press cuttings, visitors' books etc., and correspondence from a wide range of people.

Further correspondence can be found in the Conway of Alington papers, Cambridge University Library.

PEASE, Edward Reynolds (1857–1955)

Socialist administrator. Secretary of the Fabian Society, 1890–1913; Hon. Secretary, 1914–38. Member of the Executive, Labour Representation Committee, later Labour Party, 1900–13.

Two volumes of papers collected by Pease, under the title 'Infancy of the Labour Party', are available in BLPES. They include minutes, letters and other papers reflecting the early work of the LRC and the Labour Party and his participation in it, and cover the period 1900–12, with one paper of 1918. Other material is available in the Labour Party archive, including correspondence on the Party's proposed newspaper (refs. LRC: Index; LPGC: Index; LP NEW/06).

Pease's work is also strongly reflected in the archives of the Fabian Society, deposited in the Library of Nuffield College, Oxford. Reference should also be made to the Passfield Papers at BLPES, while there are letters from Pease and his wife to G. B. Shaw in the British Library, 1888–1946 (Add. MS 50547). Ten letters to Pease from Shaw, 1890–1900, are also in the British Library (Add. MS 59784).

The International Institute of Social History has a few letters, including two letters to Bernstein, 1906; and letters in the Socialist League collection. Correspondence can also be found in the H. G. Wells archive, University of Illinois.

PEIERLS, Sir Rudolf Ernst (1907–)

Scientist. Fellow of the Royal Society. Professor of Mathematical Physics, Birmingham University, 1937–63. Professor of Physics, Oxford University, 1963–74. Worked on Atomic Energy Project in Birmingham, 1940–3; in USA, 1943–6.

The papers of Sir Rudolf Peierls have been listed by the Contemporary Scientific Archives Centre and are now deposited in the Bodleian. The collection consists almost entirely of correspondence, written and received by him, and covers all aspects of his career, including scientific research, service on committees, advisory boards, publications, appointments, overseas visits, etc. The biographical and personal material includes biographical notes, papers on his early work and career, honours, formal and congratulatory letters, files of personal correspondence, autobiographical and historical reminiscences, and correspondence of a personal or semi-personal character. Many papers cover his university and academic work, and relate to the Universities of Birmingham and Oxford, general educational policy and ideas, university examinations etc. The scientific correspondence is extensive, with a wide range of scientists including F. C. Barker, J. S. Bell, Hans Albrecht Bethe, P. M. S. Blackett, Niels Bohr, W. L. Bragg, G. E. Brown, Sir John Cockcroft, W. M. Fairbairn, J. W. Gardner, J. B. S. Haldane, Fred Hoyle, N. F. Mott, J. R. Oppenheimer, Wolfgang Pauli etc. Other papers relate to publications, broadcasts, reports, etc., and include correspondence with publishers and editors, correspondence and typescripts for broadcasts. There are also correspondence and papers concerning conferences, lectures, visits, appointments, etc. Most of this material dates from after 1962. Other material concerns committees on which he served, societies which he supported or corresponded with, consultancies, etc., e.g. the Atomic Energy Research Establishment, British Association, Pugwash Conference, the Royal Society, CERN (European Organisation for Nuclear Research).

PENROSE, Lionel Sharples (1898–1972)

Biologist. Galton Professor of Eugenics, University College London, 1945–65. Director, Kennedy-Galton Centre, Harpenbury Hospital, St Albans, from 1965.

The Library of University College London has an extensive collection (at present not completely listed) of some 50 boxes of material. These include working papers, case papers, correspondence and notebooks.

PENTY, Arthur Joseph (1875–1937)

Architect and social critic. His book on *The Restoration of the Gild System* published in 1906 was a forerunner of the National Guilds propaganda of the 1910s. A frequent contributor to the *New Age* and later *G. K.'s Weekly*, and various architectural and Christian social journals.

Mr .M. H. Penty (son), 59A Church Street, Old Isleworth, Middlesex TW7 6BE, retains various papers, dating from the early 1900s. Among these are press-cutting albums including cuttings from *Fabian News* and the *New Age*. There are some papers relating to the National Guilds League, including annual reports, leaflets, building guild material, etc. Other material is concerned with the Distributivist League and with the Catholic Social Movement. There is a cuttings book which includes articles by the Spanish theorist Ramiro de Maeztu, and articles on social credit; there are also albums relating to the General Strike and architecture in the 1930s. Correspondence is scattered but includes letters from many sympathetic co-thinkers, including the Italian writer Odon Por and A. R. Orage. Correspondence with Orage relates chiefly to his period as editor of the *New English Weekly*. Much of the material in this collection relates to architecture and Penty's theories about its social significance. There are typescripts of various of his works, notes for speeches and lectures, drafts of articles, etc,. as well as some correspondence. In addition to this material there are cuttings from various magazines with which Penty was sympathetic, including the *New Age* and *G. K.'s Weekly*, and runs of these magazines. Miscellaneous other material includes postcards, pamphlets and books.

Copies of some of this material are available at Hull University Library. The material includes papers on the National Guilds League, miscellaneous correspondence, press cuttings and obituary notices.

PEPLER, Sir George Lionel (1882–1959)

Town Planner. Chief Town Planning Inspector, Ministry of Health, 1919–41. Chief Technical Adviser, Ministry of Town and Country Planning, 1943–6. Chairman, Inter-Allied Committee for Physical Planning and Reconstruction, 1942–5. Planning Adviser to the Government of Singapore, 1950–4. President, International Federation for Housing and Town Planning, 1935–8, 1947–52. Chairman, Institute of Professional Civil Servants, 1937–42.

There is a collection of books, maps, drawings and correspondence with the Department of Urban and Regional Planning, University of Strathclyde, Glasgow C1. A catalogue has been prepared by the Department.

PEROWNE, Stewart Henry (1901–)

Orientalist and historian. Joined the Palestine Government Education Service, 1927. Assistant District Commissioner, Galilee, 1934. Assistant Secretary, Malta, 1934. Political Officer, Aden Protectorate, 1937. Arabic Programme Organiser, BBC, 1938. Information Officer, Aden,

1939. Public Relations Attaché, British Embassy, Baghdad, 1941. Oriental Counsellor, 1944. Colonial Secretary, Barbados, 1947–51. Principal Adviser (Interior), Cyrenaica, 1950–1. Assistant to the Bishop of Jerusalem on refugees, 1952.

The Middle East Centre, St Antony's College, Oxford, has several boxes of papers. Amongst the papers are correspondence wth the Hashemite family; notes on communications between Syria and Palestine, 1941; and personal letters to his family throughout his career.

PERRIS, George Herbert (1866–1920)

Journalist and author. Editor, *Hull Express*, 1885. On staff of *The Speaker*. Editor of *Concord*, 1898–1906. A founder, and Hon. Secretary, of Anglo-German and Anglo-Russian Friendship Committees. Secretary, Cobden Club, 1903–5. Foreign editor, *The Tribune*, 1906–7, *Daily News*, 1908–10. Originator and Assistant Editor, Home University Library, 1912–14. War correspondent, *Daily Chronicle*, 1914–18.

No personal papers are known, but there are letters to David Soskice in the House of Lords Record Office. Records of the Cobden Club are deposited in West Sussex Record Office.

PERRY, 1st B
Percival Lea Dewhurst Perry (1878–1956)

Businessman. Director, Ford Motor Co. Ltd; Firestone Tyre and Rubber Co. Ltd; President, Slough Estates Ltd. President, Motor Trade Association, 1914. Director, Food Production Department, 1916; Agricultural Machinery Department, 1917–18. Deputy Controller, Mechanical Warfare Department; Director of Traction, Ministry of Munitions, 1918–19. Business Adviser, Ministry of Food, 1939–40.

Papers, 1917–48, are in the Ford Motor Company archives, Dearborn, Michigan.

PETRE, Maud Dominica Mary (d. 1942)

Author and Catholic Modernist.

The British Library has correspondence and papers relating to her involvement in the Modernist movement. Add. MSS 45361–2 consist of some 100 letters from Baron F. von Hügel to Maud Petre on religious matters in general and the Modernist controversies in particular, Dec 1899–June 1922. Some of this correspondence was printed in B. Holland, *Baron Frederick von Hügel: Selected Letters* (1927). Add. MSS 45744–5 include further correspondence between Maud Petre and the Baron. Add. MSS 52367–82 consist chiefly of correspondence and papers relating to Maud Petre's biography of Father George Tyrrell, and include letters from Tyrrell, 1892–1908; correspondence with his Jesuit superiors and others, 1900–8; autographed works of Tyrrell; 'Christianity at the Cross Roads' (1909) by Maud Petre; her diaries, 1900–42; letters to her about Abbé Henri Bremond; general correspondence, 1909–41; and the correspondence of her literary executor, 1912–54.
Further letters from Maud Petre are in the Canon A. L. Lilley collection.

PETTER, Sir Ernest Willoughby (1873–1954)

Engineer and businessman. President, British Engineers Association, 1923–5. Executive member, Federation of British Industries. Vice President, Institute of Mechanical Engineers. Conservative parliamentary candidate, 1918, 1923; Independent Conservative (St George's, Westminster), 1931.

Professor E. G. Petter (son), c/o Notre Dame University, Nelson, British Columbia VIL 3C7, Canada, states that his father destroyed nearly all his papers before he died. The only papers he has consist of photocopies of newspaper reports relating to the St George's by-election, and copies of correspondence with Lord Beaverbrook. The originals of these are in the Beaverbrook papers, now at the House of Lords Record Office.

PHELPS, Lancelot Ridley (1853–1936)

Provost, Oriel College, Oxford, 1914–29. Member of Royal Commission on the Poor Laws; Chairman of Departmental Committee on Vagrancy.

A voluminous collection of correspondence and papers can be found in the Library of Oriel College, Oxford. The correspondence begins in 1877, but it was only in 1880 that Phelps began a systematic preservation of papers. From then practically all communications he received, with the exception of advertising circulars and charity appeals, were filed in a bundle for each month. There are few of his own letters, apart from a bundle of letters written by him to his close friend, H. R. Boyce, 1894–1914, 1916–17; and a small group of letters written to his father in 1899. The letters number over 100,000 in all.

The general correspondence has been arranged in three sections, although retaining the separate bundles: 'Family letters', 'Reserved', and 'Unimportant'. The 'Reserved' letters are of most general interest, throwing light on Phelps' career and interests. The letters are most numerous for the period 1895 to 1914, the period in fact of Phelps' greatest activity. The correspondence contains a vast amount of material relating to admissions to College, etc. During the ensuing war, he maintained a high output of letters, often to Fellows on war service.

During later years, however, there is a diminution in the number of letters, and these are mainly to friends and former members of the College. Topics covered include college and university affairs, letters relating to India and Africa, the war, various committees, including Poor Law Administration, the Vagrancy Committee, the Oxford College Improvement Society Ltd. The family papers relate to family business and estate matters.

PHILLIPS, Morgan Walter (1902–63)

Labour Party Official. Secretary of Research Department, 1941–4. Secretary of the Labour Party, 1944–62. Chairman, Socialist International, 1948–57.

The Baroness Phillips (widow) holds a selection of press cuttings and an outline autobiography, which she is currently using for a book she is writing. Morgan Phillips' work can be traced in the archives of the Labour Party at Transport House (described in *Sources* Vol. 1, p. 127ff).

PHILLPOTTS, Dame Bertha Surtees, see NEWALL, Dame Bertha Surtees

PIERCY, 1st B
William Piercy (1886–1966)

Economist and businessman. A Director of the British Ministry of Food in the USA, World War I. Principal Assistant Secretary, Ministry of Supply and Ministry of Production, and Personal Assistant to the Deputy Prime Minister, World War II. Chairman, Industrial and Commercial Finance Corporation, 1945–64. A Director of the Bank of England, 1945–56. President, National Institute of Industrial Psychology, 1946–63. Chairman, Wellcome Trust, 1960–5.

A collection of papers is available at BLPES which reflects the wide range of Piercy's activities. There are papers relating to the following subjects and work: Ministry of Munitions (World War I); the British Food Mission to the USA; lectures and papers on economics during the 1920s and 1930s; the Northern Ireland Arbitration Tribunal; First Garden City; various business firms; Ministry of Production papers; miscellaneous material concerning his period as assistant to the Deputy Prime Minister; papers, memoranda, correspondence, cuttings concerning the Industrial and Commercial Finance Corporation, 1945–64; the Revolving Fund for Industry, 1953–7; material on the Acton Society Trust, 1962–6; the BBC; official papers of the Committee of Inquiry on the Rehabilitation of Disabled Persons ('Piercy Committee'); correspondence, 1950–62, of The Evelyn Trust Ltd; material concerning Ghana; the Institution of Works Managers; the Labour Party; correspondence, Court and seminar papers relating to the London School of Economics, and to London University, 1950–66; correspondence, 1947–52, concerning the National Institute of Industrial Psychology; correspondence, 1949–63, papers for meetings and accounts of the Wellcome Trust; and miscellaneous correspondence dating from the 1950s.

PIGGOTT, Sir Francis Taylor (1852–1925)

Jurist and writer on International Law. Legal Adviser to the Prime Minister of Japan, 1887–91. Chief Justice, Supreme Court of Hong Kong, 1905–12.

The British Library has a collection of Piggott's material relating to his work on the international law of blockade (Add. MSS 42523–54). It is chiefly concerned with the 'Law of the Sea' series of historical and legal works projected by him, and includes copies of, and extracts from, historical documents; extracts and notes from various authorities consulted by him; various notes and commentaries; a small quantity of contemporary correspondence; and some seven volumes of proofs.

PIGOU, Arthur Cecil (1877–1959)

Economist. Professor of Political Economy, Cambridge, 1908–43.

King's College, Cambridge, has a copy of Pigou's Fellowship dissertation of 1902, while some printed and typed material resulting from his work on the Committee on Currency and Bank of England Note Issues is available at the Marshall Library, Cambridge. Sturges, *Economists' Papers*, pp. 86–7, mentions this and correspondence in other collections (viz. J. M. Keynes, and the Macmillan deposit at the British Library, Add. MSS 55199–200). In addition a memorandum on the taxable capacity of Ireland, and correspondence arising from this (1917) can be found in the Plunkett Foundation papers.

PITT, Thomas Fox-

Secretary, Anti-Slavery Society.

Papers, 1953–62, are in the Library of the School of Oriental and African Studies. They consist of manuscripts, typescripts, press cuttings, official documents and telegrams etc, relating to the Central African Federation.

PLEDGE, Humphrey Thomas (1903–60)

Scientist. Keeper of the Science Museum Library from 1945.

A collection of manuscripts, notes, drafts and working papers, together with a small amount of correspondence is deposited in Sussex University Library. The collection includes biographical material, including an essay on his intellectual development, and notes and a draft for part of an autobiography. There are manuscript and typescript bibliographies and drafts for books and articles; and working papers and notes relating to Pledge's project for a synthesis of knowledge. Correspondence is from various colleagues and scholars, chiefly concerning his work *Science since 1500*.

PLOWMAN, Mark (Max) (1883–1941)

Writer and pacifist. Editor, the *Adelphi* from 1938. Secretary, Peace Pledge Union, 1937–8.

Papers of Max and Dorothy Lloyd Plowman are located in the Library of University College London. Amongst the material are letters from Max Plowman, 1929–36; and letters to him, 1907–36, often about literary matters, and particularly poetry. There are manuscripts and notebooks on the 'Right to Live', the 'Problems of Pacifism', and 'William Blake'; notebooks containing drafts of several works; typescripts of plays and novels; manuscripts of poems. Various drafts and notes, articles and addresses date from Plowman's period as General Secretary of the Peace Pledge Union, and there is some material (largely press cuttings) relating to Dick Sheppard. Several albums contain further articles and poems by Plowman, including articles contributed to the *Oxford Mail* and *Everyman*. There are also engagement diaries of Max and Dorothy Plowman, 1914–1940s, legal agreements with publishers, etc., press cuttings, including miscellaneous items on pacifism, and obituary notices.

Papers of Dorothy Plowman include correspondence, 1908–43; miscellaneous notes especially on D. H. Lawrence and Blake; poems, and manuscripts and typescripts of stories by her; notebooks; anthologies of Max Plowman's letters; and 'Memoirs', 1964–6.

Records of the Peace Pledge Union are described in *Sources*, Vol. 1, p. 210.

PODMORE, Frank (1856–1910)

Pioneer socialist. A founder of the Fabian Society and of the Society for Psychical Research. Author of numerous studies of psychical phenomena and of Robert Owen.

No personal papers have been located but letters from Podmore are in the Thomas Davidson papers in Yale University, while the Fabian Society archive, Nuffield College, Oxford, has relevant material.

POLAK, Henry Salomon Leon (1882–1959)

Lawyer and humanitarian. Edited *India* for British Committee of Indian National Congress, 1918–19. Founder and first secretary, Indians Overseas Association.

Papers are in Rhodes House Library, Oxford.

POLLEN, Arthur Joseph Hungerford (1866–1937)

Writer on naval affairs; expert on naval gunnery. Pioneer of naval fire control.

Churchill College, Cambridge, has a collection of material, including correspondence, articles and press cuttings. The papers are arranged in seven sections. These are Gunnery and Tactics, 1900s; printed papers on *Land and Water*, 1915–19; newspaper cuttings, c. 1907–36; articles 1910s–20s; correspondence, 1905–35; papers of Sir Reginald Custance, who collaborated with Pollen on discussions of naval tactics and gunnery, and who is the major correspondent in Pollen's letters; and miscellaneous material, including notes for articles and transcripts. The papers are under restriction.

POLLITT, Harry (1890–1960)

Communist propagandist. Secretary, Hands off Russia Movement, 1919; National Minority Movement, 1924–9. General-Secretary of the Communist Party of Great Britain, 1929–56; Chairman from 1956.

John Mahon, *Harry Pollitt, a biography* (1976) made 'full use of such papers as were preserved by Harry Pollitt', and also uses personal recollections. The papers used by Mahon are now with the Communist Party of Great Britain whose records are described in *Sources* Vol. 1, pp. 49–50.

POSTGATE, Raymond William (1896–1971)

Journalist and author. Writer of works on Labour and socialist history; edited several socialist journals; on staff of *Daily Herald*. Departmental editor, XIVth edition *Encyclopaedia Britannica*. Civil Servant, 1942–50. President, Good Food Club, from 1949; editor of its *Guide* from 1951.

No substantial grouping of papers survived after Postgate's death. The University of Kent at Canterbury has a few relevant items. The International Institute of Social History, Amsterdam, has a small collection of National Council of Civil Liberties material given to it by Postgate. It consists of the carbon copy of a typescript (about 100 pages) with reports about tribunals; short case histories of conscientious objectors; reports about the behaviour of the tribunals, the attitudes of military and non-military members; a dissertation about Civil Liberties under the Defence of the Realm Act, 1914, 1916; about industrial conscription; reports about the treatment of C.O.s, etc. Further there is some cyclostyled material of the NCCL (22 pages). A further small Postgate collection at the International Institute contains reports and correspondence in answer to a questionnaire about the General Strike, 1926.

PRICE, Langford Lovell F. R. (1862–1950)

Economist. Fellow and Treasurer, Oriel College, Oxford, 1888–1918; Fellow, 1918–23. Lecturer to the Toynbee Trust, 1886–7. Reader in Economic History, Oxford, 1909–21. Hon. Secretary. Royal Economic Society.

Copies of lecture notes and his typescript memoirs are in Leeds University Library. Other copies of parts of the memoirs are in the Royal Statistical Society Library and at Oriel College, Oxford.

PROSSER, David Lewis (d. 1950)

Ecclesiastic. Bishop of St David's from 1927. Archbishop of Wales, 1944–9.

The National Library of Wales has diaries, 1912–50; records of his ecclesiastical preferments; scripts of his addresses to the Governing Body of the Church in Wales; and correspondence, press cuttings and pamphlets on the history of the Church in Wales.

PROTHERO, Sir George Walter (1848–1922)

Historian. Professor of History, Edinburgh University, 1894–9. President of the Royal Historical Society, 1901–5. Director of the Historical Section, Foreign Office, 1918–19. Member of the British Peace Delegation, 1919. Co-editor, *Cambridge Modern History*. Editor, *Quarterly Review*.

Papers survive in the archives of the Royal Historical Society, University College London. Correspondence, 1915–19, is in the Dawson papers, Birmingham University Library, and there is correspondence with the A. C. Swinburne papers, University of Texas, Austin.
    Further letters are in the Oscar Browning collection.

QUELCH, Harry (1858–1913)

Marxist propagandist. Leading member of the Social Democratic Federation, and editor of *Justice*. Manager, Twentieth Century Press.

No private papers have been found. However, correspondence can be found in various collections. In the Labour Party archive there is correspondence in the International File (ref. LP/INT/11/1) material in the LRC archive 1902–6 (ref. LRC: INDEX), and elsewhere. The International Institute of Social History has a few further items of correspondence, e.g. seven letters, 1903–10, in the Kautsky collection; 11 letters, 1897–8, in the Kleiner papers. Papers relating to the Social Democratic Federation, in BLPES, the Marx Memorial Library, and the National Library of Scotland, are described in *Sources* Vol. 1, pp. 236–7.

RADFORD, Ernest (d. 1919)

Poet, art critic and pioneer socialist. Early member of the Fabian Society. Secretary of the Arts and Crafts Movement.

Dr Muriel Radford (daughter-in-law), 43 Hillfield Court, Belsize Avenue, London NW3 4BJ, has certain papers.

RASHDALL, Hastings (1858–1924)

Theologian. Fellow of New College, Oxford, 1895–1917. Dean of Carlisle from 1917.

Family correspondence and sermon notes, 1866–1923, are in the Library of New College, Oxford.

The Bodleian Library has letters and papers, 1871–1924, together with material concerning him, 1924–53. There are letters to his mother, 1869–79, 1907; letters to Rashdall, with copies of some from him, including letters from H. Montagu Butler, 1875–1917; drafts of lectures; papers and a few letters about ecclesiastical matters, 1891–1921; letters and papers about his life; miscellaneous papers such as agreements with publishers, royalty statements, testimonials, memoranda on university reform, lecture notes to Carlisle WEA; and printed prize essays, pamphlets, reviews, etc.

RATCLIFFE, Samuel Kirkham (1868–1958)

Journalist and lecturer; supporter of ethical movement. Editor, *The Echo*, 1900. Acting editor, *The Statesman*, Calcutta, 1903–6; the *Sociological Review*, 1910–17.

No information on papers was made available. Mr Nicolas Walter of the Rationalist Press Association may have information.

RATTENBURY, John Ernest (1870–1963)

Methodist minister. Superintendent of West London Mission (with headquarters at Kingsway Hall), 1907–25. President, National Free Church Council, 1936; Methodist Sacramental Fellowship, 1939–50.

Letters and papers are in the Methodist Archives and Research Centre, now placed on permanent loan with the John Rylands University Library of Manchester. There are letters to and from Rattenbury, the chief correspondents being Harold C. Morton, Secretary of the Weekly Bible Union, and J. A. Kensit of the Protestant Truth Society. There are also press cuttings, articles, offprints, tracts, and a collection of 24 unpublished hymns. Miss Grace Rattenbury (daughter), states that, at her father's request, she destroyed all his private letters and diaries after his death.

READ, Sir Herbert (1893–1968)

Author: writer on poetry, fine art, anarchism, etc. Assistant Principal, H. M. Treasury, 1919–22. Assistant Keeper, Victoria and Albert Museum, 1922–31. Professor of Fine Art, Edinburgh University, 1931–3. Lecturer in Art, Liverpool University, 1935–6. Editor, *Burlington Magazine*, 1933–9. Leon Fellow, London University, 1940–2. Professor of Poetry, Harvard University, 1953–4.

A large collection of papers and published works is in the McPherson Library of the University of Victoria, British Columbia. It has been described in detail by Howard Gerwing, 'A Checklist of the Herbert Read Archive', in Robin Skelton (ed.), *Herbert Read: A Memorial Symposium* (1970). The manuscript and typescript material in the collection includes drafts of many of his articles, reviews, pamphlets, and books; notebooks with notes, drafts, comments, lectures, speeches, BBC radio talks etc; and corrected proof sheets, newspaper cuttings, etc. There is extensive correspondence including letters to Sir Herbert Read from Joe Ackerley, Richard Aldington, Julien Benda, John Berger, André Breton, W. R. Childe, Richard Church, Alex Comfort, D. Cooper, Edward Dahlberg, G. Lowes Dickinson, Bonamy Dobrée, T. S. Eliot, Ford Madox Ford, Naum Gabo, Barbara Hepworth, Patrick Heron, Richard Hull, C. G. Jung, Jacob Kramer, F. V. Morley, Henry Miller, J. Middleton Murry, A. R. Orage, George Orwell, Robert Payne, Hans Richter, Bertrand Russell, Stephen Spender, Allen Tate, Henry Treece, Beatrice Webb, H. G. Wells, Colin Wilson. There are carbons of letters from Sir Herbert to John Berger, Edward Dahlberg, T. S. Eliot, C. G. Jung, Stephen Spender, H. G. Wells and others. A number of other papers concern the Freedom Defence Committee and the Freedom Press. The former papers include a constitution; draft letter to sponsors and friends; and replies to letters appealing for funds from E. M. Forster, George Orwell, Bertrand Russell, Stephen Spender, Graham Sutherland, Julian Symons and Leonard Woolf. Freedom Press material includes a copy of a circular letter, 25 Oct 1944, several letters from Read and newspaper cuttings. Correspondence concerning the Progressive League is in Washington University Library, St Louis, Missouri.

READ, Margaret Helen (1889–   )

Anthropologist. Social work in India, 1919–24; lecturer on international affairs in Great Britain and USA, 1924–30; student and occasional lecturer, London School of Economics, 1930–4; Assistant Lecturer, 1937–40. Research Fellow, International African Institute, 1934–9. Professor of Education in Tropical Areas, London Institute of Education, 1940–55. Professor of Education, University College, Ibadan, 1955–6.

BLPES has a collection of material which includes field notes, published and unpublished papers, reports, conference papers and correspondence, notes and drafts for works by Margaret Read.

RECKITT, Maurice Bennington (1888–   )

Journalist and religious writer. Founder member, National Guilds League, 1915. Member, Church Socialist League, and editor *Church Socialist*, 1915–19. A founder of the League of the Kingdom of God and the High Anglican Chandos Group, 1926. Editor, *Christendom: A Journal of Christian Sociology*, from 1931.

M. B. Reckitt's papers are to be bequeathed to the University of Sussex. They include printed material concerning the range of Mr Reckitt's interests, and correspondence etc.

Reckitt papers on microfilm at Hull University Library include material on National Guilds, the Building Guilds, and the Industrial Parliament Scheme; the National Building Guild and Guild of Builders (London) Ltd, 1922–3; the Furnishing Guild, Engineering Guild and Guild of Clothiers; certain material on the New Town Trust Ltd, the New Town Agricultural Guild Ltd, and Workers' Control League.

REDDIE, Cecil (1858–1932)

Educationalist. Founded Abbotsholme School, 1889; Headmaster until 1927.

Abbotsholme School, Rocester, Uttoxeter, Staffs, has a collection of correspondence, sermons, diaries, etc. Papers have been quoted in Bernard M. Ward, *Reddie of Abbotsholme* (1934).

REDFERN, Percy (1875–1958)

Co-operative movement journalist.

Manchester Central Library has a collection of letters to Percy Redfern (ref. MS f 091.5 Re 1) consisting of letters from Robert Blatchford, Leo Tolstoy, H. G. Wells, Sidney and Beatrice Webb, Philip Snowden, John Galsworthy, H. J. Laski and J. R. MacDonald, and covering the period 1896 to 1940.

REES, Sir (James) Frederick (1883–1967)

Economic historian. Professor of Commerce, Birmingham University, 1925–9. Principal of University College, Cardiff, 1929–49. Vice Chancellor, University of Wales, 1935–7, 1944–6. Visiting Professor in Economics, Ceylon University, 1953–4. Head of Economic History Department, Edinburgh, 1956–8. Member or Chairman of various commissions and inquiries, e.g. Advisory Council on Welsh Reconstruction Problems, Ceylon Constitutional Commission, Boundary Commission, etc.

Glamorgan Record Office has three files of papers and correspondence relating to inquiries and public bodies which Rees chaired. One file relates to the inquiry held into the labour position in the ship-repairing industry in the Bristol Channel ports, Nov 1940, and includes minutes of meetings, copies of the report, and some correspondence. A second file concerns a survey of manpower in South Wales, which was part of the Beveridge national survey, and includes miscellaneous papers and correspondence. A third file contains reports, minutes, statistics and letters concerning the National Service Tribunals for the South Wales coal-mining industry.

REES, Sir Richard Lodowick Edward Montagu, 2nd Bt (1900–70)

Author. Hon Attaché, H. M. Embassy, Berlin. Hon. Treasurer and lecturer, London District, Workers' Educational Association, 1925–7. Editor, the *Adelphi*, 1930–6. Specialist in the work of Simone Weil.

Rees's papers are located in the Library of University College London. These include autograph manuscripts and typescripts of books, published and unpublished; lectures and essays, including Workers' Education Association lectures, 1924–7, manuscript drafts of talks, reviews and articles; fragments of diaries, 1920s and 1930s; notebooks and the manuscript draft of the opening chapter of his autobiography. Other material includes papers concerning the Spanish Civil War, including press cuttings, a few letters, and the text of 13 telegraph reports from Frank Jellinek concerning the settlement of Spanish refugees in Mexico. Other material includes minutes and papers and some correspondence of the International Commission for War Refugees; papers concerning Rees' war service; and material on his membership of the Committee of the Pilgrim Trust. Some material relates to the sales of his books (royalties, statements, etc.). A grouping of literary correspondence, 1922–c.66 includes letters from Hon. David Astor, Vanessa Bell, Leon Chestor, Lord Gladwyn, Victor Gollancz, Frieda Lawrence, Stephen Spender, Geoffrey Sainsbury, Hugh Trevor-Roper, Colin Wilson.

Certain correspondence, in French, concerns his work on Simone Weil. Correspondence from 1965–70 includes letters from Mark Benney, Iris Murdoch, H. T. Moore, Malachi Whitaker, Professor J. M. K. Vyvyan. There is correspondence with publishers and with A. D. Peters, his literary agent. Rees also retained copies of his various letters to the press, and a foolscap notebook contains reviews or drafts of letters to editors. There are some 100 letters from Rees to his mother, c. 1938–42, and correspondence with his sister and Surgeon-Captain Harald E. B. Curfel; and there are letters from J. Middleton Murry. Many of these relate to the *Adelphi*. Rees also retained a collection of press cuttings, including items on literature and art, politics, and colleagues and friends, such as Middleton Murry and George Orwell.

In addition to the personal material the Rees archive includes papers concerning George Orwell, Simone Weil and R. H. Tawney. The Orwell material includes material concerning his literary estate, legal correspondence, general correspondence, material on the George Orwell Archive Trust (including correspondence and records of Trust Meetings); and a folder of Orwell material, including some 20 press cuttings, mostly obituary notices and typescript transcripts of six poems by Orwell contributed to the *Adelphi*, 1933–6.

The Weil material includes typescripts and proofs of his work on her, including his translations; plus correspondence and photographs. The Tawney material includes letters from various correspondents to Tawney, material relating to Rees's tasks as Tawney's literary executor, and a file of Rees's correspondence as literary executor.

Correspondence, 1960–5, with Arthur Creech Jones, Allen & Unwin, and Tawney's solicitors about the administration of Tawney's will and publication of his works, are in the Creech Jones papers, Rhodes House Library, Oxford.

REEVES, William Pember (1857–1932)

Journalist, politician and economist. Editor of several journals in New Zealand. Member of the New Zealand Parliament, 1887–96; Minister of Education, Labour and Justice, 1891–6. Later Agent-General for New Zealand, and High Commissioner for New Zealand in London, 1905–8. Director of the London School of Economics, 1908–19. Chairman, National Bank of New Zealand from 1917.

The Alexander Turnbull Library (the National Library of New Zealand), Wellington, New Zealand, has the largest collection of papers. The material includes official correspondence concerning appointments, 1892–1920; and personal correspondence, 1852–1929. Among the correspondents are his father, M. Reeves, Charles Trevelyan, J. R. MacDonald, Sidney Webb, William Clarke, Sir Henry Newbolt, Philip Snowden, G. B. Shaw, the Earl of Onslow, Gilbert Murray. Other correspondence concerns the Anglo-Hellenic League, of which Reeves was Chairman, 1915–19. The collection also includes copies of a number of his verses; lectures, on Imperial Federation, Britain and the Colonies, and Greek affairs; portraits and sketches, mostly of political figures of the time; personalia, such as menus, invitations, photographs, etc.; newspaper clippings, mostly on Old Age Pensions, feminism in New Zealand, and Liberalism; and a biographical study on Reeves and brochures by Sidney Webb and others. A later deposit of papers includes typescript reminiscences in the form of short articles or chapters (perhaps intended as a newpaper series); a typescript account of a visit to France during World War I; typescript extracts from a diary or commonplace book, 1889–1906; and a pamphlet, 'Notes on the Family of Pember', with MS annotations. There are also three volumes of newspaper cuttings, c. 1888–1900, chiefly from New Zealand newspapers. These largely relate to political matters, and include a few MS notes, and interleaved letters and cards. A commonplace and birthday book of the Reeves family dates from 1865.

Further Pember Reeves material can be found in other collections at the Alexander Turnbull Library. It also holds a microfilm of the Henry Demarest Lloyd collection at the State Historical Society, Madison, Wisconsin (including correspondence with Reeves, press cuttings and notebooks on his New Zealand visit) and of the Pember Reeves collection in BLPES.

The BLPES has one volume of material, 1895–1908, including letters written from important figures in New Zealand to Reeves as Agent-General. Additionally there are letters from Reeves in the Herbert Samuel collection at the House of Lords Record Office.

Keith Sinclair, *William Pember Reeves: New Zealand Fabian* (Oxford 1965) makes use of the available manuscript sources.

RENDEL, 1st B
Stuart Rendel (1834–1913)

Liberal politician. M.P. (Lib.) Montgomeryshire, 1880–94. President, University College of Wales, Aberystwyth, from 1895.

The National Library of Wales has a large collection of papers and correspondence. There are letters and papers relating to the University College of Wales and the proposed National Library; letters from Principal T. F. Roberts, 1892–1913; papers and letters on the Intermediate Education Act, 1889; other papers and letters on the University and Disestablishment; letters and papers on the Welsh Land Commission, 1890–6; drafts of speeches and addresses, 1882–1909. There is extensive correspondence, including many letters from A. C. Humphreys-Owen. There are also letters from Lord Aberdare, David Davies, T. E. Ellis, S. T. Evans, Sir Lewis Morris, J. Herbert Lewis, Lord Sudeley, Sir John Williams, Sir Michael Hicks-Beach, Sir William Harcourt, Charles Hobhouse, John Morley, A. J. Mundella, W. H. Smith, Sir G. O. Trevelyan. There are also letters from W. E. Gladstone and other members of his family. Topics covered include Welsh politics, Liberalism, the supply of gunboats to China, etc.

Tyne and Wear County Record Office has business correspondence and papers of Stuart Rendel and W. G. Armstrong. Correspondence with H. N. Gladstone is in the Gladstone family papers, at St Deiniol's Library, Hawarden, which may be seen at the Clwyd Record Office.

RENDEL, Harry Stuart Goodhart- (1887–1959)

Architect. Slade Professor of Fine Art, Oxford, 1933–6. Director of Architectural Association, School of Architecture, 1936–8. President, Royal Institute of British Architects, 1937–9.

The RIBA has relevant material, including his correspondence with W. Begley. Guildford Muniment Room has estate papers and papers concerning his membership of non-architectural clubs and societies.

RHODES, Cecil John (1853–1902)

Imperialist. Treasurer-General, Cape Colony, 1884; Commissioner of Crown Lands, 1890–4; Minister of Native Affairs, 1894–6; Premier, 1890–6. Managing Director, British South Africa Company.

Many papers were believed destroyed during World War II. Rhodes House Library, Oxford, has correspondence, including letters to Sir Graham Bower and photocopies of letters to C. D. Rudd, 1874–1901.

Yale University Library has the Howell Wright collection of Cecil Rhodes material.

Letters to Sir John Sprigg, 1889–98, are in the Cory Library, Rhodes University, Grahamstown, South Africa. Some 422 folios of correspondence (mainly photocopies) are in the National Archives, Salisbury, Rhodesia.

The Milner papers at the Bodleian Library, Oxford, contain correspondence and material on his death and the early years of the Rhodes Trust. John Flint, *Cecil Rhodes* (1974) uses manuscript sources.

RHONDDA, 2nd Viscountess
Lady Margaret Haig Thomas (d. 1958)

Author and journalist. Editor, *Time and Tide*, and Chairman, Time and Tide Publishing Co. Ltd.

Lady Rhondda deposited papers of her father in the National Library of Wales in 1941. Items relating to her own career include a grant of sùpporters, 1920, and two volumes of press cuttings.

RHYS, Ernest Percival (1859–1946)

Author and editor. Editor, Everyman's Library.

Correspondence, 1886–1935, is in the British Library (Egerton MSS 3247–8). It includes letters from Joseph Conrad, R. Jefferies, Lord Leighton, G. Moore, Ezra Pound, G. B. Shaw, A. Symons, Walt Whitman and W. B. Yeats.

RHYS-WILLIAMS, Lady
Juliette Evangeline Rhys-Williams (née Glyn) (1898–1964)

Social worker and publicist. Founder and subsequently Chairman of the National Birthday Trust, which undertook medical surveys and research work on the prevention of maternal and infant mortality. Founder member of the Economic Research Council. Hon. Secretary, United Europe Movement; and British Section of European League for Economic Co-operation. Liberal Parliamentary candidate, 1938, 1945. Worked for Liberal Party Publicity Department but after 1946 supported attempts at an Anti-Socialist Union of Liberals and Conservatives. Chairman, Cwmbran New Town Development Corporation, 1955–60.

Miss Elspeth Rhys-Williams (daughter), 47 Eaton Place, London SW1, has a large collection of papers. A number of boxes contain papers relating to the Birthday Trust. Amongst these is material relating to nutrition and feeding schemes in South Wales between the wars. Other material reflecting her social work between the wars includes correspondence, including letters to the Prime Minister, papers on taxation and economic policy, press cuttings, etc. There are a number of box-files of correspondence relating to Europe, chiefly during the 1950s. The correspondents include Sir Winston Churchill, Harold Macmillan, Lord Eccles, Duncan Sandys, Peter Thorneycroft, Sir Piers Dixon, Sir Roger Makins, etc.; and leaders of European nations; and the letters concern the European Movement, the European League for Economic Co-operation, the Commonwealth, the role of sterling, etc. Lady Rhys-Williams' work for the Liberal Party and her anti-socialist activities are reflected in further correspondence, including correspondence with Churchill. Other box-files and folders contain articles and reviews, letters to editors, invitations to speak, domestic material, papers on taxation policy, material concerning the Married Women's Association, hospitals, the Population Commission, science, the Economic Research Council, Christian Action, the National Council of Social Service, the BBC (of which Lady Rhys-Williams was a governor), etc. In addition, there is a considerable amount of personal material including papers concerning the novelist Elinor Glyn, her mother.

RICHARD, Timothy (1845–1919)

Baptist Missionary and adviser to the Chinese Government. General Secretary, Society for the Diffusion of Christian and General Knowledge among the Chinese (the Christian Literature Society for China). Founded the Modern Imperial University, Shansi. Arbitrator after the Boxer rising. Author of works on Christianity and national progress, in English and Chinese.

Some letters, 1905–19, and papers are in the National Library of Wales. The collection includes notes, extracts from a diary, obituary notices, notes collected for a biography, etc. Other material includes 31 letters and postcards from Richard to his mother, 1882–6; family correspondence and personalia, 1888–1910; and some papers on the need for reform in international relations and in missionary methods. The Baptist Missionary Society has correspondence.

RICKMAN, John (1891–1951)

Leading Quaker.

Papers on Russia are in Friends' House Library (ref. Temp. MSS 99/5).

RIDDELL, 1st B
Sir George Allardice Riddell, 1st Bt (1865–1934)

Newspaper proprietor. Chairman of *News of the World*, George Newnes Ltd. and C. Arthur Pearson Ltd. One-time Chairman, Newspaper Proprietors Association.

Papers and diaries, 1908–24, are in the 'reserved' collection at the British Library. They will not be available until 1985. Political and social correspondence with Lloyd George, 1912–21, 1933–4, is in the House of Lords Record Office. There is some correspondence, 1918–19, in the Douglas Sladen collection. Parts of Riddell's diaries have been published: *Lord Riddell's War Diary, 1914–18* (1933); *Lord Riddell's Intimate Diary of the Peace Conference and After, 1918–23* (1933); *More Pages from my Diary, 1908–14* (1934).

RIDDING, George (1828–1904)

Headmaster and ecclesiastic. Headmaster of Winchester, 1868–84. Bishop of Southwell from 1884.

Nottinghamshire Record Office has 11 volumes of newspaper cuttings, 1868–1907, concerned with national and local government affairs and politics, education, and all aspects of national and provincial church life, Southwell diocesan activities, etc. Southwell Minster library has various papers of Bishop Ridding (NRA 7879). There are letters to Roundell Palmer, 1878–85, in the Selborne collection at the Bodleian Library, Oxford, while correspondence, 1898–9, concerning the furtherance of Christianity in Egypt is in Lambeth Palace Library.

RILEY, Athelstan (1858–1945)

Prominent layman in the Church of England. Chairman of the Anglican and Eastern Churches Association. Author of books, pamphlets and articles on education, Eastern Christians, foreign affairs. He was prominent in the creation of the Church Assembly.

Lambeth Palace Library has a collection of material which reflects his wide range of interests in Church and educational matters. Correspondents include Archbishop Davidson, Lord Hugh Cecil, W. J. Birkbeck, W. H. Frere, 4th Marquess of Salisbury, Bishop Gore and Lord Phillimore, as well as, in other spheres, Robert Bridges and Ralph Vaughan-Williams. The collection also includes several volumes of journals kept by Riley on visits to the Eastern Churches, and his engagement books which give an insight into his wide ranging interests.

ROBERTS, Robert Davies, (1851–1911)

Educational administrator. Secretary to the London Society for Extension of University Teaching, 1885–94, and Secretary for Lectures of Local Examinations and Lectures Syndicate, Cambridge, 1894–1902. Chairman of the Executive Committee, University of Wales, 1910–11. Secretary of the Congress of the Universities of the Empire, 1912. Secretary–Lecturer of the Gilchrist Educational Trust.

The National Library of Wales has a collection of correspondence and other items. This includes letters from Sir John Gibson to Robert Davies Roberts, 1878–1911; press cuttings from the *Cambrian News*; and the warrant of appointment of R. D. Roberts as High Sheriff of Cardiganshire. There is also correspondence, 1878, between Roberts and Lord Aberdare, Edward Breese, David Davies, T. C. Edwards, Sir Lewis Morris, Sir Hugh Owen, John Robertson, Evan M. Richards, F. W. Rudler, and O. Williams, concerning the University College of Wales, Aberystwyth.

ROBERTSON, Sir Dennis Holme (1890–1963)

Economist. Fellow of Trinity College, Cambridge, 1914–38, and from 1944. Reader in Economics, Cambridge, 1930–8. Professor of Economics, London University, 1939–44. Adviser to the Treasury, 1939–44. Professor of Political Economy, Cambridge, 1944–57. President of the Royal Economic Society, 1948–50.

Papers are held by his executor, Professor S. Dennison of Hull University, who is preparing a study of Robertson. There are letters to Beveridge and Cannan in BLPES, to Sir Hubert Henderson in Nuffield College, Oxford, and to Keynes in the Marshall Library, Cambridge.

ROBERTSON, John Henry
John Connell* (1909–65)

Journalist and author. On staff of *Evening News* from 1932; leader-writer, 1945–59. Served in Middle East and India, World War II; Chief Military Press Censor, India, 1944. Co-opted member, London County Council Education Committee, 1949–58; Deputy Mayor, St. Pancras Borough, 1951–2. Biographer and military historian.

McMaster University Library, Ontario, has a collection of papers. This contains a considerable quantity of correspondence (amounting to some 14,000 pieces) with literary, political and military figures. The papers also include typescripts of four of his novels and three of his biographical works, *Winston Churchill* (1956), *Auchinleck* (1959) and *Wavell* (1964), together with typescripts of numerous articles and reviews for newspapers, radio and television, and of many unpublished articles and drafts. The archives also include research material used by Robertson.

*Pseudonym.

ROGERSON, Sydney (1894–1968)

Publicist. Served in army in France, 1916–19. Publicity Manager for Federation of British Industries, 1923–30; Publicity Controller, ICI Ltd., 1937–52. Publicity and Public Relations Adviser to Army Council, War Office, 1952–4.

A collection of typescript and final drafts of Rogerson's book *Propaganda in the Next War* and his autobiographical works *Unorthodox Endeavour* and *Stirling Times* are held at the Imperial War Museum. The collection also includes some typescript articles and his diaries for the period 1939–47.

ROSS, William McGregor

Engineer and critic of British colonial policies in Africa. Author of *Kenya from Within* (1927), etc.

There are papers with the family, including diaries and correspondence. Enquiries should be directed to Mr Hugh McGregor Ross (son), 5 Kingsley Place, London N6.

ROTH, Cecil (1899–1970)

Historian. Reader in Jewish Studies, Oxford University, 1939–64. President of the Jewish Historical Society, 1936–45, 1955–6. Editor, *Encyclopaedia Judaica* from 1965.

The Mocatta Library, University College London has a collection which includes correspon-dence, genealogical and biographical notes, lecture notes, press cuttings, texts of lectures and articles, a draft for a 'Modern Jewish History', book reviews, offprints and miscellaneous items. Correspondents include S. Alexander, Yigal Allon, Sholem Asch, W. G. W. Barnard, Richard Barnard, 2nd Vt Bearsted, N. Ben-Menahem, B. Blumenkranz, Eddie Cantor, Lord Cecil, Lord Cohen, Cynthia M. Crews, M. Eisenbeth, Benno Elkan, Levi Eshkol, Cesare Foligno, Arthur E. Franklin, N. Goldmann, Philip Guedalla, A. M. Hyamson, Hilary Jenkinson, Neville Laski, Seymour B. Liebman, 2nd Lord Melchett, Pierre Mendès-France, Sir Robert Ludwig Mond, Lord Nathan, H. G. Richardson, Herbert Samuel, Charles Singer, Arnold Wiznitzer and Abraham Yaari.

ROTHA, Paul (1907–)

Film producer and director. Author and journalist. Specialised in the making of documentary films, for the Empire Marketing Board, UNESCO, The Times, the Scottish Office, National Council of Social Service, etc. Head of Documentaries, BBC Television, 1953–5.

The University College of Los Angeles has a large collection of material. The archive includes the original typescripts and/or manuscripts with the author's corrections, additions, etc., for his books: The Film Till Now, (1930), Celluloid: The Film Today (1931), Documentary Film (1936), Portrait of a Flying Yorkshireman (1951), Rotha on the Film (1958), The Flaherty Biography (i.e. the completed manuscript which the publishers considered too specialised for the general public and was edited by Arthur Calder-Marshall as The Innocent Eye (1962)).

In addition there are scripts, revisions, set drawings, etc., for films directed by Paul Rotha: Contact, 1932, Shipyard and The Face of Britain, 1934–5, The Peace of Britain, 1936, The Fourth Estate (the Times film), 1939, World of Plenty, 1942, Land of Promise, 1944, A City Speaks, 1947, The World is Rich, 1947, No Resting Place, 1950, World Without End, Cat and Mouse, 1958, Cradle of Genius (the Abbey Theatre Film), 1959, The Life of Adolf Hitler, 1961, The Silent Raid, 1962, plus scripts, story treatments, etc. for projects and unrealised films. Scripts for television include Fight to Survive, 1949; The Challenge of Television, 1955.

A collection of material relates to Paul Rotha's work as a journalist, comprising folders of the manuscripts and typescripts of his articles (some unpublished), reviews, criticisms, etc., from 1928 to 1959, together with some printed journals and extracts. There is a unique collection of approximately 20 volumes and folders of press cuttings and extracts from 1920 to 1962. These have been compiled from two points of view: first, material relating to the cinema in general (but not fan material), i.e. important articles and published correspondence, government decisions on film-making, criticism, certain reviews, etc., by the most competent cinema writers of this time. Each cutting is identified and dated, and forms an invaluable record of the cinema during the last forty years. Secondly, there is an enormous volume of cuttings relating to Paul Rotha and his work as film historian, critic, director, producer, lecturer, supporter of film societies, etc.

ROWNTREE, (Benjamin) Seebohm (1871–1954)

Sociologist and manufacturer. Chairman of Rowntree and Co. Ltd, 1925–41.

Papers remain with the family. It is likely that they will be deposited with York University Library. Correspondence, 1930–7, can be found in the Lothian papers at the Scottish Record Office, and there are 13 letters to Lloyd George, 1923–43, in the House of Lords Record Office. Family papers were used in Asa Briggs, Social Thought and Social Action: A Study of the Work of Seebohm Rowntree, 1871–1954 (1961).

ROWNTREE, Joseph (1836–1925)

Manufacturer and philanthropist. Temperance reformer. Chairman of Rowntree and Co. Ltd.

Papers survive with the family. They may be deposited with York University Library. A few items of correspondence, 1905, concerning an invitation to Ramsay MacDonald to be Vice-President of the Temperance Legislative League are in the archives of the Labour Party at Transport House. Family papers were used in Anne Vernon, *A Quaker Businessman: The Life of Joseph Rowntree, 1836–1925* (1958).

ROYDEN, (Agnes) Maude
Mrs G. W. H. Shaw (1876–1956)

Feminist, preacher, writer and broadcaster. On Executive Committee, National Union of Women's Suffrage Societies, 1908. Editor, *The Common Cause*, 1912–14. Assistant Preacher at the City Temple, 1917–20.

Some letters can be found in the autograph collection at the Fawcett Library, but it is believed that the bulk of her papers has been destroyed.

RUSSELL, 3rd E
Bertrand Arthur William Russell (1872–1970)

Philosopher and publicist. Fellow of Trinity College, Cambridge. Lecturer at London School of Economics, Cambridge, Sorbonne, Peking, California, New York, Pennsylvania, etc. President of the Aristotelean Society. First Reith Lecturer. Awarded Nobel Prize for Literature, 1950. Founder member of No-Conscription Fellowship, the Campaign for Nuclear Disarmament and Committee of 100. Author of works on various topics – German Social Democracy, philosophy, logic, mathematics, social policy, political theory, marriage and morality, education and issues of war and peace.

The Bertrand Russell Archive at McMaster University, Hamilton, Ontario, contains by far the largest accumulation of Russell material, being based on his own collection, and supplemented by further acquisitions, including copies of papers and correspondence in collections elsewhere. The McMaster collection includes family papers, covering the political work of his parents and his brother Frank, the 2nd Earl Russell. (Selections were published by Bertrand and Patricia Russell, *The Amberley Papers*, 1937.) There are several drafts and versions of Russell's autobiography, and the manuscripts of books and articles (some 1100 separate works, many unpublished). The earliest MS is of a notebook, c. 1878–9. There are a number of unpublished essays on mathematics, incuding drafts of *The Principles of Mathematics*, and early work on *Principia Mathematica*. There is also an incomplete MS of an unpublished book on epistemology; a collection of some very early work on politics, and a more or less complete run of his political writings from the 1930s, both published and unpublished, together with an unpublished novelette and the MSS of short stories.

There is a vast collection of correspondence, comprising some 25,000 letters to and from a wide range of correspondents. Apart from some highly personal correspondence with his wives and family, there is personal, political and social correspondence with, among others, Clifford Allen, Lord Attlee, A. J. Ayer, the Duke and Duchess of Bedford (1940s), Lord Boothby, Prof. Max Born, Fenner Brockway, colleagues at Cambridge, G. D. H. Cole, Margaret Llewelyn Davies, G. Lowes Dickinson, Lucy Martin Donnelly, Albert Einstein, T. S. Eliot, Dr Simon Flexner, E. M. Forster, the Fabian Society, Michael Foot, Ernest Gellner, Emma Goldman, Florence Halévy, J. L. Hammond, G. H. Hardy, Sir Roy Harrod, Stephen Hobhouse, H. A. Holland, Julian and Juliette Huxley, the Homosexual Law Reform Society, C. E. M. Joad, Ernest Jones, J. M. Keynes, Sir Stephen King-Hall, H. J. Laski, D. H. and Frieda Lawrence, A. Lynch, B. Malinowski, Miles and Lady Constance Malleson, Catherine Marshall, G. E. Moore, E. D. Morel, Gilbert Murray, A. S. Neill, Philip Noel Baker, Dr Victor Purcell, Sir Herbert Read, Eleanor Roosevelt, Ralph Shoenman, Albert Schweitzer, G. B. and Charlotte Shaw, Lord Simon of Wythenshawe, Marie Stopes, Lytton Strachey, C. A. Strong, Arnold and Philip Toynbee, C. P. and G. M. Trevelyan, Beatrice and Sidney

Webb, Wittgenstein, Allan and Mary Wood. The correspondence with A. N. Whitehead, his wife Evelyn and children, 1895–1940s, and with Lady, Ottoline Morrell, her husband Philip and daughter, 1910–30s, is extensive, and grouped separately. Also in a separate grouping are drafts of letters, 1952–66, dictated to Edith, Lady Russell. There is, in addition, a large number of letters from the general public, some 10,000 in all, reflecting his wide-ranging impact on world opinion.

A great deal of correspondence can also be found in other sections of the Archive. There are papers and letters concerning various legal actions with which Russell was involved, especially during World War I and from the 1940s to 1960s. A considerable part of the Archive is devoted to papers and correspondence concerning various social and political organisations and activities in which he was involved – the Liberal Party, Women's Suffrage (including the 1907 by-election), the Union of Democratic Control, the No-Conscription Fellowship, the Labour Party, ILP, 'Save Europe Now', the United Europe Movement, the New Commonwealth, World Government, Congress for Cultural Freedon, Family Planning Association. Finally, there is a great deal of material – articles, letters, handouts, papers – concerning Russell's work for world peace; the 1955 peace initiative (his 'Man's Peril' broadcast of 1954, the Einstein–Russell Declaration and the Scientists' conference of 1955), the Pugwash Movement, CND, the Committee of 100, the Bertrand Russell Peace Foundation, the International War Crimes Commission, the Vietnam Solidarity Campaign, his correspondence with Heads of State.

In addition to this manuscript collection the Archive contains collections of photographs and drawings; tape recordings of interviews, speeches, talks and messages; honours, medals, and personal documents, such as passports and appointment diaries; greetings cards; a vast collection of press cuttings, dating from the end of the nineteenth century and including reviews of most of his works; and a collection of books, articles, pamphlets, typescripts and manuscripts by people in whose work Russell was interested. The original Archive is described in B. Feinberg (ed.), *A Detailed Catalogue of the Archives of Bertrand Russell* (1967). Additions are described in successive issues of *Russell*, bulletin of the Archive.

Russell's varied activities are represented in a number of other collections. The most important of these is that of Lady Ottoline Morrell in the University of Texas, Austin. This contains more than 1900 letters written by Russell, 1911–38, and the latter portion of a private and intimate journal kept by him, 1888–1905. Trinity College, Cambridge, has relevant material, including correspondence with Mrs Robert Trevelyan. King's College, Cambridge, has material, particularly in the J. M. Keynes papers. BLPES has a diary of a visit to Germany in 1895, while the Passfield Collection in BLPES and the Woolf and Kingsley Martin papers in Sussex University Library have further letters. There are letters from Russell in the Marie (Mattingly) Meloney collection, the National Emergency Civil Liberties Committee records and the E. P. Sheehy papers in Columbia University Library; the Coronet Magazine collection and the Laski material in Syracuse University Library; the Benjamin W. Huebsch papers and the Van den Poel literary collection in the Library of Congress; and the H. B. Liveright papers in the University of Pennsylvania Libraries (Philadelphia). Some correspondence with Sir Norman Angell can be found in Ball State University Library, and with Frank Swinnerton in Arkansas University Library. Some Russell letters are in the Bancroft Library, Berkeley, California. There are also letters from Russell in the Emma Goldman collection at the International Institute of Social History.

The Public Record Office has material concerning Russell's activities during World War I, while the BBC archive also has relevant material. The Fabian Society archive at Nuffield College, Oxford, should also be consulted. Various papers concerning the No-Conscription Fellowship are described in *Sources* Vol. 1, pp. 206–7. The Catherine Marshall papers at the Cumbria Record Office are of particular relevance. The Union of Democratic Control collection at Hull University Library may also be consulted (see *Sources* Vol. 1, p. 269). Records of the Campaign for Nuclear Disarmament are in BLPES (*Sources* Vol. 1, pp. 32–3).

Much original material was quoted by Russell in his *Autobiography* (3 vols, 1967–9) while *The Life of Bertrand Russell* by Ronald Clark (1975) has made use of most of the available papers.

RUSSELL OF LIVERPOOL, 1st B
Sir Edward Richard Russell (1834–1920)

Journalist. M.P. (Lib.) Glasgow Bridgeton, 1885–7. Editor, *Liverpool Daily Post*, from 1869.

Liverpool University Library has some 33 letters to Russell from the 5th Earl of Rosebery, with copies of three replies. They cover the period 1888–1901. The 2nd Baron Russell of Liverpool has family and personal material only, and the *Liverpool Daily Post* states that it has no papers whatever concerning the 1st Baron.

RUTHERFORD, 1st B
Sir Ernest Rutherford (1871–1937)

Physicist. Fellow of the Royal Society. Professor of Physics, McGill University, 1898–1907. Professor at Manchester, 1907–19. Cavendish Professor of Experimental Physics and Director of Cavendish Laboratory, Cambridge University, from 1919. Director of Royal Society, Mond Laboratory, Cambridge, from 1936. Professor of Natural Philosophy, Royal Institution. Chairman of Advisory Council of Department of Scientific and Industrial Research from 1930.

Papers are housed in Cambridge University Library. They include correspondence, especially with other scientists; papers on scientific matters; and miscellaneous material, including papers on the Academic Assistance Council. There are nine volumes of facsimile correspondence in the Science Museum Library.

SACHER, Harry (1881–1971)

Journalist and lawyer. Pro-Zionist publicist. On the editorial staff of the *Manchester Guardian*, 1905–9, 1915–19; *Daily News*, 1909–15. Practised at the Bar in Palestine, 1920–30. Member of the Executive, World Zionist Organisation, 1927–31. Director, Marks & Spencer Ltd, 1932–62.

Political papers were deposited in the Central Zionist Archives, Jerusalem. They include reports on meetings between Zionist leaders and officials in the British Government in Palestine and in Britain; Abdullah-Golda meetings; and protocols from the Jewish Agency Executive meetings. Other papers remain in private hands in Britain. Martin Gilbert is using the available papers for a study.

SADLER, Sir Michael Ernest (1861–1943)

Educationalist. Secretary of the Oxford University Extension, 1885–95. Director of Special Inquiries and Reports in the Education Department, 1895–1903. Professor of the History and Administration of Education, Manchester, 1903–11. Vice-Chancellor, Leeds University, 1911–23. Master of University College, Oxford, 1923–34.

The Bodleian Library, Oxford, has a collection of letters, papers and diaries, 1882–1941. The collection includes letters from both Sadler and his wife, and various other correspondents; letters and papers concerning education, 1885–1947, but particularly relating to his work at the Board of Education, 1895–1903; papers relating to the Oxford Preservation Trust, 1925–41; papers and letters relating to the Bodleian, 1924–40. A number of commonplace books, dating from 1899, survive, together with a notebook, 1923, and diaries (with gaps), 1912–42. Correspondence with Laurence Binyon is at the British Library (Add. MS 49997).

Papers relating to Michael Sadleir (1888–1957) publisher and author, and son and biographer of Sir Michael Sadler, are available in the Houghton Library, Harvard University.

SALAMAN, Redcliffe Nathan (1874–1955)

Botanist, expert on the potato. Supporter of Zionist aspirations. Director of the Potato Virus Research Station, Cambridge. Governor, Hebrew University, Jerusalem. Author of works on heredity, and on anthropology of the Jews.

Material concerning the heredity of the Jews, Zionism, and his work on the genetics of the potato, are in Cambridge University Library.

SALEEBY, Caleb Williams (1878–1940)

Eugenicist. Chairman, National Birthrate Commission, 1913–16. Founder (1929) and Chairman, Sunlight League. Author of works on evolution, eugenics, temperance, etc.

No personal papers have been traced.

SALT, Henry Stephens (1851–1939)

Author and humanitarian. Secretary, Humanitarian League, 1891–1920.

No personal collection of papers is known, but the British Library has relevant material, including letters to G. B. Shaw and other papers in the Shaw collection (Add. MS 50549). Correspondence can be found in the Edward Carpenter collection, Sheffield City Libraries, where there is in particular, an extensive correspondence between Carpenter and Salt's wife, Kate. There are also letters in the Fabian Society archive, Nuffield College, Oxford.

SALVIDGE, Sir Archibald Tutton James (1863–1928)

Conservative politician. Leader of Liverpool City Council. President, Liverpool Constitutionalist Association. Chairman, National Association of Conservative and Liberal Unionist Associations, 1913.

The surviving papers of Salvidge are in the care of his grandson, Mr M. A. Nicholson, Keate House, Eton College, Windsor, Berks, SL4 6EN. They consist of some 50 letters, which were almost all used in Stanley Salvidge's *Salvidge of Liverpool* (1934). The 'diary notes' used by Stanley Salvidge no longer appear to survive.

SANSOM, Sir George Bailey (1883–1965)

Specialist in Japanese Studies. Served in Consular posts in Japan from 1904. Commercial Counsellor, British Embassy in Tokyo, 1925–40. Civilian member, Far Eastern War Council, 1941–2. Minister, British Embassy, Washington, 1942–7; British member, Allied Far Eastern Commission, 1946–7. Professor of Japanese Studies, Columbia University, 1947–53, and Director, East Asian Institute, 1949–53. Consultant Professor, Stanford University, from 1955.

St Antony's College, Far East Centre, has a small amount of material from his private papers, including some press cuttings for the inter-war period.

SARA, Henry (1886–1953)

Socialist activist. Founder member of the Trotskyist Left Opposition in Britain.

The Modern Records Centre, University of Warwick Library, has a collection of material (ref. Maitland/Sara papers). This includes correspondence, leaflets, booklets, duplicated documents and press cuttings, chiefly relating to the International Left Opposition and to the national and international socialist movements. There are leaflets on various Trotskyist groups and the Labour Party, ILP and Communist Party; together with discussion documents and letters concerning internal controversies; press cuttings and scrap books on working-class budgets, British Labour history, the Spanish Civil War, the Moscow trials, political activity during World War II, the post-war period, etc.

SAROLEA, Charles (1870–1953)

Academic and editor. First Lecturer and Head of French and Romance Department, Edinburgh University; Professor of French Literature. Belgian consul in Edinburgh from 1901. Founder, editor and proprietor, *Everyman*, 1912–17. War correspondent of the *Daily Chronicle*, 1914. Visiting Professor of Political History, Cairo, 1926–7. Political Adviser to King of Belgium in Brazil and West Africa, 1920.

The papers and correspondence of Sarolea were purchased by Edinburgh University Library in 1954. The collection consists of 234 files, in 81 folio boxes, and covers the years 1897–1952, reflecting the wide range of his interests. Various papers relate to the editorial and business sides of *Everyman*. The editorial papers consist mainly of correspondence between Sarolea, his assistants and contributors. There are also a few manuscripts of articles. The files also contain various letters from correspondents, such as Norman Angell, 1912–14; A. J. Balfour, Hilaire Belloc, 1911–15; G. K. Chesterton, 1916, 1925; G. B. Shaw, H. G. Wells and Rebecca West. The business side is represented by the correspondence of the office with J. M. Dent, publisher, and correspondence and papers relating to financial, legal, advertising and printing matters, plus letters of advice, appreciation and criticism, applications for posts, etc.

Several files relate to Sarolea's university work, including correspondence relating to lectures, university administration, the administration of the French Department, etc. The collection also includes various writings by Sarolea, mostly typescripts with some autograph corrections and including drafts of books, articles, lectures, addresses, and radio talks. Amongst these are articles on Germany, 1914–17; the text of six public lectures on foreign policy, 1917; and papers relating to his controversy with the Duchess of Atholl over Spain, 1938.

There is also a considerable amount of personal and general correspondence. This includes correspondence with publishers, 1909–43; correspondence with prominent individuals and organisations, including W. Rathenau, 1919–21, editors of British papers, the National Constitution Defence Movement, the Scottish–American Association. Sarolea was on close terms with the Belgian Royal Family and there is correspondence with the King and Queen, Belgian Consular correspondence, correspondence about the behaviour of King Leopold in May 1940, after the German invasion, and papers relating to Belgian relief and refugee questions. There is also correspondence with and concerning various foreign countries, including files on Russia containing drafts and correspondence on his books; papers and correspondence on Germany, 1920–40; Spain, 1938–9, 1944–6; Czechoslovakia, 1919–42; Italy, 1928–40; Yugoslavia, 1921–6; Poland, 1913–47; Central Europe, 1921–4. Finally, the collection contains various miscellaneous items, such as personal financial, legal and medical papers, letters of introduction and personalia.

SAUNDERS, George (1859–1922)

Journalist. Berlin correspondent of the *Morning Post*, 1888–97; and of *The Times*, 1897–1908. Paris correspondent of *The Times*, 1908–14. Served in Department of Information and other Government Departments, 1915–20.

Churchill College, Cambridge, has a collection of family material which includes papers and correspondence of George Saunders. There are letters from him to his father, 1870s to 1890s, reflecting the issues of the day as well as dealing with family matters; letters to his mother; to his sister, Margaret, 1880s–1920s; to his wife, 1903–19; to his children 1910–21; and miscellaneous German correspondence, 1920–2. There are also letters to and from Gertrude Saunders, 1893–1922; Margaret Saunders, 1886–1905 (including correspondence with her parents); correspondence of Malcolm Saunders; and other family correspondence, not directly concerning George Saunders. Amongst other papers are George Saunders' memoranda book, 1872–3; notes made on visits to Paris, Glasgow, Vienna, Prague, 1870s; notes on books read; personal notebooks and other appointment diaries; and press cuttings of articles written for *The Times*, 1889–1917.

Reference should also be made to the archives of *The Times*, which contain relevant material, including correspondence.

SCHREINER, Olive (1855–1920)

South African novelist and feminist. Author of *The Story of an African Farm*, and *Women and Labour* (1911), etc.

Papers can be found in the South African Public Library, Cape Town. The surviving letters of · her extensive correspondence with Havelock Ellis are with the University of Texas, Austin. Over 100 letters to Edward Carpenter are in Sheffield City Libraries. Correspondence has been published as *The Letters of Olive Schreiner*, ed. S. C. Cronwright-Schreiner (1924). Ruth First and Ann Scott are preparing a major biography.

SCOTT, Charles Prestwich (1846–1932)

Journalist and editor. Editor, *Manchester Guardian*, 1872–1929. M.P. (Lib.) Leigh, 1895–1906.

The British Library has papers, 1870–1928 (Add. MSS 50901–909). These consist of memoranda and notes on interviews with leading politicians, and some correspondence (two vols). The archives of the *Manchester Guardian*, in John Rylands University Library of Manchester (described in *Sources* Vol. 1, p. 104) contain diaries and miscellaneous papers relating to Scott, from 1870. There is correspondence with G. B. Dibblee, 1891–1905, and with L. T. Hobhouse, 1896–1925. Political diaries cover the period 1911–28. Other papers, 1896–1930, are in Manchester Central Library (ref. MS f. 920 SS 84), and contain letters and articles. Balliol College, Oxford has certain other correspondence.

The Dawson papers in Birmingham University Library contain correspondence, 1905–25, particularly relating to Germany. The Lloyd George papers at the House of Lords Record Office contain correspondence, 1911–29; and there are also letters to Viscount Samuel, 1928–30, in that Library. There are letters to Lord Lothian 1927–30 in the Scottish Record Office.

The Political Diaries of C. P. Scott (ed. Trevor Wilson) were published in 1970.

SCOTT, John William Robertson (1866–1962)

Journalist and author. Worked for *Pall Mall Gazette*, *Westminster Gazette*, *Daily Chronicle*, etc. Editor of *New East* (Japan) during World War I; *The Countryman* thereafter. Member of the Councils of National Education Association, National Society for the Abolition of Cruel Sports, Rationalist Press Association, Liberation Society, etc.

There are a few papers at St Antony's College, Far East Centre, including some Japanese press notices, 1917–20. Correspondence, 1947–56, with Sir Sydney Cockerell is in the British Library (Add. MS 52752) as is correspondence with the Society of Authors, 1909–55 (Add. MSS 56801–02).

SCOTT, William Robert (1868–1940)

Economist. Lecturer in Political Economy, St Andrews, 1899–1914. Professor of Political Economy, Glasgow University, from 1915. President, Royal Economic Society, 1935–7.

Glasgow University Library has seven boxes of papers, chiefly relating to Scott's work on Adam Smith. Some correspondence and manuscripts relate to his other work, mainly from the 1930s. Family papers, including letters to Scott, 1891–1935, and manuscripts, are deposited in the Public Record Office of Northern Ireland. Sturges, *Economists' Papers*, pp. 97–8, mentions these papers, administrative records in the St Andrews University archives, and correspondence in other collections.

SEAMAN, Sir Owen, 1st Bt (1861–1936)

Poet and satirist. On the staff of *Punch* from 1897; editor, 1906–32.

John Adlard made use of unpublished correspondence, diaries and other material for his biography, *Owen Seaman: His Life and Work* (1977). The British Library has correspondence with T. A. Guthrie, 1906–26 (Add. MS 54272) and with the Society of Authors, 1912–35 (Add. MS 56803). There are letters to Douglas Sladen, 1915, concerning recruitment to the army; and letters, 1919–20, about the After Dinner Club. There is further correspondence in the Galsworthy and Edmund Gosse papers.

SEDGWICK, Thomas E. (d. 1929)

Advocate of juvenile emigration.

The Royal Commonwealth Society Library has three albums of 'migration scrapbooks', 1910–14, describing his efforts to promote juvenile migration to the Empire. They contain cuttings, letters, photographs, handbills, reports etc.

SHACKLE, George Lennox Sharman (1903–)

Economist. Served in Admiralty and Cabinet Secretariat, World War II. Reader in Economic Theory, Leeds University, 1950. Brunner Professor of Economic Science, University of Liverpool, 1951–69.

Papers are deposited with Liverpool University Library (the Sydney Jones Library) and a microfilm is retained in the University Archives. The collection includes correspondence on economic theory, his publications and work, both letters received and copies of letters sent by Shackle.

SHARP, Clifford Dyce (1883–1935)

Journalist. Editor of *New Statesman*, 1913–31.

No personal papers are known but relevant material may be found in the Passfield papers at BLPES.

SHAW, George Bernard (1856–1950)

Playwright and socialist publicist. Edited *Fabian Essays* (1889) and wrote numerous tracts on socialism for the Fabian Society. Awarded the Nobel Prize for Literature, 1925.

The British Library has a large collection of papers and correspondence, some 236 volumes, arranged in two series (Add. MSS 50508–743). The first series consists of general correspondence, special correspondence, works by other authors, and photographs relating to Shaw. The general correspondence covers the period 1857–1950. The special correspondence dates chiefly from the 1880s and includes correspondence with Sir George Alexander, 1900–13; William Archer, 1885–1923; Lady Astor, 1930–46; Sir James Barrie; Max Beerbohm, 1898–1935; Annie Besant, 1885–1919; Rutland Boughton, 1912–45; Hon. Sylvia Brett, 1910–14; Pakenham Thomas Beatty, 1878–89; Sir Hall Caine, 1904–28; Mrs Patrick Campbell,

1901–39; Sir Lewis Casson and Sybil Thorndyke, 1925–46; Sir Sydney Cockerell, 1897–1950; Walter Crane, 1885–1904; R. B. Cunninghame Graham, 1888–1913; Charles Charrington and Janet Achurch, 1889–1924; Lord Alfred Douglas, 1931–44; Havelock Ellis, 1888; St John Ervine, 1916–48; Sir Johnston Forbes-Robinson, 1897–1935; Harley Granville-Barker, 1905–43; Lady Gregory, 1909–25; Elinor Huddart, 1878–94 (three volumes); Lord Haldane, 1900–19; Rev. James Hannay, 1908–12; Keir Hardie, 1906–14; Frank Harris, 1898–1924; Austin Harrison, 1910–22; H. M. Hyndman, 1884–1920; Dean W. R. Inge, 1921–50; Frederick Jackson, 1910–14; Augustus John, 1915–44; T. E. Lawrence, 1922–45 (including relevant papers); William Morris, 1884–96; May Morris, 1885–1913; Gilbert Murray, 1900–50; Sydney Olivier, 1887–1937; Mrs Jenny Patterson, 1882–8 (two volumes); Mrs Kate Perugini, 1887–1903; Hesketh Pearson, 1938–44; Marjory Davidson (Mrs Edward Pease), 1888–1946; Sir Arthur Pinero, 1908–17; Sir Horace Plunkett, 1915–20; J. M. Robertson, 1885–1927; Auguste Rodin, 1906–14; G. W. Russell ('AE'), 1914–34; H. S. Salt, 1889–1939 (with papers relating to Salt, 1939–50); W. T. Stead, 1887–1911; Henry Sweet, 1901–11; Sir Herbert Beerbohm Tree, 1892–1913; F. H. Trench, 1908–17; H. G. Wells, 1901–41; Graham Wallas, 1889–1929; Diana Watts, 1923–50; Beatrice and Sidney Webb, 1883–1938; Sir A. E. Wright, 1906–43; Sir Charles Wyndham, 1895–1911; W. B. Yeats, 1901–32; and letters and papers relating to phonetics and spelling reform, 1852–1956 (Add. MS 50554–6); the Fabian Society, 1884–1944 (Add. MS 50557); and letters and memoranda of Shaw's biographers (Professor Archibald Henderson, 1905–46; Demetrius O'Bolger, 1910–22; Dr F. E. Loewenstein, 1947–8.

Works by other authors are chiefly typescripts, and include works by James Bridie, Mrs Rosie Dobbs (sister of Beatrice Webb, consisting of an unpublished autobiography); Harley Granville Barker; Frank Harris; Marie Stopes; and translators of Shaw. There are also some 20 volumes of photographs of Shaw, his family, friends, his plays and productions.

The second series in the British Library includes plays and other writings, lectures, Fabian Society material, notebooks, etc. (Add. MSS 50593–743). The plays are in longhand and typescript, and date from his 'Passion Play', 1878. There are also rehearsal notes, and notebooks on the plays and productions. Nine volumes concern his poems, novels and short stories, 1883–1950; and 21 volumes relate to his critical writings and essays. There are a further 11 volumes on the Fabian Society, including memoranda and other papers relating to the internal affairs of the Fabian Society and its relations with other bodies, 1888–1920; lectures by Shaw given to or arranged by the Fabian Society, 1885–1933; Fabian writings, including prefaces to the *Fabian Essays* 1888–1948; and Fabian tracts and reports by Shaw, 1884–1930. Add. MSS 50691–9 include Shaw's contributions (articles, letters, reviews, etc.) on miscellaneous subjects written for or published in newspapers and periodicals. Add. MSS 50700–705 consist of notes and drafts for lectures and public addresses by Shaw, 1884–1933. There are 13 volumes of autobiographical writings and personal memoranda (Add. MSS 50706–18), and including drafts, notes on Shaw's character as revealed in phrenology, index of travels, 1894–1934, index of articles written, passports, wills, daily lists of correspondence to be dealt with, address books and personalia. In addition some 21 notebooks contain notes on miscellaneous subjects, personal memoranda and drafts of letters and articles etc, 1871 onwards (Add. MSS 50719–39). Finally, there are four volumes of miscellaneous material, including press cuttings (two volumes) and miscellaneous notes and memoranda.

Also at the British Library are letters from Shaw to his wife, Charlotte, 1896–1934 (Add. MSS 46505–7; other correspondence and papers of Charlotte Shaw are Add. MSS 45903–04, 45922). The material includes letters and lettercards written before their marriage, 1896–8; letters written at various dates after marriage, 1912–34; and typewritten copies of the above; Add. MS 56364 relates to the 'forgery' of a newspaper article by Shaw, with letters from him, 1940–5.

The British Library also has the manuscript of an unpublished comedy, 'Why She Should Not', 1950 (Add. MS 48201); and there are letters of Ellen Terry to Shaw on theatrical and personal matters, 1892–1923 (Add. MSS 43800–2, with four further letters at Add. MS 46172G, and copies of Shaw's to her at MS Facs 496). There is correspondence with the

Society of Authors, (Add. MSS 56627–37); and correspondence with Marie Stopes (Add. MS 58493). There is correspondence with Lady Aberconway, 1925–30 (Add. MS 52556); with Sir Sydney Cockerell, 1907–43 (Add. MS 52752).

The Fabian Society archive at Nuffield College, Oxford, has extensive correspondence and papers. BLPES has diaries, 1885–97, in shorthand, together with typescript transcripts by his secretary. There are also appointment diaries, 1877–1950; and correspondence and papers relating to Shaw's publishing operations and personal and domestic expenditure. There are royalty statements, correspondence with publishers, translators, bank statements, papers relating to real estate, bills, etc. Much relevant material can also be found in the Passfield papers at BLPES.

According to the editor of his *Collected Letters*, there is a large collection of manuscript and typescript letters in the T. E. Harley collection at the University of Texas, Austin. This library has some Shaw manuscripts, including personal accounts, 1885–1917, a manuscript in shorthand of *Pygmalion*, and a diary. There are over 300 letters in Boston University Library, Mass., while the Burgunder Collection, Cornell University Library, Ithaca, New York, has a large collection of his letters.

The British Theatre Museum collection has notes on the Theatre Guild, *Aesthetic Science*, and the first production of *The Apple Cart* (1929); correspondence, 1928–49; proof copies of Maurice Colbourne's *The Real Bernard Shaw* (1930) with autograph notes by Shaw.

The Kingsley Martin collection in Sussex University Library has correspondence and five files of papers on Shaw, including his letters to the *New Statesman*, drafts, proofs, letters, notes on Shaw, press cuttings, etc.

Correspondence can be found in the Astor papers at Reading University Library; in collections at King's College, Cambridge; in Edinburgh University Library (the Sarolea papers); in the National Library of Scotland; in the J. H. Lloyd papers in Hull University Library; in the Sir Horace Plunkett papers; in the Sladen papers; and in the Herbert Samuel papers at the House of Lords Record Office. At the International Institute of Social History there is correspondence in the Socialist League archive and with Emma Goldman. There is correspondence in the Rom Landau collection, University of California, Santa Barbara Library; the Ada Rehan papers, University of Pennsylvania Libraries, Philadelphia; the Herman Deutsch collection, the State Historical Society of Wisconsin collections (Madison); the Sir Percy Bunting collection, University of Chicago Library; the W. B. Yeats collection, University of California, Berkeley, Bancroft Library. Columbia University Libraries has correspondence, MSS and documents relating to his speech on 'The Future of Political Science in America', 1933 (107 items, 1933–40)

The University of North Carolina Library, Manuscripts Department, has copies of papers at BLPES, including correspondence with his publishers and letters to Beatrice and Sidney Webb. Relevant material can be found in the correspondence of Mrs Patrick Campbell in Chicago University Library. There is correspondence with Thorvald Solberg in the Library of Congress, and other papers in the Houghton Library, Harvard University.

Various parts of Shaw's correspondence have been published. The major collection is Dan H. Lawrence (ed.), *Collected Letters* (1965), which also describes the fate of some of his correspondence (e.g. Shaw destroyed much family material and letters to Annie Besant). Other collections include *Letters from George Bernard Shaw to Miss Alma Murray*, printed for private circulation (Edinburgh, 1927); *Ellen Terry and Bernard Shaw; a correspondence*, ed. Christopher St John (1931); *Florence Shaw, Bernard Shaw and W. B. Yeats*, ed. Clifford Bax (Dublin, 1941, London, 1946); *Bernard Shaw and Mrs Patrick Campbell*, ed. Alan Dent (1952); *Bernard Shaw's Letters to Granville Barker*, ed. C. B. Purdom (1956); *Advice to a Young Critic. Letters 1894–1928* (1956); *To a Young Actress. The Letters of Bernard Shaw to Molly Tompkins* (1960).

A major biography of Shaw, using all the available sources, is being prepared by Michael Holroyd.

SHEPPARD, Hugh Richard Lawrie (1880–1937)

Churchman and pacifist. Priest from 1905. Vicar, St Martin-in-the-Fields, 1914–27. Dean of Canterbury, 1929–31. Canon of St Pauls, 1934–7. With William Temple founded the Life and Liberty Movement, 1917. Founder of the Peace Pledge Union.

Carolyn Scott, *Dick Sheppard* (1977) uses the available papers. A note on the records of the Peace Pledge Union appears in *Sources* Vol. 1, p. 210. There are letters to Claud Jenkins in Lambeth Palace Library; and letters to Lord Ponsonby of Shulbrede, 1919–37, in the Bodleian Library, Oxford. Correspondence with Laurence Housman has been published, *What Can We Believe? Letters exchanged between Dick Sheppard and Laurence Housman* (1939)

SHEPPARD, Sir John Tresidder (1881–1968)

Classical scholar. Provost, King's College, Cambridge, and Senior Fellow of Eton College, 1933–54.

King's College Library, Cambridge, has a collection of material. It includes correspondence on personal, theatrical and political matters from his family, from friends in the Bloomsbury circles, and from other Kingsmen, including Rupert Brooke, J. M. Keynes, and Lytton Strachey. There are also intermittent diaries, and other material, including papers read by him to societies.

SIEFF, Baron
Israel Moses Sieff (1889–1972)

Businessman. Vice Chairman and Joint Managing Director, Marks & Spencer Ltd, from 1926; Chairman, 1964; President from 1967. Secretary, Zionist Commission, 1918. Vice President, World Jewish Congress, and Chairman, European Executive. Member of the Executive, Jewish Agency. Hon. President, Zionist Federation of Great Britain. Chairman, Political and Economic Planning (PEP), 1931–9; Vice Chairman, 1939–64; then President.

The main collection of his papers, including the more important political material, is with the Central Zionist Archives, Jerusalem. The remaining papers are at the Head Office of Marks & Spencer Ltd, London.
Records of PEP are described in *Sources* Vol. 1, pp. 213–4.

SIMMS, Frederick R. (1863–1944)

Engineer, inventor and entrepreneur. Founder of the Daimler Motor Car Syndicate Ltd, 1893. A founder of the Aero Club of the United Kingdom (now Royal Aero Club) and the Royal Automobile Club.

A collection of papers is deposited in London University Library. The most complete section of the papers consists of the minute and agenda books, correspondence and papers of the Daimler Motor Car Syndicate, 1893–6. Simms acted as consulting engineer to the resulting companies, and in addition to correspondence addressed personally to Simms, to Simms and Co., Consulting Engineers, or to the Motor Carriage Supply Co. Ltd, the papers contain publicity material issued by the Daimler and associated companies, under the direction of Harry J. Lawson. The collection also includes correspondence relating to the foundation of the Aero Club and the Automobile Club, including rules and regulations, memoranda, leaflets etc. There is also correspondence on early Motor Shows, and the military use of motor vehicles, such as the Simms 'Motor Scout', and correspondence with and concerning foreign, especially German, motor vehicle firms.
Further material remains with the Veteran Car Club. The archives of the Royal Automobile Club, 83–5 Pall Mall, London SW1Y 5HW, contain material complementary to that in the Simms collection. Personalia are retained by Simms' daughter. Details are available at the Historical Manuscripts Commission.

SIMON, Kathleen, Viscountess
Kathleen Harvey (d. 1955)

Social Worker. Joint President of the Anti-Slavery Society, 1944–5.

A number of papers were deposited with the Anti-Slavery Society by her son and are now in Rhodes House Library, Oxford. They cover the period 1927–52, and most of these papers are directly connected with her work for the Society, the lectures she gave on slavery, and the articles she wrote. There are a few papers also on Lady Simon's other interests, such as the Zionist movement, the League of Coloured Peoples, Ethiopia, plus some of personal interest. The collection is in four parts: correspondence; notebooks containing lecture notes and notes for her writings; newspaper cuttings; and other papers, relating to the anti-slavery movement and arranged by territory.

The papers of the 1st Viscount Simon (husband) are in the possession of the present Viscount and are described in Hazlehurst and Woodland, pp. 131–2. Papers of the Anti-Slavery Society are described in *Sources* Vol. 1, pp. 9–10.

SIMON, Sir Leon (1881–1965)

Public Servant. Member of Zionist Commission to Palestine, 1918. Director of Telegraphs and Telephones, GPO, 1931–5; Director of Savings, 1935–44. Member of Commission of Inquiry into Jewish Education in Palestine, 1945–6. Chairman, Executive Council of the Hebrew University, Jerusalem, 1946–9; and of its Board of Governors, 1949–50. President of the Israel Post Office Bank, 1950–3. Writer on Jewish and Zionist topics.

His diary of the 1918 Zionist Commission is in the Hebrew University Library. Other relevant correspondence is believed to be in the Sacher papers. More details may be available in the findings of the British Academy's Anglo-Palestinian Archives Project.

SIMON, (William) Glyn Hughes (1903–72)

Ecclesiastic. Priest from 1928. Dean of Llandaff, 1948–54. Bishop of Swansea and Brecon, 1954–7; Llandaff, 1957–71. Archbishop of Wales, 1968–71.

The papers are deposited in the National Library of Wales, under a 30-year closure.

SINNETT, Alfred Percy (1840–1921)

Journalist and Theosophist.

Sinnett's correspondence and papers in connection with the Theosophical Movement (1880–90) are available at the British Library (Add. MSS 45284–9). This material formed the basis of his published works on theosophy. The letters were published as A. T. Barker (ed.), *The Mahatma Letters to A. P. Sinnett* (1923) and *The Letters of H. P. Blavatsky to A. P. Sinnett* (1925). Another edition (ed. T. C. Humphreys and E. Benjamin), *The Mahatma Letters*, was published in Madras in 1962.

SLADEN, Douglas Brooke Wheelton (1856–1947)

Popular novelist, journalist and writer. First Professor of History, Sydney University. Editor of *Who's Who*, 1897–9; *The Green Book*, 1910–11.

Papers are preserved by Richmond Borough Libraries, The Green, Richmond, Surrey. They consist of his personal, literary and business manuscripts, which consist of 74 volumes of wet-copy letterbooks, into which have been stuck Sladen's correspondence, drafts of books, mementoes and miscellanea. There is personal, literary and general correspondence, 1888–1920, with a wide range of literary personalities, including Rider Haggard, Conan Doyle, Walter Besant, Marie Corelli, Hall Caine, etc., but also left-wing journalists such as Robert Blatchford and

H. M. Hyndman. There is correspondence about the Vagabonds and Authors' Clubs, 1893–1904, the Argonauts' Club, 1897–8, the After Dinner Club, the Recruiting Bands, 1915; and with his literary agents; and material on various books and projects, 1888–1918.

SLOTKI, Israel Wolf (1884–1973)

Hebraic educationalist. Director of Education, Manchester Central Board for Hebrew Education. Principal, Manchester Talmud Torah Schools, 1911–50. Hon. Superintendent of Hebrew in Manchester and Salford County Schools, 1912–50. Manchester Editor of the *Jewish Guardian*, 1919–31.

Papers concerning his published work and research are in Manchester Central Library, at present uncatalogued.

SMITH, Arthur Lionel (1850–1924)

Historian. Master of Balliol College, Oxford, from 1916. Associated with the Workers' Educational Association.

Papers are at Balliol College, Oxford. Records of the WEA are described in *Sources* Vol. 1, p. 286.

SMITH, Goldwin (1823–1910)

Historian, journalist and controversialist. Regius Professor of Modern History, Oxford, 1858–66. Professor of History, Cornell University, Ithaca, New York, 1868. Journalist in Toronto from 1871.

Cornell University Library has a collection of correspondence and other papers, mainly concerned with English, Canadian and American political questions. Subjects covered include Canadian–American Union, free trade v protection, party problems, Irish Home Rule, Imperialism, the yellow press, women's suffrage, the Jew in modern society, socialism and labour questions. Correspondents include C. F. Adams, the Duke of Argyll, Matthew Arnold, Ashbourne, W. J. Ashley, A. H. Beesley, John Bright, James Bryce, Joseph Chamberlain, A. V. Dicey, Sir Charles Dilke, E. A. Freeman, Lord Lansdowne, Lords Minto, Morley and Peel, Horace Plunkett, Lord Rosebery, James Strachey, G. O. Trevelyan, Viscount Wolseley. Cornell has further correspondence in the A. D. White collection.

A collection of papers relating to his work in Canada is in the University of Toronto. Letters to James Bryce concerning politics and public life in Canada are in the Bodleian Library. There is correspondence in the Cobden papers (Add. MS 43665); the Grey of Howick, J. E. Thorold Rogers, Escott, and Ashbourne papers. There is correspondence in the W. B. Cockran collection, New York Public Library; and the Edwin Palmer papers, Honnold Library, Claremont, California.

His *Reminiscences* were published in 1911 and *Correspondence* in 1913.

SMITH, Norman Kemp (1872–1958)

Philosopher. Lecturer in Glasgow University, 1897–1906. Professor of Psychology, Princeton, 1906. Served in Government Information Department, 1916–18. Professor of Logic and Metaphysics, Edinburgh University, 1919–45.

Letters, notebooks and papers, 1908–57, are preserved in Edinburgh University Library. There are some 302 letters, from correspondents such as Henri Bergson, Max Born, Bernard Bosanquet, W .M .Dixon, William James, Friedrich von Hügel, Sir Henry Jones, J. H. Muirhead, A. S. Pringle-Pattison, W. R. Sorley, A. N. Whitehead, Edmund Wilson and Woodrow Wilson. There are 16 notebooks of philosophical lectures, etc., and the collection is completed by miscellaneous papers, offprints, etc.

SMITHELLS, Arthur (1860–1939)

Scientist. Fellow of the Royal Society. Professor of Chemistry, Leeds University, 1885–1923. Director, Salters' Institute of Industrial Chemistry from 1923. President of the Institute of Chemistry, 1927–30. Chief Chemical Adviser, GHQ, Home Forces, 1916–19. Encouraged better training of chemists. In later life, he was concerned to arouse public opinion about the dangers of chemical .warfare.

Leeds University Library has a collection of papers, including personal material, printed materials, and miscellaneous items.

SOLLY, Henry (1813–1903)

Social reformer; sponsored workmen's education. Founder of the Workingmen's Club and Institute Union.

BLPES has 18 volumes of correspondence and papers which cover a wide range of interests. Papers on education include material concerning the Work Men's Social Educational League, the London Artizans' Club and Institute, the Trades Guild of Learning, the Artizans' Institute and the Artizans' Technical Association. Other material concerns ethics, morality and religion; material on social issues, including housing and land, the Society for Promoting Industrial Villages, the Villa and Cottage Homes General Land and Building Company, the London Association for the Prevention of Pauperism and Crime, the Charity Organisation Society and the 'Autobiography of John Bebbington'. A number of papers concern Labour issues, and there is material concerning the Labour Publications with which Solly was involved; and there are papers on the Working Men's Club and Institute Union. Other material concerns politics and temperance issues.

In addition there are personal papers and material on his printed works. Persons and topics referred to include the Addiscombe Liberal and Radical Club, the Alexandra Park and Palace Company, T. G. Anson, 2nd Earl of Lichfield, the Atlas Club, John Bebbington, Thomas Burt, the Charity Organisation Society, Thomas Fardon, Friends of Co-operative Production, James Hole, George Jacob Holyoake, George Howell, the *Inquirer*, Sir J. R. Seeley, Social Purity Alliance, Society of Christian Disciples, Samuel Morley, C. G. Lyttelton, and the 8th Viscount Cobham.

SORABJI, Cornelia (1867–1954)

Indian feminist. Lady Assistant to the Court of Wards in Bengal, Bihar, Orissa and Assam, 1910–22.

The India Office Library has a collection of papers concerning all aspects of her life and career, including three boxes of her letters, 1916–29, to Elena, Lady Richmond. The papers reflect her hostility to Gandhi and the Independence Movement, and also cover her promotion of infant welfare, maternity and district nursing in India.

SOSKICE, David (1869–1943)

Russian emigré. An active member of the Society of Friends of Russian Freedom (founded 1890).

The House of Lords Record Office has a collection of Soskice family papers. There is miscellaneous printed and manuscript material, including financial papers of the Soskice and Madox Brown families; a file of correspondence and papers on David Soskice's investments; miscellaneous notebooks in Russian containing Soskice's notes on Russian history and economics; a book of early twentieth-century press cuttings from the Russian press, c. 1910–20; five notebooks of Juliet Soskice recording her experiences in Russia and her hatred of Bolshevism. There is extensive literary and personal correspondence including letters from

E. S. Alderton, Asherley Johns, W. E. Ayrton, Karl Blind, H. N. Brailsford, Jane Cobden Unwin, R. Donald, Eric Drummond, Constance Garnett, J. F. Green, William Heinemann, J. A. Hobson, George Howard, H. W. Lee, G. H. Perris, Aylmer Maude, C. P. Scott, Donald Murray, Gilbert Murray, H. W. Nevinson, Robert Bell, J. L. Garvin, F. W. Pethick-Lawrence, Lord Phillimore, Sir F. Pollock, J. M. Robertson, Charles Rowley, A. M. Scott, G. M. Trevelyan, Robert Spence Watson, and Lucien Wolf. There are also draft articles and notes, mainly on Russian history and politics. There are papers on the situation of Jews in Russia, 1914–17, material on the Kerensky government, his views on Bolshevism. Additionally, there are 40 bundles of Soskice's correspondence in Russian, largely with his mother and relatives and friends; and there is personal correspondence with his wife and family in English.

SPARKES, Malcolm (1882–1933)

Quaker businessman. Involved in the Guild Socialist Movement during and after World War I; sponsored the establishment of Building Guilds.

An MS biography compiled by his wife entitled 'Malcolm Sparkes – Constructive Pacifist', together with correspondence and other items are preserved at Friends' House Library, London, and a microfilm of this material is in Hull University Library.

SPARROW, Walter Shaw (d. 1940)

Writer, particularly on art and architecture. Editor of the Art and Life Library.

The British Library has six volumes of papers relating to his *The Fifth Army in March 1918* (Add. MSS 48203–8). They include correspondence with F. S. Oliver and General Sir H. Gough; general correspondence; various accounts of the engagements; notes; a manuscript of the book; and maps.

SPENDER, John Alfred (1862–1942)

Journalist and author. Editor of the *Westminster Gazette*, 1896–1922. Member of the Royal Commission on Divorce and Matrimonial Causes and of the Royal Commission on the Private Manufacture of Armaments. Member of the Special Mission to Egypt, 1919–20.

The British Library has a collection of correspondence and papers (Add. MSS 46386–94). This includes correspondence of Spender with Private Secretaries to the Monarch (Francis Knollys, Stamfordham, etc.); Professor M. Temperley's questionnaire concerning the Cabinet's declaration of war in 1914, with relevant documents; letters to Spender from W. Mackenzie King, the Canadian Prime Minister, 1931–7; correspondence with 5th Lord Rosebery, including letters to Spender's wife, Mary, 1895–1927; and correspondence with other Prime Ministers. The correspondence and material relating to Campbell-Bannerman includes Spender's autograph memorandum on the formation of the 1905 Government, and papers relating to his *Life* of Campbell-Bannerman, together with letters from Queen Victoria used in the *Life*, and some copies of Campbell-Bannerman's letters to Sir J. B. Smith.The correspondence with Asquith and his wife covers the period 1897–1927. There is also correspondence with Lloyd George, J. R. MacDonald, Winston Churchill, and Louis Botha. Other correspondents include Grey of Falloden (together with drafts of Grey's *Twenty-five years*), Lord Fitzmaurice, Foreign Under-Secretary, 1905–8; Lord Fisher, 1908–19; and R. B. Haldane, 1899–1919. There are also four volumes of general correspondence, 1886–1941. This material was used in Spender's *Life, Journalism and Politics* (1927) and *Fifty Years of Europe* (1933) and was also used by H. W. Harris in his biography, *J. A. Spender* (1946).

Correspondence can be found in the Samuel collection (1902–40), the Lothian papers (1934–40), and in the Asquith, Chamberlain and W. H. Dawson collections.

SPRIGG, Sir John Gordon (1830-1913)

Imperialist. Premier of Cape Colony, 1878-81, 1886-90, 1896-8, 1900-04.

Personal and political papers, including correspondence from Joseph Chamberlain, Sir Bartle Frere, Lord Grey, Lord Milner, Cecil Rhodes, Lord Wolseley, etc., are in the Cory Library for Historical Research, Rhodes University, Grahamstown, South Africa.
Correspondence with Joseph Chamberlain, 1881-98, is in Birmingham University Library. The P. L. Gell collection has a memorandum recounting Milner's opinion of Sprigg.

STACY, Enid (1868-1903)

Socialist publicist and lecturer. Campaigner for women's suffrage.

A collection of letters, diaries and papers is currently in the care of Angela Tuckett (niece), 5 Liddington Street, Swindon, Wilts, who is using them for a biography of her aunt. They are owned by Mr Gerard Widdrington of Toronto, son of Enid Stacy. There is a group of letters written to her by Ramsay MacDonald, 1894-5, referring to Fabian Society and ILP matters. There are also letters from her husband Canon Widdrington to Enid Stacy while she was in the USA on a lecture tour in 1902; letters about the Starnthwaite Colony row involving the Rev. H. Mills, Dan Irving and Katherine Bruce Glasier as well as Enid Stacy; letters of a personal nature; and letters of condolence on her early death. The collection also includes a series of pocket diaries. The fullest are for the years 1894-5, with a few entries in later years. The entries include notes on her lectures, the name of the lecture organiser and her hostess, and occasionally some words of description.

STALLYBRASS, William Teulon Swan (1883-1948)

Academic. Principal of Brasenose College, Oxford, from 1936. Vice-Chancellor, Oxford University, from 1947. Hon. Secretary, Oxford branch of League of Nations Union, 1918-20. Member of Inter-Varsity Council for Higher Education in the Colonies.

Stallybrass's notebooks are at Brasenose College, Oxford.

STAMP, Sir (Laurence) Dudley (1898-1966)

Geographer. Professor of Geology and Geography, Rangoon University, 1923-6. Sir Ernest Cassel Reader in Economic Geography, London University, 1926-45. Professor of Social Geography, London University, at London School 'of Economics, 1948-58. From 1936 to 1944 he directed the compilation and publication of the report of the Land Utilisation Survey of Great Britain. Chief Adviser to the Ministry of Agriculture on Rural Land Utilisation, 1942-55. Director of the World Land-Use Survey (International Geographical Union).

Sussex University Library has a collection of papers, amounting to some 53 boxes. Amongst the material are addresses; papers on Africa; Agricultural Land Service; Allied Post-War Requirements Bureau; articles and reviews, 1933-66; books by Dudley Stamp; papers relating to the British Association Committee on Inland Water Survey, Burma, Canada, Colleges of Estate Management, conferences; correspondence and early notes; material on the Council for the Preservation of Rural England, the International Geographical Union, Iraq, Land Transfer Committee, the Land Utilisation Survey, London Planning Group; personalia and press cuttings, reports and plans, reviews; papers on Romania, the Royal Commission on Common Land, 1955-8, Rural Land Utilisation, UNESCO.

STARK, Dame Freya Madeline

Writer and traveller. In government Service in Middle East and elsewhere, 1939-45. Author of works on Arabia, etc.

The Middle East Centre, St Antony's College, Oxford, has various letters, including correspondence with Elizabeth Monroe, 1943–4, on a visit to the USA to combat Zionist propaganda and state the British case on Palestine.

The Public Record Office has various relevant papers. Correspondence, 1949, can be found in the W. P. Ker papers.

STEAD, William Thomas (1849–1912)

Journalist and author. Editor, Darlington *Northern Echo*, 1871–80, *Pall Mall Gazette*, 1883–9. Founder and editor, *Review of Reviews*, from 1891. Author of various propagandist works, including *Maiden Tribute of Modern Babylon* (1885).

Papers are believed to survive with his grandson, Mr W. K. Stead, but no information on these was available. The Fawcett Library has a file of his correspondence, chiefly with Mrs Fawcett, in its autograph collection. The Bodleian Library, Oxford, has a group of some 140 letters, 1877–1908, addressed to Olga Novikoff (Ms Eng. Misc. D. 182).

Correspondence can be found in a number of other collections. At the British Library there is correspondence with G. B. Shaw, 1887–1911 (Add. MS 50549) and with John Burns, 1891–1910 (Add. MS 46287). The George Holyoake papers contain correspondence, 1899–1903, while further letters can be found in the papers of Sir Oliver Lodge. The Samuel papers at the House of Lords Record Office contain letters, 1901–12, and there are letters to the 3rd Earl Grey in the Grey of Howick papers; to Thomas Huxley in the Huxley papers; and to Viscount Wolseley at Hove Central Library. The Edward Carpenter collection with Sheffield City Libraries contains a few items, and some letters from Stead can also be found in the Labour Party archive, Transport House.

J. W. R. Scott, *The Life and Death of a Newspaper* (1952) quotes from a diary.

STEBBING, William (d. 1926)

Journalist and author. On staff of *The Times*, as journalist, leader-writer and deputy to the editor.

Several volumes of press cuttings from *The Times*, plus an annotated copy of his biography of Sir Walter Ralegh and an envelope of material collected by Stebbing relating to Ralegh are in the London Library. Volumes of letters received by Stebbing when he worked on *The Times* were sold by the London Library. Reference should be made to the archives of *The Times*.

STEED, Henry Wickham (1871–1956)

Journalist. Foreign Editor of *The Times*, 1914–19. Editor, 1919–22. Lecturer on Central European History, King's College, London, 1925–38. Proprietor and editor, *Review of Reviews*, 1923–30. Broadcaster on Overseas Affairs, BBC, 1937–47.

Papers are held by Miss Joan Stevenson, 4, Priory Mansions, Drayton Gardens, London SW 10. Further material, including correspondence, is in the archives of *The Times*. The British Library has correspondence with Lord Cecil (Add. MS 51156).

STEIN, Leonard Jacques (1887–1974)

Lawyer and pro-Zionist publicist. He served on the political staff of the military administration in Palestine, 1918–20. Political Secretary, World Zionist Organisation, 1920–9. Hon. Legal Adviser, Jewish Agency for Palestine, 1929–39; represented the Jewish Agency before the 1937 Peel Commission. Vice President Anglo-Jewish Association, 1939–49. President, Jewish Historical Society, 1964–5. Author of *The Balfour Declaration* (1961) and joint editor of 2 vols of *Letters and Papers of Chaim Weizmann*.

Papers concerning his political activity are in the Central Zionist Archives, Jerusalem. The transcript of an interview about his career is in the Oral History Archive, Institute for Contemporary Jewry, Hebrew University, Jerusalem.

Personal papers, including correspondence, diaries and material collected for his historical works are held by the Bodleian Library, Oxford. The material includes a large collection of papers concerning Chaim Weizmann (copies of correspondence, notes, diaries, etc.) and a large accumulation of material used in the preparation of his definitive work on *The Balfour Declaration*. There is a diary of Stein's visit to Palestine, 1909, papers concerning the naturalisation controversy, 1919, the Peel Commission, attitudes to the Palestine question in the 1940s, etc. plus correspondence concerning his publishing activities and the range of his interests.

STENTON, Sir Frank Merry (1880–1967)

Historian. Professor of Modern History, Reading, 1912–46. Deputy Vice-Chancellor, 1934–46. Vice-Chancellor, 1946–50.

Reading University Library has papers and correspondence. They include family papers, concerning Sir Frank's parents; and personal papers of Sir Frank and Doris Mary Stenton, including correspondence, 1898–1971, certificates and diplomas, 1880–1959, diaries and journals, 1892–1965, financial papers, 1927–70, and photographs. The historical papers include original documents (deeds, charters, wills, letters, etc.), transcripts, notes for lectures, books and articles, drafts of publications, speeches, radio scripts, etc., proofs of books and articles, reviews. Other papers include committee papers, 1918–70, and press cuttings, notebooks, brochures, 1880–1970.

STEPHEN, Sir George, 1st Bt, see MOUNT STEPHEN, 1st B

STOCKS, Baroness
Mary Danvers Stocks (1891–1975)

Author and broadcaster. Lectured on economics from 1911. General Secretary, London Council of Social Service, 1938–9. Principal of Westfield College, London. 1939–51.

Mrs Ann Patterson (daughter), 42 Campden Hill Square, London W8, states that her mother did not make a habit of retaining many papers. Letters from Lady Stocks can be found in the Marie Stopes papers at the British Library.

STOPES, Marie Carmichael (d. 1958)

Birth control pioneer. Founded Mothers' Clinic for Constructive Birth Control, 1921. President, Society for Constructive Birth Control and Racial Progress. Author of numerous works on contraception, etc.

The British Library has a large collection of correspondence and papers (Add. MSS 58447–770). Add. MSS 58447–462 consist of family correspondence and papers. There is a diary of her father, 1880; correspondence of Henry Stopes with his daughters, 1882–1902; correspondence of Mrs Charlotte Carmichael Stopes with her daughters, 1887–1928; a diary of Mrs Stopes relating to Marie, 1880–6; letters to Mrs Stopes from Constance Wilde and Oscar Wilde, as editor of *Woman's World*, 1888–90; correspondence of Marie with her sister Winifred, 1897–1923; correspondence of Marie Stopes with her husband, Humphrey Verdon Roe, 1917–49; correspondence of Marie Stopes with her son, Dr Harry Stopes-Roe and his wife, 1940–56; and general correspondence , 1915–47. Various other correspondence concerns Marie Stopes' school and university career, 1893–1920, scientific correspondence from c. 1900–55, with Professor F. W. Oliver, Henry Woodword, Professor K. Soebel, Dukinfield Henry Scott, 1905–34, Charles Gordon Hewitt, 1907–14, Sir Julian Huxley, 1929–49, and many others. Literary correspondents include Aylmer Maude, 1912–42, George Bernard Shaw, 1916–52, Lord Alfred Douglas, 1938–54, H. G. Wells, 1915–45, Israel Zangwill, Arnold Bennett, Austin Harrison, 1919–28, E. M. Forster, 1940–57, the Society of Authors, and there are letters to publishers, newspapers, the BBC, and others such as George Bedborough, 1918–40 (Add. MSS 58532–4), Lady Stocks, 1923–56. There are agenda, evidence, etc., on the Cinema Commission of Enquiry sponsored by the National Council of Public Morals, 1916–17; and papers of the National Birth Rate Commission, 1918–21. Church correspondents include the Rev. Sir James Marchant, 1917–50, Dean Inge,.1918–53, Canon Percy Dearmer, correspondence relating to a questionnaire to Anglican clergy, 1920–4 etc. Political correspondents include Lord Beaverbrook, 1919–56; Lady Astor, 1935–53; Lord and.Lady Pethick-Lawrence, 1921–54, 2nd Lord Russell, 1921–31; Bertrand and Dora Russell, 1922–54, the 12th Duke of Bedford, 1924–52, Sir Richard Acland, 1930–47. There is also a considerable correspondence with doctors, including Havelock Ellis, 1915–39 (Add. MS 58564), Norman Haire, 1921–34 (Add. MS 58567) and others, in Britain, America, Europe and the empire.

Various papers relate to the Society for Constructive Birth Control and Racial Progress, and to clinics. There are agenda, minutes, accounts, correspondence and miscellaneous papers of the Society, and the Mother's Clinic, London 1921–58; and papers relating to the Aberdeen Clinic and Mrs Margaret Rae, nurse, 1934–50; the Belfast Clinic, 1936–47; the Caravan Clinic, 1926–33; the Cardiff Clinic, 1937–47; the Leeds Clinic, 1923–41; the Swansea Clinic, 1936–47; the Women's Welfare Clinic, Wolverhampton, the Norwich Mother's Clinic and the Royal Institute of Public Health. There is also an extensive correspondence with the manufacturers and suppliers of contraceptives, 1920–57. Other papers and correspondence relate to societies with which Marie Stopes had contact, including the National Birth Control Association, 1930–40; the Eugenics Society, including correspondence with Dr C. P. Blacker as secretary, 1920–30, 1931–56 (Add. MSS 58644–5). Some 23 volumes contain papers relating to legal cases into which Marie Stopes was drawn, 1914–52. Other correspondence includes letters from persons requesting advice on sexual matters, 1918–58 (reserved until A.D. 2008); and there are some 58 volumes of general correspondence, 1880–1958. Amongst the remaining papers are appointment diaries, and fragmentary diaries and autobiographical memoranda, 1903–53; miscellaneous memoranda; and photographs, 1919–39.

The Society of Authors archive, also in the British Library, contains further correspondence, 1909–57 (Add. MSS 56823–4). At Hull University Library papers presented by the Marie Stopes Memorial Foundation include letters to Thomas Joseph Haslam and Mrs Anne M. Haslam, relating to work for birth control and women's suffrage, and letters to Marie Stopes. Some 18 letters from Marie Stopes to F. J. Kitchin, 1906–20, are in the Institute of Geological Science.

The biography by Ruth Hall (1977) makes use of the available papers.

STRACHEY, Joan Pernell (1876–1951)

Principal of Newnham College, Cambridge, 1923–41.

Certain material deposited in the Fawcett Library includes literary papers and lecture notes, and papers and correspondence relating to Newnham.

STRACHEY, John St Loe (1860–1927)

Journalist..A Liberal Unionist from 1886; co-editor of the party paper. Contributor to the *Spectator* from 1887. Editor, *Cornhill Magazine*, 1896–7. Editor and proprietor of the *Spectator*, 1898–1925.

A collection of papers, formerly deposited in the Beaverbrook Library is now housed in the House of Lords Record Office. Although a relatively small collection (some 41 boxes), the

Strachey papers provide an excellent insight into the political and social atmosphere of British public life, particularly within the Conservative Party, from 1885–1927. The collection has ben arranged into five sections. The first (arranged alphabetically by name of correspondent) consists of correspondence between Strachey and prominent politicians on topics ranging from the situation in Ireland and the role of the Unionist Party to the budget debate of 1909 and the Parliament Act of 1911, from the fight against Socialism to plans for strengthening imperial ties. There are letters from all Prime Ministers, 1902–27, but Unionist politicians (e.g. Chamberlain, Carson and Craigavon) are most prominently represented. The second section, 'Political–General', supplements the previous section. Correspondents include journalists, politicians, government officials, religious leaders, and the major political events, 1885–1927, are fully represented. Three boxes relating to America, 1899–1927, include correspondence with President Theodore Roosevelt. The third section, 'Social–General', consists largely of invitations and responses. Herbert Warren, Principal of Magdalen College, Oxford, is well represented in this group of papers. A fourth section covers Strachey's correspondence with professional writers, including Joseph Conrad, Aldous Huxley, Rudyard Kipling and J. A. Symonds (his uncle). Three boxes contain correspondence with other journalists, editors and publishers concerning articles in the *Spectator* and Strachey's own books. A fifth section comprises four boxes of Strachey's own articles, and some of the drafts. A final section concerns family correspondence, the majority of which is with his brother Harry, with whom he corresponded on a wide range of matters. Further correspondence can be found in the Londonderry, Samuel, Sladen, Edward Carson and Earl Roberts papers.

STRACHEY, Lytton (1880–1932)

Author; biographer.

Correspondence of Lytton and James Strachey has been purchased by the British Library.

STRACHEY, Philippa (1872–1968)

Feminist. Hon. Secretary of the London and National Society for Women's Service, later the Fawcett Society. A governor of Bedford College, London.

The Fawcett Library has full records of the Society and its predecessor organisations (described in *Sources* Vol. 1, pp. 280–1). Amongst these are papers of Philippa Strachey, including correspondence and papers, 1936–48.

STREATFEILD, Lucy Anne Evelyn (d. 1950)

Civil Servant; Senior Inspector of Factories. Member, War Office Commission of Inquiry on Concentration Camps during South African war. Member, Royal Commission on the Civil Service. First Woman Organising Officer, National Health Insurance Commission.

The Modern Records Centre, University of Warwick Library, has copies of papers, the originals of which are in the care of Mr Martin Wright, Director of the Howard League for Penal Reform. The copied material includes business diaries as Inspector of Factories, 1893–7, together with cuttings and notes contained in these; a file of cuttings and ephemera relating to conditions of employment, and covering subjects such as lead poisoning in potteries, 'phossy jaw' in match factories, laundries, women's suffrage, sweated industry and Irish outworks. There is a series of files of correspondence and related papers concerning the Boer War Concentration Camp Commission, plus a scrapbook of cuttings, 1901–2, transcripts of letters from Lucy Deane to her sister, 1901, and manuscript notes on the situation in South Africa. Correspondence and papers also survive relating to World War I.

STUART, Sir Campbell (1885–1972)

Civil servant. Served in Washington, 1917. Deputy Director of Propaganda in Enemy Countries, 1918. Managing editor, *Daily Mail*, 1921. Director of *The Times*, 1919–60. Managing Director, 1920–4. Chairman, Imperial Communications Advisory Committee, and its successor, the Commonwealth Communications Council, 1933–45. Director of Propaganda in Enemy Countries, 1939–40.

Papers relating to the Board and Commonwealth communications are deposited with the Royal Commonwealth Society Library, including memoranda, reports and correspondence.

The archives of *The Times* contain papers concerning his work for that newspaper, 1910–60. Reference should also be made to the Northcliffe papers in the British Library.

STUART, Sir Louis (1870–1949)

Served in Indian Civil Service from 1891. Chief Judge of Oudh Chief Court, 1925–30. Hon. Secretary, Indian Empire Society, and editor, *Indian Empire Review*, from 1932.

The Bodleian Library, Oxford, has a collection of papers, 1922–49, the greater part relating to Stuart's work in England and for the Indian Empire Society. The material includes correspondence relating to the Indian Empire Society, 1930–48; letters from Lord Sydenham to Stuart, 1931–3; and correspondence from various notables, including Wedgwood· Benn, Sir J. M. Clay, Lord Croft, Curtis Brown, Sir L. Gammans, Lord Gretton, the Duke of Devonshire, Lord Rothermere, Sir A. W. F. Knox, Sir H. V. Lovett and the Marquess of Zetland. Amongst other papers are summaries of press messages from Burma and India, 1941–4; typescript notes and memoranda; miscellaneous papers on various aspects of Indian affairs; material relating to Indian Pensioners, and to the Sir Michael O'Dwyer Memorial Fund; and notes on his various judgments during his legal career.

SWAFFER, Hannen (1879–1962)

Journalist and dramatic critic. On the staff of the *Daily Herald* from 1931. Edited the *Weekly Despatch* and *The People*.

Hannen Swaffer's papers were used by Tom Driberg (later Lord Bradwell) for a biography. They were still in his care at the time of his death in 1976. Enquiries should be directed to his literary executors, David Higham Associates. Copyright belongs to Dr Richard Rathbone, School of Oriental and African Studies, London.

SWANWICK, Helena Maria (1864–1939)

Feminist journalist and author. First editor of *The Common Cause*. President, Women's International League (British Section).

No personal papers are known but records of the Women's International League, in BLPES, are relevant. They are described in *Sources* Vol. 1, p. 278.

Some 12 letters, 1935–9, are in the Ponsonby of Shulbrede papers, Bodleian Library, Oxford.

TALBOT, Edward Keble (1877–1949)

Member of the Community of the Resurrection from 1906; its Superior, 1922–40.

The Borthwick Institute of Historical Research, York, has a small collection of material formerly at the Community of the Resurrection. This includes a small amount of personal material (reminiscences, school records, his Crockford entry), a memoir of the Community, letters from Brendan Bracken concerning an offer of a bishopric; information about the Community and articles by Talbot; occasional letters concerning the Community, Reunion, Cosmo Gordon Lang, Prayer Book Reform, Church Schools, the General Strike. Additionally, there are copies of addresses, notes on 'The Community of Prayer' and notes on Retreats, various books read and lectures attended.

TALBOT, Edward Stuart (1844–1934)

Theologian and Churchman. Warden, Keble College, Oxford, 1870–1888. Vicar of Leeds, 1889–95. Bishop of Rochester, 1895–1905; of Southwark, 1905–11; of Winchester, 1911–23.

Lambeth Palace Library has correspondence, 1917–19, and correspondence, 1881–1928, can be found in the Selborne papers at the Bodleian Library, Oxford.

TAWNEY, Richard Henry (1880–1962)

Historian and Christian Socialist. Tutor for Tutorial Classes Committee of Oxford University, 1908–14. Member of the Executive, Workers' Educational Association, 1905–47; President, 1928–44. Director of Ratan Tata Foundation, University of London, 1913–14. Member of Coal Industry Commission, 1919. Professor of Economic History, University of London (London School of Economics), 1931–49.

Papers are preserved at BLPES. They include Tawney's lectures on Economic History, 1785–1800, given at the London School of Economics; lectures given in Bristol, Oxford and Chicago, Denmark and Sweden; drafts of chapters for his book on Cranfield; notes and talks on the French Revolution, given 1910–13; notes for classes or lectures on nineteenth-century economic history; syllabuses and bibliographies for his LSE course on the economic history of the great powers in the nineteenth century; lectures on nineteenth-century agriculture; notes on early nineteenth-century reform movements, and hand-loom weavers; public lectures given in Chicago, 1939, on democracy and the current political situation; notes and speeches on education, chiefly for the WEA, c. 1930–40; a paper by G. D. H. Cole, 'Thoughts for the Nuffield College Survey Education Committee', Mar 1942; various lectures given in the USA, 1941–2, and lectures given in the USA on the Labour Government, 1946; lectures on education, given to the New Education Fellowship, 1934, and in Cambridge, 1935; speeches on various occasions, chiefly on education; correspondence and other papers concerning education, especially the WEA and the policy of the Labour Party, education and post-war reconstruction, etc. There are letters from Morgan Phillips, H. E. Clay and others on educational matters. Another group of papers concerns the Webbs, and in particular Tawney's proposed biography of Sidney Webb. There are letters from Bishop Bell, Sir A. Carr-Saunders, Margaret Cole, R. H. Dobbs, J. L. Hammond, Stephen Hobhouse, Storm Jameson, F .J .Kenyon, Harold Laski, H. M. Pelling, Lady Simon, Lady Stocks, Arnold Toynbee, F. M. Unwin, Brian Wormald and others. There are drafts and preparatory notes for his Webb Memorial Lectures, and press cuttings on the interment of the Webbs in Westminster Abbey. Other correspondence in the collection includes letters from G. P. Gooch and Richard Titmuss. There are also notes for reviews and copies of the reviews.

Other material includes a paper by Tawney for the War Cabinet, 'The Abolition of Economic Controls, 1918–1921', including letters to Tawney about the paper; letters from R. H. Tawney to Brian Pearce and letters to Frank Hardie. The Beveridge papers at BLPES contain many further relevant papers and correspondence.

Tawney's *Commonplace Book*, in the possession of Michael Vyvyan, Trinity College, Cambridge, has been published (ed D. M. Joslin and J. M. Winter, 1972).

The Sir Richard Rees collection in University College Library, London, includes letters from various correspondents to Tawney and material concerning Rees's work as literary executor. The Creech Jones papers, Rhodes House Library, Oxford, have letters from Tawney, 1929–61, correspondence about his 80th birthday celebrations and testimonial fund, and material on his death and the posthumous publication of his works.

Further correspondence can be found in the Passfield and Wallas papers at BLPES, in the Hammond papers at the Bodleian Library, Oxford, and in the Sir R. D. Denman correspondence at the India Office Library.

Records of the Workers' Educational Association, Temple House, 9 Upper Berkeley Street, London W1H 8BY contain three files of Tawney correspondence: 1907–8 on early tutorial classes; 1913–14 on tutorial classes and matters of general policy; and 1958–62, general correspondence. Other records are in the papers on Rewley House, Oxford, to be deposited in the Bodleian Library, Oxford.

TEMPLE, William (1881–1944)

Churchman. Headmaster of Repton School, 1910–14. Canon of Westminster, 1919–21. Bishop of Manchester, 1921–9. Archbishop of York, 1929–42. Archbishop of Canterbury, 1942–4. Editor of *The Challenge*, 1915–18; *The Pilgrim*, 1920–7. President, Workers' Educational Association, 1908–24.

Lambeth Palace Library has relevant papers. The British Library has his correspondence with Lord Cecil, 1921–43 (Add. MS 51154) and with Macmillan, 1905–42 (Add. MSS 55100–1).

THOMAS, Sir Daniel Lleufer (1863–1940)

Lawyer and administrator. Secretary, Welsh Land Commission, 1893–6. Member of Industrial Unrest Commission (Chairman of Panel for Wales), 1917. President, Workers' Educational Association for Wales, 1915–19. Member of Departmental Committee on the Welsh Language, 1925–7. Stipendary Magistrate for Pontypridd and Rhondda, 1909–33.

The National Library of Wales has correspondence and papers, 1893–1940. There are letters from J. Romilly Allen, Lord Amulree, Davies of Llandinam, Sir O. M. Edwards, J. P. Ellis, Ivor L. Evans, Lord Gladstone of Hawarden, Lloyd George, Sir D. Brynmor Jones, H. Stuart Jones, Sir J. Herbert Lewis, Ellis Lloyd, Lord Merthyr, Sir Lewis Morris, Thomas Rees, Stuart Rendel and Sidney Webb. Amongst the topics covered are the Royal Commission on Licensing, 1929–30, the Welsh Land Commission, the Welsh Agricultural Labourer, Welsh versions of Government Publications, the Welsh Church Commission, Welsh settlers in Russia, the Glamorgan Sessions, etc.

THOMPSON, Alexander Mattock (1861–1948)

Journalist. Founded *The Clarion* with Robert Blatchford in 1891; part proprietor, business manager and contributor.

Four volumes of letters from Blatchford to Thompson, 1885–1943 are available at Manchester Central Library, Archives Department. This library also has a collection of other material relating to the Clarion Newspaper Company Ltd. For further details, see Robert Blatchford.

THOMSON, Sir George Paget (1892–1975)

Scientist. Fellow of the Royal Society. Professor of Natural Philosophy, University of Aberdeen, 1922–30. Professor of Physics, Imperial College, London, 1930–52. Chairman, first British Committee on Atomic Energy, 1940–1. Scientific Adviser, Air Ministry, 1943–4. Awarded Nobel Prize for Physics, 1937. Master of Corpus Christi, Cambridge, 1952–62.

Papers are preserved in Trinity College, Cambridge.

THORSTON, Herbert (1856–1939)

Prominent Jesuit. Writer on ecclesiastical subjects.

Letters and papers are in the Archives of the English Province of the Society of Jesus.

THURSFIELD, Sir James Richard (1840–1923)

Naval historian and journalist. Contributor to *The Times, Naval Annual*, etc.

The Thursfield collection at the National Maritime Museum contains papers and correspondence. The material includes naval articles and pamphlets, mostly written by Thursfield, 1906–10; reports on naval manoeuvres, 1894–1901; and letters and printed papers sent by Sir John (Lord) Fisher, 1900–8. Correspondence can be found in the J. S. Corbett papers, and the archives of *The Times* contain further relevant material. '

TITMUSS, Richard Morris (1907–73)

Social theorist. Historian in the Cabinet Office, 1942–9. Professor of Social Administration, London School of Economics, from 1950. Deputy Chairman, Supplementary Benefits Commission from 1968.

Working papers are in BLPES. The bulk of the papers are currently with the family but information will be available with the archivist, BLPES.

TOMLINSON, Henry Major (1873–1958)

Author and traveller. On staff of *Morning Leader* from 1904, and later of *Daily News*. War correspondent in Belgium and France from Aug 1914. Literary editor, *Nation and Athenaeum*, 1917–23.

Yale University Library has a collection of relevant material.

TOYNBEE, Arnold Joseph (1889–1975)

Historian. Government service during World War I; in Political Intelligence Department, Foreign Office, 1918. Professor of Byzantine and Modern Greek Language, Literature and History, London University, 1919–24. Director of Studies in the Royal Institute of International Affairs from 1925; and Research Professor of International History, London University. Director, Research Department, Foreign Office, 1943–6. Author of *A Study of History* (1934–61).

Professor Toynbee's library and personal papers (correspondence, diaries and unpublished papers) are presently in the care of his family. They will eventually be deposited in the Bodleian Library, Oxford. The Royal Institute of International Affairs at Chatham House has papers relating to his work there as author and Director of Studies. The archives of the Institute are subject to a thirty-year rule. Letters can be found in the Herbert Samuel collection and the Lothian papers.

TRENT, 1st B
Sir Jesse Boot, 1st Bt (1850–1931)

Businessman and philanthropist. Founder of Boots the Chemist.

The Boots Company Ltd, Nottingham NG2 3AA, has certain records, largely of a formal nature. They have been used in Stanley Chapman, *Jesse Boot of Boots the Chemist*, who also made use of oral testimony from surviving members of the family. It appears that neither of Lord Trent's daughters knows of any papers. Correspondence with Asquith concerning the

Nottingham Daily Express, 1916–23, is in the Asquith papers, Bodleian Library, Oxford.

TREVELYAN, George Macaulay (1876–1962)

Historian. Regius Professor of Modern History, Cambridge University, 1927–40. Master of Trinity College, Cambridge, 1940–51.

Trinity College Library, Cambridge, has various letters, some 300 in all. Most of these are of family interest. In addition there are some 20 letters written by Trevelyan, the manuscript draft of the first ten chapters of his *Garibaldi's Defence of the Roman Republic* and his 'Address to the Navy Records Society', 1938. Correspondence with Sir Sydney Cockerell, 1946–56, is in the British Library (Add. MS 52756) as is correspondence with the Society of Authors, 1909–46 (Add. MS 56835). There are four letters, 1895–1930, in the Bernstein collection, International Institute of Social History, Amsterdam.

TREVOR, John (1855–1930)

Unitarian minister. Founder of the Labour Church.

The Modern Records Centre, University of Warwick Library, has a deposit of relevant material. It consists of the working papers of the late Rev. G. W. Brassington, collected in preparation for a study of Trevor. As well as extensive research correspondence, particularly relating to the Johnsonian Baptists, among whom Trevor was brought up, and to his family connections, the collection includes Vols I, II and IV of the *Labour Prophet*, contemporary photographs of Trevor and his family, and two letters from Trevor himself.

A few surviving records relating to the Labour Church movement are described in *Sources* Vol. 1, p. 126. The most substantial collection is that relating to the Birmingham Labour Church, in Birmingham City Libraries.

TUCKWELL, Gertrude Mary (1861–1951)

Secretary, Women's Trade Union League, 1892–1904; later its President. President, Women Public Health Officers' Association. Chairman, National Association of Probation Officers.

The British Library has a small collection of letters (24 in number) from Mark Pattison, Rector of Lincoln College, Oxford, to Gertrude Tuckwell (Add. MS 44886). The letters cover the period 1879–1883, and deal frequently with personal matters, but also include many general observations on questions of philosophy, education, etc. Copies of these letters are available at the Bodleian Library (MS Patt. 140), together with other letters of Mrs Pattison, Lady Dilke, to Gertrude Tuckwell, 1868–88 (MS Patt. 139).

The Tuckwell Collection in the Library of the Trades Union Congress includes material relating to the Women's Trade Union League. This is described in *Sources* Vol. 1, p. 285.

TUKER, Mildred Anna Rosalie

Writer on women and the Roman Catholic Church.

Papers in the Fawcett Library cover the years 1887–1951. They include literary and general correspondence and cuttings, 1888–1939; correspondence on her book *Ecce Mater*, 1914–18; letters and cuttings on her article 'Women Preachers', 1916–17; and similar material relating to her book on Cambridge, 1906–28.

TUOHY, James M. (1859–1923)

Journalist. London correspondent, *Dublin Freeman's Journal*, 1881–1912; European Manager, *New York World* from 1897.

The National Library of Ireland has two volumes of material, containing *inter alia* about 20 autograph letters to Tuohy from Irish Nationalist politicians including William O'Brien, John Dillon and T. M. Healy; and a number of House of Commons members' cards signed by anti-Parnellite M.P.s, 1883–1920.

TURNOR, Christopher Hatton (1873–1940)

Land reformer and author.

Lincolnshire Archives Office has papers and correspondence. They include a series of loose-leaf files covering the period 1903–34, and consisting of articles and lectures, together with relevant letters, extracts from printed books, etc. (24 vols and 12 files); further bundles of papers and correspondence; journals of tours, in Yucatan, Germany, Denmark, the Mediterranean, Canada, New Zealand, Australia, India, South Africa; nine volumes of press cuttings, 1911–36; pamphlets and offprints of articles, 1912–36; pamphlets on land, agricultural and educational topics, 1908–29; and miscellaneous journals, notebooks, drafts, etc.

UNWIN, Sir Raymond (1863–1940)

Architect and town planner. With R. B. Parker designed Letchworth Garden City and Hampstead Garden Suburb. Lecturer in Town Planning, Birmingham, 1911–14. Responsible for town planning successively at Local Government Board, Ministries of Munition and Health. Visiting Professor, Columbia University.

The Royal Institute of British Architects has a number of Unwin's working papers and other miscellaneous items. Amongst the papers are notes and miscellaneous material on 'City Planning – Education', 1908–14; 'City Planning – Economic Aspects', 1938–40; 'Population; Ethics and Industrial Relations' (with quotes from Ruskin, etc.); 'Housing General, 1926–39', with papers on cottages, England, architects; texts of his USA lectures, 1936–8. There are also obituary notices collected by his widow, and some miscellaneous letters and papers, chiefly for the late 1930s. There is also an exercise book containing an address, on 'The Dawn of a Happier Day', 1886; and an address to the Sheffield Socialist Education League, 1897, with full text and selections from the works of Ruskin, Morris, Carpenter and Lethaby.

There are a number of letters from Unwin in the Socialist League collection at the International Institute of Social History. The Ashbee Journals, King's College, Cambridge, contain a few items, 1911–23. Relevant material can also be found in the Edward Carpenter papers, Sheffield City Libraries.

Walter L. Creese examines his work in *The Legacy of Raymond Unwin. A Human Pattern for Planning* (1967).

UNWIN, Thomas Fisher (1848–1935)

Publisher. Joint Founder, Publishers' Association. Founder and Council member of Friends of Russian Freedom. Member of South African Conciliation Committee. Treasurer, Cobden Club. Hon. Librarian, Gladstone Memorial Library. Chairman, Political and Economic Circle of the National Liberal Club.

The Cobden and Unwin papers at the West Sussex Record Office contain correspondence, papers relating to publishing and personalia. The material includes letters to Thomas Fisher Unwin and Emma Jane Cobden (Mrs Fisher Unwin), 1877–1939; correspondence between them, 1890–1934; and correspondence between Jane and her sisters. Other papers include publishing material, including the Memorandum and Articles of Association of the Fisher Unwin firm; papers and correspondence on Ireland; correspondence dating from 1887 from various sources, and scrapbooks on Ireland which include cuttings, pamphlets, notices of lectures, photographs and broadsheets. There are miscellaneous personal records, including the birth, marriage, and cremation certificates of Fisher Unwin, personalia, passports, correspondence about Dr Johnson's house, a list of members of the South African Conciliation Commission, scrapbooks of miscellaneous items, a record of Fisher Unwin's last words. There are also scrapbooks containing various personal and political items, broadsheets, minutes, agenda, press cuttings, photographs, pamphlets, cartoons, memoranda, correspondence on various topics. The family papers generally contain relevant papers, including material on the Cobden Clubs in London and Heyshott.

The National Liberal Club collection includes a box of unsorted correspondence and papers chiefly relating to Mrs Cobden Unwin, and containing material on the Boer War period and radical organisations with which she was involved. There is correspondence with Lord Hardinge, 1912–15, in Cambridge University Library, while the Bernstein collection in the International Institute of Social History, Amsterdam, contains some items of correspondence, 1896–9. The Norman Angell collection, Ball State University, also has some relevant correspondence.

VARLEY, Julia (1888–1953)

Trade unionist and suffragette.

Hull University Library has a collection of papers. There is some correspondence with members of the royal household, plus press cuttings, photographs, poems and some publications.

VEITCH, George Stead (1885–1943)

Historian. Professor of Modern History, Liverpool University from 1923.

Papers in the Liverpool University Archives reflect Professor Veitch's academic and professional interests. There are various notes taken from primary and secondary sources covering a range of historical topics; and there are lectures and notes for lectures and syllabuses on various subjects – Industrial History, Communications, the Teaching of History, etc. The collection also includes the drafts, typescripts and manuscripts of books and articles, together with relevant correspondence concerning publication. The miscellaneous papers include material relating to his period as a student and later a member of the staff of Liverpool University, plus papers on the history of the University; material relating to work as an examiner at the University and for the Civil Service; illustrative material (slides); personal material such as insurance policies and photographs (slides); plus press cuttings, etc. There is also correspondence with Ramsay Muir, 1908–37, concerning professional and political matters.

VERNEY, Hon. Richard Greville, see WILLOUGHBY DE BROKE, 19th B

VICKERS, Albert (1838–1919)

Businessman. Chairman of Vickers Ltd, shipbuilders and maker of armaments.

Vickers Ltd, Vickers House, Millbank Tower, Millbank, London SW1, has many relevant papers, including Chairman's letterbooks, directors' report books, minutes of boards, and general correspondence.

VOIGT, Frederick Augustus (1892–1957)

Journalist. On staff of *Manchester Guardian* from 1918, specialising as a foreign correspondent; Diplomatic Correspondent, 1933–9. Author. Editor of *Nineteenth Century and Afterwards*, 1938–46.

Reference should be made to the archives of the *Manchester Guardian* in John Rylands University Library of Manchester.

WADSWORTH, Alfred Powell (1891–1956)

Journalist. On staff of *Manchester Guardian* from 1917; editor, 1944–56.

Miscellaneous papers can be found in the archives of the *Manchester Guardian* in John Rylands University Library of Manchester.

WALKER, Eric Anderson (1886–)

Historian. Professor of Imperial and Naval History, Cambridge, 1936–51.

The African Studies Centre, University of Cambridge, has 23 box-files of material, containing chiefly manuscript notes on various aspects of Southern Africa which Professor Walker once worked on. There are some press cuttings, the majority relating to his work, though some are of a more personal nature; and there are several letters concerned with his writings.

WALLACE, Alfred Russel (1823–1913)

Naturalist and author. President, Land Nationalisation Society. Author of works on evolution, botany, vaccination, progress, etc.

The British Library has manuscripts and correspondence, 1856–1912 (Add. MSS 46414–442). They include drafts of *Bad Times*; *Darwinism, The Wonderful Century, My Life*, etc.; his contributions to periodicals, 1890–1908; and correspondence, general, scientific (with Charles Darwin, among others) and concerning spiritualism, land nationalisation, socialism and anti-vaccination. Notebooks are in the Natural History Museum, and there are letters and notebooks with the Linnean Society. There is correspondence with the Hope Department of Entomology, Oxford University. The Zoological Society of London also has material.

There is correspondence in the Darwin papers, Cambridge University Library.

WALLACE, Sir Donald Mackenzie (1841–1919)

Journalist and author. Private Secretary to Viceroys of India, 1884–9. Director of the Foreign Department, *The Times*, 1891–9. Editor of 10th edition, *Encyclopaedia Britannica*.

Cambridge University Library has papers collected by Wallace. They consist chiefly of notes for his unpublished 'History of Foreign Policy' and notes on the Russian Revolution of 1905. There is also some correspondence with Chirol.

Three boxes of office papers and correspondence are in the archives of *The Times*. The London Library has a small collection of manuscript notes of the 1st and 2nd Dumas, and the Russian revolutionary movements, 1861–1914.

There is a bundle of official papers, 1886, in the Kimberley papers, while the Lord Randolph Churchill papers also contain correspondence.

WALLACE, William (1891–1976)

Businessman and philanthropist. Served in various government agencies, World War I, and as industrial adviser and director, Ministry of Food, World War II. On staff of Rowntree and Co. Ltd from 1919. Secretary, 1929–31, Director, 1931–52, Chairman, 1952–7. Chairman, Joseph Rowntree Memorial Trust, 1951–63; and the Social Service Trust, 1959–69. Chairman of the Industrial Co-Partnership Association. A founder member, British Institute of Management. Author of several works on private enterprise and the state's relations with industry. He drafted Lloyd George's election manifesto of 1929, 'We Can Conquer Unemployment'.

Papers remain with the family, c/o 26 Clifton, York. They include correspondence and an unpublished autobiography.

WALLAS, Graham (1858–1932)

Political Scientist. Member of the Fabian Society, 1886–1904 (contributor to *Fabian Essays*, 1889). Member, London School Board, 1894–1904. Member, London County Council, 1904–7; member of LCC Education Committee, 1908–10. Lecturer at the London School of Economics from 1895. Professor of Political Science, University of London, 1914–23.

BLPES has a collection of correspondence and papers. The collection includes letters to Wallas, 1882–1932, mainly arranged chronologically, and including correspondence with the Webbs and G. B. Shaw, letters about *Human Nature in Politics*, letters on Francis Place, and letters from Lowes Dickinson. There is also a series of letters from Wallas of various dates. Other material includes lecture notes and syllabuses; papers on the British Neutrality Committee, World War I; manuscripts and drafts of reviews and essays, notes on reading; manuscripts of *Great Society*, *Human Nature in Politics*, *Our Social Heritage*, *Social Judgement*, *Men and Ideas*, *Francis Place*, including notes etc.; reviews of these books; notes and cuttings made by Wallas on Bentham, the Poor Law, the Army, Education, International Affairs, USA; biographical material dating from 1858; engagement books; private letters; and Ada Wallas's diaries. Reference should also be made to the Passfield papers, also at BLPES. Papers of Mary Wallas at Newnham College, Oxford, contain further relevant material. The British Library has correspondence with Shaw, 1889–1929 (Add. MS 50553). Further letters can be found in the Marvin papers at the Bodleian Library, the Samuel papers at the House of Lords Record Office, and in the Fabian Society archive in Nuffield College, Oxford.

WALSH, William J. (1841–1921)

Roman Catholic Archbishop of Dublin and Primate of Ireland from 1885.

Archbishop Walsh's papers are housed in the Dublin Diocesan archives. General access is not given. Twenty-five letters to W. R. Moss on bimetallism are in the John Johnson Collection (NRA 16952).

WALSTON*, Sir Charles (1856–1927)

Historian of ideas and Hellenist. Director of the Fitzwilliam Museum, Cambridge, 1883–9. Reader in Classical Archaeology, Cambridge University, 1883–1907. Slade Professor of Fine Art, 1895–1901, 1904–11. Director, American Archaeological School, Athens, 1889–93. Fellow of King's College, Cambridge.

King's College, Cambridge, has a collection of papers, including his lectures on classical archaeology and art history; London University Extension Lectures; Gilchrist Lectures;

correspondence on the foundation of the British Academy, 1902; lectures on 'Anglophobia' given during World War I; notes and press cuttings on *Chauvinism*, *The English Speaking Brotherhood*, and *The Jewish Question* (1890s–1900).

*Formerly Waldstein.

WALTER, Arthur Fraser (1846–1910)

Proprietor and Chairman of *The Times*.

The archives of *The Times* contain much relevant material.

WARD, Sir Adolphus William (1837–1924)

Historian. Professor of History and English Literature, Owen's College, Manchester, 1866; Principal, 1890–7. Vice-Chancellor, Victoria University, 1886–90, 1894–6. Master of Peterhouse, Cambridge, from 1900. Vice-Chancellor, Cambridge University, 1901.

The Library of Peterhouse, Cambridge, has a collection of papers, chiefly relating to Ward's historical interests: lectures, notes, etc. There are also papers of his father John.

Letters to H. E. Roscoe are in John Rylands University Library of Manchester; there are letters, 1881–1918 in the Spenser Wilkinson papers; and eight letters, 1919–24, in the W. H. Dawson collection.

WARD, Mary Augusta
Mrs Humphry Ward (1851–1920)

Novelist and social worker. Founded the Passmore Edwards Settlement and the Play Centres for London, 1897. A founder of the Women's National Anti-Suffrage League in 1908.

Pusey House, Oxford, has a substantial collection of papers relating to Mrs Ward's career. It contains a considerable amount of correspondence, including letters by Mrs Ward to members of her family from 1870 onwards (letters to her daughter, Dorothy M. Ward; to her son, A. S. Ward; to her husband, T. Humphry Ward and others); a number of letters concerning her novels, many of them from other prominent literary and political figures; miscellaneous correspondence with Bishop Mandell Creighton, A. J. Balfour, J. A. Froude, Mrs T. H. Green, Lords Jellicoe, Rosebery, Milner, Curzon and Lansdowne, Violet Bonham-Carter, Theodore Roosevelt, H. H. Asquith and others; and family correspondence, 1870–1935. The collection also includes drafts of publications and manuscripts of various speeches, as well as some published material.

University College London has other relevant Ward material, including diaries of T. H. Ward and Dorothy Mary Ward. These are obviously relevant to Mary Ward's career. There are also a number of press cuttings, dating from 1891 to 1920. Some 20 boxes of material are held by the Hannold Library, Claremont Colleges, Claremont, California. These papers chiefly relate to her literary activity and include correspondence of Mary Ward and her agent and publisher, Smith Elder & Co., together with letters to and from other publishers; and 41 volumes of manuscript notes and drafts, 1863–1919.

The Mary Ward Centre, 9 Tavistock Place, London WC1, has other relevant material, including twelve folders of correspondence relating to the Settlement, 1890–1907, including correspondence with Passmore Edwards, the Duke of Bedford and Philip Wicksteed (Warden).

The manuscript of the novel *Robert Elsmere* is in the Berg collection, New York Public Library, while the British Library has the autograph manuscript of *The Story of Betty Costrell* (Add. MS 43505).

Mrs Humphry Ward's daughter, Janet Penrose Trevelyan published a *Life* of her mother in 1923 and Enid Huws Jones, *Mrs Humphry Ward* (1973), made use of manuscript sources.

WARD, Thomas Humphry (1845–1926)

Journalist and author. Fellow of Brasenose College, Oxford, 1869; tutor, 1870–81. Contributor and leader writer, *The Times*.

Papers can be found in collections of Ward family papers at Pusey House, Oxford, and in University College Library, London, as described above. These include correspondence, diaries and appointments books.

Social correspondence, 1910–12, is in the Sladen papers, while his publishing correspondence with Macmillans, 1869–1901, can be found in the British Library (Add. MS 54927). The University of Texas, Austin, has correspondence with Thomas Hardy and Henry James.

WARE, Sir Fabian Arthur Goulstone (1869–1949)

Administrator and author. Acting Director of Education, Transvaal, 1901; Director, 1903–5. Editor of the *Morning Post*, 1905–11. Founder, Imperial War Graves Commission; Vice Chairman, 1917–48. Chairman, Parents' National Educational Union.

No papers are known, but there is correspondence with Richard Jebb, 1907–17, in the Institute of Commonwealth Studies. Papers of PNEU are in London University Library.

WARREN, Sir (Thomas) Herbert (1853–1930)

President of Magdalen College, Oxford, 1885–1928. Vice-Chancellor, University of Oxford, 1906–10.

Magdalen College, Oxford, has Warren's 'official' papers in the College records. They chiefly relate to tutorial and bursarial matters. Family and personal papers are in the care of Mr C. A. Brodie, Squires Farm, Coldharbour, near Dorking, Surrey. They are contained in several deed boxes, but are at present unsorted. There is correspondence with Douglas Sladen, 1908–9, concerning his book on Egypt, and letters, 1915, on recruitment for the army. Letters to Ruskin are in Hull University Library, and there is correspondence in the Edward Arber collection (NRA 10731).

WATSON, Robert Spence (1837–1911)

Political, social and educational reformer. Helped found Armstrong College, Durham, 1871; first President, 1910. Pioneer of University extension teaching in North of England. President of the National Liberal Federation, 1890–1902. President of the Peace Society.

The House of Lords Record Office has photocopies of correspondence and papers, including correspondence with John Morley. It also has some 25 letters from Spence Watson in the Soskice collection.

WEAVER, Harriet Shaw (1876–1961)

Feminist and literary patron. Editor of *The New Freewoman*, later known as *The Egoist*, and of the *Egoist Press*. Patron of James Joyce.

The British Library has a collection of correspondence and papers both literary and business, and including material relating to James Joyce (Add. MSS 57345–65). There is a substantial grouping of letters from' or concerning Joyce, 1914–41, together with letters from Nora and Lucia Joyce and other members of the family. Other correspondents include Archibald Macleish, Ezra Pound, John Quinn, G. B. Shaw, H. G. Wells, Sylvia Beach, T. S. Eliot, Edmund Gosse, Virginia Woolf and Dora Marsden (1912–35). There are also literary and business papers concerning *The New Freewoman*, and *The Egoist*, such as articles of association, press cuttings, articles, minutes, notices to shareholders, accounts, etc.

Other Joyce material deposited by Harriet Shaw Weaver is at Add. MSS 47471–89 (autograph drafts of *Finnegan's Wake*, proof sheets, etc.); and Add. MS 49975, which includes part of an early draft of Joyce's autobiography, and notes for the last seven chapters of *Ulysses*, 1919–21. Some of the correspondence is reproduced in Jane Lidderdale and Mary Nicholson, *Dear Miss Weaver* (1970).

WEBB, (Martha) Beatrice
Beatrice Potter (1858–1943)

Political scientist and socialist author. Contributed to Charles Booth's *Life and Labour of the People*. Member of Royal Commission on the Poor Law and Unemployment, 1905–9, and joint author of the Minority Report. Member of various government committees. With her husband Sidney Webb wrote numerous works of social investigation and labour history.

BLPES has a large collection of the papers of both Beatrice and Sidney Webb (1st Baron Passfield) (ref. Passfield Papers). The collection consists of both public and private papers. The former include 350 volumes of material collected for the Webb's history of English local government, two volumes of papers related to their Board of Trade activities, 1911–18, twenty volumes relating to *New Statesman* special supplements, 1915–17 (the Webbs founded the *New Statesman* in 1913), and six volumes of papers on East African politics, 1929–31. There are also nine boxes of papers from the reconstruction committee of the Ministry of Reconstruction, 1916–18, and five boxes on the relief of distress, 1914–15.

The most important section of the private papers is Beatrice Webb's diaries, 1873–1943. The manuscript version fills 58 notebooks and includes some letters and photographs. A typescript copy exists. Beatrice Webb herself typed out many of her diaries and began editing them for publication. They were published as follows: Beatrice Webb, *My Apprenticeship* (1926), *Our Partnership*, ed. Margaret I. Cole and Barbara Drake (1948), *Beatrice Webb's Diaries 1912–1924* and *1924–32*, ed. Margaret I. Cole (1952–6), *Beatrice Webb's American Diary 1898*, ed. David A. Shannon (Madison, Wisc., 1963), and *The Webbs' Australian Diary 1898*, ed. A. G. Austin (Melbourne, 1965). Margaret Cole has also written a memoir, *Beatrice Webb* (1945). Kitty Muggeridge, Beatrice Webb's niece, has written a biography (co-author Ruth Adam), *Beatrice Webb:A Life* (1967), based on Potter family papers as well as the Webb collection.

In addition to the diaries, the papers include Potter family letters, Sidney Webb's letters to Beatrice, 1890–1940, and letters from the Webbs given to the library after an appeal in 1956 and subsequently. There are personal papers concerning the various honours and certificates granted to the Webbs, their personal finances and their houses, including a catalogue to the sale of contents in 1948. There are papers related to the Webbs' political and public work, including a collection of papers made by Sidney Webb concerning the 1931 crisis. There is material concerning their many publications, lecture notes, articles, broadcasts and speeches, their bibliographies on various subjects such as the poor law and syndicalism, six boxes of Fabian Society papers, particularly concerning resident summer schools, and papers concerning the foundation, history and administration of the London School of Economics. Two volumes of the letters of Beatrice and Sidney Webb are to be published (ed. Professor Norman Mackenzie). A microfilm of Beatrice Webb's diary is also being prepared.

The Fabian Society archive at Nuffield College, Oxford, contains a mass of correspondence of Beatrice and Sidney Webb, 1891–1941. There are also letters in the War Emergency Workers National Committee papers in the Labour Party archive at Transport House.

Correspondence can be found in a number of collections. There are five letters, 1881–1903, in the Herbert Spencer papers (NRA 16255). At the British Library there are letters to George Bernard Shaw, 1913–42 (Add. MS 50553) and John Burns (Add. MS 46287). The Horace Plunkett papers include letters concerning the *New Statesman* supplement on Ireland, and German Industrial Development. The W. A. S. Hewins papers in Sheffield University Library contain further letters. At the Bodleian Library, Oxford, there is correspondence with Asquith,

1895–1909, particularly concerning the Poor Law; and with Mrs Marvin. The House of Lords Record Office has her correspondence with Lloyd George, 1933–42, and with Herbert Samuel, 1902–44.

Some relevant items are also to be found in the Laski and Evan Durbin papers.

WEBSTER, Sir Charles Kingsley (1886–1961)

Academic; expert on international relations. Professor of Modern History, Liverpool University, 1914–22. On general staff, War Office, 1917–18. Secretary, Military Section, British Delegation to the Paris Peace Conference, 1918–19. Wilson Professor of International Politics, University of Wales, Aberystwyth, 1922–32. Ausserordentlich Professor, University of Vienna, 1926. Professor of History, Harvard University, 1928–32. Stevenson Professor of International History, London School of Economics, 1932–53. Served with the Foreign Research and Press Service, 1939–41. Director of the British Library of Information, New York, 1941–2; Foreign Office, 1943–6. Member of the British Delegation at Dumbarton Oaks and San Francisco, 1944–5; Member of the Preparatory Commission and General Assembly, United Nations, London, 1945–6. President, British Academy, 1950–4.

BLPES has a large collection of papers. There is little on his early career or his period at Liverpool University, but more has survived for the 1930s and the papers are fullest on Webster's work during World War II and afterwards. Correspondence dates from 1906, and includes early family letters, 1906–11; letters on his work on Castlereagh; his marriage; his army service; requests for articles; letters from fellow scholars; correspondence concerning his various posts; his research; his work during and after the war. There is a 'Private File', 1941–2, being semi-official correspondence as Director of the British Library of Information, New York; and a file of 'Miscellaneous correspondence from F.O.', 1945–6; letters on UNESCO and other conferences, and correspondence regarding his later publications. There are some papers for the early part of his career, dating from 1901, and including examination papers, and his application for the chair at Liverpool, 1914. Some further material, small in quantity, reflects his work there. General papers relate to his military service, 1916–19, but the material concerning the Paris Peace Conference is more extensive. There are papers on the arrangements for the Peace Conference, Zionism, the foundation of the Institute of International Affairs, treaties. There are later papers, correspondence, leaflets, agenda, etc., on the League of Nations Union, papers on disarmament, European Union, etc. His work at Aberystwyth is reflected in committee papers, memoranda, examination papers, and articles. There are also papers on his visits abroad, and teaching notes for Harvard and Radcliffe students. There is similar material for his period at the London School of Economics including lists of students, notes on work, correspondence, drafts of theses, memoranda, LSE committee papers, agenda and minutes of *Politika*. Another section of the collection relates to committees, meetings and visits, 1934–40, including the League of Nations Union, the Royal Institute of International Affairs, English Speaking Union, British Council, University Sub-Committees, the Research Committee and its sub-committees. Miscellaneous papers, including memoranda, correspondence with Bracken, Halifax, Sir Gerald Campbell, etc., concern the British Library of Information, and there are similar papers concerning the Foreign Office Research Department. A large number of papers relate to the post-war settlement and the new world organisation. There are memoranda and minutes concerning the war-time planning of the United Nations, papers relating to the UK Delegation to the Dumbarton Oaks conference, official conference papers, papers preparatory to the San Francisco conference, papers on the United Nations Conference on International Organisation, Apr–July 1945, conference documents and background files of the UK delegation for technical committees, papers concerning the post San Francisco Preparatory Commission of the United Nations, July 1945–Mar 1946, material relating to the United Nations General Assembly, Jan–Apr 1946, the final assembly of the League of Nations, and papers on UNESCO. There are also papers relating to Webster's other activities and committee work after the war – in the university, on various committees and organisations, including the

Anglo-Israel Association, the Weizmann Archives, Friends of Atlantic Union, the Great Britain–USSR Society, etc., as well as material on his various visits abroad. The Webster collection also includes copies of his lectures and speeches, 1906–60; papers relating to his published work, 1911–62, including manuscripts, typescripts, galley proofs, transcripts, press cuttings etc., letters to *The Times* and to other journals; personalia; press cuttings, 1909–61; photographs, obituary notices and letters of condolence to his family.

Webster's library was purchased by Queen Mary College, London, where it is housed in the History Department. The college library holds a small collection of residual Webster material, including passports, some photographs and certificates and a few letters to Webster.

Webster's diaries up to 1949 were bequeathed to Professor P. A. Reynolds and have been published as *The Historian as Diplomat: The Diaries of Sir Charles Webster 1939–46*, edited by P. A. Reynolds and E. J. Hughes (1977). Originals are at BLPES. Diaries subsequent to 1949 were bequeathed to Dr Noble Frankland.

WEDD, Nathaniel (1864–1940)

Academic. Fellow and Librarian, King's College, Cambridge. University lecturer in Ancient History. Active in Fabian politics in Cambridge.

The Bulmer–Wedd correspondence in King's College Library, Cambridge contains letters between Wedd and Edward Frederick Bulmer (1865–1941), joint founder of the firm of H. P. Bulmer & Co. The correspondence covers the period 1889–1939 (677 letters). Other items include drafts of a talk on 'The British Empire' given in 1933.

WELBY, 1st B
Reginald Earle Welby (1832–1915)

Civil Servant. Served in Treasury from 1856; Assistant Financial Secretary, 1880; Auditor of the Civil List, 1881; Permanent Secretary, 1885–94.

The Welby collection at BLPES (in nine volumes) includes papers of Arbuthnot on currency, edited by V. Delves-Broughton; papers of Welby on the organisation of Government departments (including minutes, reports, etc.); papers on gold coinage (including minutes, etc.); papers and correspondence on Indian currency and bimetallism; further papers on coinage and the Bank of England (correspondents including W. S. Jevons, H. C. E. Childers, Campbell-Bannerman); and miscellaneous letters and papers.

Official and personal papers of Lord Welby are deposited with the Lincoln Archives Office (Welby (Allington) MSS). They include volumes of Departmental reports, bills, written memoranda, correspondence etc.; four volumes of correspondence relating to his official positions, including material on the Gold Standard Defence Association; a series of volumes containing notes and extracts on various historical matters, with cuttings from various printed sources (e.g. Navy and Ordnance, Army, Civil Finance, Church Government, etc.); and a number of miscellaneous volumes of a personal nature.

Other papers are in the British Library (Egerton MSS 3291). These include official papers, among which are memoranda, printed material and some correspondence relating to expenditure on defence, mainly as Permanent Secretary at the Treasury, but including a few papers of an earlier date. The material covers the period, 1853–95.

Letters to Lord Rendel are in the National Library of Wales. Correspondence on financial affairs can also be found in the Iddesleigh papers.

WELDON, Walter F. R. (d. 1906)

Fellow of the Royal Society. Professor of Comparative Anatomy and Zoology, University College London, to 1899. Linacre Professor of Comparative Anatomy, Oxford, from 1899. Associated with Sir Francis Galton and Karl Pearson in study of heredity, etc.

Weldon's papers passed to his literary executor, Karl Pearson, and are now in the Pearson collection in the Library of University College London. They include working papers, correspondence and papers relating to *Biometrika*. A substantial grouping of correspondence can also be found in the Galton papers in University College London.

WELLS, Herbert George (1866–1946)

Novelist and social critic. Author of many works of fiction, science fiction, political pamphlets and articles (with socialist themes), etc.

The University of Illinois Library has a large collection, some 65,000 items in all, covering the years 1880–1946. The correspondence consists of some 60,000 letters received, from a large range of political and literary correspondents, and around 1500 letters from Wells. There are also the typescripts and proofs of 40 novels, 37 sociological books and 11 pamphlet typescripts and clippings of some 150 unpublished articles, stories, speeches, plays, films and other papers. Personal papers include pocket diaries, personal financial material, family records, contracts and publishers' statements, address books, house inventories, photographs etc. Correspondence concerning his publications, and a collection of his wife's letters are in the University of Virginia Library (Charlottesville). Correspondence of Wells and his family with William Baxter and notes by Baxter concerning Wells are in Bromley Central Library. Correspondence with the Society of Authors, 1909–39, and with Macmillans the publishers, 1895–1944, can be found in the British Library (Add. MSS 56843–4 and 54943–5 respectively). The British Library also has Wells' correspondence with G. B. Shaw and his wife 1901–4 (Add. MS 50552) and with Lady Aberconway, 1925–46, (Add. MSS 52551–3). The Wells letters in the PEN archive have been purchased by the University of Texas, Austin.

Wells' correspondence with Frank Swinnerton is in Arkansas University Library; with William Smith Culbertson and with Charles Anderson Dana in the Library of Congress; with H. J. Laski and with Coronet Magazine in Syracuse University Library; with Howard Vincent O'Brien in the Newberry Library, Chicago; with Marie Meloney in Columbia University Libraries; and with Norman Angell in Ball State University. There are also letters to Sir Edmund Gosse, 1897–1912, in Leeds University Library; to R. Murray Gilchrist in Sheffield City Library; personal, social and literary correspondence with Douglas Sladen, 1915–20; letters to Lloyd George, 1927, 1934–9, in the House of Lords Record Office. The Ashbee journals at King's College, Cambridge, also have references.

The Fabian Society archive at Nuffield College, Oxford, contains correspondence and lectures by Wells, and papers relating to the H. G. Wells controversy, 1907, including reports of the Special Committee and the Executive Committee, the report on the reconstruction of the Fabian Society, printed circulars, various letters and notes, letters to Wells, agenda, etc.

The Kingsley Martin collection in Sussex University Library has relevant papers, including general correspondence to Martin, and three files of manuscript, typescript and printed material specifically concerning Wells. These include his letters to the *New Statesman*; drafts, notes by Martin and others on Wells, a bibliography, etc.

Norman and Jeanne Mackenzie, *The Time Traveller: The Life of H. G. Wells* (1973) made full use of the Wells archives in Illinois and elsewhere. Lovat Dickson, *H. G. Wells: His Turbulent Life and Times* (1969), quotes from correspondence. Gordon N. Ray, *H. G. Wells and Rebecca West* (1974) uses the c. 800 letters from Wells to Rebecca West in her care (hers to Wells have been destroyed). Ray is also editing the *Life and Letters*.

WHITE, Arnold Henry (1848–1925)

Author and journalist. Writer on social problems, colonisation, Jewish settlement. Advocate of a strong navy as 'Vanoc' of the *Referee*.

The papers were deposited on permanent loan in the National Maritime Museum by the Bedford Estate Office in 1972. They consist of 202 files arranged alphabetically, as White left them, by subject. The topics covered by the collection include gunnery, 1903 to 1905; naval policy and strategy, on which White exchanged letters with Lord Fisher, Lord Charles Beresford, and Sir Percy Scott. On lower-deck conditions the correspondence is largely with Lionel Yexley, and there are general papers on Ireland, emigration and eugenics. A number of original letters were removed by White but it was his practice to leave typed copies in their place; those of Lord Fisher come into this category. Correspondence, 1911–16, can be found in the Blumenfeld papers, House of Lords Record Office.

WICKSTEED, Philip Henry (1844–1927)

Economist. Unitarian minister from 1867. University Extension Lecturer, 1887–1918.

Wicksteed stated that he kept 'next to no documents' (see Sturges, *Economists' Papers*, p. 128). BLPES has one volume of papers, including MSS, typed and printed material connected with his work on economics. It includes a few notes for University Extension lectures, a syllabus for lecture courses, two letters to and one from Wicksteed and some printed pamphlets, and covers the period 1887–1924. Correspondence with F. E. Colenso concerning colonial affairs is in Rhodes House Library, and further correspondence is available in the Cannan and Wallas papers (BLPES) and James Macluckie Connell collection (Dr Williams' Library).

WIDDRINGTON, Percy Elborough Tinling (1873–1959)

Anglo-Catholic priest. Advocate of a Christian Sociology. A founder member of the League of the Kingdom of God, and founder of *Christendom*.

Papers, including correspondence with his first wife Enid Stacy (q.v.) are in the care of his son, Mr Gerard Widdrington of Toronto. Enquiries may be directed to Mrs Angela Tuckett (niece), 5 Liddington Street, Swindon, Wilts. Maurice B. Reckitt, *P. E. T. Widdrington* (1961), quotes from correspondence and papers in the care of family and friends.

WILKINSON, (Henry) Spenser (1853–1937)

Military historian; author and journalist. Fellow of All Souls, Oxford. Chichele Professor of Military History, University of Oxford, 1909–23.

Material with the Army Museums Ogilby Trust includes letters concerning the Niger and Congo Conference, Berlin, 1885; 37 letters from Lord Milner about political questions in South Africa, 1888–1918; letters from General Sir Ian Hamilton, mainly about South Africa, 1898–1931; and letters and papers dealing with the setting up of the Navy League, 1894–1919. There is correspondence from the Duke of Devonshire, Asquith, Haldane, Fisher, Methuen, Sir John Colomb, M.P., Sir William Robertson, Kitchener, General Sir Aylmer Haldane, Admiral Sir Reginald Custance, Colonel J. L. A. Colin and US Admiral William S. Sims. In addition, the Trust holds various draft articles and leaders, letters to newspapers, typescripts and notes, lectures, press reviews, appreciations of his books, press cuttings, etc.

Two boxes of notebooks, containing many of Wilkinson's lectures and research notes were given to the National Army Museum by the Royal United Service Institution, of which he was Secretary.

In addition, correspondence 1891–1909 can be found in the papers of Earl Roberts, also at the National Army Museum.

WILLERT, Sir Arthur (1882–1973)

Journalist. Chief correspondent of *The Times* in the USA, 1910–20. Secretary of the British War Mission, USA, 1917–18. Head of the News Department and Press Officer, Foreign Office, from 1921. Head of the Ministry of Information Office for Southern Region, 1939–45.

Sir Arthur Willert's papers were bequeathed to Yale University Library.

WILLIAMS, Harold Whitmore (d. 1928)

Journalist, closely involved in Russian emigré work after 1917.

The British Library has 41 volumes of papers, partly in Russian, covering the period 1918–29 (Add. MSS 54436–76). Most of the papers relate to the activities of the Russian Liberation Committee in London, and include letters to Williams from Russian figures (e.g. Peter Struve, A. I. Guchkov); general correspondence from a variety of people, 1918–29; telegrams received by the Russian Liberation Committee from Omsk, Irkutsk, Helsingfors, Archangel, Reval, Vladivostok, etc., 1919–20; miscellaneous papers relating to the Liberation Committee, 1918–23; reports of the Special Committee to investigate Bolshevik atrocities, attached to the C.-in-C., Armed forces in Southern Russia; miscellaneous papers relating to the Commission's work and to the question of the Orthodox Church under Bolshevik rule; and miscellaneous papers relating to Russian affairs, 1918–27.

WILLIAMS, Robert (1881–1936)

Trade union leader and Labour politician. Secretary, National Transport Workers' Federation, 1912–25. President, International Transport Workers' Federation, 1920–5. Member of Labour Party Executive Council, 1918–21, and from 1922; Chairman, 1926. Labour Propaganda Officer, *Daily Herald*.

The Labour Party archive at Transport House contains papers and correspondence: in the War Emergency Workers National Committee files; and in the file on seamen, 1922. Records of the National Transport Workers' Federation survive in the records of the Transport and General Workers Union (*Sources* Vol. 1, p. 264). Relevant material can also be found in the archives of the International Transport Workers' Federation, deposited in the Modern Records Centre, University of Warwick Library.

WILLOUGHBY DE BROKE, 19th B
Hon. Richard Greville Verney (1869–1923)

Conservative politician. M.P. (Con) Rugby, 1895–1900. Leading 'Diehard'.

The papers, including diaries, are housed in the House of Lords Record Office.

WILSON, Alexander Cowan (1866–1955)

Quaker, particularly concerned with Indian and international affairs.

The Library of Friends' House, London, has a collection of material, including South African and Indian journals; correspondence on secular education; personal material, including some relating to H. T. Wilson, M.P.; political material, concerning pacifism, armaments, the Incitement to Disaffection Act, 1934, slavery and native races, War on Want, Korea, Germany and EDC; together with a collection of pamphlets.

WINTRINGHAM, Tom (d. 1949)

Socialist writer and publicist. One-time member of the Communist Party. Officer in British contingent, International Brigade in Spain. Leading member of Common Wealth during World War II.

It is believed that papers are with Mr Benjamin Wintringham (son), The Old Boathouse, Llanfair Hale, near Caernarvon, Gwynedd. The archive of Common Wealth, in Sussex University Library, contains relevant material.

WITHERS, Hartley (1867–1950)

Economic journalist. With the City office of *The Times* from 1894. City Editor, 1905–10. City Editor, *Morning Post*, 1910–11. Director of Financial Inquiries in the Treasury, 1915–16. Editor, *The Economist*, 1916–21; and of the Financial Supplement of *Saturday Review*, 1921–3. Director, Allied Investors' Trust.

Sturges, during his survey of the papers of economists, found that no papers survive with his daughter, Miss E. M. Withers.

WOLF, Lucien (1857–1930)

Journalist. Prominent Anglo-Jewish anti-Zionist. Sub-editor and leader-writer, *Jewish World*, 1874–93; editor, 1906–8. Assistant editor, *Public Leader*, 1877–8. Foreign editor, *Daily Graphic*, 1890–1909. He opposed the Balfour Declaration. Secretary of the Conjoint Foreign Committee of the Board of Deputies and Anglo-Jewish Association, 1917–30. He represented the Anglo-Jewish community at the Paris Peace Conference, 1918–19. Founder and delegate, the League of Nations Advisory Committee on Refugees. President of the Jewish Historical Society.

The main collection of his papers are at the YIVO Institute for Jewish Research, New York. The Central Zionist Archives includes a diary from the Peace Conference, 1919; the British Foreign Office interpretations of the Balfour Declaration; suggestions for various sorts of administration in Palestine. The Anglo-Jewish Archives, University College London has minutes of the Conjoint Committee, for 1917; shorthand notes by his secretary, Ruth Phillips, and some letters. The Mocatta Library has his genealogical notes and notes on Anglo-Jewish history (53 boxes). There are also relevant papers in the records of the Board of Deputies of British Jews (briefly described in *Sources* Vol. 1, pp. 20–1). The Soskice papers in the House of Lords Record Office contain 13 letters, 1905.

WOLFF, Henry William (1840–1931)

Propagandist for Agricultural Co-operation. A founder and President of the International Co-operative Alliance.

Records of the International Co-operative Alliance are described in *Sources* Vol. 1, pp. 78–9. There is correspondence, 1909–18, on agricultural matters, in the Sir Horace Plunkett papers.

WOODHEAD, Henry George Wandesford (1883–1959)

Journalist and publicist on the Far East. Editor, *Peking and Tientsin Times*, 1914–30; *Oriental Affairs*, 1933–41. Chairman, Shanghai British Residents Association, 1932; China Association, Shanghai, 1938–40. Head of Far Eastern Reference Section, Ministry of Information, December 1942. Correspondent for *The Times*, Hong Kong, 1946–8. Editor, *Far East Trader*, 1950–4.

Mrs E. Higham (daughter), Owl Cottage, Church Path, Ashwell, near Baldock, Herts, states that few papers survive. His library and papers were seized when he was captured by the Japanese during World War II. Mrs Higham has some appointment and other diaries. The diaries for 1904–6 are being edited by Dr Ann Trotter of the Department of History, University of Otago, Dunedin, New Zealand.

WOOLF, Leonard Sidney (1880–1969)

Author and publisher. Served in the Ceylon Civil Service, 1904–11. Editor, *International Review*, 1919. Editor of the International Section, *Contemporary Review*, 1920–1. Literary editor, *The Nation*, 1923–30. Joint editor, *Political Quarterly*, 1931–59. Founded Hogarth

Press, 1917. Secretary of Labour Party Advisory Committee on International Affairs.

The University of Sussex Library has a collection of Woolf's papers. This includes boxes of miscellaneous letters, from the 1930s to 1969; family correspondence and two boxes of letters from eminent persons; 11 boxes of work and business papers, up to 1968; and papers relating to his autobiographical volumes, *Sowing, Growing, Beginning Again, Downhill All The Way* and *The Journey not the Arrival Matters*. Political papers include documents relating to the Labour Party International Advisory Committee, the Fabian Society Research Group, the League of Nations, reviews of political works, and miscellaneous political letters and papers. Amongst literary material are university essays and translations, volumes of university notes, papers, articles and reviews relating to Ceylon, correspondence and reviews relating to Virginia Woolf and to his own books, unsorted manuscripts and typescripts, offprints of articles, etc. There is in addition, a collection of domestic papers, and 'bills paid'. Other miscellaneous material includes a box-file of papers on Africa, War, League of Nations Mandates, plus reviews, press cuttings, photostats, etc.

Correspondence regarding Labour Party policies towards the colonies can be found in the Creech Jones papers at Rhodes House Library, Oxford. Letters of Virginia and Leonard Woolf can also be found in the J. M. Keynes papers at King's College, Cambridge, and in the Charleston papers there. A considerable amount of material relating to Virginia Woolf, Leonard's wife, can be found in the Berg collection, New York Public Library.

Documents of the Labour Party Advisory Committees on International and Imperial Affairs at Transport House are briefly described in *Sources*, Vol. 1, p. 130. The Greenidge papers contain miscellaneous notes and papers, while correspondence concerning Ceylon is in the Cambridge Centre for South Asian Studies.

WORSFOLD, William Basil (1858–1939)

Barrister, lecturer and author. Confidant of Lord Milner in South Africa. Editor of the *Johannesburg Star*, 1904–5.

A collection of material survives at Rhodes House Library, Oxford. The papers cover the years 1902–33 and are concerned almost entirely with his association with Milner until his death in 1925. Correspondence in the collection reveals the accord between the two men, and the extent to which Milner influenced the *Star*'s editorial policy. There are also letters between them concerning the publication of books by Worsfold on Milner's South African policy. There is a draft of his 1913 book on *The Reconstruction of the New Colonies under Lord Milner 1902–1905*, together with notes and extracts made by Worsfold from Milner's diaries and correspondence with Chamberlain and others.

There are also articles by Worsfold on Imperial questions, which appeared in the *Nineteenth Century* and a file of papers is concerned with the memoir of Milner prepared by Worsfold at the request of *The Times*, and printed after Milner's death in May 1925. Other files contain drafts and other papers connected with a biography of Milner originally intended to form one of a series of biographical sketches entitled 'Empire Builders', edited by Worsfold. It was unfinished at the time of Milner's death, and his widow did not feel able to give permission for Worsfold to complete it in an extended form.

A further file of papers was listed by Worsfold under the heading 'Obituary Packet'; it includes his memoir of Milner, printed in *The Times* of 14 May 1925. There are also articles and papers which Worsfold wrote about the Doullens Conference held on 26 Mar 1918, in which Milner took part and at which was established the single command of the Western Front under Foch. These papers include pencil sketches made by Worsfold in 1925 at Doullens and Beauvais. Twenty bound volumes of photographs, line drawings and watercolour sketches made by him in various parts of the world have been deposited in the Bodleian Library, Oxford. The Milner papers are also in the Bodleian Library and should be referred to.

WRENCH, Sir (John) Evelyn Leslie (1882–1966)

Writer and politician. Promoter of Commonwealth unity. Founder of the Overseas Club (later League) and of the English-Speaking Union of the Commonwealth, 1918. Chief Private Secretary, Air Minister, 1917–18. Deputy controller, British Empire and USA Section, Ministry of Information, 1918. American Relations Officer to government of India, 1942–4. Editor of *The Spectator*, 1925–32; its chairman from 1925.

Correspondence and diaries are located in the British Library (Add. MSS 59541–597). The correspondence chiefly consists of letters addressed to Wrench and dates from 1887. One volume, Add. MS 59541, consists chiefly of letters to his father, Rt. Hon. Frederick Wrench. Vol. VIII of the correspondence, Add. MS 59548 consists of six letters from T. E. Lawrence to Francis Yeats-Brown of *The Spectator*, 1926–7. The diaries cover the years 1897–1950, and are mostly records of travel abroad, including some typewritten versions, consisting of copies of, or extracts from, the diaries.

Correspondence can be found in the Edward Carson papers, Public Record Office of Northern Ireland.

YOUNG, Sir Frederick (1817–1913)

Colonial Administrator; advocate of Imperial Federation. Secretary of the Royal Colonial Institute.

The Royal Commonwealth Society Library has a collection of material. It includes both correspondence to him personally and letters addressed to him as Secretary of the Institute (these are filed in the main collection of autograph letters). There are two letterbooks, including letters from Young, dating from 1837, and letters to him. There is also an 85-page manuscript autobiography. In addition, there are two volumes of press cuttings on his activities, covering subjects of interest to him. Three files contain letters and memoranda, and copies of pamphlets by Young.

YOUNG, George Malcolm (1882–1959)

Historian.

Material concerning his biography of Stanley Baldwin is in Cambridge University Library. All Souls College, Oxford, has some typescripts by Young.

ZANGWILL, Israel (1864–1926)

Man of letters. Author of novels, poetry, plays, essays. President of the Jewish Historical Society.

The bulk of his papers are in the Central Zionist Archives, Jerusalem, including diaries and notes from meetings with Foreign Office officials. Relevant items can be found in the Anglo-Jewish Archives, University College London. His unfinished novel 'The Baron of Offenbach' is in the British Library (Add. MS 41485). There is correspondence, 1894–1900, 1915–20, on social, business and literary matters in the Douglas Sladen papers. Correspondence with Annie

Meyer is in the American Jewish Archives, Cincinnati, Ohio, and there is correspondence with Emma Goldman in the International Institute of Social History, Amsterdam.

ZIMMERN, Sir Alfred (1879–1957)

Political scientist. University Secretary of Joint Committee on Oxford and Working Class Education, 1907–8. Staff Inspector, Board of Education, 1912–15. At Political Intelligence Department, Foreign Office, 1918–19. Wilson Professor of International Politics, University College, Aberystwyth, 1919–21. Acting Professor of Political Science, Cornell University, 1922–3. Deputy Director, League of Nations Institute of Intellectual Co-operation, Paris, 1926–30. Montague Burton Professor of International Relations, Oxford University, 1930–44. Deputy Director Research Department, Foreign Office, 1943–5. Adviser, Information and External Relations, Ministry of Education, 1945. Secretary General, Constituent Conference of UNESCO, 1945. Director, Greater Hartford Council for UNESCO, 1950. Director, Geneva School of International Studies, 1925–39.

The Bodleian Library, Oxford, has a collection of material, including correspondence and miscellaneous papers. There is a collection of general correspondence with various figures (eight boxes), 1895–1957; and special correspondence, including correspondence with Oliver Wendell Holmes, 1911–17; Sir Reginald Coupland, 1908–47; Sir R. W. Livingstone, 1914–56; A. J. Toynbee, 1909–57; W. F. Wilcox, 1922–57; K. A. Busia, 1942–56; Alexis Photiades, 1947–53; J. R. MacDonald, 1928. There are also a variety of other letters, including correspondence relating to UNESCO, 1946–54, and to the Geneva School of International Studies, 1928–39, and letters of congratulations, and letters to Lady Zimmern on his death. Other papers in the collection include minutes and papers of the Geneva School; papers relating to the League of Nations, UNESCO, Inter-Allied Economic Organisation, 1917–19, and the World Council of Churches, 1939–46; miscellaneous typescript material and manuscripts and drafts of books and reviews; essays, notes on the *Greek Commonwealth*, etc., 1910–16; manuscripts of lectures and broadcasts, mainly in the 1950s; articles and addresses, 1947–50; press cuttings and assorted material.

Appendix
A select list of major libraries mentioned in the text, with their archival holdings

The following is an alphabetical list of the libraries which hold the main archival collections described in the text of this book. It does not include the addresses of libraries holding related collections which are mentioned but are not themselves described in the book. It was felt that this would make a list of inordinate length. For up-to-date addresses of libraries and archives departments in Britain, readers are referred to the Royal Commission on Historical Manuscripts, *Record Repositories in Great Britain* (5th ed., 2nd impression, HMSO, 1976). For international addresses, reference may be made to *The World of Learning* (26th ed., 2 vols, 1975), the *National Union Catalog* and similar sources.

Under each address in the following list there is a name guide to the major relevant collections. Readers are advised in each case, however, to check with the main entry in the text to ensure that the collection is relevant to their interests. In several cases the addresses of major institutions (e.g. the Labour Party, Board of Deputies of British Jews) have been supplied, with a note on relevant material. In these cases, it should be understood that what are referred to are not complete collections, but rather relevant files in the institution's records.

Anglo-Jewish Archives, Mocatta Library, University College London, Gower Street, London WC1E 6BT
 S. Brodetsky; Sir R. W. Cohen; I. M. Greenberg; P. Guedalla; Sir B. L. Q. Henriques; S. A. Hirsch; N. J. Laski; L. Wolf; I. Zangwill
Army Museums, Ogilby Trust, Ministry of Defence (Army), 85 Whitehall, London SW1A 2NP
 H. S. Wilkinson
Baillie's Library, 69 Oakfield Avenue, Glasgow W2, G12 8LP
 G. A. Aldred; R. E. Muirhead
Baker Library, Dartmouth College, Hanover, N.H. 1658, USA
 R. B. C. Graham
Ball State University, Department of Library Services, Muncie, Indiana 47306, USA
 Sir R. N. Angell
Balliol College, Oxford
 J. E. C. Bodley; C. P. Scott; A. L. Smith

Birkbeck College, Malet Street, London WC1
J. D. Bernal
Birmingham Public Libraries, Birmingham B3 3HQ
G. Cadbury; G. J. Holyoake
Birmingham University Library, P.O. Box 363, Edgbaston, Birmingham B15 2TT
Sir W. J. Ashley; Sir C. R. Beazley; G. Cadbury; W. H. Dawson; Sir O. J. Lodge
Bishopsgate Institute, 230 Bishopsgate, London EC2
G. J. Holyoake; G. Howell
Board of Deputies of British Jews, Woburn House, Upper Woburn Place, London WC1
I. Cohen; Sir L. L. Cohen; Sir R. W. Cohen; P. Guedalla; N. J. Laski; L. Wolf
Bodleian Library, Oxford OX1 3BG
Sir E. T. Backhouse, 2nd Bt; J. M. Baldwin; E. C. Bentley; J. E. C. Bodley; V. Brittain;
Sir H. Burdett; A. J. L. Cary; Lady Clark; F. Clifford; C. A. Coulson; W. M. Crook;
L. G. Curtis; Lady Dilke; P. Guedalla; H. A. Gwynne; J. L. L. B. Hammond; L. B. Ham-
mond; J. A. Hobson; E. R. Hughes; C. Jenkins; T. E. Lawrence; R. V. Lennard;
A. P. Magill; F. S. Marvin; Viscountess Milner; G. G. A. Murray; Sir L. B. Namier;
H. W. Nevinson; 1st Vt Northcliffe; Sir R. E. Peierls; H. Rashdall; Sir M. E. Sadler;
W. T. Stead; L. J. Stein; Sir L. Stuart; G. M. Tuckwell; W. B. Worsfold; Sir A. Zimmern
Borthwick Institute of Historical Research, St Anthony's Hall, Peaseholme Green, York
YO1 2PW
1st B Davidson; J. N. Figgis; W. H. Frere; 1st B Lang of Lambeth; E. K. Talbot
Boston Public Library, Boston, Mass, USA
F. P. Cobbe; Sir S. C. Cockerell; H. H. Ellis; W. A. Knight; Sir F. Meynell; G. B. Shaw
Brasenose College, Oxford
W. Stallybrass
Brisbane, John Oxley Library, Brisbane, Queensland, Australia
Sir R. W. G. Herbert
Bristol University, Wills Memorial Library, Queens Road, Bristol BS8 1RJ
Dame K. Furse
BBC Written Archives Centre, Caversham Park, Reading RG4 8TZ
3rd E Russell
British Library, Dept. of Manuscripts, Great Russell Street, London WC1B 3DG
Sir W. J. Ashley; 1st B Avebury; Archbishop J. H. Bernard; R. S. Briffault; 1st Baroness
Burdett-Coutts; W. B. Carpenter; Sir S. C. Cockerell; Sir E. T. Cook; E. C. W. Elmy;
T. H. S. Escott; Hon Sir J. W. Fortescue; Sir J. G. Frazer; F. J. Furnivall; Baron Gar-
diner; F. E. Garrett; 1st B Keynes; R. Kipling; J. Lane; T. E. Lawrence; J. McCarthy;
A. Mansbridge; Sir C. R. Markham; C. E. Montague; E. B. I. Müller; H. W. Nevinson;
1st Vt Northcliffe; D. S. Northcote; F. S. Oliver; G. Orwell; Dame C. Pankhurst;
E. S. Pankhurst; M. D. M. Petre; Sir F. T. Piggott; E. P. Rhys; 1st B Riddell; C. P. Scott;
G. B. Shaw; A. P. Sinnett; W. S. Sparrow; J. A. Spender; M. C. Stopes; G. L. Strachey;
G. M. Tuckwell; A. R. Wallace; H. S. Weaver; 1st B. Welby; H. W. Williams;
Sir J. E. L. Wrench; I. Zangwill
British Library of Political and Economic Science, London School of Economics, Houghton
Street, Aldwych, London WC2A 2AE
1st B Anderson; T. S. Ashton; Dame H. O. Barnett; S. A. Barnett; Sir H. E. C. Beaver;
J. Bonar; C. Booth; H. Burrows; E. Cannan; H. Chevins; 1st B Citrine; 1st B Courtney;
M. L. Davies; C. V. Drysdale; F. W. Galton; A. G. Gardiner; Sir R. Giffen; M. Ginsberg;
Sir T. E. G. Gregory; F. Harrison; H. M. Hyndman; W. R. Jeffreys; F. Johnson;
F. N. Keen; L. C. A. Knowles; E. M. H. Lloyd; Sir A. McFadyean; B. K. Malinowski;
V. R. Markham; J. E. Meade; D. Mitrany; S. F. Nadel; E. R. Pease; 1st B Piercy;
M. H. Read; W. P. Reeves; 3rd E Russell; G. B. Shaw; H. Solly; R. H. Tawney;
R. M. Titmuss; G. Wallas; M. B. Webb; Sir C. K. Webster; 1st B Welby;
P. H. Wicksteed

British Theatre Museum, Victoria and Albert Museum, Cromwell Road, London SW7 2RL
Sir F. C. Burnand; 1st B Lang of Lambeth; G. B. Shaw
Building Research Establishment, Garston, Watford
E. M. Denby
Calgary University Library, 2920 24 Ave N.W., Calgary, Alberta, Canada T2N 1N4
J. M. Murry
California: University of California, Los Angeles, California 29007, USA
H. H. Ellis; A. L. Huxley
California: University of California, Santa Barbara, California
A. L. Huxley
Cambridge University, African Studies Centre, Cambridge
E. A. Walker
Cambridge University Library, West Road, Cambridge CB3 9DR
1st B Acton; A. J. Arberry; Sir F. C. Bartlett; J. D. Bernal; M. Creighton; Sir J. G. Frazer; T. R. Glover; M. G. S. Grey; A. C. Haddon; C. C. Hurst; Sir J. E. L. Jones; J. N. Keynes; B. Kidd; R. Kipling; J. M. Ludlow; F. W. Maitland; A. Manning; H. C. G. Moule; 1st B Rutherford; R. N. Salaman; Sir D. M. Wallace; G. M. Young
Cardiff Central Library, The Hayes, Cardiff CF1 2QU
Sir H. Owen
Cashel Diocesan Archives, Thurley, Tipperary, Republic of Ireland
T. W. Croke
Central Zionist Archives, P.O. Box 92, Jerusalem, Israel
H. Bentwich; N. de M. Bentwich; S. Brodetsky; I. Cohen; J. L. Cohen; M. D. Eder; M. Gaster; P. Goodman; P. Guedalla; L. Kessler; S. Landman; 1st B Marks of Broughton; Sir L. B. Namier; H. Sacher; Baron Sieff; L. J. Stein; L. Wolf; I. Zangwill
Chicago University Library, Chicago, Illinois 60637, USA
1st B Acton; Sir P. Bunting; G. G. Coulton; Sir B. Pares
Christ Church, Oxford
G. Drage; C. Jenkins
Churchill College, Cambridge CB3 0DS
H. M. Belgion; H. M. Cam; Baron Carron; G. P. Chapman; H. Clausen; Sir J. D. Cockcroft; V. M. Crawford; P. Einzig; Sir W. S. Farren; Baron Francis-Williams; Sir R. G. Hawtrey; Sir J. E. L. Jones; Sir J. R. Leslie; Dame E. Lyttelton; D. H. McLachlan; A. J. H. Pollen; G. Saunders
Cincinnati Library, Eighth and Vine Streets, Cincinnati 45202, USA
J. M. Murry
Claremont Colleges, Hannold Library, Claremont, California, USA
M. W. Ward
Clwyd Record Office, The Old Rectory, Hawarden, Deeside, Clwyd CH5 3NR
H. Gladstone
Colby College, Waterville, Maine, USA
L. Housman; V. Paget (Vernon Lee)
Columbia University Libraries, New York, NY 10027, USA
Sir R. N. Angell; A. Austin; Sir H. R. Haggard; L. Housman; R. Kipling; E. V. Lucas; A. Maude; G. B. Shaw
Co-operative Union Library, Holyoake House, Hanover Street, Manchester M60 0AS
E. O. Greening; G. J. Holyoake
Cornell University Library, Ithaca, N.Y. 14853, USA
R. Kipling; P. W. Lewis; G. Smith
Corpus Christi College Library, Cambridge
A. Boutwood
Corpus Christi College, Oxford
Sir R. C. K. Ensor

Cumbria Record Office, The Castle, Carlisle CA3 8UR
    C. E. Marshall
Dalhousie University Library, Halifax, Nova Scotia, Canada
    R. Kipling
Devon Record Office, Concord House, South Street, Exeter EX1 1DX
    Lady Acland; Sir A. H. D. Acland, 13th Bt.
Dublin Diocesan Archives, Dublin, Republic of Ireland
    W. J. Walsh
Dublin, University College Library, 82 St Stephen's Green, Dublin 2, Republic of Ireland
Duke University, Durham, North Carolina 27706, USA
    1st B Courtney; Sir W. Maxwell
Dundee University Library, Dundee DD1 4HN
    Sir T. M. Knox
Durham University Library (Oriental Section), Palace Green, Durham DH1 3RN
    G. M. L. Bell
Edinburgh University Library, George Square, Edinburgh EH8 9LJ
    Sir A. Gray; C. M. Grieve (Hugh McDiarmid); D. B. Horn; A. B. Keith; R. E. Muirhead;
    C. Sarolea; N. K. Smith
Essex Record Office, County Hall, Chelmsford, CM1 1LX
    S. L. Bensusan
Essex University Library, Wivenhoe Park, Colchester CO4 3SQ
    S. L. Bensusan
Fawcett Library, City of London Polytechnic, Calcutta House Precinct, Old Castle Street, London E1 7NT
    J. E. Butler; W. A. Coote; Dame K. D'Olier Courtney; Dame M. Fawcett; T. B. Greig;
    A. M. Royden; J. P. Strachey; P. Strachey; M. A. R. Tuker
Fitzwilliam Museum, Trumpington Street, Cambridge
    W. S. Blunt; R. Kipling; G. Le Strange
Friends' House Library, Euston Road, London NW1 2BJ
    V. G. Bailey; P. Bartlett; C. L. Braithwaite; E. Grubb; A. M. Harrison; H. T. Hodgkin;
    J. Rickman; M. Sparkes; A. C. Wilson
Girton College, Cambridge
    K. T. B. Butler; H. M. Cam; S. E. Davies; Dame B. S. Newall
Glamorgan Record Office, County Hall, Cathays Park, Cardiff CF1 3NE
    Sir J. F. Rees
Glasgow University Library, Glasgow G12 8QQ
    J. Bonar; A. V. Dicey; W. R. Scott
Greater London Record Office, County Hall, London SE1 7PB
    Dame H. O. Barnett; S. A. Barnett
Guildhall Library, Aldermanbury, London EC2P 2EJ
    1st Vt Bearsted
Harvard University, Cambridge, Mass., 02138, USA
    T. Bosanquet; H. S. Foxwell; R. Kipling; T. E. Lawrence; Sir M. E. Sadler
Hastings Public Library, John's Place, Cambridge Road, Hastings, Sussex
    O. Browning
Hebrew University, Institute of Contemporary Jewry, The Hebrew University of Jerusalem, Jerusalem, Israel
    N. de M. Bentwich; Sir L. Simon; L. J. Stein
Heriot-Watt University Library, Edinburgh EH1 1HX
    Sir R. Blair
Hertfordshire Record Office, County Hall, Hertford SG13 8DE
    Sir E. Howard
House of Lords Record Office, London SW1A 0PW
    R. D. Blumenfeld; Sir R. Donald; Sir F. C. Gould; Countess Lloyd-George; D. Soskice;

J. S. L. Strachey; R. S. Watson; 19th B Willoughby de Broke
Hull University, The Brynmor Jones Library, Hull, Humberside HU6 7RX
F. W. Dalley; M. L. Davies; S. G. Evans; J. Haston; J. A. Hobson; W. Horrabin; T. E. Hulme; W. E. Jones; H. J. Laski; J. H. Lloyd; C. L. D. R. Noel; A. J. Penty; M. B. Reckitt; M. Sparkes; M. C. Stopes; J. Varley
Humberside Public Libraries (Hull and Bridlington), Central Library, Albion Street, Hull
W. Holtby
Huntington Library, San Marino, California 91108, USA
F. P. Cobbe; F. J. Furnivall; Sir H. R. Haggard
Illinois University, Urbana, Illinois 61801, USA
J. Bonar; H. G. Wells
Imperial War Museum, Lambeth Road, London SE1 6HZ
R. D. Blumenfeld; R. Colby; Dame K. D. 'O Courtney; G. E. R. Gedye; J. W. Harvey; J. Hughes; T. E. Lawrence; R. MacColl; J. Moffat; S. Rogerson
India Office Library, Foreign and Commonwealth Office, 197 Blackfriars Road, London SE1 8NG
Sir F. H. Brown; W. Digby; Sir P. J. Hartog; W. A. Hirst; C. Sorabji
Indiana University Library, Bloomington, Indiana 47401, USA
H. H. Ellis
Institute of Archaeology Library, University of London, 31 Gordon Square, London WC1
V. G. Childe
Institute of Commonwealth Studies, University of London, 27 Russell Square, London WC1
Sir W. K. Hancock; R. Jebb
Institute of Psycho-Analysis, 63 New Cavendish Street, London W1
A. E. Jones
International Institute of Social History, Herengracht 262–6, Amsterdam, Netherlands
H. N. Brailsford; G. D. H. Cole; H. J. Laski; J. M. Middleton; E. S. Pankhurst; R. W. Postgate
Iowa University Library, Iowa City, Iowa 52242, USA
A. Austin
Jesus College, Oxford
L. G. Curtis
Kansas City University Library,
J. McCarthy
Keele University Library, Keele, Staffs, ST5 5BG
1st B Lindsay of Birker
Kent Archives Office, County Hall, Maidstone, Kent
Sir M. W. Collet; Viscountess Milner
Kent: University of Kent at Canterbury, Canterbury, Kent
R. W. Postgate
King's College Library, Cambridge
C. R. Ashbee; Sir J. H. Clapham; G. L. Dickinson; E. M. Forster; R. E. Fry; 1st B Keynes; J. N. Keynes; G. E. Moore; A. C. Pigou; Sir J. T. Sheppard; Sir C. Walston; N. Wedd
King's College, Liddell Hart Centre for Military Archives, Strand, London WC2R 2LS
Sir B. L. Hart; J. L. Garvin
King's College, University of London, Strand, London WC2R 2LS
F. J. 'Furnivall; R. R. Gates
Labour Party Archives, Transport House, Smith Square, London SW1
H. N. Brailsford; G. Cadbury; S. Coit; G. D. H. Cole; A. J. Cook; Dame K. D'O Courtney; Sir R. Donald; J. B. Glasier; H. M. Hyndman; J. Larkin; H. J. Laski; J. S. Middleton; M. Middleton; E. R. Pease; M. W. Phillips; H. Quelch; J. Rowntree; R. Williams
Lady Margaret Hall, Oxford
M. L. D. Grier

Lambeth Palace Library, London SE1 7JU
Dame H. O. Barnett; S. A. Barnett; G. K. A. Bell; 1st Baroness Burdett-Coutts; W. O. Burrows; M. Creighton; 1st B Davidson; Sir L. T. Dibdin; Baron Fisher of Lambeth; C. Gore; M. G. Haigh; A. C. Headlam; M. H. Henson; H. Hodge; C. Jenkins; H. Johnson; H. H. Kelly; T. A. Lacey; 1st B Lang of Lambeth; G. Ridding; A. Riley; E. S. Talbot; W. Temple

Leeds City Libraries, Archives Dept., Sheepscar Branch Library, Chapeltown Road, Leeds LS7 3AP
Sir M. Burton

Leeds University: The Brotherton Library, Leeds LS2 9JT
Sir W. L. Andrews; L. L. F. R. Price; A. Smithells

Leo Baeck Institute, 129 East 73rd Street, New York, N.Y. 10021, USA
L. Feuchtwanger

Library of Congress, Washington DC 20540, USA
C. R. Ashbee

Liddell Hart Centre for Military Archives
see King's College, Liddell Hart Centre for Military Archives

Lincolnshire Archives Office, The Castle, Lincoln LN1 3AB
E. L. Hicks; E. King; C. H. Turnor; 1st B Welby

Liverpool: Picton Library, William Brown Street, Liverpool
J. Holt

Liverpool University Archives, P.O. Box 147, Liverpool L69 3BX
J. H. Forshaw; Baron Holford; D. C. Jones; G. L. S. Shackle; G. S. Veitch

Liverpool University Library, P. O. Box 123, Liverpool L69 3DA
C. Booth; J. E. Butler; 1st B Russell of Liverpool

London Borough of Bromley: Central Library, Bromley BR1 1EX
H. G. Wells

London Borough of Camden: Swiss Cottage Library, 88 Avenue Road, London NW3 3HA
A. Craig

London Borough of Richmond Libraries, The Green, Richmond, Surrey
D. B. W. Sladen

London Library, 14 St James's Square, London SW1Y 4LG
C. R. Ashbee; W. Stebbing; Sir D. M. Wallace

London University Library, Senate House, Malet Street, London WC1E 7HU
H. H. L. Bellot; C. Booth; E. Cammaerts; H. S. Foxwell; C. M. S. Mason

London University, Institute of Education, Bedford Way, London WC1
Sir F. Clarke; K. Mannheim

McMaster University, Hamilton, Ontario, Canada
V. Brittain; Sir G. E. G. Catlin; J. Grierson; J. H. Robertson; 3rd E Russell

Magdalen College, Oxford
Sir T. H. Warren

Manchester Central Library, St Peter's Square, Manchester M2 5PD
R. P. G. Blatchford; Dame M. Fawcett; N. J. Laski; Dame C. Pankhurst; P. Redfern; C. P. Scott; I. W. Slotki; A. M. Thompson

Manchester: John Rylands University Library of Manchester, Deansgate, Manchester M3 3EH
H. H. L. Bellot; E. Carpenter; W. P. Crozier; J. E. Rattenbury; C. P. Scott; A. P. Wadsworth

Marshall Library of Economics, Sidgwick Avenue, Cambridge CB3 9DB
1st B Keynes; J. N. Keynes; A. Marshall

Marx Memorial Library, Marx House, 37A Clerkenwell Green, London EC1
J. Connolly; H. Crawfurd; W. Hannington

Mary Ward Centre, 9 Tavistock Place, London WC1
M. A. Ward

Mass-Observation Archive, Sussex University, Brighton BN1 9QL
  T.. Harrisson
Menninger Foundation, Box 829, Topeka, Kansas 66601, USA
  H. H. Ellis
Merton College Library, Oxford
  F. H. Bradley
Michigan University, William L. Clements Library, Ann Arbor, Michigan, USA
  J. F. Finerty; Sir C. R. Markham
Ministry of Defence Library (Navy), Empress State Building, Lillie Road, Fulham, London SW6
  Sir H. J. Newbolt
Mitchell Library, Sydney, New South Wales, Australia
  G. E. Morrison
Mocatta Library, University College London, Gower Street, London WC1E 6BT
  M. Gaster; C. Roth; L. Wolf
Museum of London, Barbican, London EC2
  Dame C. Pankhurst
Museum of the History of Science, Oxford
  Sir F. Galton
National Archives of India, Janpath, New Delhi, India
  D. Naoroji
National Archives of Malaysia, Federal Government Building, Jalan Sultan, Petaling Jaya,
  Malaysia
  T. Harrisson
National Army Museum, Royal Hospital Road, London SW3 4HT
  Hon. Sir J. W. Fortescue; H. S. Wilkinson
National Liberal Club, Whitehall Place, London SW1
  T. F. Unwin
National Library of Australia, Parkes Place, Canberra, ACT 2600, Australia
  R. Jebb; G. G. A. Murray
National Library of Ireland, Department of Manuscripts, Kildare Street, Dublin 2, Republic of
  Ireland
  Sir R. D. Casement; E. Ceannt; R. E. Childers; J. Connolly; R. L. Crawford; T. W. Croke;
  M. Davitt; J. Devoy; F. Gallagher; T. P. Gill; A. S. A. S. Green; B. Hobson; T. Johnson;
  J. Larkin; J. McCarthy; M. G. Moore; R. Mulcahy; A. P. O'Briain; S. T. O'Kelly;
  P. Pearse; J. M. Tuohy
National Library of New Zealand, Alexander Turnbull Library, Wellington 1, New Zealand
  W. P. Reeves
National Library of Scotland, Department of Manuscripts, George IV Bridge, Edinburgh
  EH1 1EW
  1st B Davidson; G. Dott; Sir J. G. Frazer; Sir P. Geddes; R. B. C. Graham; Sir A. Gray;
  C. M. Grieve; Sir J. Kirk; T. E. Lawrence; J. Macgregor; J. Maclean; F. M. McNeill; Sir
  F. C. Mears; R. Meinertzhagen; N. M. Mitchison; R. E. Muirhead; Sir H. J. Newbolt
National Library of Wales, Department of Manuscripts, Aberystwyth, Dyfed, SY23 3BU
  D. R. Daniel; G. Davies; T. I. Ellis; Sir E. V. Evans; G. I. Evans; A. P. Graves;
  H. S. Jevons; Sir C. B. Jones; D. C. Jones; T. Jones; J. Owen; Sir D. H. Parry;
  W. J. Parry; D. L. Prosser; 1st B Rendel; 2nd Viscountess Rhondda; T. Richard;
  R. D. Roberts; W. G. H. Simon; Sir D. L. Thomas
National Maritime Museum, Greenwich, London SE10
  E. Altham; L. Cope-Cornford; L. G. H. Horton-Smith; Sir J. R. Thursfield; A. H. White
New College Library, Oxford
  H. W. B. Joseph; H. Rashdall
New York Public Library, Manuscripts Department, Fifth Ave., New York 10018, USA
  H. H. Ellis; F. Harris

Newcastle University Library, Queen Victoria Street, Newcastle upon Tyne, NE1 7RU
G. M. L. Bell; B. Bosanquet
Norfolk Record Office, Norwich NOR 57E
Sir H. R. Haggard
Nottinghamshire Record Office, County House, High Pavement, Nottingham NG1 1HR
G. Ridding
Nuffield College, Oxford OX1 1NF
W. Ball; Sir H. Clay; G. D. H. Cole; F. T. Edgeworth; J. Edwards; A. Loveday; 1st Vt Nuffield
Oriel College, Oxford
L. R. Phelps; L. L. F. R. Price
Oxford Central Library, St Aldate's, Oxford OX1 1DJ
1st Vt Nuffield
Pembroke College, Cambridge
J. N. Keynes
Pennsylvania State University, University Park, Pennsylvania 16802, USA
E. Gore-Booth
Peterhouse Library, Cambridge
Sir A. W. Ward
Public Archives of Canada, 395 Wellington Street, Ottawa, Ontario K1A ON3, Canada
Sir G. R. Parkin; 1st B Mount Stephen
Public Record Office, Kew, Richmond, Surrey TW9 4DU
Sir L. P. Abercrombie; Sir R. D. Casement; M. Gonne; J. M. Hamill; 3rd E Russell; Dame
F. M. Stark
Public Record Office of Ireland, Four Courts, Dublin, Republic of Ireland
T. R. Harrington
Public Record Office of Northern Ireland, 66 Balmoral Avenue, Belfast BT9 6NY Northern
Ireland
Sir R. H. H. Baird; Sir R. D. Casement; C. R. Fay; J. K. Ingram; E. F. V. Knox
Pusey House, St Giles', Oxford
M. A. Ward; T. H. Ward
Queen Mary College, University of London, Mile End Road, London E1
Sir C. K. Webster
Queen's University, Douglas Library, Kingston, Ontario, Canada
Sir W. H. Fyfe
Reading University Library, Whiteknights, Reading, Berks RG6 2AE
S. A. Brooke; Sir A. D. Hall; V. Klein; Sir F. M. Stenton
Reform Club Library, Pall Mall, London, SW1Y 5EW
W. M. Eagar
Rhodes House Library, Oxford
H. L. Clarke; Sir R. Coupland; E. Gedge; C. W. W. Greenidge; Sir F. H. Hamilton; R. Hinden; J. Holt; Sir L. S. Jameson, 1st Bt; L. Kessler; A. J. Loveridge; R. Meinertzhagen;
S. Moody; H. S. L. Polak; C. J. Rhodes; Viscountess Simon; W. B. Worsfold
Rhodes University, Cory Library for Historical Research, Grahamstown, South Africa
Sir J. G. Sprigg
Royal Anthropological Institute, 36 Craven Street, London WC2
M. E. Durham
Royal Commonwealth Society Library, Northumberland Avenue, London WC2N 5BJ
Sir H. R. Haggard; T. E. Sedgwick; Sir C. Stuart; Sir F. Young
Royal Geographical Society, 1 Kensington Gore, London SW7
Sir C. R. Markham
Royal Historical Society, University College London, Gower Street, London WC1E 6BT
Sir G. W. Prothero

Royal Institute of British Architects, British Architectural Library, 66 Portland Place, London W1N 4AD
W. W. Coates; W. R. Lethaby; H. S. G. Rendel; Sir R. Unwin

Royal Institute of International Affairs, Chatham House, 10 St James's Square, London SW1Y 4LE
A. J. Toynbee

Royal Society of Medicine, 1 Wimpole Street, London W1
Sir J. Y. W. Macalister

Royal Statistical Society, 25 Enford Street, London W1
Sir A. L. Bowley; L. L. F. R. Price

St Andrews University Library, St Andrews, Fife, KY16 9TR, Scotland
J. E. Butler; A. L. Lilley

St Antony's College, Oxford OX2 6JF
Sir J. W. W. Bennett; Sir G. B. Sansom; J. W. R. Scott

St Antony's College, Middle East Centre, 137 Banbury Road, Oxford OX2 6JF
G. M. L. Bell; N. de M. Bentwich; H. P. Gordon; D. G. Hogarth; L. Kessler; S. H. Perowne; Dame F. M. Stark

St. Hilda's College, Oxford
C. M. E. Burrows

School of Oriental and African Studies, University of London, Malet Street, London WC1E 7HP
L. Barnes; T. F. Pitt

School of Slavonic and East European Studies Library, University of London, Malet Street, London WC1
Sir B. Pares

Science Museum Library, South Kensington, London SW7 5NH
1st B Rutherford

Scott Polar Research Institute Archives, Cambridge, CB2 1ER
Sir C. R. Markham

Scottish Record Office, PO Box 36, HM General Register House, Edinburgh, EH1 3YY
G. G. Dawson

Sheffield City Libraries, Surrey Street, Sheffield S1 1XZ
E. Carpenter

Society for Psychical Research, 1 Adam and Eve Mews, London W8
Sir O. J. Lodge

Somerville College, Oxford
V. Paget

South African Public Library, Queen Victoria Street, Cape Town, South Africa
O. Schreiner

South Carolina University Library, Columbia, South Carolina, 29208 USA
1st B Allen of Hurtwood

Southampton University, Parkes Library, Southampton SO9 5NH
J. Parkes

Southern Illinois University Library, Carbondale, Illinois 62901, USA
N. Cunard

Southwell Minster Library, Southwell, Notts
G. Ridding

State Historical Society of Wisconsin, Madison, Wisconsin, USA
R. Kipling

Stirling University, Stirling, FK9 4LA
J. Grierson

Strathclyde Regional Archives Office, PO Box 27, City Chambers, Glasgow G2 1DU
G. A. Aldred

Strathclyde University Library, McCance Building, 16 Richmond Street, Glasgow
G. A. Aldred

Strathclyde University, Department of Urban and Regional Planning, George Street, Glasgow G1 1XW

Sir G. L. Pepler

Street Library, 1 Leigh Road, Street, Somerset

L. Housman

Sussex University Library, Falmer, Brighton BN1 9QL

W. W. Bartlett; L. G. Curtis; Sir R. A. Gregory; B. K. Martin; H. T. Pledge; Sir L. D. Stamp; L. S. Woolf

Sussex University, History and Social Studies of Science Division, Falmer, Brighton BN1 9QL

F. A. E. Crew; L. Darwin; A. Ferguson; L. Hogben

Swansea University College Library, Singleton Park, Swansea, West Glamorgan

A. L. Horner

Sydney University Library, New South Wales 2006, Australia

N. Haire

Syracuse University Library, New York, NY 13210, USA

R. Kipling; H. J. Laski

Texas University Library, Austin, Texas 78712, USA

1st B Acton; E. Chesser; N. Cunard; H. H. Ellis; E .M .Forster; J. L. Garvin; R. B. C. Graham; C. M. Grieve (Hugh McDiarmid); M. R. Hall; Sir B. L. Hart; L. Housman; T. E. Hulme; G. C. Ives; T. E. Lawrence; N. M. Mitchison; G. B. Shaw

Theosophical Society, International Headquarters, Adyar, Madras, India

A. Besant

The Times, PO Box 7, New Printing House Square, Gray's Inn Road, London WC1X 8EZ

C. A. S. Austin; C. F. M. Bell; J. O. P. Bland; J. D. Bourchier; D. D. Braham; A. C. Brock; C. W. Brodribb; Sir F. H. Brown; G. E. Buckle; J. B. Capper; W. F. Casey; Sir I. V. Chirol; 1st B Courtney; H. G. Daniels; G. G. Dawson; R. Deakin; N. Ebbutt; D. S. Fraser; L. Fraser; J. L. Garvin; H. P. Gordon; P. P. Graves; W. B. Harris; Sir B. L. Hart; L. James; A. L. Kennedy; Sir W. H. Lewis; B. K. Long; 1st Vt Northcliffe; G. Saunders; W. Stebbing; H. W. Steed; Sir C. Stuart; Sir J. R. Thursfield; Sir D. M. Wallace; A. F. Walter

Toronto University Library, Toronto 181, Ontario, M5S 1A1, Canada

J. O. P. Bland; C. R. Fay; G. Smith

Trades Union Congress Library, Great Russell Street, London WC1

Lady Dilke; G. M. Tuckwell

Trinity College, Cambridge

3rd E Russell; Sir G. P. Thomson; G. M. Trevelyan

Trinity College, College Street, Dublin 2, Republic of Ireland

C. F. Bastable; Archbishop J. H. Bernard; M. Davitt; J. K. Ingram; Sir J. R. Leslie; Sir J. P. Mahaffy; D. O'Brien

Tyne and Wear County Record Office, 7 Saville Place, Newcastle upon Tyne, NE1 8DQ

1st B Rendel

University College London Library, Gower Street, London WC1E 6BT

Sir W. J. Ashley; E. S. Beesly; H. H. L. Bellot; A. Comfort; Sir T. G. Foster, 1st Bt; H. S. Foxwell; Sir F. Galton; J. B. S. Haldane; D. Hannay; L. Housman; H. J. Laski; Sir O. J. Lodge; F. C. Montague; G. Orwell; K. Pearson; L. S. Penrose; M. M. Plowman; Sir R. L. Rees; M. A. Ward; T. H. Ward

Ushaw College Library, University of Durham, DH1 3HP

Cardinal F. A. Bourne

Victoria University, McPherson Library, Victoria, British Columbia, Canada

Sir H. Read

Victoria and Albert Museum, Cromwell Road, London SW7 2RL

C. R. Ashbee; Sir S. C. Cockerell; W. R. Lethaby

Virginia University Library, Charlottesville, Virginia 22903, USA

S. Higginbottom; H. G. Wells

Wadham College, Oxford
Sir C. M. Bowra
Warwick University Library: Modern Records Centre, Coventry CV4 7AL
Lady Allen of Hurtwood; Sir L. Cannon; C. E. Collet; C. Fenby; Sir V. Gollancz; J. H. Harley; S. K. Hocking; H. Sara; L. A. E, Streatfeild; J. Trevor
Weizmann Archives, Rehovot, Israel
B. E. C. Dugdale
West Sussex Record Office, West Street, Chichester, West Sussex PO19 1RN
L. J. Maxse; T. F. Unwin
Westminster City Libraries, Marylebone Library, Marylebone Road, London NW1
O. Hill
Westminster City Libraries, Victoria Library, Buckingham Palace Road, London SW1 9TR
A. Burdett-Coutts
Westminster Diocesan Archives, Archbishop's House, London SW1P 1QJ
Cardinal F. A. Bourne; C. W. Godfrey; E. J. Oldmeadow
William Morris Gallery, Water House, Lloyd Park, Forest Road, Walthamstow, London E17
A. H. Mackmurdo
Wisconsin University, Memorial Library, Madison, Wisconsin 53706, USA
G. Hayler
Worcester College, Oxford
G. E. Hadow; Sir W. H. Hadow
Yale University Library, New Haven, Connecticut, 06520, USA
H. H. Ellis; Sir W. T. Grenfell (Medical Library); H. M. Hole; H. Macfall; B. K. Malinowski; K. Mayo; H. M. Tomlinson; Sir A. Willert
YIVO Institute for Jewish Research, 1048 Fifth Ave, New York 10028, USA
L. Wolf
York Minster Library, York
C. F. Garbett
York University, J. B. Morrell Library, Heslington, York
J. De Blank